CW00549394

Lys de Bray's
MANUAL OF
Old~Fashioned Shrubs

The Oxford Illustrated Press

© Lys de Bray 1986

ISBN 0 946609 25 X

All rights reserved. No part of this book may be reproduced or transmitted in any form or by any means, electronic or mechanical, including photocopying, recording or by any information storage or retrieval system, without permission of the publisher.

Published by:
The Oxford Illustrated Press, Sparkford, near Yeovil, Somerset BA22 7JJ, England

Haynes Publications Inc
861 Lawrence Drive, Newbury Park, California 91320 USA

Printed in England by:
J.H. Haynes & Co Ltd., Sparkford, near Yeovil, Somerset BA22 7JJ

British Library Cataloguing in Publication Data
De Bray, Lys
  Lys de Bray's manual of old-fashioned shrubs.
  1. Shrubs — Dictionaries
  1. Title
  635.9'76'0321   SB435

ISBN 0-946609-25-X

Library of Congress Catalog Card Number
86-81828

Other books by Lys de Bray:
Lys de Bray's Manual of Old-Fashioned Flowers (Oxford Illustrated Press, 1984)
The Wild Garden (Weidenfeld & Nicholson, 1978)
Midsummer Silver (Weidenfeld & Nicholson, 1980)
Fantastic Garlands (Blandford Press, 1982)
Cottage Garden Year (J.M.Dent, 1983)

CONTENTS

ACKNOWLEDGEMENTS

I am indebted to the following people for their help to me during the gestation period of this book.

Peter Chappell allowed me to take photographs of his peaceful woodland garden 'Spinners'; Mr and Mrs Hill of 'Headland' gave me similar freedom in their fascinating wind-blown cliff-side garden at Polruan in Cornwall. Tim and Barbara Hooker were, as always, immensely patient and helpful. John May let me photograph his interesting and well-grown shrubs at 'The Knoll', while Charlie Marchant never seemed to mind me prowling about in his tranquil acres at Keeper's Hill. Roger and Francis Pring afforded me the same facilities in their garden which I have come to rely on. The Marchioness of Salisbury has been most kind in permitting me to take photographs in the always beautiful gardens at the Manor House at Cranborne, and Mrs. Freda Taylor at the garden centre there solved many questions of nomenclatural nature. I was most fortunate in being able to ask Mr David C. Trehane of the International Camellia Society to read, criticise and correct the section on Camellias, on which he is an acknowledged authority.

Finally — no home runs well without help and, as always, Sue was a tower of cheerful strength during some very difficult times; Maurice kept my own shrubs from engulfing the rest of the garden and Hilary achieved miracles in her interpretation of my hand-written manuscript, reducing its hieroglyphs to a very presentable pile of typing. Without her efforts the manuscript would not have been ready on time. My husband, Larry Blonstein, endured the house — and particularly the garden — being almost permanently full of strangers, and so I appreciate his patience and encouragement in what I always feel is a selfish and solitary occupation, that compulsive urge to write which has resulted in this book. To you all, my thanks.

Lys de Bray

Picture credits

T. Hooker
Rhododendron ponticum; Corylopsis pauciflora; Clematis macropetala; Rosa Cerasocarpa; Rose 'Madame Isaac Pereire'.

R. Pring
Berberis stenophylla.

INTRODUCTION

This book is the natural sequel to *Old Fashioned Flowers** and in it you will find all the familiar flowering shrubs that I promised to write about, including climbing plants and roses.

What *is* a shrub? And when does it stop being a shrub and become a tree? The answer to the first question may be defined as follows: a shrub is a perennial plant with many woody stems at or near its base — that is, at ground-level. The botanical term 'sub-shrub' is often applied to some species or varieties; this means that the plant is woody at the bottom with soft growth at the top. A tree is generally defined as a woody-stemmed perennial with a single definite trunk: by the very nature of things, some shrubs are large enough to take tea under in comfort, while some trees are just about the right height for Alice (at her smallest) to do the same, and these are fine in rockeries, tubs and containers for many years, providing that they are nourished.

Shrubs are no longer a relic of Victorian gardens, where a group of evergreens such as Laurel, Privet, Aucuba and sometimes Rhododendron would have formed the nucleus of that now out-moded term 'shrubbery', to which might have been added equally easy-tempered plants such as Hydrangeas, Lilacs, 'Mock-Orange' and a clump of whispering Bamboo. But such days are gone, and so are the shrubberies, which is just as well. The slate is clean and now we can see shrubs for the beautiful and individual flowering plants that they are, or, just as important, as foliage contrast that provides a solid and well-upholstered background for the soft or vivid flower colours of the shrubs themselves, as well as roses, herbaceous plants, annuals and bulbs.

There are other reasons for the increasing popularity of shrubs (as may be seen by the large number of specialist nurseries). Perhaps the main one is that they can make a new garden look well-established even in their first season, and even more so in their second. They are, on the whole, quite trouble-free and most need little or no attention except from compulsive pruners. This means that a garden can be designed and planted for shrubs alone — although I would suggest an underplanting of spring bulbs to provide colour in early spring — because they can be chosen for any aspect and any height, from absolute ground level to about 20ft (6m), after which the climbers will take care of any bare spaces that are left. Such a garden, composed mainly of shrubs, has tremendous appeal for busy working people who want their gardens to look magically tidy without having to do too much about it. Shrubs seem to me to be the vegetable equivalent of leprechauns, because they look after themselves almost unaided without the obligatory dish of porridge. Perhaps it has something to do with all those solidified leprechauns called gnomes — you never see *them* in untidy gardens.

Then there are the elderly folk who may have houses in quite large gardens; for reasons of sentiment they are unwilling to leave their homes, but a large garden becomes as frightening as a jungle when one cannot cope with the annual exuberance of spring and summer growth. This is where carefully chosen medium-sized and dwarf shrubs, planted in groups, will solve most of this maintenance problem without too much loss of form and flower.

Small town gardens lend themselves to shrubs, or perhaps it is the other way about; either way, shrubs can make a small, often shady garden look almost permanently neat and well-furnished throughout the year, especially if evergreen species are chosen.

I cannot end this introduction without speaking of roses, which, of course, really deserve a book to themselves in any case. I have had to finish my lists of plant introductions at or around 1914, to correspond with the preceding book on flowers and because one has to stop at a logical date in history. In the intervening 70 years rose-breeding has made giant strides in quantity, if not always in quality, but, fortunately, many of the old roses have survived the ebb and flow of fashion. They are so easy and undemanding in the garden, needing so little of that dedicated care that is essential to keep the modern varieties looking as if they'd just stepped out of a catalogue.

To sum up, a garden without shrubs is as formless as a blancmange and it will collapse to nothing in winter. With them, a garden has a strong bone formation which is interesting throughout the year. In winter there will be a subtle beauty of bark, branch and swelling bud, or the strong and shining leaves of evergreens. In spring the tracery of bare brown twigs slowly mists with green to tell you that another season has come to the garden.

I hope that this book will remind you of some favourite old shrubs and introduce you to others that are even older.

Lys de Bray

Wimborne,
Dorset,
ENGLAND

December 1985

---

* *Lys de Bray's Manual of Old-Fashioned Flowers,* published by Oxford Illustrated Press, 1984

ABELIA *(Caprifoliaceae)*. The Abelia takes its name from Dr Clarke Abel 1780-1826, physician to Lord Amhurst's Embassy to China in 1817. Dr Abel was keenly interested in all branches of natural history and by 1816 had made a fine collection of plants and seeds, many of them being new discoveries. Having loaded this living cargo on to the vessel 'Alceste', he left Canton for the long voyage to England, but was almost immediately wrecked on an uncharted reef. There were no fatalities but all the precious seeds and plants were lost, and pirates and belligerent natives made rescue work difficult and dangerous. Eventually all were saved, though with few possessions, and they joined another ship, the 'Caesar', for the interrupted voyage home.

Because of the precarious nature of plant collecting in those days, it was customary to give duplicate plant collections to friends, in case of disaster; fortunately, before he left Canton, Dr Abel had previously given a small selection of his plants to Sir George Staunton who immediately gave them back when he heard of the shipwreck. Among the plants was *A. chinensis*.

Robert Fortune discovered another Abelia in China in 1849 whilst on an expedition in search of black tea. (Tea processing consists of withering, rolling, fermentation, drying, sifting and grading, during which the tea-leaves turn from green to black. Green tea is made by heating the leaf to prevent it fermenting.)

As was customary in those days, Fortune travelled by boat and by sedan-chair, from Foochow to Hochow, and to the delight of the chairmen he walked most of the way through the mountains along the route because he wished to examine the native flora. On this journey he discovered several new plants (a hydrangea, *A. uniflora* and *Spiraea japonica fortunei*) and proceeded to dig them up, though he had great difficulty in making the chairmen carry them — the Chinese regarded such plants as weeds of no value. But, as is usual with travellers of experience and determination, he succeeded in his efforts in getting the new discoveries to Shanghai and thence to England.

A. chinensis (1844) grows to 4ft (1.2m) with fragrant, funnel-shaped white flowers from July-September. A tender deciduous spreading shrub from China.

A. floribunda (1841) grows to 5ft (1.52m), sometimes more, with rose-coloured flowers on previous year's growth from May-July. A tender evergreen shrub from Mexico, needing wall protection.

A. triflora (1847) grows to 15ft (4.5m) with a spread of 8ft (2.5m) and has deliciously scented pale pink flowers in June. A hardy deciduous shrub from the Himalaya.

A. uniflora (1845) grows to 6ft (1.9m) with pale pink flowers in June. An evergreen shrub from China needing wall protection.

Requirements: Good well-drained soil, and a sheltered situation against a sunny wall.

Cultivation: Take 3-4″ (8-10cm) woody cuttings of current season's growth in July. Insert into a pot of rooting compost (equal parts of peat and sand) and set in a propagator at a temperature of 16-19°C (61-64°F). When the cuttings are rooted they may be potted on, but they must be protected during the first winter.

Pruning: None needed. Tidy bush after flowering to encourage new growth before the winter. Thin out old growth on evergreen varieties.

Uses: As fragrant wall shrubs.

Shrubs: Bodnant, Highfield, Hilliers, Hopleys, Jackman, Kaye, Knaphill, Knoll Gardens, Lime Cross, Marchant, Marten's Hall, Meare Close, Notcutts, Orchard (E.J.Pascoe), Otter, Reuthe, Rosemoor, Scotts, Shepton, Sherrard, Southcombe, St. Bridget, Stonehouse, Toynbee, Treasures, Treseder, Warley, Woodland, W.W., Wyevale.

ABUTILON *(Malvaceae)*. On the whole, this genus should be regarded as tender and requiring special care in siting. They really do need that south-facing aspect with a wall at the back for reflected warmth, except perhaps in the most southerly parts of the British Isles. Most Abutilons are greedy for food and extra water (though they should never be planted in wet situations). An ideal compost for pot-grown plants is equal parts of good loam, peat and sand with some fine grit added. The pots should be well crocked and when the plants begin to grow in the spring they can be given fortnightly feeds of weak manure water. *A. vitifolium* grows too large for any pot, and needs a sheltered corner where its attractive grey-green felted leaves remain throughout the year, forming a pleasing foil to the delicate flowers of white, pale blue, azure or lavender. In the autumn the dangling clusters of seeds make an interesting feature in the garden and are good in dried arrangements. The variegated form of *A. megapotamicum* is still seen as a 'dot' plant in municipal planting schemes where it is treated as an annual. It is more delicate than *A. vitifolium* and is really best in a conservatory, though there are many sheltered gardens along the south coast where mature specimens are a great credit to their owner's care. The flowers have scarlet calyces, yellow petals and dangling dark stamens and are instantly recognisable. This shrub should be planted where one can look up into the bell-shaped flowers.

A. megapotamicum (1864) grows to 6ft (1.9m) with red and yellow flowers from May until the frosts. A delicate wall shrub from Brazil for a sheltered site. May be grown as a large pot plant, on a conservatory wall or as an annual. The variety *A. megapotamicum* 'Variegatum' has attractively yellow variegated leaves.

A. vitifolium (1837) grows to 15ft (4.5m) or much more in sheltered areas. White, pale blue, azure or lavender flowers 2″ (5cm) wide in loose panicles of three to five from May-August. Greyish evergreen leaves. Best against a south wall.

Requirements: Site, soil and feeding as described. Protect stems of young plants with sacking during first winter outside.

Propagation: Take 4" (10cm) half-ripe cuttings from June-August and insert in pots of John Innes No.1 at a temperature of 15-18°C (59-64°F). When well rooted transfer into individual pots of the same compost and grow on. Protect during first winter, harden off in late May. *A. vitifolium* can be grown from seed. Sow in spring in a temperature of 15-18°C (59-64°F) in pots of seed compost. Grow seedlings on in the usual way, keep in greenhouse or conservatory for first winter.

Pruning: Little required. Cut out frost-damaged shoots in late March or April. The stems of greenhouse plants should be cut back by half and lateral branches shortened.

Uses: As tender wall shrub, *A. megapotamicum* as a container plant, *A.m.* 'Variegatum' as a foliage plant (in sun). Seed heads of *A. vitifolium* for winter arrangements.

Shrubs: Brackenwood, Peter Chappell, Farall, Hilliers, Hyden, Knoll Gardens, Marchant, Notcutts, Scotts, Sherrard, St. Bridget, Stonehouse.

Seeds: Chiltern, Thompson and Morgan.

ACTINIDIA (*Actinidiaceae*). The best known member of this genus of climbers is *A. Kolomikta* which has tri-coloured leaves of green and white tipped with pink. The shrub is grown for its decorative foliage though it has small ½" (1cm) wide white flowers in June.

In 1855 Carl Maximowicz (1827-1891), Conservator of the Herbarium of St Petersburg Botanic Gardens, discovered this very attractive shrub and many other plants whilst returning from China across Siberia. Maximowicz was an authority on the plants of Manchuria and Japan, and like all plant collectors of the time he endured much hardship on his travels: like all plant collectors he kept returning to these often inhospitable countries, to the ultimate benefit of the gardens of today. (His name is commemorated in the honeysuckle, *Lonicera maximowiczii.*)

Another plant collector, Charles Maries (1851-1902), spent many years in the Far East for the great horticultural firm of Veitch. Plants new to Europe were often to be found in nurseries in those countries, but the collectors, whilst availing themselves of this convenience, still spent a great deal of their time looking for new plants in the wild and uninhabited areas. In 1877 Maries found the fascinating Balloon flower, *Platycodon grandiflorum mariesii*, deservedly named after him, as was a new fir, *Abies mariesii*. During that same year he found *A. Kolomikta*, in the district of Sapporo on the Japanese island of Hokkaido.

For some reason cats are very attracted by this particular shrub, and may damage the stems of newly-set plants, so protect them with some wire netting until the Actinidia is truly established.

A. chinensis — Chinese Gooseberry, Kiwi fruit (1900) grows to 30ft (9m) with large leaves 8" (20cm) long. Sprays of creamy yellow flowers in August followed by hairy brown fruit tasting like apples. A large and vigorous climber from China for covering old trees and large areas of wall. Best in full sun in good soil. Male and female plants needed for pollination and subsequent fruit.

A. Kolomikta (1877) grows to 20ft (6m) with heart-shaped green leaves in spring that later become tinged or tipped with white and pink. Fragrant white flowers in June, followed by egg-shaped edible yellow fruit. A rather tender twining shrub for a sheltered position, variegation is better when planted in full sun.

Requirements: Good rich, well-drained soil and a sunny situation. Strong trellis, wire or wire netting for support.

Propagation: Take 3-4" (8-10cm) woody cuttings in July and insert in a rooting compost of sand and peat. Place in a propagator in a temperature of 16°C (61°F). When well rooted transfer into individual pots. Seeds may be sown as soon as ripe (in October). Sow in a box or pan of seed compost and leave in a cold frame for the winter. Prick out when large enough and grow on in individual 5" (13cm) pots.

Pruning: None generally needed unless plants get too large (it should be remembered that *A. chinensis* is a very big plant which should not be planted against a very small shed).

Uses: *A. chinensis* is excellent drapery for large, old, dead or unsightly trees, tall walls, or where screening is needed.

Shrubs: Busheyfields, Goscote, Hilliers, Hopleys, Jackman, Lime Cross, Marchant, Meare Close, Notcutts, Otter, Reads, Reuthe, Roger, Russell, Scotts, Shepton, Sherrard, St. Bridget, Stonehouse, Treseder, Woodland, Wyevale.

Seeds: Thompson and Morgan.

AKEBIA (*Lardizabalaceae*). *A. quinata* is a delightful creeper having such attractive leaves that the scented dark crimson flowers come as an extra bonus. This climber takes a little while to become established, and then, suddenly, the garage will vanish beneath a canopy of pleasing leaves. In April racemes of pink flower buds appear and soon the whole plant is a curtain of crimson flowers that have an almost tropical perfume. I planted mine against the shed wall (built as two privies 200 years ago) and now I can't see out of the windows when I am inside, and half the time I can't get in through the door, especially on wet days when the damp makes the leafy swags sag. It is a deceptively innocent-looking creeper which is another one that should not be planted in a confined position. It will grow in a shady situation but is lusher and lustier in full sun. In mild winters the plant is evergreen, and it looks very beautiful when planted to curtain an old Victorian verandah where the crimson flowers can be seen in their season with the sun shining through them. In the right position greyish-purple sausage-shaped fruits appear, though this is very rare. The ground beneath an established plant will soon be a coiling mass of purple-stemmed runners seeking fresh territory: these will inhibit other things, so be ruthless and cut them away at the base of the plant. It won't even notice. These new stems will root if left alone in any case, so if more plants are needed they can be layered in spring and in six months will be well rooted. The plants take from three to five years to become established and will then flower regularly.

A. quinata (1845) grows to 40ft (12m) with pendant racemes of heavily perfumed flowers in April-May. A (usually) evergreen twining climber from China, Japan and Korea for covering large areas. Best in sun though does well enough in semi-shade.

Requirements: Plenty of space, ordinary well-drained soil, strong trellis or wires.

Propagation: Best method is to layer the runners in April/May or take woody cuttings in July. Insert these in rooting compost (equal parts of peat and sand) and put in a propagator at 10°C (50°F).

Pruning: Not necessary if the plant has sufficient growing space. If it becomes a neglected tangle it can be thinned out in early spring, though much of the season's flowers will be sacrificed. In hard winters it may shed most of its leaves and it is easier to see where to thin out while it is in this state. If pruned after flowering (April-May) it is better, though the plant may look untidy well into the summer. It is a matter of choice and pruning can be done to suit the gardener's time or social programme.

Uses: As an excellent and very beautiful evergreen cloak for unsightly garages or large sheds. Leaves for floral decoration, flowers for pot-pourri.

Shrubs: Bodnant, Busheyfields, Knoll Gardens, Marchant, Notcutts, Otter, Reuthe, Roger, Scotts, Sherrard, St. Bridget, Stonehouse, Woodland, Wyevale.

Seeds: Chiltern, Thompson and Morgan.

AMELANCHIER — Snowy Mespilus, Shadbush, Juneberry (Rosaceae).

The most commonly grown and easily obtainable Amelanchier is *A. canadensis*, easily recognisable in spring because of its cloudy white blossom. No halfmeasures here — this bush can be counted on to do its stuff every year, and as it is a vigorous grower the gardener can cut branches of blossom to bloom indoors without any of the usual feelings of guilt.

The Amelanchiers are a rather variable and confusing genus, often hybridising naturally in their native North America.

This shrub likes moist soil to grow in and is often seen along river banks in eastern North America where it flowers as the shad come up the tidal rivers to spawn, hence the name 'Shadbush'.

The fruits, small though they are, are very edible, and if the wild creatures would leave them alone, it would be easy to pick enough to do something with. But in this country the garden birds are busy in the bush as soon as the berries are ripe, and in America skunks, raccoons, bears, moose, rabbits, foxes, squirrels and chipmunks, as well as all the birds, will squabble over the tiny fruits. Even the twigs are tasty, because moose, rabbits, deer and beaver browse on them. It really is a wonder that there is anything left to bear flowers in the following year, but as I have said, it is a vigorous grower. The leaves colour to yellow and crimson in autumn.

A. canadensis — Shadbush, grows to 20ft (6m) or more with white flowers in May and (usually) good autumnal colour. A deciduous suckering shrub from N. America or small tree, not for cramped places or very small gardens.

A. florida (1826) (sometimes confused with *A. alvifolia*) grows to 20ft (6m) or more with white flowers in May. A deciduous shrub or small tree from N. America with black-purple fruits and yellow leaves in autumn.

A. ovalis — Snowy Mespilus (1596) grows to 9ft (2.7m) with large white flowers in May. A deciduous shrub from S. Europe with good autumn colour.

Requirements: An open, sunny situation, lime-free moisture-retentive soil.

Propagation: Sow seeds as soon as ripe (June-July) in individual pots of seed compost. Layer low branches in September, leave in position for a year before separating. Some of the suckers may have separate roots, sever from parent during winter.

Pruning: Not needed, except to keep shrub shapely. Suckering stems may be cut away if liked.

Uses: Beautiful spring-flowering and autumn-colouring shrubs with currant-sized fruit, though the birds always get up earlier in the morning.

Shrubs: Barcock, Brackenwood, Daisy Hill, Farall, Goatcher, Hilliers, Hyden, Jackman, Kaye, Kershaw, Knaphill, Marchant, Meare Close, Notcutts, Otter, Reuthe, Roger, Russell, Scotts, Sherrard, Smith, St. Bridget, Stonehouse, Warley, Woodland, Wyevale.

Seeds: Chiltern.

AMPELOPSIS — Porcelain-berry (Vitaceae).

A genus of climbing plants, taking their name from *ampelos*, vine, and *apsis*, like. Most of them are very vigorous — a gardening synonym for rampant-if-not-controlled and the most beautiful (and easy) of these is *A. heterophylla*, sometimes sold as *A. brevipedunculata*. However, *A. brevipedunculata* differs from *A. heterophylla* in having slightly hairy young shoots, hairy stalks and it is bristly-hairy underneath the leaves. Those of *A. heterophylla* are shiny. The only way to tell the two apart is by the leaves — those of *A. heterophylla* are shaped like a hop though sometimes they are five-lobed or heart-shaped, all on the same plant. *A. brevipedunculata* is more consistent, with three-lobed leaves all over. Both have anticipatory greenish-cream cymes of flowers that look as if about to burst into something spectacular in the way of bloom, but never do. For this they can be forgiven, because when the grape-like sprays of berries form they begin to turn pale blue at first, changing to beautiful shades of turquoise, verdigris, cobalt, ultramarine, violet and indigo, all with dark speckles on them like a thrush's egg. The sprays of berries are spectacular — after a good hot summer and autumn — and depend on the plant being grown in a warm south-facing position against a wall. In dry years, when the garden-watering is not always as thorough as it might be, the leaves turn lime-green and then yellow which sets off the berries to perfection. Grow some asters (Michaelmas daisies) in shades of blue nearby, with the late dark spikes of *Salvia superba*. I have a gift-Helianthus next to my plant, whose name I do not know and its yellow flowers make a pleasing picture among the trailing blue-berried vine stems.

The stronger growing species need to be grown where their roots can be confined, as those of figs should be. It will be apparent from the following names and descriptions that the taxonomy is, as they say, unclear.

A. brevipedunculata, syn. **Cissus brevipedunculata,** syn. **A. heterophylla — Porcelain-berry** (1868) grows to 20ft+ (6m+) with unremarkable flowers in June and very beautiful berries in shades of blue from late August onwards. A very vigorous deciduous plant from N.E. Asia, climbing by means of tendrils. Excellent for warm walls, pergolas, low fences (when pruned) and to clothe steep banks. Var. *A. Maximowiczii* syn. *A. heterophylla* differs in the variation of leaf-shape on one plant and in having shinier leaves. For a focal position in a sunny place.

A. heterophylla, syn. **A. brevipedunculata** var. **Maximowiczii — Porcelain-berry** (1860) grows to 25ft+ (7.5m+) with shining, mostly three-lobed leaves, cymes of greenish flowers in June and sprays of remarkably beautiful berries in every shade of blue, turquoise, mauve and violet. A vigorous deciduous plant, from China, Japan and Korea, climbing by means of tendrils. For a focal position in a sunny place.

Requirements: Good garden soil, a sunny position and strong supports.

Propagation: Take heel cuttings in July or August and place in a rooting compost of sand and peat. When rooted transfer into individual pots of John Innes No.1 and grow on, keeping in a cold frame for the winter. Pot on and plunge pots in a nursery area in early spring or transplant into open ground to grow on for a season. Berries will germinate if planted when ripe in boxes or pots of seed compost. Keep in a cold but ventilated frame for winter. Seedlings will be found near plants in the following summer if the ground has not been disturbed. These can be potted up and grown on. Purchased plants will take from three to five years to come

to flowers and berrying.

Pruning: No special pruning needed. If vine is too large for its space, cut back in early March, otherwise allow to grow, which it certainly will.

Uses: As excellent wall, post, pillar, pergola and trellis covering, also for clothing banks and low fences. Berried sprays superb in arrangements.

Shrubs: Highfield, Hilliers, Kaye, Kershaw, Lime Cross, Marchant, Notcutts, Reads, Roger, Scotts, Shepton, Sherrard, Smith, St. Bridget, Warley, Woodland, W.W., Wyevale.

Seeds: Butcher.

ARBUTUS — Strawberry Tree *(Ericaceae).* This is a colourful shrub (or small tree in maturity) particularly in autumn, when the preceding season's fruit ripen to redness at the same time as the current season's pendant white flowers appear. The neat evergreen leaves are a pleasing foil to scarlet fruits and white flowers, and the rough shreddy bark is another interesting feature. If there is only room for one good specimen tree in the garden, then this is a good choice unless the soil is strongly alkaline. The Arbutus grows wild in Southern and S. W. Europe and parts of S.W. Ireland where at one time charcoal burners cut it down to such a degree that its incidence was permanently reduced. In Spain and Corsica wine was formerly made from the fruits, though these are thought to be narcotic when consumed in large quantities. Arbutus has been grown for centuries because of its attractive appearance throughout the year.

The Arbutus was sacred to the Romans and particularly to the goddess Cardea who was one of Apollo's sisters. Using a root of Arbutus wood, Cardea drove away witches and protected little children when they were ill.

Water distilled from the leaves and flowers was considered to be a potent remedy against poison and the plague, and branches of the wood were ceremonially laid on the coffins of the dead.

It is interesting to read that Pliny gave *A. Unedo* this name because it was said that he who ate one of the fruits would eat no more. In the interests of the true researcher (and it being the right time of year for my own small shrub) I sampled the ripest fruit and found it to be so bland as to be almost tasteless: Pliny was right.

A. andrachne (1724) grows to 15ft (4.5m) though much taller in its native Greece. A tender evergreen shrub when young but much hardier (if it survives) in maturity. White urn-shaped panicles of flowers in March and April, with orange-red fruits, attractive peeling bark. For a very sheltered garden.

A. Unedo — Strawberry Tree, eventually grows to 30ft (9m) with dangling clusters of white, urn-shaped flowers at the same time as the red and orange strawberry-like fruit. A tall evergreen shrub or small tree for a warm position protected from north or east winds, and particularly good in sheltered seaside gardens, where it will grow taller.

Requirements: Lime free soil, though *A. Unedo* tolerates more lime than other members of this genus. A warm and sheltered situation.

Propagation: Plant ripe seeds (after the winter) in a compost of 2 parts of peat to one of sand. Grow on and transplant into individual pots of John Innes No.2. Keep in a cold frame for two seasons, potting on if necessary. Plant into final positions in the third or fourth year. (Once established, Arbutus should not be moved.) Cuttings of half-ripe wood with a heel may be taken in July, insert these in a rooting compost of half peat and half sand and put into a propagator at a setting of 16-18°C (61-64°F) until the cuttings have rooted. Transfer rooted cuttings very carefully into individual pots and grow on.

Pruning: None needed.

Uses: As handsome evergreen fruiting and flowering shrubs. The fruit is edible but insipid and is better as decoration on the tree than in a pie.

Shrubs: Ballalheannagh, Bodnant, Brackenwood, Peter Chappell, Dobbies, Goatcher, Goscote, Hilliers, Hopleys, Hyden, Jackman, Kaye, Kent, Knaphill, Marchant, Meare Close, Reuthe, Roger, Rosemoor, Russell, Scotts, Shepton, St. Bridget, Stonehouse, Toynbee, Treasure, Treseder, Warley, Woodland, W.W., Wyevale.

Seeds: Butcher, Chiltern, Thompson and Morgan.

ARISTOLOCHIA — Dutchman's Pipe *(Aristolochiaceae)*.

This is a handsomely leaved climber that will only flower well in a warm sheltered place. My own plant languished, flowerless on a windy pergola pillar until just such a special situation materialised and the plant now produces its fascinating flowers each year in June. It has also become more rampant (along with all the other tender things on the same wall) and remembering that it needs either great height (which I have not) or a great width sideways, I have wired the wall so that its main stem can grow busily backwards and forwards. It can also be spirally trained round pillars in the same way, with only a few inches between the turns so as to save space.

This is one of the many valuable garden plants introduced by the Quaker botanist John Bartram (1699-1777) who made many plant collecting journeys during his life, though only two of them were properly recorded.

The Latinised name of Aristolochia comes from the Greek words for 'best delivery' and the common name of *A. clematitis* (a rare British wild flower) is Birthwort, which had a powerful reputation in former times for all things connected with childbirth from the conception, through to delivery and later in expelling the afterbirth. For good measure the plant protected mother and newborn babe from evil the whilst.

A. macrophylla, syns. **A. durior, A. sipho.** grows to 30ft (9m) in ideal conditions. The fascinating pipe-shaped yellow, brown and black flowers appear on mature plants in June. A hardy deciduous climber from eastern North America. The heart-shaped leaves are very attractive even if the plant is flowerless.

A. elegans — Calico Flower (1883) grows to 10ft (3m) with curious hooded flowers of rich purple-brown streaked with white that look rather like old-fashioned ships' ventilators. A tender evergreen greenhouse climber from Brazil for a border in a frost-free greenhouse or conservatory.

Requirements: *A. macrophylla* does best in good well-drained garden soil, and will appreciate an annual mulch of manure. Full sun is best, though if the position be warm and sheltered it will do in partial shade. It needs plenty of upward or sideways space. Pinch out the growing points of young plants, if sideways branching is required. Strong trellis or wiring is necessary. *A. elegans* is best grown in a greenhouse or conservatory border with a minimum winter temperature of 10°C (50°F). Water well during the growing seasons but keep much drier in winter. *A. elegans* needs shade in summer and more light in winter.

Propagation: For *A. macrophylla* take tip cuttings in July and insert into a rooting compost of half peat and half sand. Put pots into a propagator set at 18°C (64°F) until well rooted. Transfer cuttings to individual pots of John Innes No.2. Grow on for a year in a deep cold frame or a cold greenhouse, harden off before planting out in spring. For *A. elegans* take cuttings of lateral growths in June and put into a peat and sand rooting compost in a propagator set at 21-24°C (70-75°F). When rooted, transfer into individual pots of John Innes No.2. Aristolochias may be grown from seed sown in March at a temperature of 13-16°C (55-61°F), pricked out and grown on in the usual way. Give each young plant its own cane.

Pruning: Do this in February for *A. macrophylla* when it is outgrowing the available space. For *A. elegans,* reduce lateral growths by two-thirds and nip out main shoots.

Uses: *A. macrophylla* is a useful and unusual climber for large areas of wall. *A. elegans* is a striking plant for a warm greenhouse or conservatory.

Shrubs: Busheyfields, Hilliers, Jackman, Marchant, Notcutts, Sherrard.

Seeds: Chiltern, Thompson and Morgan.

ARTEMISIA *(Compositae)*.

This is a large genus of (usually) aromatic shrubs many of which have delicate grey or silver foliage. One of the best known is *A. Abrotanum* — Southernwood or Lad's Love, sometimes called 'Old Man' which has deliciously aromatic foliage. A sprig of it was always included in posies that were constructed with loving care by country lads for their lasses. There is a cousin to it, *A. camphorata,* which has leaves that smell strongly of camphor. The two plants look very similar and if a herb garden is planned then both should be grown.

A. Absinthium is Wormwood, used in the manufacture of absinthe. I always think of Toulouse Lautrec when autumn-tidying this aromatic, short-lived shrub. It pays to take insurance cuttings of this and *A. Abrotanum* which seems to have a slightly longer life.

In former days wormwood was used to counteract hemlock and toadstool poisoning, also the much rarer bites of the Sea Dragon. It was used in magic, and an old love charm ran as follows:

'On St Luke's day, take marigold flowers, a sprig of Marjoram, thyme, and a little Wormwood, dry them before a fire, mak them to powder, then sift it through a fine piece of lawn and simmer it over a slow fire, adding a small quantity of virgin honey, and vinegar. Anoint yourself with this when you go to bed, saying the following lines three times, and you will dream of your partner that is to be:

"St Luke, St Luke, be kind to me,
 In dreams let me my true love see."'

Wormwood is a good plant for seaside gardens, and is useful because it is quite happy in partial shade, unlike most silver-leaved plants.

A. Abrotanum — Southernwood, Lad's Love, Old Man (1548) grows to 4ft (1.2m). An aromatic deciduous shrub from S. Europe with delicate green-grey foliage and small dull yellow flowers from July-September. A shrub to plant where it can be brushed against so as to release the scent of the leaves. Best in a sunny, sheltered position but will grow in partial shade.

A. Absinthium — Wormwood grows to 3ft (92cm) with silvery-grey leaves. A pungently aromatic deciduous shrub, source of the particularly bitter flavour of absinthe. Used medicinally since earliest times. Will tolerate a degree of shade.

Requirements: Ordinary soil, and best in a sunny, sheltered position.

Propagation: Take woody cuttings with a heel in August, insert in a compost of sand and peat until rooted. Transfer into individual pots and keep in a cold frame for the winter.

Pruning: None necessary except for shaping. Cut *A. Absinthium* to within 6″ (15cm) of the ground in April. Tidy away frost killed branches of *A. Abrotanum* in spring, as soon as the new shoots can be seen.

Uses: As foliage plants, and in pot-pourri.

Shrubs: Ballalheannagh, Beth Chatto, Margery Fish, Great Dixter, Hilliers, Jackman, Kaye, Kershaw, Lime Cross, Marten's Hall, Notcutts, Oak Cottage, Old Rectory, Rampart, Scotts, Shepton, Sherrard, Stoke Lacy, Stonehouse, Toynbee, Treasure, Weald, Woodland, Wyevale.

Seeds: Chiltern, Thompson and Morgan.

AUCUBA — Spotted Laurel (*Cornaceae*). Surely the most good-natured and tolerant of all shrubs, the Aucuba, along with privet, laurel and ferns is only just beginning to live down its association as a founder-member of the Victorian shrubbery. Aucubas are unisexual, that is, male and female plants should be planted close to each other in order to produce the bright scarlet long-lasting berries. All gardens have bad or difficult corners and these can be instantly improved by an Aucuba, which even in infancy is a plumply substantial bush; the spotted kinds are best for dark walls and under trees, as they will light up these hard to plant situations with their sun-speckled leaves.

Some nurseries sell Aucubas under varietal names: these are generally types of *A. japonica*. When ordering more than one plant always specify (and check that you have received) male and female plants, which should be clearly labelled.

If a married pair of Aucubas have to be separated in your garden you can practise artificial insemination with a camel-hair paint brush. If the male flowers open first, the mature pollen can be collected and kept in a sterile glass jar until the lady is ready.

A. japonica (1783) grows to 12ft (3.7m) with clusters of small crimson flowers in March and April followed by scarlet berries on the female plants. An exceedingly useful evergreen shrub for difficult garden positions, as it will tolerate almost any situation. *A. Maculata* syn. *'Variegata'* is the most commonly grown female kind, having yellow-spotted leaves.

Requirements: Almost any soil, though good soil will make better furnished plants. Sun or shade, but the yellow-spotted types stay more brightly coloured in an open situation. Good in town gardens and by the sea. If grown in containers they should be planted in John Innes No.2 and fed several times during the summer and they should not be allowed to dry out. They will eventually grow too large and will have to be replaced with new small plants.

Propagation: Sow seeds in autumn for a large quantity of plants. Take heel cuttings in August and insert in a rooting compost of sand and peat and keep in a cold frame for the winter. The cuttings will have rooted by spring and can be potted on or planted out in nursery rows to grow on.

Uses: Myriad. As container plants in sun or shade, as indoor house plants, as wall-shrubs under tall trees and anywhere that other plants would not thrive.

Shrubs: Ballalheannagh, Bees, Bodnant, Brackenwood, Caldwell, Daisy Hill, Dobbies, Fairley's, Goatcher, Goscote, Great Dixter, Highfield, Hilliers, Jackman, Kershaw, Knaphill, Lime Cross, Marchant, Meare Close, Reuthe, Roger, Russell, Scotts, Shepton, Sherrard, Smith, St. Bridget, Treasures, Treseder, Warley, Woodland, W.W., Wyevale.

Seeds: Butcher, Chiltern.

AZALEA — see RHODODENDRON

Shrubs: Cunnington, Daisy Hill, Dobbies, Exbury, Glendoick, Goatcher, Hilliers, Hyden, Meare Close, Otter, Roger,

Russell, Scotts, Shepton, Sherrard, Smith, St. Bridget, Toynbee, Warley, Wyevale.

Seeds: Chiltern, Thompson and Morgan.

BALLOTA — *(Labiatae)*. *Ballota pseudodictamnus* is a rather tender shrub with felted silver-grey foliage. From June onwards whorls of tiny perfect doll's hat flowers appear and these persist on the plant until destroyed by winter frosts. They are much in demand by flower-arrangers because the stems do not wilt, and the small flowers are so perfect as to seem artificial — they look as though they have been cut out of pale green suede. These are the calyces, the flowers are rather inconspicuous, being white with purple spots.

B. pseudodictamnus grows to a rounded bush 2ft (61cm) high with neat green 'flowers' from June onwards. A grey-leaved shrub from Crete for a position in full sun.

Requirements: Ordinary free draining soil, full sun, a sheltered situation. The plants dislike wet and need protection in cold areas.

Propagation: Take woody cuttings with a heel in August and insert in a rooting compost of peat and sand and keep in a cold frame for the winter. The rooted cuttings should be potted on in spring and kept in a sheltered place for another season before being planted out.

Pruning: Tidy away frost-damaged branches in April.

Uses: As a contrast shrub, excellent for floral arrangements.

Shrubs: Peter Chappell, Beth Chatto, Margery Fish, Great Dixter, Hilliers, Knoll Gardens, Marten's Hall, Oak Cottage, Ramparts, Sherrard, Stonehouse, Treasure.

BERBERIDOPSIS — **The Coral Plant** *(Flacourtiaceae)*. This is an unusual evergreen shrub for a shady and sheltered position. It needs protection in cold areas, where it may not survive the British winters. It is best grown against a wall, or it will make a handsome plant in a cold greenhouse or conservatory. It has racemes of interesting flowers.

B. corallina — The Coral Plant. An evergreen scrambling bush or 'leaner' with coral-coloured flowers in July. A tender plant from Chile, needing a sheltered position against a wall.

Requirements: Ordinary garden soil, winter protection and shade.

Propagation: Layer branches in autumn or take cuttings in spring.

Uses: As an unusual wall-plant for shaded places.

Shrubs: Peter Chappell, Farall, Knoll Gardens, Marchant, Meare Close, Notcutts, Otter, Reuthe, Roger, Russell, Sherrard, St. Bridget, Stonehouse, Treasure.

BERBERIS — **Barberry** *(Berberidaceae)*. This large genus of usually prickly shrubs takes its name from the Arabic Berberys, though the distribution of the shrubs occurs mainly in Asia, with others in Africa, Europe and North and South America.

Because of their thorniness these shrubs are often used as very ornamental hedges, and *B. vulgaris* is known to have been grown for this purpose as far back as the 15th century. Some Berberis are evergreen but most garden forms are deciduous, often colouring beautifully in autumn thus having three periods of interest — flowers, fruit and autumn foliage. The fruit of *B. vulgaris,* the European wild Berberis, was formerly eaten as a rather pleasant form of medicine, and until the end of the 18th century the berries were gathered to make jelly. *B. Darwinii* is most often seen, its branches loaded down with the very characteristic flowers of orange-yellow that later turn to blue-bloomed berries. If several different kinds are grown together, hybrid seedlings will probably appear which are seldom as good as the parents. Berberis stamens are particularly sensitive when touched by bees or other insects seeking the abundant nectar, and clouds of pollen will be showered on the backs of the visitors which will thus be carried to the next flower or neighbouring plant. Most Berberis grow to a large size and this should be remembered when planting a minute slip-of-a-thing. When the slip has metamorphosed into a solid and exceedingly prickly, path-blocking monster it will be too late to say 'I told you so'. It is not kind to any large plant to attempt to keep it pruned into submission, so plant it with growing space and wait with a little patience and then you can enjoy it in its maturity. In any case, there is too much else that needs doing in the average garden to waste time peering at the gaps between bushes. Plant some interesting herbaceous things, which you will soon get to love; if you plant peonies they will outlast almost everything else in the garden, including you.

B. aggregata (1908) grows to 5ft (1.5m) with spiny leaves and yellow flowers in July followed by heavy clusters of soft red berries. Good autumn colouration altogether. A deciduous shrub from China for a focal position against a wall or dark evergreens.

B. candidula (1895) grows to 2ft (61cm) with yellow flowers and blue-black berries. An evergreen shrub from China for the rock-garden, with a pleasing shape and pale undersides to the leaves. (Sometimes sold as *B. Wallichiana hypoleuca*).

B. Darwinii (1849) grows to 6ft (1.8m) often more with evergreen leaves, golden yellow flowers in April and May and blue berries. A spiny shrub from China for hedging.

B. Hookeri (1848) grows to 5ft (1.5m) with a similar spread, with pale yellow flowers in April and May followed by black berries. A spiny shrub from Sikkim with glossy evergreen leaves.

B. pruinosa (1883) grows to 6ft (1.8m) with lemon flowers and black fruits. Spiny sea-green leaves, with white undersides. An evergreen shrub from Yunnan.

B. Thunbergii (1883) grows to 4ft (1.2m) with a spread of about 6ft (1.8m). Pale yellow flowers in spring turn to small scarlet, jewel-like berries that remain on the leafless branches. A deciduous shrub from Japan with superb autumn colouration. Var. *atropurpurea* has purple leaves.

Requirements: Ordinary free-draining garden soil, many will do quite well in semi-shade, though they will not be as compact.

Propagation: Seeds grow well (sow in November) but the seedlings may not be true to type. Or take heel cuttings in July-August and insert in a peat and sand rooting compost in pots in a cold frame. Grow on in John Innes No.1 for deciduous kinds and John Innes No.2 for evergreen varieties.

Pruning: None regularly: a spring tidy-up of deciduous kinds is advisable, evergreen varieties after flowering. Do not plant quart size Berberis into pint size positions.

Uses: Large vigorous kinds as effective, pretty, dog and people-proof hedges; as autumn foliage and berries, and for floral decoration.

Shrubs: Ballalheannagh, Barcock, Bees, Bodnant, Brackenwood, Bressingham, Caldwell, Peter Chappell, Daisy Hill, Dobbies, Farall, Goatcher, Goscote, Highfield, Hillier, Hopleys, Hortico, Hyden, Jackman, Kaye, Kershaw, Knaphill, Knoll Gardens, Lime Cross, Marchant, Meare Close, Notcutts, Orchard, Otter, Potterton and Martin, Reuthe, Robinsons, Roger, Scotts, Shepton, Sherrard, Smith, Southcombe, St. Bridget, Stonehouse, Toynbee, Treasure, Treseder, Warley, Woodland, Wyevale.

Seeds: Chiltern, Thompson and Morgan.

BILLARDIERA *(Pittosporaceae)*. For shady sheltered places, this is an unusual climber from Australia which has neat evergreen leaves and rather gentle ways. The genus was named after Jacques Julien Houtou de la Billardière (1755-1834), a French botanist. It is a good plant to use for clothing walls and has yellow-green bell-shaped flowers followed by very blue berries in October which come as a pleasing bonus. Surprisingly, these are edible. *B. longiflora* is hardy enough to be grown in the open in the southern half of the United Kingdom.

B. longiflora (1810) grows to 10ft (3.1m) or more with yellowish flowers and interesting blue berries. A twining small-leaved evergreen climber from Tasmania for a shaded warm wall.

Requirements: A north-facing position, ordinary garden soil and trellis or wires.

Propagation: Take cuttings in July and insert in a sandy rooting compost. Place in a propagator set at 16°C (60°F) and grow on in the usual way. Keep in a warm greenhouse for the first winter. If seed can be obtained it should be sown in March.

Uses: As soft evergreen cover for walls and pillars.

Shrubs: Busheyfields, Knoll Gardens, Marchant, Rosemoor, Sherrard, St. Bridget, Stonehouse, Wyevale.

Seeds: Chiltern

BOUGAINVILLEA — Paper Flower *(Nyctaginaceae)*. The genus is named after Louis Antoine de Bougainville (1729-1811), a French navigator who sailed round the world between 1766 and 1769. Whilst on his journey through the Pacific Ocean he claimed Tahiti and the Society Islands for the French, though the islands had also been discovered by Samuel Wallis during the same period (1766-1768) whilst circumnavigating the world in the hope of finding a habitable southern continent.

The brilliant magenta 'flowers' of Bougainvillea (in reality they are bracts) are a characteristic part of most Mediterranean towns where the shrubs are neatly clipped into shape against walls, around pillars and pergolas or as cascading colour over and through balustrades. Alas, such virtuosity of performance cannot be repeated under the greyer skies of Northern Europe, though good plants can be very floriferous when grown against a wall in a south-facing greenhouse which should be a large one, as established shrubs can attain a height of 20ft (6.1m) in the course of time. *B. glabra* can be grown in a large pot and will flower when still young, but there will come a time when it will have to be planted in the greenhouse or conservatory border. Or given away.

B. glabra — Paper Flower (1861). A showy plant for a large, moderately warm greenhouse, though in warmer latitudes it is a rampant climber, covering tall buildings, trees and cliffs with its mantle of 'flowers'. (The actual inflorescence has three small white flowers that are surrounded by the large, semi-transparent bracts that are commonly called the 'flowers'.) It makes a sturdy and useful hedge because the stems are thorny. There are red, orange, salmon, pink and white cultivars but the magenta coloured one is the most characteristic. A vigorous, deciduous thorny climber from Brazil which must be grown in a greenhouse or conservatory in Northern Europe, where it will flower in late summer and early autumn. In warmer climates it is in flower for most of the year.

Requirements: In the greenhouse a hole 2ft (61cm) deep should be dug and a 9″ (23cm) layer of brick rubble placed in the bottom (ideally, the site should be over a drain but this is seldom possible). Fill the hole with a compost of 3 parts good loam, 1 part leaf mould and 1 part or more of horticultural grit or sharp sand. Water once a week with liquid manure during the growing season, allow to rest after flowering (November-December) when watering should decrease. When being grown in large pots it needs the same compost, feeding and 'rest' period. Bougainvillea will need canes for support when being grown in pots and a strong framework to tie the (ultimately) heavy plants to when grown in the greenhouse border where they will climb up to the roof. Water well in the growing season and more so in hot weather. Syringing is beneficial at these times. They need a minimum winter temperature of 7°C (45°F) and increase to 10°C (50°F) in March. Pot on at this time.

Propagation: Take half-woody cuttings in summer and insert in individual pots of peat and sand rooting compost. Put into a propagator set at 21-24°C (70-75°F) until well rooted.

Pruning: Cut out weak and spindly growth in February, shorten main stems by about one third, and prune lateral branches according to available space *or* reduce to one strong growth on each spur.

Uses: In warmer climates Bougainvillea is used as hedging, as wall, arch, tree, pillar and pergola covering and as standard shrubs. In Northern Europe it is a brilliant-flowered greenhouse climber or large pot specimen.

Shrubs: Roger.

Seeds: Butcher.

BUDDLEIA, BUDDLEJA — Butterfly Bush *(Loganiaceae).* The genus was named after Adam Buddle, a seventeenth-century English botanist, and it does have other (and very attractive) members besides the ubiquitous *B. Davidii,* that determined and vigorous colonizer of railway embankments, old walls and post-second world war bomb-sites. This very beautiful shrub is much scorned because it grows so easily (and quickly) but if it is grown as a specimen plant it looks like a fountain of flowers when in full bloom. It is usually called the Butterfly Bush because in late summer it is a mass of butterflies of all kinds, particularly Red Admirals, who like best the nectar in the half-dead flower panicles. (Many of the world's most beautiful butterflies have some very un-beautiful appetites, such as ash, warm tar, carrion, dung, urine and human sweat.) The wood of mature Buddleias is very brittle (particularly *B. Davidii)* and during winter or summer gales the stems can and do snap. Even Buddleias die of old age and when this happens the roots are deep, strong and difficult to get out. This is just a reminder not to plant them where their demise can cause considerable upheaval, such as beside an established rockery, as mine was. I now have a much larger rockery, but at fearful cost to muscle and sinew. The white forms of *B. Davidii* are very beautiful indeed when in full bloom, but as the flowers age and turn brown they become unattractive, though not to the butterflies.

B. globosa has orange bobble flowers that are sweetly scented. It was mentioned by William Houstoun (1695-1733), a ship's surgeon who travelled and collected extensively in the West Indies where he died of heat in 1733. He sent plants, seeds and specimens to Philip Miller at the Chelsea Physic Garden, and it is thought that he discovered this shrub in a garden long before its recognised date of introduction in 1774.

B. Davidii — Butterfly Bush (1896) grows to 15ft (4.5m); more if planted against a warm wall, with spikes of mauve flowers in June. (Flowering time can be extended by pruning.) A deciduous shrub from China, best grown as a specimen plant in the open where the many butterfly visitors can be enjoyed. Any soil.

B. globosa — Orange Ball Tree (1774) grows to 15ft (4.5m) with globose heads of scented orange flowers in June. A semi-evergreen shrub from Chile for a reasonably sheltered position — can be damaged by severe frosts.

Requirements: Any soil, full sun and space to grow. Do not plant *B. Davidii* too near to a wall or in a corner.

Propagation: *B. Davidii* self-sows like dragon's teeth and the tiny shrubs can be moved as soon as recognised. Take half-ripened cuttings with a heel in July or August. Insert into a potting compost of peat and sand and grow on in a cold frame. Young shrubs can be moved when dormant.

Pruning: Cut *B. Davidii* hard back in early spring, to within 3″ (7.5cm) of the old wood, to produce large panicles of flower on long stems in July and August. Alternatively, leave shrub unpruned and it will flower in June. If a group of shrubs of different colours are grown together they may be pruned, or not, to flower at the same time or successively. Tidy winter-killed branches in early spring. Prune *B. globosa* after flowering by cutting dead heads off, down to a good pair of leaves.

Uses: *B. Davidii* can be used as a large flowering hedge, where space permits. It should not be used as a cut flower because though it lasts well enough, it has an unpleasant smell. The scented *B. globosa* is good for cutting, lasting well in water.

Shrubs: Ballalheannagh, Bees, Brackenwood, Caldwell, Daisy Hill, Dobbies, Farall, Margery Fish, Goatcher, Goscote, Highfield, Hilliers, Hopleys, Hortico, Hyden, Jackman, Kaye, Kershaw, Knaphill, Knoll Gardens, Lime Cross, Marchant, Meare Close, Notcutts, Otter, Reuthe, Roger, Rosemoor, Russell, Scotts, Shepton, Sherrard, Smith, Stonehouse, Toynbee, Treasure, Treseder, Warley, Woodland, W.W., Wyevale.

Seeds: Chiltern, Fothergill, Unwins.

CALLICARPA — Beautyberry *(Verbenaceae).* This is a genus of uncommon shrubs that are grown for their attractive fruits or berries. These are lilac-to-violet and make a pleasing picture with the autumn leaf colouration of yellow, pink and mauve. Their name comes from the Greek *kallos,* beauty, and *karpos,* fruit, and they are doubtfully hardy only in the southern counties of the British Isles — and then best against a sunny wall, and in groups of three so as to fruit more abundantly. The berries are not consumed by birds.

C. Giraldiana syn. **Bodinieri Giraldii** (1907) grows to 6ft (1.8m) with axillary clusters of lilac flowers in July followed by shining blue-violet berries. A deciduous shrub from China for a sheltered, sunny position.

C. japonica grows to a neat 4ft (1.2m) with pale pink axillary flower clusters in August followed by violet-blue berries. A deciduous shrub from Japan for a similarly sheltered place.

Requirements: Ordinary good garden soil, sun and shelter. Best grown against a wall in groups.

Propagation: Take heel cuttings in June and insert into a rooting compost of peat and sand. Place in a propagator at a temperature of 16-18°C (61-64°F) until rooted, then transfer into individual pots of John Innes compost.

Pruning: Very little, cut back to the previous year's wood.

Uses: Berried branches excellent for floral arrangements.

Shrubs: Barcock, Bodnant, Goatcher, Hilliers, Hopleys, Jackmans, Knoll Gardens, Marchant, Notcutts, Rosemoor, Russell, Shepton, Sherrard, St. Bridget, Stonehouse, Toynbee, Wyevale.

Seeds: Chiltern.

CALLISTEMON — Bottle-brush *(Myrtaceae).* This plant is another that takes its name from the same Greek word — *kallos,* beauty, and *stemon,* stamens. This genus comes from the Antipodes and mature shrubs are interesting at all times of the year, even when not in flower, because generations of flowers have hardened into knobbly bands that remain forever on the stem. The fascinating scarlet (or yellow) flowers are formed at the tip of the shoot, but after the flower dies, another shoot grows directly out of the remains of the brush-like inflorescense leaving it behind like a bead on a string. In time the flower stems take on a fossilized appearance, much appreciated by flower arrangers for their more permanent creations.

The leaves of *C. citrinus* have a lemon fragrance when they are crushed. The genus is tender in the British Isles and needs a home against a warm wall where a mature plant in full flower is an arresting sight. In the event of an exceptionally cold winter the aerial parts of the plants may be killed but new growths often spring from the roots if they are left in situ, as happened in my own garden. Plant a spring-vigorous thing like an Oriental poppy near the stump and forget about it, and there may well be a nice surprise in late summer when you clear away the poppy leaves to find a brave new shoot of the Callistemon. Young plants can be grown on in pots and taken into the greenhouse or conservatory for the winter. They will need potting on every other year, requiring only a growing medium of loamy garden soil, peat and sand. They need no feeding at all.

C. citrinus (1788) grows to 8ft+ (2.4m+) and more in maturity. An evergreen shrub from Australia with striking red bottle-brush flowers in June for a very sheltered and sunny position outside or in the cold greenhouse.

C. linearis (1788) grows to 5ft (1.5m) with crimson-green flowers in July. A more hardy evergreen shrub from New South Wales for a sunny corner.

Requirements: A warm and sheltered site against a sunny wall and ordinary garden soil (though not chalk).

Propagation: Take half-ripe heel cuttings in July and insert them in a rooting compost of sand and peat in a propagator set at 18-21°C (64-70°F). When rooted, transfer to a growing compost of equal parts of loam, peat and sand. Sow seeds in seed compost in March at a temperature of 16-18°C (61-64°F) and grow on in the usual way. Protect for two winters before planting out either cuttings or seedlings.

Pruning: None needed, as cutting off the old branches with their 'permanent' woody fruits would spoil the appearance of this interesting Antipodean plant.

Uses: Both flower spikes and old stems are excellent for arrangements. As a striking wall shrub, but not red-flowered spires against new red brick.

Shrubs: Ballalheannagh, Bodnant, Brackenwood, Crarae, Goscote, Hilliers, Kaye, Knoll Gardens, Lime Cross, Marchant, Orchard, Otter, Reuthe, Shepton, Stonehouse, Treasure, Treseder, Wyevale.

Seeds: Chiltern.

CALLUNA — Heather, Ling *(Ericaceae).* The name of the genus is taken from *kallunein,* to sweep: heather branches were much used as brooms in former days. In Cornwall men with brushes of heather were stationed on the headlands above the fishing villages to watch for the vital shoals of fish so necessary for survival. My father could remember the shout of 'hevver' when a shoal was sighted, accompanied by the jubilant waving of the heather branches as the watcher ran down the cliff path to join the fishing fleet. Heather was an essential plant in the northern parts of Great Britain for centuries providing springy mattresses to sleep on, thatch for the houses, fuel for the fires, brooms to sweep with and the wherewithal for basket-making and even rope. Heather honey is famous for its dark colour and extra flavour, and nowadays the plant is preserved along with the grouse that it shelters. There is only one species of Calluna, though there are hundreds of named modern varieties with green, grey, red, crimson, orange, gold and yellow coloured scaly leaves. Modern varieties of Calluna have flowering times from July until November, and it is as well to try to see a heather garden (with named cultivars) in full bloom before planning your own. Foliage colour often changes with the seasons, and this should also be taken into account — some of the petunia purples do not look harmonious with orange-leaved kinds. 'Garden' heathers will be found under 'Erica'. Heather-gardens can be a lovely feature in areas of acid soil, but there is little point in trying to grow them in all their colourful beauty unless you have the right conditions.

C. vulgaris — Heather, grows to 18″ (46cm) (more in natural moorland conditions) with characteristic purple-pink bell-shaped flowers from July to September. An evergreen plant of moorlands and acid bogs, not really suitable for any but wild gardens.

For requirements, propagation and uses see *Erica.*

Shrubs: Dobbies, Frye, Highfield, Hilliers, Ingwersen, Knoll

Gardens, Otter, Potterton and Martin, Reuthe, Russell, Scotts, Sherrard, Smith, Speyside, Treasure, Ward, Warley, Woodland, Wyevale.

Seeds: Chiltern, Thompson and Morgan.

CAMELLIA *(Theaceae)*. This most beautiful genus of evergreen flowering shrubs and trees was named after Georg Joseph Kamel (1661-1706), a Jesuit priest who spent the whole of his life as a missionary in the Philippines, whence he corresponded with John Ray about botany. In 1704 he wrote a book on the plants of Luzon, the most northerly island of the Philippines. One of the earliest travellers to discover the Camellia was Engelbert Kaempfer (1651-1715), a German physician employed by the Dutch East India Company. Japan had expelled all missionaries and foreign nationals because the so-called Christians were supporting a revolutionary coup. Ports were closed to all foreigners and any Japanese who left the country was not allowed to return. The Dutch had sent no trouble-making missionaries and were therefore permitted to trade in a minor way at the port of Nagasaki. Conditions were difficult — the Dutch were given a small artificial island called Deshima where they built their warehouses and where their permanent officials lived. At first, three ships a year were permitted to enter and leave the harbour; later this was reduced to two. The seas around Japan were notoriously dangerous in every way for shipping — storms, typhoons, uncharted reefs and pirates were the main hazards. In addition to the natural difficulties of the area, the Dutch were expected to send an annual embassy with traditional presents to the court of the Emperor in Tokyo. Botanizing was exceedingly difficult under these conditions. Kaempfer went on two of the embassies in his capacity as physician to the Dutch governor, and it is very likely that he welcomed the journeys as an opportunity to collect specimens, because it is known that he travelled with a large box perched in front of his saddle, into which he put all kinds of flowers and plants and even branches of trees (it must have been a very large box), which he later described and 'figured' (drew). Hidden under the box was a compass so that he could make exact notes of his travels (this was a forbidden practice — possession of Japanese maps ranked as treason and was punishable by death). When the cavalcade reached Tokyo, Kaempfer was expected to entertain the Emperor (and his concealed women) by singing and dancing and miming current European manners and behaviour. After his return to Europe Kaempfer wrote his famous book *Amoenitates Exoticae* (1712), in the fifth section of which he described very many plants and shrubs then quite new to European gardeners, including nearly thirty different kinds of Camellia.

Camellia japonica has always been considered to be the hardiest of the more well known species, though *C. oleifera*

(with its strong and leathery leaves) is actually hardier; this has small fragrant white flowers in spring. Camellias and their characteristic leaves can be recognized from some distance. These are broadly oval, toothed, and a shining dark green above. Camellias have very specific needs which must be catered for or the plants will not thrive. Gardeners with lime-free soil are the most fortunate when it comes to Camellia culture, as they do not have the nuisance of mixing up vast quantities of Camellia-type compost, though the siting of the plants is just as important. Camellias should be planted in sheltered places, either close to (but not rammed up against) a west or north-facing wall or where they can be sheltered from frosts by an overhead canopy of mature woodland trees. Camellias should not be planted facing to the east, especially if it is in an exposed position. After a night of frost, the morning sun will damage the flowers. At this time of year a frosted open flower would in any case be pulped. They can be grown in large tubs or pots or in a cold greenhouse, though they will need to be shaded in summer. Bud-drop is a worry to those gardeners who have not got it quite right: it is caused by drought at the roots or by poor drainage and once a happy medium is achieved the Camellias will settle down and grow away. Frost does not cause actual bud-drop unless the plants have had an earlier set-back like drought, or a cold, wet unripening sort of summer. A better and more sheltered situation will generally induce multiple bud-clusters, among which the later buds are too small and immature. These will drop when winter comes, or spring.

Blue tits are often seen 'at work' among the Camellia buds, just when they show colour. The tits tear open the buds or strip the opening flowers to get at the plentiful supply of nectar at the base of the stamens. Inevitably, buds (unready and uncoloured) get knocked off as well during this activity. It will be noticed that the formal flowers without stamens are not so attacked. The blue tits are a real problem in certain gardens and dry bird-food is not always the answer, though a slab of bee-candy will be an inducement to keep the birds out of your bushes, but they need unfrozen water to drink as well. Netting can be used to protect the bushes as a last resort. Camellias do quite well in full sun if their root-run is moist though they will do even better in Cornwall where the air is moister. They are best in the shelter of larger shrubs, in the shade of tall-tree canopy and in woodland conditions in humus-rich soil that does not dry out. Pink and white-flowered kinds can be badly damaged by sun and dew, whereas frost burns show less (from a distance) on red, crimson or cerise flowers.

Camellias may be used as exotic hedging plants, and for this should be planted 2½ft (76cm) apart. They should be clipped after flowering, when the dead flowers are cut off. Shape the hedge so that it is wider at the base than at the top.

Camellias (pronounced Ker-mell-ia if you want to be correct but most people say Ker-meel-ia) have thick-petalled flowers in all shades of pink, salmon, red, crimson and white, with splashed, striped, shaded, single, semi-double and double flowers. They have been separated into the following categories: single, semi-double, anemone-flowered, paeony-flowered, double, rose form double and formal double (the latter have very beautiful and unreal-looking flowers with perfectly overlapping round or pointed petals and no stamens). *C. reticulata* is best grown outside only in the south of England, and a fine example of this Camellia, 'Captain Rawes', is in Joseph Paxton's greenhouse at Chatsworth. It is one of those curious things that the progeny of *C. reticulata* when used as a pollen parent on *C. saluenensis* are as hardy as the later (1930s) *C. x williamsii* hybrids. The semi-double pink form of *C. reticulata* was introduced by Captain Rawes of the 'Warren Hastings' and was named after him. *C. Sasanqua* has narrow leaves and scented flowers that begin to open from November onwards. Since the British winter is as cruelly unpredictable as a sleeping tiger, *C. Sasanqua* is seldom likely to flower with abundance and is best grown in a cold greenhouse except in southern gardens by the sea, in Cornwall and the Scilly Islands, or against a protective wall. Camellias do not always shed their dead flowers. Many gardeners cut them off, risking damage to forming shoots. If the browned blossoms remain obstinately on the bush they will generally yield to a smart tap on the branches with a stout walking stick or a hoe-handle. In favourable situations, particularly in Cornwall, Camellias that are average sized shrubs elsewhere grow into very beautiful trees. But as their situation has to be very favourable indeed for this to happen it need not prevent you purchasing what the catalogue may describe as 'ultimately large-growing'. *C. x williamsii* varieties are well mannered about this, and it will be found that all the species shed their flowers except when frosted.

Plants in tubs may produce too many buds — this is indeed an ideal to aim for; disbudding is not necessary except when show flowers of greater quality are wanted.

There are many thousands of named cultivars with too many new hybrids or seedlings appearing every year. *C. japonica* is by far the easiest type to start with and one of the most popular (and recognisable) varieties is the red semi-double ADOLPHE AUDUSSON (1877) which is the most amiable and easy-going of plants, forming a large glossy-leaved bush in maturity that in the right conditions will be covered with typical Camellia-shaped flowers. Midseason flowering (early is defined as February).

The following are some old varieties which are still obtainable:

Arejishi (1891) has larger, pointed leaves, a more open habit and bright red paeony-like flowers. Early.

Australis (1862). Medium sized flowers, characteristic round leaves, good for tubs. Midseason-late.

Bokuhan (date not known but a very old variety). **Tinsie** in the USA. Anemone-flowered with red petals and a white boss of petalodes. Early-midseason.

C.M. Hovey (USA 1853) has large 4½″ (11.5cm) dusky red flowers with an occasional pale stripe. Midseason.

Contessa Lavinia Maggi (Italy 1860). A formal double with pale pink and carmine stripes on a white ground. (Branches which have red flowers should be cut out immediately they are seen or the whole bush will revert.) Early-late.

Elegans (London 1831). Large rose-pink anemone-form flowers with notched petals and some white petalodes. Characteristic lax wavy leaves and close, spreading habit. Never prune the leading shoot.

Gloire de Nantes (France 1895) has rose red semi-double flowers under glass and paeony flowers out of doors, 3″ (7.5cm) wide. Early flowering, sometimes in November through to late season.

Jupiter (England 1900). Carmine red single or semi-double with 4″ (10cm) flowers. Characteristic dark, glossy leaves with sideways-turned point. Midseason.

Lady Clare (Japan 1887 as **Akashi-Gata**) forms a round, spreading bush with large semi-double salmon-pink flowers with reflexing petals. Midseason-late.

Lady Loch (Australia 1889). A picotee paeony Camellia, dark-veined pink shading to a white fringe on broad reflexing outer petals. Inner petals small and erect. Upright bush with good dark leaves. Early-late.

Magnoliflora (Japan 1886). Pink flushed white semi-double flowers with narrow recurving petals. Midseason.

Mrs Bell (Australia 1879). Formal double white on a neat bush. For greenhouse cultivation with midseason flowers.

Rubescens Major (France 1895). Formal double with rose-red flowers on a densely-leaved bush. Midseason.

The Czar (Australia 1913). Semi-double with salmon-red petals and a barrel of creamy stamens. Midseason-late.

Reticulata varieties:

Captain Rawes (China 1820). Full semi-double carmine rose-pink flowers. Late. Grows into a tree in Cornwall.)

Robert Fortune syns **Flore Pleno, Songzilin, Pine Cone** (China 1857) Crimson-red formal or rose form. Midseason.

Requirements: Camellias need rather light acid soil with a pH of 5 to 6.5. They cannot be grown easily or successfully on chalk and usually look most inappropriate if this is attempted. They need plenty of humus such as peat and leafmould. If grown in pots these must be large enough for the variety (check its size and growth habit, there are many small-growing types) and filled with ericacious compost. Pots, tubs or containers should be well crocked and stood off the ground, and placed in situations that suit them (some varieties like the sun more than others). Pots should not be in situations where frost can penetrate to the roots as these will be killed before the aerial parts by intense cold and chilling winds. Unsightly though it may be, it is at times necessary to wrap the larger and more immovable pots (and, in any case, where can one put them?) with comforters of sacking, straw, newspaper and plastic outside all. Camellias need semi-shade and do well in north facing positions. They do not like draughty corners near buildings though they do not mind wind. Many types grow and flower better (and larger) under glass, often the difference is quite marked. Greenhouse conditions should be humid, shaded and airy, with heat only at times of hard frost. Use sphagnum peat when planting. Spread this 3″ (7.5cm) deep on sq.yd (metre) dig out top spit with peat into a heap; break up bottom spit with fork and return heap to hole. Sprinkle John Innes Base fertiliser before planting, plant to same soil level and tie to stake or cane if necessary. After planting, mulch with 2″ (5cm) peat or firbark.

Water newly planted Camellias well during their first season in your garden, particularly if they are in dry places near walls, large hedges or under trees. If there is a dry period at the roots of new or any Camellias during July and October this is generally the cause of bud-drop. Feed with complete fertiliser according to directions and sulphate of ammonia or dried blood in April, always on damp soil. When watering shrubs in tubs, give liquid feeds between March and early August, but stop then, or the leaves will turn brown and drop off. Use liquid feed carefully according to directions, do not use animal manure. Get all this right and Sequestrene will never be necessary.

Propagation: Take cuttings of 3-4″ (7.5-10cm) long lateral shoots from June to August and place in a rooting compost of peat and sand in a propagator set at 13-16°C (55-61°F).

C. reticulata is best layered and separated 18 months later, or rooted as cuttings directly into a 3″ (7.5cm) pot. It has been discovered that transplanting them from the cuttings beds formerly killed them.

Pruning: None generally needed except to cut back extra long or unbalanced growth in February. Clip hedges or wall shrubs at or just after flowering time.

Uses: As long-lasting cut flowers (quite beautiful when floated in a crystal or silver bowl) and as greenhouse, wall and container shrubs.

Shrubs: Antony, Ballalheannagh, Barcock, Bees, Bodnant, Brackenwood, Caldwell, Peter Chappell, Crarae, Daisy Hill, Dobbies, Exbury, Farall, Glendoick, Goatcher, Goscote, Hillier, Jackman, Kaye, Kent, Knaphill, Knoll Gardens, Marchant, Notcutts, Otter, Reuthe, Rosemoor, Russell, Scotts, Sherrard, St. Bridget, Toynbee, Treasure, Tregrehan, Trehane, Warley, Wyevale.

Seeds: Chiltern.

CAMPSIS — Trumpet vine, Trumpet creeper *(Bignoni-*

aceae). Campsis is a beautiful and unusual creeper that is not often seen. It needs a warm wall to climb up, preferably one that is forty feet high and faces south-west. Its name comes from *kampe,* a bending, because of its curved stamens and it is often confused with Bignonia which it much resembles except for one important difference, Bignonia climbs by means of tendrils while *Campsis radicans* climbs by means of ivy-like aerial rootlets, though when in full leaf it is a heavy thing and needs proper support and tying. There are only two species of Campsis, *C. chinensis* syn. *C. grandiflora* and *C. radicans,* both have similarly coloured orange trumpet flowers, though those of *C. chinensis* are the largest. In China it is called with very literal simplicity 'sky-approaching flower' and it has been cultivated for centuries both for its beauty and as a medicinal plant. In Northern Europe it is shy-flowering and will only oblige in drought-type summers, of which we have had three in the last ten years and during which all the Campsis climbers rejoiced and scrambled happily skywards. There is a hybrid of the two called 'Madame Galen' which is hardier than both parents. *C. radicans* comes from North America where its flowers are pollinated by humming birds. Both species have attractive pinnate leaves.

C. chinensis syn. **C. grandiflora** (1800) grows to 30ft (9.5m) in ideal conditions with brilliant orange-scarlet trumpet shaped flowers in August and September. A vigorous deciduous creeper from China and Japan for a large, hot, sheltered wall.

C. radicans — Trumpet Creeper, Trumpet Vine (1690) grows to 40ft (12m) in similar conditions, with smaller orange-scarlet trumpets in August and September. A vigorous deciduous climber from S.E. United States.

C. x tagliabuana (1880) is a variable hybrid having characteristics of both parents. It has salmon-red trumpets in August and September and is hardier.

Requirements: A warm summer, a tall wall or buildings to grow up and over, shelter, adequate support and good rich soil.

Propagation: Take 4″ (10cm) cuttings in July and August and insert in a rooting compost of peat and sand. Put into a propagator at 16-21°C (61-70°F). Grow on in the usual way and protect in a warm greenhouse or conservatory for the first winter. Plant in manure enriched soil in full sun against a trellis or wires, tie in as the plant grows, or until the aerial roots of *C. radicans* appear. Long branches can be layered into pots in October or November, these will take a year to form roots and can then be separated. Sow seeds in March in a temperature of 10-13°C (50-55°F) and grow on in a frame. Transfer into larger pots with supporting canes and plunge in a 'nursery' area, protect in a frost-free greenhouse for the first winter and plant out in the spring. Bud-drop can occur because of cold summer nights or lack of water in the growing season.

Pruning: Cut back second year plants to within 6″ (15cm) of the ground to encourage strong new growth. Prune mature plants in February, cutting back the previous year's growth (if you can sort it out from the tangle) to within 3-4″ (7.5-10cm) of the base of each shoot.

Uses: As handsome wall covering creepers even if shy-flowering.

Shrubs: Busheyfields, Farall, Hilliers, Hortico, Jackman, Knaphill, Lime Cross, Marchant, Notcutts, Otter, Reuthe, Russell, Scotts, Shepton, Sherrard, St. Bridget, Stonehouse, Toynbee, Treasure, Woodland, Wyevale.

Seeds: Butcher, Chiltern, Thompson and Morgan.

CARYOPTERIS *(Verbenaceae).* These are small shrubs for hot sunny walls, with flowers of a rather indeterminate shape that are the truest of blues. Non-gardeners notice this and always ask what the plant is called, and when told they never remember — it is always 'that greyish plant with the fuzzy blue flowers'. The name Caryopteris comes from the Greek *karyon*, nut, and *pteron*, wing (fruit winged), which may make botanists happy but does not make the plant memorable. Bees love Caryopteris and it should always be one of a bee-garden's plants because its flowers are so rich in nectar and come in late summer.

If the shrub needs to be moved, do this in its dormant period. The early species were not very strong growing and have been superseded by more recent hybrids which are outside the scope of the book because of their later dates. *C. Mastacanthus* was discovered by Robert Fortune who brought a fine shipload of plants back with him in 1846, fighting off pirates and fever in order to protect himself, his precious plants and indeed the whole crew and the captain of the Chinese junk in which he had taken a passage. The story is as follows:

Fortune set sail for Chu-san from the port of Foo-chow, where he had made his last purchases from those few nurseries that he was allowed to visit. No European ships called at the port, so Fortune was obliged to take a passage in a timber-carrying junk. At that time he was ill with a fever and as soon as he was aboard he went to his cabin. The China seas were as infested with pirates as a stray cat is with fleas, and soon after the junk had left port Fortune, still sick of his fever, was informed that a number of pirate junks were in sight. The crew fled below in terror as soon as the first shots were fired from the nearest junk, though the two helmsmen remained at the tiller for a few moments longer. They, too, were about to scuttle below for temporary safety, but Fortune drew his pistol and forced them to stay in control. The leading pirate drew ever nearer, firing as she came; Fortune allowed the shots to pass harmlessly through the rigging and told the two helmsmen to lie down for safety, while he waited until the pirate vessel had sailed close in. He had previously loaded his double-barrelled gun and, holding his fire, he waited with the calmness of true courage until the enemy ship was within twenty yards.

Then he took aim and fired, causing great losses among the pirates. The enemy vessel fell away, its place being taken by another pirate, and Fortune did the same thing, waiting until the last moment before firing. This double massacre aboard the pirate junks frightened the others off as they were unused to retaliation of any kind. The Chinese captain, the crew and all the passengers came and kowtowed before Fortune, who accepted their thanks and went back to his bunk to nurse his fever. There were further encounters with pirates before the junk docked at Chu-san, and arguments with the captain who wanted to divert to Ning-po, there to leave his courageous passenger who had saved their lives several times over.

C. Mastacanthus syn. **C. incana** (1844) grows to 5ft (1.5m) with violet-blue flowers in September and October. A tender deciduous wall-shrub from China and Japan for a sunny site.

Requirements: A chalky, free-draining soil, and a hot, sunny position against a wall.

Propagation: Take half-ripe cuttings of lateral shoots in August or September; insert in a rooting compost of peat and sand. Protect in a frame or cold greenhouse for the winter and plant out in late summer.

Pruning: Cut back previous year's strong growth in April to the base of the shoots. Remove weak growth.

Uses: As a bee plant and as good colour in the late summer garden.

Shrubs: Barcock, Bodnant, Brackenwood, Caldwell, Peter Chappell, Daisy Hill, Dobbies, Farall, Goatcher, Highfield, Hilliers, Hopleys, Hyden, Jackman, Kaye, Kershaw, Knaphill, Lime Cross, Marchant, Meare Close, Notcutts, Orchard, Otter, Reuthe, Roger, Russell, Scotts, Shepton, Sherrard, Smith, St. Bridget, Stonehouse, Toynbee, Treasure, Treseder, Warley, Woodland, W.W., Wyevale.

Seeds: Thompson and Morgan.

CASSIOPE *(Ericaceae).* Cassiopeia was the wife of Cepheus, the king of Ethiopia. The beautiful Andromeda was their daughter, who was later chained to a rock as a meal for an unaesthetic but permanently hungry sea monster. Fortunately, as in most good Greek myths, being beautiful, she was rescued in the nick of time by Perseus who happened to be passing in his *Argo*. Some members of this genus were formerly called Andromeda.

Cassiopes are delightful, evergreen dwarf shrubs and mat-formers for rock gardens with acid soil, and they do best in the more northerly counties of the United Kingdom, and particularly so in Scotland. If grown in the (generally) warmer southern counties they should be planted in a north-facing aspect. There is a great deal to be said for constructing a shaded north-facing end or side to the more usual south-facing rockery; many plants, notably ferns, are happiest in this kind of home and there are certain delicate and very beautiful alpine plants such as Haberleas and Ramondas which dislike direct sunlight.

Cassiopes prefer an open aspect, and should not be planted where there is drip from trees or in dense shade. They are rigid little plants with overlapping scales instead of leaves, with many large (for the size of the plant) solitary bell-shaped flowers on delicate stems.

C. fastigiata (1849) grows to 10″ (25.5cm) with white flowers in April and May. A dwarf shrub from the Himalaya for an un-sunny situation.

C. lycopodioides is prostrate, growing only to 1½″ (3.8cm) with white bells in April and May. A beautiful evergreen mat-former from N.E. Asia and N.W. America for a north-facing ledge.

C. tetragona (1810) grows to 10″ (25.5cm) with sometimes pink-tinged white flowers in April and May. A more erect ever-green shrublet, best planted in groups.

Requirements: A peaty or acid humus-rich soil, moist but not water-logged and with an open but not sunny situation. Best in Scotland, the northern, north-west and western counties. Does not mind cold.

Propagation: Take 1½″ (3.8cm) cuttings in August and insert in a rooting compost of peat and sand. When rooted transfer to individual pots of acid soil and leafmould, grow on for a year in the pots which should be plunged in a shaded pos-ition. Plant out in the second spring.

Uses: As evergreen plants for specific types of rock garden, in association with choice heathers chosen for contrast of foliage or flowers (see *Erica* for list).

Shrubs: Ballalheannagh, Jack Drake, Glendoick, Glenview, Goscote, Hilliers, Ingwersen, Marchant.

CEANOTHUS — Californian Lilac *(Rhamnaceae)*.

The name Ceanothus is from the Greek *keanothus,* which means 'spiny plant': an example of the shifts and changes of nomenclature. (The name would better have been given to Colletia which is as spiteful as a cactus.) These beautiful mostly evergreen shrubs are often called 'Californian Lilac' because nearly all of them originate from that part of the United States. The taller and more vigorous kinds should not be bought on impulse and just popped in, against any old wall — they demand the gardener's ability to plan ahead. Some species, such as *C. thyrsiflorus* grow to 30ft (9m) and as most are evergreen they make an imposing plant in the right place, where they will flower for months, cover-ing themselves with puffs of blue which is a rare colour among large shrubs. Honeysuckle *(Lonicera* vars.) with pink to red flowers looks delightful when scrambling among this blue mist, as does pale pink Clematis, but do not overload the Ceanothus with passengers because Loniceras are stranglers, carving deep diagonal weals in the trunks of their host-plant, as I know to my cost. My own Ceanothus was somewhat neglected for two years owing to pressure of

work, and by the time I noticed the delightful harmony of honeysuckle and Ceanothus in flower together the damage was done and the Ceanothus will bear the spiralling scars for life. I have apologised to it and have moved the honey-suckle further away, where its innocent pink flowers can still twiddle through its former friend but where its chokingly powerful stems can do no more damage. Most Ceanothus today are hybrid plants, grown to combine as much hardiness as possible together with a good blue colour and evergreen or semi-evergreen foliage. Two deep blue flowering kinds, *C. dentatus* and *C. rigidus,* were discovered by Theodor Hartweg, a German plant collector who, in 1846, was plant-hunting for the Horticultural Society as it then was. By 1847 he had already spent seven years in the Americas, and must have become accustomed to the hazards and delays of his occupation. The war between America and Mexico was about to break out and travel, whether by land or sea, was difficult, dangerous and expensive. Like many travellers of the times he was periodically ill, with no possibility of proper medical advice or help. He carried on with his collecting journeys though often ill of a 'quotidian fever and ague'* because all the complex arrangements had been made, and it was also the right season for the plants that he was seeking. He cured himself as best as he could from the contents of his own medicine chest, and carried on his search for the Society's plants and trees, though he was often so ill that he could hardly sit on his horse. (It makes one ashamed to be a fair-weather gardener, as most of us are.) Eventually he had made up his collection, and crossed Central America by mule, ox-cart and canoe to the port of San Juan. After delivering his plants safely he retired from collecting and accepted a deservedly comfortable position as Inspector of Gardens to the Duke of Baden at Schwetzingen.

Ceanothus take some time to become established even when soil and aspect are apparently just right. They do best in acid-to-neutral soils, disliking lime. But in due course the first few bud-knobs will appear and after that they will cover themselves in blue glory.

All those listed require good sunny wall positions where the tall-growing kinds can keep going without let or hindrance. Check on eventual height when purchasing and plant out from the wall appropriately — mature plants can be very large and will need fixings so that they are not damaged by high winds or the weight of snow.

C. dentatus (1848) grows to 6ft (1.8m) with abundant panicles of rich blue flowers in May. An evergreen shrub from California for a wall position.

C. rigidus (1847) grows to 12ft (3.7m) with deep purple-blue flowers from April-June (borne on previous year's growth). A tall evergreen shrub from California for a wall position.

C. thyrsiflorus (1837). A very large shrub, demanding space of up to 30ft (9m) in height into which to grow, with panicles

an intermittent fever, recurring daily

of pale china blue flowers in May and June. A tall, wide shrub from California for a good position against the house wall.

C. x Veitchianus (1853) grows to 10ft (3m) with clustered panicles of deep bright blue flowers on previous year's growth. An evergreen shrub from California for a wall position, hardiest of the evergreen types.

Requirements: Ceanothus are a better colour and more floriferous when grown on acid soil and need full sun and good free-draining soil together with a south or west-facing wall of appropriate height. Once installed and growing strongly only a foolish gardener will attempt to move them — they resent disturbance and will retaliate by dying a lingering, shrivelling death.

Propagation: Take heel cuttings of lateral shoots in July, insert into a rooting compost of peat and sand and put into a propagator set at 16°C (61°F). When rooted set out into individual pots of John Innes No.2 and grow on, protect in a cold frame for first winter. Pot on into larger pots in spring and plunge in a nursery area. They can be planted out into their final position in autumn.

Pruning: Evergreen kinds need no pruning unless they are growing too large for their positions — do not plant large, vigorous kinds in narrow borders. Tidy away winter-damaged shoots: if there are too many of these the plant may take time to recover, consider not having Ceanothus if this keeps happening. The more modern deciduous hybrids (not covered in this book) need hard pruning in April.

Diseases: In wrong chalky soil the leaves will show signs of chlorosis — they will turn yellow between the veins, or the whole leaf will become pale. This means that they cannot be grown successfully in that particular place in your garden, and a really sick shrub is difficult to nurse back to health because it will not stand being moved. Dig it up and start again elsewhere with soil that is carefully prepared for it. Ceanothus are sometimes prone to Honey fungus — if badly affected dig plant up and burn it.

Uses: Good blue flowering shrubs. A strong support for gentler climbers. As cut flowers, though not long lasting.

Shrubs: Ballalheannagh, Bodnant, Brackenwood, Busheyfields, Daisy Hill, Dobbies, Fairley's, Farall, Goatcher, Hilliers, Hyden, Jackman, Kaye, Kershaw, Knaphill, Knoll Gardens, Lime Cross, Marchant, Meare Close, Notcutts, Otter, Reuthe, Roger, Rosemoor, Russell, Scotts, Shepton, Sherrard, Smith, St. Bridget, Stonehouse, Toynbee, Treasure, Treseder, Warley, Woodland, Wyevale.

Seeds: Chiltern.

CELASTRUS — Staff vine, Asiatic Bittersweet (*Celastraceae*). This is an easy climber, very demanding of space but seldom seen either in nurseries or as a mature plant. Its flowers are unmemorable: these are followed by strings of brown packets which split open in autumn to reveal brilliant scarlet seeds set off by the yellow capsule lining. Most members of the genus are unisexual, and to berry there must be two plants near each other. This is uneconomic of space, since the plants can get very large indeed and therefore the bisexual *C. orbiculatus* is a blessing. Celastrus are not fussy as to soil, provided it is not too wet nor too dry and chalky. They will ramp away on south or west-facing walls if this is what is needed — do not grow this plant if space is at a premium. Another very beautiful way of displaying it is to start it off near a large conifer such as the strong-growing *Cypressus Leylandii;* when the leaves of the vine are gone the tree will be garlanded with the bright orange-scarlet berries.

C. orbiculatus syn. **C. articulatus** (1870) grows to 40ft (12m) with cymes of small green flowers in summer followed by strings of orange-scarlet berries in October. A very striking, strong-growing deciduous twiner for a wall that is not cold, or as a companion for a large evergreen tree.

Requirements: Any good soil, well prepared, a wall with support, a large pergola or equally large, solid fence and a reasonably sheltered position.

Propagation: Sow seeds in November in boxes of seed compost and put in a cold frame. Grow on in the usual way. Take cuttings of half ripe wood in July or ripe wood late on in Octtober. Insert in a rooting compost and put both kinds in a propagator set at 13-16°C (55-61°F). When well rooted, pot on into individual pots of John Innes No.1 and protect during winter, pot on in spring and plunge in a nursery area. Plant out in summer and stand back — this twining climber really will.

Uses: As an excellent wall covering — plant to show off the strings of seeds. Good against white or grey backgrounds.

Shrubs: Bodnant, Goatcher, Hilliers, Jackman, Marchant, Marten's Hall, Meare Close, Notcutts, Otter, Reuthe, Roger, Sherrard, Southcombe, St. Bridget, Stonehouse, Wyevale.

Seeds: Chiltern.

CERATOSTIGMA — Plumbago, Leadwort (*Plumbaginaceae*). This is not the tender, true Plumbago, which has to live under glass in Northern Europe, but it is a close relative and a lovely genus in its own right. It has an abundance of small cobalt-blue flowers in late summer which seem to harmonize with everything in the late summer garden. *Fuchsia magellanica* 'tricolor' is beautiful with it, having small crimson and purple flowers that harmonize with the scattered scarlet leaves the Ceratostigma produces in autumn. *Lobelia cardinalis* often goes on absent-mindedly flowering late and its flowers are the same tone as the red leaves of Ceratostigma, particularly the very tender *C. Griffthii.* The stalwart pink and crimson Sedums look plumply substantial beside it, as they always do anywhere; Schizostylis is good with it and all the yellows (though one has to watch out for those Hannibal's hordes, the sunflowers, lest they engulf it): the Ceratostigma is a polite plant and doesn't talk back. Autumn crocus (particularly the white kinds) are very beautiful when grown with it, with some silver leaved Cinerarias, the shocking pink of Nerines, and blue and lavender Michaelmas daisies. But this garden symphony needs good weather in late autumn to succeed and the first few frosts will blacken all the beauty for another year. Ceratostigmas are most attractive to butterflies and day flying moths, particularly the rare Humming-bird Hawk-moth which behaves as its name indicates. It has often been my delight to watch this creature feeding from the flowers in my garden — it likes phlox and jasmine as well — and it hangs, a brown blur, in front of its chosen bloom, uncoiling its proboscis which is three times as long as itself. This is another fascinating thing — when not in use the proboscis is coiled up like a watch-spring.

The moth will hang there, drinking nectar from the blue flowers for a few seconds, then it will dart to another flower and repeat the process. I have observed that it does not coil up its drinking-tube completely when it intends to stay about the bush, and the sound of its wings vibrating (they are moving too fast to see) is like the sound of a pack of cards being quickly riffled by a Mississippi gambler. *C. Willmottianum* was first grown in England by that dedicated but eccentric lady gardener, Ellen Willmott, who obtained the seeds from E.H. Wilson, the plant collector responsible for a great deal of our garden glory.

C. plumbaginoides (1846) grows only to 12in (30cm) with intense blue flowers from July to November. A deciduous low shrub from China very suitable for large sunny rockeries, walls, edging and ground cover.

C. Willmottianum (1908) grows to 4ft (1.2m) with clusters of brilliant blue flowers from July-October or later, until the frosts. A deciduous shrub from W. China for any sunny position. In autumn many of the leaves turn red, which contrasts well with the flowers. Take care with establishment.

Requirements: Any good soil and full sun. All do better if grown against a wall or in a sheltered place.

Propagation: Take half-ripe cuttings in July, best with a heel. Insert in a peat and sand rooting compost and put pots in a propagator set at 16-18°C (61-64°F). When rooted pot on into John Innes compost and protect in a frost-free greenhouse, conservatory or frame for the first winter. *C. plumbaginoides* may be divided in April. The plants come into leaf late.

Pruning: None necessary except to tidy up plant in spring.

Shrubs: Ballalheannagh, Barcock, Bodnant, Brackenwood, Bressingham, Caldwell, Peter Chappell, Beth Chatto, Daisy Hill, Dobbies, Farall, Goatcher, Great Dixter, Highfield, Hillier, Holden Clough, Hopleys, Ingwersen, Jackman, Kaye, Knaphill, Lime Cross, Marchant, Meare Close, Notcutts, Orchard, Otter, Reuthe, Robinsons, Roger, Russell, Scotts, Shepton, Sherrard, Smith, Stonehouse, Toynbee, Treasure, Treseder, Warley, Woodland, Wyevale.

Seeds: Thompson and Morgan.

CHAENOMELES — Cydonia, Japanese quince, Japonica, Pyrus japonica *(Rosaceae).* This lovely spring-flowering shrub has had the misfortune of having its name changed three times and the last, and I hope, final one is the most difficult to pronounce and spell. The true quince is *Cydonia oblonga,* and though closely related the two differ in that the quince is grown for its aromatic fruit and as a pear rootstock for grafting. Chaenomeles is a true ornamental shrub with perfectly edible but usually wooden-tasting fruits that look like thick-skinned apples. Leave them on the bush — they look better there. The first plant of *C. speciosa* was brought back to England from China by James Main (1770-1846), a young gardener to a Mr Gilbert Slater who was rich enough and keen enough to fund the trip. Main set sail on one of Slater's ships, the *Triton,* and the vessel made good time on her voyage, though there was a temporary delay while the ship put in at Madras — she was needed to assist in the siege of Pondicherry. Later, and further along on the journey, the *Triton* met with a French frigate which had a fine collection of some half a dozen prize ships. Since the war between Britain and France had just broken out the frigate was fair game, and so were the prize ships; the *Triton* attacked the Frenchman, who promptly fled, leaving his prizes to the *Triton* and two other ships. (Today's gardeners lead more placid lives, much removed from pirates, privateers and those long ago perils.) Once the *Triton* had reached her destination Main was able to purchase his plants from the nurseries that he was allowed to visit — there were still very many restrictions as to where foreigners could go. Main had had plant cases made to fit the available space on the *Triton,* on which ship he returned; being conscientious he looked after his plants with the utmost care, sometimes sitting up with them all night. Main seems to have innocently generated excitement and incidents (see *Chimonanthus* for the next instalment).

Chaenomeles are easy, lusty-growing shrubs, much liking full sun and good soil, where they will grow to a height of ten or twelve feet. The abundance of bright, cup-shaped flowers on the dark leafless branches is a lovely sight, much reminiscent of their country of origin. They do even better against walls. My own two shrubs are in what was once a hedge, so have a decided list sunwards, but now that they have more space the red-flowered one blooms intermittently as a 'thank-you' all the summer through. The long weeping stems of the old-fashioned *Forsythia suspensa* look very well growing through it — the two colours, yellow and bright rose-pink, might be thought to clash but they do not. Perhaps it is because one is grateful for an abundance of flower early in the year, but in the later midsummer plenty, one becomes much more condemning of colour dis-harmony. And since this is an old garden and they were here when I came I am happy to let them be. Chaenomeles hybridise all too readily, so seedlings are not likely to be true if other types are nearby.

C. speciosa syn. *C. lagenaria* (1796) grows to 10ft (3m), with spiny stems and pink, salmon, white or crimson flowers from January to April, followed by apple-like fruits in autumn. A deciduous shrub from Japan for a sunny position or a wall. Many modern named hybrids now grown: these are propagated vegetatively.

C. cathayensis (about 1800) grows to 10ft (3m) with white flowers in April followed by large (6″) (15cm) long oval green fruits that make good jelly. A strong, rather gaunt deciduous shrub from China for a sunny position.

Requirements: Sun, shelter, good soil and a wall if there is one to spare.

Propagation: If a strong but beautiful hedge is wanted, grow Chaenomeles from seed — it is cheaper, and there may be several colours which will make the hedge most attractive. Sow seeds when ripe (cut open the 'apples' in September) in seed compost in a cold frame. Grow on in the normal way: they should flower in about four years. Or take lateral cuttings in August, insert into a rooting compost of peat and sand and put in a propagator set at 16°C (61°F). When rooted transfer into pots of John Innes No.1 and protect in a cold frame for the winter.

Pruning: None needed unless the shrub grows over-large, which means that it has been planted in the wrong place for its eventual size. Wall shrubs can be pruned hard after flower-ing by cutting back to within two or three buds of the base of the previous season's growths. They will flower very pro-fusely in the following year.

Uses: Superb for flower-arranging (this is the best kind of pruning), as hedging and wall plants.

Shrubs: Goatcher, Goscote, Hilliers, Hyden, Kent, Kershaw, Knaphill, Lime Cross, Marchant, Meare Close, Notcutts, Otter, Reuthe, Roger, Russell, Scotts, Shepton, Sherrard, Smith, St. Bridget, Stonehouse, Toynbee, Treasure, Warley, Woodland, Wyevale.

Seeds: Chiltern.

CHIMONANTHUS — Winter sweet *(Calycanthaceae)*.

Winter sweet is a pleasant looking shrub in summer, with shining, rather willow-like mid-green leaves. But in the depths of winter little pear-shaped bumps appear on the bare branches and one cold, sunny day you walk past it, all unthinking, and a positive blast of perfume meets you. It is difficult to believe that the heavy, spicy deliciousness of it emanates from the curiously nondescript flowers, but it does. These last for about two months, sometimes, and you always vow never, never to root it up for something more showy. *Chimonanthus praecox*, the Winter sweet, was

another of the shrubs brought back from China by James Main. In those days, the plants had to survive a six months' long voyage, with two equator crossings and many other discomforts. Miniature (but heavy) greenhouses were built for the transportation of the plants, and these were fixed high up on the poop-deck of the sailing ships. The captains were never very happy about all this extra weight so wrongly placed (they had to be high up to avoid the spray) and made every excuse to throw them overboard if there was a crisis. Many shipmasters refused altogether to take them as cargo, because of their cumbersome fragility. In any case, despite the old belief that seafaring folk can't wait to return ashore and grow vegetable marrows, most sea-captains felt that gardening did not come under the heading of cargo-care, and many of the plants must have perished. This is why James Main was sent to China to purchase and bring home as many as he could of the 'new' Chinese plants. The voyage home on the *Triton* was comparatively peaceful compared to the journey out, until the ship reached the island of St Helena. Here Main was told that his employer, Gilbert Slater, had died suddenly. This was dreadful news for the young gardener who had liked and admired his employer, though there had been no written agreement between them. But worse was to come. In the English Channel the *Triton* collided with a frigate and was dismasted. In falling the main and mizzen-masts crashed on top of the plant-cases, which were utterly smashed. The wrecked ship was towed into the Thames and the broken remains of the precious plants, so carefully tended, were sold to a keen gardener called George Hibbert. What a challenge for a good gardener — it is to be hoped that many of his purchases were nursed back to health. It is thought that Main went to work for Hibbert for a while — certainly it would have been the logical thing to do as Main's knowledge of the new plants, coupled with his gardening abilities would have made him a valuable asset. Later he went to work for Loudon on the 'Gardener's Magazine' and became quite well known as a gardening writer.

Chimonanthus is a tender shrub, always needing a sunny south or west facing wall where in time it will grow quite large. Established shrubs should not be moved.

C. praecox syn. **C. fragrans** (1766) grows to 8ft (2.4m) or taller against a wall. Heavily perfumed yellow flowers from November to March. A delicate shrub from China for a sheltered site.

Requirements: A sheltered sunny site and good soil.

Propagation: From layers made in September: sever after two years. Or from seed sown in September into boxes of seed compost in a cold frame. Prick out when large enough into John Innes No.1 and plunge pots in a nursery area. Pot on as necessary. These plants will take about ten years to come to flowering. Chimonanthus is a shrub for gardeners who aim to stay put.

Pruning: Cut back all flowered shoots in March to within a few joints of their bases. This will keep the shrub to a manageable size, or it can be left to grow, with the removal of dead shoots being the only form of tidying.

Uses: As a winter-flowering shrub in the garden and as wonderfully perfumed cut flowers.

Shrubs: Ballalheannagh, Bodnant, Brackenwood, Bressingham, Busheyfields, Caldwell, Dobbies, Goatcher, Great Dixter, Highfield, Hilliers, Hopleys, Jackman, Knaphill, Knoll Gardens, Lime Cross, Marchant, Meare Close, Notcutts, Otter, Reuthe, Roger, Russell, Scotts, Shepton, Sherrard, St. Bridget, Toynbee, Treseder, Woodland, Wyevale.

Seeds: Butcher, Chiltern, Thompson and Morgan, Unwin.

CHOISYA — Mexican Orange (*Rutaceae*).

Choisya was named after a Swiss botanist, M J D Choisy (1799-1859), and this is a pleasing and attractive evergreen shrub with handsome shiny leaves which, except for colour, are like those of *Cytisus battandieri*. It is very useful as a sculptural plant because of its all-year-round good looks, and is much used by up-market garden designers. However, sweeping them and their follies aside, Choisya is a good plant for real gardeners, with aromatic foliage (smelling of leather when crushed) and orange-blossom-scented flowers in quantity if the plant is in the sun. It will grow in semi-shade but will become 'thrawn' and will all but cease to flower. It is really too big for any container though for the first few years of its life it can be grown in large pots and kept on a sheltered sunny patio or other warm corner, where it will do well if planted in John Innes No.2 and watered regularly in warm weather. In winter it can be moved to where its shiny leaves will furnish a dull corner. After about four years the Choisya (needing annual re-potting with the absolute minimum of disturbance) will have become root-bound in its pot and must be settled in the garden if it is to be saved. It likes a warm wall, and will have earned it by now. Choisya grows to a plumply rounded shape that is very satisfying in its middle years. A large mature shrub will yield branches for picking, and the flower buds can be seen as early as the November of the previous year. Intermittent flowers will appear throughout summer and autumn. My every day dinner service of olive green and white was inspirationally named 'Choisya' by the local firm of Poole Pottery, and I mourn the fact that they have ceased making it.

C. ternata — Mexican Orange (1825), grows to 10ft (3m) and as much wide, with a mass of white flowers in April and May. A tender evergreen from Mexico for a sheltered or wall position.

Requirements: Any well drained good garden soil and a sunny, sheltered situation.

Propagation: Take cuttings of half-ripe lateral shoots in August and insert in a rooting compost of peat and sand. Put into a propagator set at 16-18°C (61-64°F). When rooted, pot on into individual pots of John Innes No.2 and grow on, keep in a cold frame for the first winter. Examine root system in spring and pot on if necessary, plunge in a nursery area.

Pruning: None necessary, except to cut away winter-killed shoots in March.

Uses: As a sculpturally shaped evergreen for patios and temporarily in large tubs. Scented flowers for cutting.

Shrubs: Ballalheannagh, Barcock, Bees, Bodnant, Brackenwood, Bressingham, Cladwell, Daisy Hill, Dobbies, Farall, Goatcher, Goscote, Great Dixter, Highfield, Hilliers, Hopleys, Jackman, Kaye, Kershaw, Knaphill, Knoll Gardens, Lime Cross, Marchant, Marten's Hall, Meare Close, Notcutts, Orchard, Otter, Reuthe, Roger, Russell, Scotts, Shepton, Sherrard, Smith, Southcombe, St. Bridget, Stonehouse, Toynbee, Treasure, Treseder, Warley, W.W., Wyevale.

CISTUS — Rock Rose, Sun Rose, Gum Cistus (*Cistaceae*).

These are truly 'flowers for a day' with the petals of each crushed paper flower falling by mid or late afternoon. Cistus is a Mediterranean shrub and it needs as much sun as it can get together with a very dry situation. Cistus are not guaranteed as hardy, and severe winters will often kill them; my pink flowered *C. x purpureus,* planted in an ideally sunny corner, succumbed at least seven winters ago. But *C. ladanifer,* which was once in a fully south-facing situation, is now shaded by substantial trees such as Eucalyptus and a purple-leaved plum, and yet the Cistus still continues to be the most focal plant in the garden when it is covered in bloom in late May and June. It is also taller and larger than I expected, and dislikes the paths on each side of it but there is nothing I can do for it except grovel.

C. ladanifer and *C. creticus* were the plants from which Ladanum (not Laudanum, which comes from the Opium poppy *P. somniferum)* was obtained. Ladanum is an aromatic, bitter resin from which medicines, incense, perfume and 'myrrh' were made in Biblical times. However, the true Biblical myrrh is *Commiphora opobalsamum* (often called the Balm of Gilead) which is the source of the third gift given by the Magi to the infant Jesus. Gold, frankincense and myrrh were always royal gifts and it was formerly the custom for the British sovereign to make a presentation of them at the Chapel Royal on the feast of Epiphany, a ceremony dating back to the reign of Edward I. For centuries myrrh was considered to be efficaceous in curing disorders connected with the reproductive organs, though it is now known that this ancient belief is wrong. The Cistus plants also produce a bitter and aromatic resinous gum, which is still collected for medicinal purposes such as catarrh, dysentery and as an expectorant. Clean strips of cloth are drawn over and through the bushes during the hottest part of the day, and the beards of browsing goats are carefully combed in the evening so as to collect further small amounts. If there was a miraculous cure for some serious malady to be had from such laborious methods one could understand it, but there are many better and quicker natural remedies for catarrh and dysentery than combing goats' beards in the evenings, pleasant though this task may be, since an oil smelling of ambergris has been made from the resin. Bacon knew of this and in his 'Natural History' he says '. . . There are some teares of trees, which are kembed from the beards of goats; for when the goats bite and crop them, especially in the morning, the dew being on, the teare cometh forth and hangeth on their beards: of this sort is some kind of Ladanum'.

Cistus plants must have the dryest, warmest place in the garden and a forgotten south-facing bank is ideal, because they need good drainage and no cosseting whatsoever. The flowers are no use for picking, since the petals drop so quickly, but the abundance of blooms in their season makes them very colourful. Plant them in groups of different types and colours if space permits, as long as they all flower together, and carpet the hot ground in front of them with the nearly-related and similarly named Helianthemums whose flowers are so like, though much smaller (and a touch longer-lasting).

C. ladaniferus syn. **C. ladanifer** (1629) Rock rose, Sun rose, Gum Cistus grows to 5ft (1.5m) with downy dark evergreen leaves and white flowers with a dark crimson or purple blotch at the base of each petal in June. A tender shrub from S. W. Europe and North Africa for poor, hot well drained soils.

C. x lusitanicus (1830) grows to 2ft (60cm) with white crimson-blotched slightly longer lasting flowers in June and July. A usefully low shrub for a sunny place. Var. *decumbens* spreads to 4ft (1.2m) and is excellent as ground cover on a hot bank.

C. populifolius (1656) grows to 6ft (1.85m) with white, yellow blotched flowers in June. A hardier shrub from S W Europe for a hot place.

C. x purpureus (1790) grows to 4ft (1.2m) with red-purple, crimson blotched flowers in June. A tender lovely shrub for a hot poor place, much needing protection in winter.

C. villosus (1650) grows to a neat compact 3ft (90cm) with downy leaves and rose-purple flowers in June. *C.v. alba* has white flowers. *C.v. creticus* is the other source of ladanum or labdanum.

Requirements: Cistus can never be classed as truly hardy, even the so-called 'hardy' sorts, so do not take them for granted. Small shrubs can be protected with bracken or the trimmings from the *C. Leylandii* hedge. Cistus need a light, poor, sandy soil and should be planted to face south. They do well in coastal areas.

Propagation: A few cuttings of the more delicate kinds should be taken periodically as an insurance — a series of mild winters lull one into a sense of foolish security. (The cuttings make good presents or exchanges if not needed.) Take half-ripe heel cuttings in July or August and insert in a peat and sand rooting compost in a propagator set at 16°C (61°F). When rooted, pot up individually in John Innes No.1 and keep in a cold frame for the winter. Pot on and plunge in a nursery area.

Uses: Shorter or dwarf kinds as excellent colour and ground cover on south-facing banks. A Cistus hedge is a lovely indulgence in the south-west.

Shrubs: Ballalheannagh, Peter Chappell, Beth Chatto, Goatcher, Hilliers, Hyden, Ingwersen, Jackman, Knoll Gardens, Marchant, Meare Close, Notcutts, Orchard, Otter, Reuthe, Robinsons, Roger, Russell, Scotts, Shepton, Sherrard, Smith, Southcombe, St. Bridget, Stonehouse, Toynbee, Treasure, Treseder, Warley, Woodland, W.W., Wyevale.

Seeds: Thompson and Morgan.

CLEMATIS — Virgin's Bower *(Ranunculaceae)*. This huge genus is somewhat daunting to new gardeners because there are so many kinds and colours and shapes. In addition, when visiting a nursery or garden centre there is such a large collection of pots and such a matching forest of canes, like ships' masts at a marina, that the new gardener might very well snatch at the nearest plant (having read its description, one hopes) to add to his barrow-load of treasures. Once home he may plant it without any of the special care that it should have and then rush away to see to all the other jobs. If he is very lucky (and most new gardeners seem to be protected by St. Phocas, the patron saint of gardeners) the Clematis will get sun and rain when it needs them and will grow, despite the fact that the new gardener has completely forgotten where he planted it until it flowers to enchant and reproach him.

Some of the species Clematis have interesting histories. *C. Armandii* and the herbaceous *C. heracleifolia davidiana* were discovered in China by Father Armand David (1826-1900), who will be remembered forever because of the Père David's deer named after him, which would have been extinct but for his efforts. Father David was a naturalist who in 1862 went to China as a missionary. He had a preference for zoology, and the specimens that he sent back to the Natural History Museum in Paris so interested the authorities there that they obtained a release for him from his theological duties so that he could be sent on a scientific expedition to Mongolia. He made several perilous journeys to that huge and little known area, courageously ignoring the local wars and insurgencies. His constitution was not strong and he was often ill, as were most European travellers in the Far East where bubonic plague, typhus, malaria and all the other tropical diseases were as common as our common cold though terminally quicker. Father David remarked that 'if he took any notice of such things he would never get anywhere'. During his many expeditions he discovered *Rosa xanthina*, the lovely Handerchief tree *Davidia involucrata*, and found silk-worms in the wild, as well as the giant panda and the rare musk-deer. The conflicting interests of zoology and botany must have made his journeys very difficult, because there was never enough time to investigate thoroughly the regions that he was passing through. In the twelve years that he was engaged on his scientific expeditions, he was responsible for many new introductions and the confirmation of hitherto uncertainly named species. He was able to return to Paris where he established a small museum; here he gave lectures to missionaries until his peaceful death in 1900.

Clematis can be used in many ways other than clothing bare walls, which is the easiest and least interesting way to grow them. Certain kinds can be grown as eye-catching tub-plants, though they must be well and regularly fed and watered. Clematis look best when grown in association with other climbers or wall shrubs, and by consulting the lists and visiting gardens, delightful planting associations can be established. It is better to spend a season looking, reading up and asking questions before making purchases, as hastily-planted Clematis will have to be moved when confidence and better ideas come to the gardener. The shrubs, trees and bushes that are chosen as 'hosts' to the Clematis should have an exact note of average flowering times made in this first year so that the Clematis can be carefully chosen to flower with them or afterwards to continue a succession of colour in the garden. Large evergreen trees such as pines, hollies, yews, and conifers of various sizes and shapes make excellent hosts. The more rampant species-type Clematis such as *C. montana*, *C. vitalba*, and *C. orientalis* should not be used to cover trees that have winter-interest, such as Holly, as too much of their essential but often untidy-looking growth is left like forgotten spiders' webs. Save these strong kinds for old fruit trees that have ceased bearing or sad and ugly trees that have had too many branches lopped. Suggestions for colour combinations are as follows: lilac, pink, violet or white large-flowered varieties with Ceanothus (these will be mainly from group three), violet *C. Jackmannii* with mauve Buddleia, blue flowered *C. macropetala* with laburnum at flowering time (check exactly when your laburnum flowers). Violet *C. Jackmannii* with the yellow-leaved hop — *Humulus lupulus* 'aurea'. Mauve-pink large-flowered kinds such as the more modern 'Hagley Hybrid' with old rambling roses such as 'Vielchenblau' or 'William Lobb' — the colours harmonize beautifully. Late pink honeysuckle with any red-flowered group three varieties: the scarlet species *C. texensis* (group one) with *Rhus coggygria*, and *C. alpina* 'Ruby' with the white flowers of Pyracantha or Crataegus. The rose-pink pea flowers of wall-growing *Robinia hispida* look even prettier when contrasted with purple or crimson (not blue) large-flowering varieties. Big spring-flowering shrubs such

as Vibernums can again become a real focal point by planting some group three kinds such as *C. Viticella* and its varieties, or delicate *C. alpina* (group one) can be planted to flower with the handsome flower-clusters of the Viburnums. Large-flowered white varieties from groups two or three can be carefully chosen to flower where their luminous blooms can be enjoyed when sitting in the garden in the dusk. The white flowers of Philadelphus look even more charming with those of a deep-pink or lilac June-flowering Clematis growing through them and the dullness of lilac bushes in mid-summer can be enlivened by any of the large-flowering kinds that suit the prevailing colour scheme nearby. *C. montana* (this comes in white, pale pink, mauve-pink and bright pink) need not be grown to steeple-height proportions, though it can and will fling dripping swags of bloom over the largest of trees. The *montanas* can be grown to solidly clothe low fences — to 3 or 4ft (90cm-1.2m) — where their abundance of flowers can be better seen and the scent enjoyed — it may not be generally known that a more modern variety of *C. montana*, 'Elizabeth', is sweetly scented, and *C. flammula* with its multitude of small white flowers from August to October has a delicious scent of vanilla. The permutations of flowering are endless, and this duality of planting is even more important and satisfying in small gardens where every inch counts, as I know only too well.

Clematis have been divided into three main types as follows (never mind the inevitable sub-divisions for the moment). This has been done to help with Clematis culture and more particularly with pruning, which, if done at the wrong time of year will mean no flowers on your plants. Group one consists of the species Clematis, most of which have remained unchanged since their various dates of introduction. They flower in spring, before the end of May, and are mainly deciduous, though there several handsome-leaved evergreen sorts such as *C. Armandii*, *C. cirrhosa* and others. This group contains such popular and usefully rampant growers as the pink or white *C. montana* and the only yellows, *C. tangutica* and *C. orientalis*. Other beautiful species are the blue and pink flowered *C. macropetala*, the upright crimson tulip-like flowers of *C. texensis*, and the various colours of *C. alpina* and *C. Viticella*. All these have smallish, sometimes 4-petalled flowers which arise as axillary buds usually on stems which have developed during the previous year, therefore correct pruning at the right time is essential (see pruning notes).

Group two has larger (usually) five-petalled flowers which are also produced from the previous year's growth. The first flowers begin to open from May until the end of June, and a favourite old variety is 'Nelly Moser' which has pale pink petals with a mauve or cerise bar in the centre of each. 'Nelly Moser' keeps her colours better in the shade and will often be in flower for most of the summer. Other kinds belonging to group two are 'Henryi', creamy-white; 'Jackmannii', off white; 'Lasurstern', blue; 'Marie Boisselot', white; 'Perle d'Azur', azure.

Group three contains those Clematis which flower on the current season's growth, the flowers appearing from July onwards. In this group there are many modern varieties which flower until the first frosts. These have been bred from *C. florida, C. Jackmannii, C. lanuginosa, C. patens* and *C. Viticella.*

Clematis climb in a very determined way by means of their flexible leaf petioles or stalks which wind round the nearest convenient support to anchor the growing plant. Frequently they wind round each other and the plant has to be disentangled from itself, and it will be found that an unwound leaf petiole will refuse point-blank to be of further service — it usually snaps in any case, but if not it will not coil itself helpfully around anything again. The coiling action happens very quickly, sometimes in a few hours in good growing weather and to some extent the plant can be programmed to twiddle its way upwards (it hates growing sideways) by gently tying the stems near their intended supports. The leaves will turn towards these and will anchor the plant with a single loop which is as surprisingly strong as the grip of a baby's finger.

There are several herbaceous Clematis which, when seen growing in a border, often fool visitors who do not associate average height herbaceous plants with the genus Clematis. They are not overly floriferous but they are interesting: *C. heracleifolia* has attractive leaves and blue hyacinth-shaped flowers from August to September. *C. recta* and *C. r.* 'purpurea' (which last is the most interesting, having pleasing purple foliage) have scented vitalba-like flowers in July, followed by the typical Clematis seed-heads. *C. integrifolia* has violet-blue nodding flowers in July and is a usefully substantial border plant, making large clumps in a sunny border of alkaline soil.

Most Clematis flowers are composed of coloured petal-like sepals, except for certain kinds such as *C. macropetala* and *C. alpina* that have staminodes, or petaloid stamens, which give these dainty flowers a petticoated semi-double appearance.

C. alpina (1792) GROUP 1 grows to 8ft (2.4m) with solitary nodding blue to violet flowers in April and May. A deciduous climber of good behaviour from N. Asia and N. Europe for wall, shrub, pergola, fence, trellis or container or any of the Clematis supports or hosts previously discussed.

C. Armandii (1900) GROUP 1 grows to 30ft (9m) with a spread of 60ft (18.5m). (Do not plant this handsome thing unless you have the right place for it.) A large and quick growing climber with leathery veined leaves and clusters of scented white or pink-tinted flowers in April and May. Needs to have its feet in shade on a north-facing wall and grow up and over into the sun. A lusty evergreen climber from

China for a favoured garden position.

C. cirrhosa (1590) GROUP 1 grows to 10ft (3m) with cream flowers from January to March. An evergreen climber from S. Europe and Asia Minor for clothing bare walls etc.

C x Durandii (C. integrifolia x C. x Jackmannii) (1870) GROUP 3 grows to 10ft (3m) with blue-violet flowers from June to September. A deciduous climber from Lyons (France) for most Clematis positions.

C. Flammula (1590) GROUP 3 grows to 15ft+ (4.5m+) with fragrant white flowers from August to October. A deciduous climber from S. Europe for a position where the scent can be enjoyed — an arbour, summerhouse, archway or near a seat against its part of the wall or fence.

C. heracleifolia (1837) grows to 3ft (90cm) with blue flowers in August and September. A handsome sub-shrub from China for the border.

C. integrifolia (1573) grows to 4ft (1.2m) with violet, blue or white flowers in July. A semi-woody herbaceous plant from S. Europe for a sunny border.

C. x Jackmannii GROUP 3 grows to 15ft+ (4.5m+) with violet flowers from July to August. Deciduous climber.

C. macropetala (1910) GROUP 1 grows to 12ft (3.7m) with nodding blue flowers from May to June. A deciduous climber from China.

C. montana (1831) GROUP 1 grows to 30 or 40ft (9-12m) with white or pink sometimes scented flowers in May and June. A usefully rampageous deciduous climber from the Himalaya to clothe fences, large old trees and whole house walls if allowed. Not for small spaces.

C. orientalis (1731) GROUP 3 grows to 20ft+ (6m+) with nodding, paired yellow flowers from August to October. A vigorous climber from N. Asia to cover old trees, buildings, fences etc. Good seed heads.

C. tangutica (1898) GROUP 3 grows to 10ft+ (3m+) with yellow lantern-shaped flowers on single stems from August to October. Good seed heads.

C. texensis GROUP 3 grows to 12ft (3.7m) with tulip-shaped flowers in shades of red from June to August. (Species rather tender.) Deciduous climber from N. America.

C. Vitalba grows to 40ft+ (12m+) with cream-green flowers from July to September. A European (and North African) wild plant where large areas need to be covered. Good seed heads.

C. Viticella (1569) GROUP 3 grows to 12ft (3.7m) with (in the species) fragrant blue or purple flowers from July to September. A deciduous climber from S.E. Europe from which many modern forms have been raised.

Requirements: All Clematis prefer limy soil and all are greedy plants, some more than others — if well decayed animal manure can be buried the season before planting your Clematis will never look back. All except the 'herbaceous' kinds need support and old castles or factory chimneys would do very nicely for the more vigorous kinds. In acid or heavy soils, work in plenty of compost and peat before planting. In really acid soils your Clematis will never thrive as they will on chalk and it is no use expecting them to — settle for Camellias and Rhododendrons instead. When planting purchased Clematis soak new plant in a bucket of water for an hour before planting, or until thoroughly damp, and dig a hole several times larger than the plant container; fork up bottom of hole to loosen soil. Put 3″ (7.5cm) of well-rotted manure in the hole, then fork sides of hole. Fill with a mixture of garden soil, peat and bone meal, remove plant from container and loosen roots if these are the thick string-like kind. If of the fibrous kind, leave as they are. Plant the Clematis so that the former soil level is 2″ (5cm) below new level (if an accident happens to the stem of the plant it will often send up a new shoot from the base). Water every day during first summer unless there is heavy rain. Put a herbaceous plant in front of the Clematis on the sunward side, to shade the roots. If the plant is to grow up or through a tree or a shrub, set a long cane in the ground at an angle leading to the host plant, and dig the Clematis hole about 2ft (61cm) away. (Leave the cane that it came with.) It is very important to keep the Clematis well watered when it or they are to grow up and through previously established plants as these will take up most of the available water.

Propagation: 4-5″ (10-12.5cm) stem cuttings of half-ripened wood should be taken in July, leaving two buds at the bottom of the stem; insert in a rooting compost of peat and sand in a large propagator with a bottom heat of 15-18°C (59-64°F). When rooted, pot on into individual pots of John Innes No.1. Keep in a frost-free greenhouse or conservatory for first winter, transplant into larger pots in spring and plunge in a nursery area. Plant out in autumn or during the second spring. Seeds of true species kinds can be sown in October (as soon as ripe) in pans or boxes of seed compost, put these in a cold frame until germination has taken place. Prick out in spring and grow on in pots that are plunged in the ground in a sheltered position. Plant out in October. Protect all small plants and new growth from slugs.

Pruning: (The most important part of Clematis growing apart from feeding, watering and admiring.) Prune GROUP 1 kinds in February. Cut back all stems to 12″ (30cm) in first year. In second year cut back all stems to 3ft (90cm) or a metre. Third and successive years prune *after* flowering, cut out weak or dead stems. Flowers will be lost during the first two seasons but strong plants will be the result. For GROUP 2 Clematis prune in February or March. Cut back all stems to 12″ (30cm). In 2nd February, cut back all stems to 1 yard (or 1 metre). In third year cut back all stems to a good pair of plump buds. Do the same each year thereafter. For GROUP 3 Clematis, cut back all stems to 12″ (30cm) in February or March. In second year, cut back all new growth to within a few inches of the start of the previous season's growth. Do the same thereafter in succeeding years. Plants

for tubs must be shortened down to 9″ (23cm) with another cut being made after three pairs of leaves have grown. After this, nip out the growing tip. Plants must have proper supports and be tied in as growth commences. They must be planted in John Innes No.3 and given fortnightly liquid feeds as well. (Never allow to dry out.)

Uses: As magnificent wall, pergola, archway, trellis, summer-house, and arbour plants. Also as companion plants to trees and shrubs. As large container plants. Choose smaller kinds for this purpose such as *C. alpina*, *C. macropetala*, and modern large-flowered cultivars. As cut flowers (condition overnight by selecting new flowers with as long a stem as possible, removing foliage and plunging into cold water, as deep as is necessary).

Diseases: 'Clematis Wilt' is the dreaded term for the unexplained collapse of stems of apparently thriving plants. If the Clematis has been set deeply enough, new, unaffected growth will usually come from the base later in the season. At the moment there is no known diagnosis (though several theories) and no cure except prayer. Spray plants for aphis and mildew.

Shrubs: Fisk, Goatcher, Goscote, Great Dixter, Hilliers, Highfield, Hopleys, Hortico, Hyden, Kaye, Kent, Kershaw, Knoll Gardens, Lime Cross, Marchant, Marten's Hall, Meare Close, Notcutts, Otter, Reads, Reuthe, Roger, Rosemoor Russell, Scotts, Shepton, Sherrard, Southcombe, St. Bridget, Stonehouse, Toynbee, Warley, Woodland, W.W., Wyevale.

Seeds: Chiltern, Thompson and Morgan.

CLERODENDRUM, CLERODENDRON *(Verbenaceae)*.

This is a large group of tropical shrubs and climbers with very beautiful flowers. Unfortunately few are grown in Northern Europe because they need warm greenhouse conditions, and *C. Bungei* and *C. trichotomum* being the hardiest and the ones most generally seen, though even these are not common in gardens. In the hotter parts of the world some species have been used medicinally and their name, *kleros*, chance, *dendron*, a tree, derives from the fact that some are useful in medicine and others not. The leaves of both smell horrible when crushed, so it is best not to plant either type too near a path where they will inevitably be brushed against.

C. trichotomum has interesting turquoise-blue berries that are still surrounded by the scarlet calyx, and sprays of these (denuded of the offensive leaves) are very beautiful in arrangements. The berries turn black eventually.

The flowers of both are pleasantly perfumed and, again, when picking for arrangements it is better to strip the stems of their leaves.

C. Bungei (1844) grows to 6ft (1.8m) with heads of fragrant rose-pink flowers in August and September. A tender shrub from China for a sheltered sunny place. The aerial parts will be killed by frost, but new shoots will come in spring. Protect as much as possible. Evil-smelling leaves.

C. trichotomum (1800) grows to 15ft (4.5m) (may form a small tree) with scented pink and white flowers in August and September followed by bright turquoise-blue berries set in pink-red calyces. A deciduous shrub from Japan for a sheltered position. Similar evil-smelling leaves.

Requirements: Any good well-drained garden soil, sun and a sheltered situation.

Propagation: These hardier species produce suckers which can be detached, best in spring though autumn is as suitable in the warmer counties. Or take 6″ (15cm) heel cuttings of lateral shoots in August. Insert in a rooting compost of sand and peat and leave in a cold frame until rooted. In spring transfer to a nursery area and grow on for two years. Transplant to final positions when dormant.

Uses: As striking flower and berry plants; berried branches for floral arrangements.

Shrubs: Barcock, Caldwell, Goatcher, Great Dixter, Hilliers, Hopleys, Knaphill, Knoll Gardens, Marchant, Notcutts, Otter, Reuthe, Russell, Scotts, Sherrard, St. Bridget, Stonehouse, Toynbee, Treasure, Treseder, Woodland, Wyevale.

Seeds: Chiltern, Thompson and Morgan.

CLETHRA — Sweet pepper bush, Coast pepperbush, Summer Sweet (Clethraceae).

Clethras are not seen as much as they could be — perhaps because they are of subtle colouration and lack the impact of more brightly-coloured shrubs. Gardeners who collect scented plants should add a Clethra to their collections — it is particularly valuable because it will tolerate a certain amount of shade. Plant it near where you sit at twilight, because the Lily-of-the-Valley scent is stronger in the evening.

C. alnifolia (1731) grows to 9ft (2.7m) with erect panicles of scented white flowers from July to September. A deciduous shrub from E. North America for a sunny sheltered place in woodland conditions in the garden.

C. tomentosa (1731) grows to 10ft (3m) with pleasing felted leaves and similar flowers to *C. alnifolia*, though flowering later: August to September. A frost-tender deciduous shrub from S.E. North America for a very sheltered place.

Requirements: Clethras need lime-free soil that is moist but well drained and rich in humus. They need shelter and sun for part of the day. *C. tomentosa* should be protected in winter, *C. alnifolia* is hardier.

Propagation: Take heel cuttings of lateral shoots in August and insert in a sand and peat rooting compost. Put pots in a propagator set at 16°C (61°F). When rooted pot on into individual pots of lime free loam mixed with peat and leafmould.

Pruning: None needed.

Uses: As long lasting scented flowers, shrubs for patio or near garden seats and dining areas. As scented cut flowers.

Shrubs: Bodnant, Goatchers, Hilliers, Jackman, Kaye, Knaphill, Marchant, Meare Close, Notcutts, Reuthe, Sherrard, Smith, St. Bridget, Stonehouse, Treasure, Treseder.

CLIANTHUS — Lobster-Claw, Parrot's Bill, Glory Pea, Sturt's Glory Pea, Sturt's Desert Pea (Leguminosae).

These exotic looking plants take their name from *kleios*, glory, and *anthus*, flower, because of their unusual and brilliantly coloured flowers which, though positively spectacular, cannot be classed as beautiful. The flowers of *C. formosus*, the Glory Pea, are scarlet and black, and look disconcertingly 'alive' as though gazing at the beholder and wondering whether or not to fly at him. This is because the purple-black blotch at the base of each of the two standard petals has a rounded eye-like appearance and these, side by side, give the flowers a boding sort of look — I wouldn't want to turn my back on them. This species of Clianthus is difficult to grow and is short lived in any case, and it has been found that if it is grafted as a seedling on to a seedling of *Colutea arborescens* it grows more strongly and has a longer life. *C. formosus* is not easy to get and, when it is, it is not cheap, but such is the cupidity of the gardener-collector that he will deprive himself of something else in order to have it, and once in his possession he will not stint in its care. This is a tender greenhouse climber which can only be grown outside in the British Isles in parts of Cornwall and the Scilly Isles. *C. puniceus*, the Parrot's Bill, is also tender, though not as demanding as the Glory Pea. In former centuries it was grown by the warlike Maoris of New Zealand, but now it has become extinct in the wild and is only found in cultivation. This species of Clianthus has all-scarlet flowers and is altogether calmer in its appearance.

C. formosus syns. **C. Dampieri, C. speciosus** — Glory Pea, Sturt's Glory Pea, Sturt's Desert Pea (1855) grows to 3ft (90cm) with pale silky leaves and shining scarlet and black flowers from March to June. A delicate and short-lived evergreen greenhouse perennial from Australia.

C. puniceus — Parrot's Bill, Lobster Claw (1831) grows to 12ft (3.7m) with brilliant scarlet flowers in May and June. A tender climber or 'leaner' from New Zealand for the sunniest of sheltered south-facing walls or for the greenhouse.

Requirements: Both kinds are tender, both need sandy, gritty compost on the dry side (John Innes No.3 with extra grit). *C. formosus* needs a minimum temperature of 7°C (45°F). Water from below. The summer temperature should not fall below 10-13°C (50-55°F) and the Clianthus would prefer it to be much warmer than this. Plant *C. puniceus* in the greenhouse border if in a cold area, otherwise try your luck with it out of doors. In winter cover the base of the plant with a mound of bracken or ashes, and protect the stems and branches with sacking during very cold weather.

Propagation: Sow seeds of *C. puniceus* in March in pots of seed compost. Put in a propagator set at 13-16°C (55-61°F), prick out with extra care when large enough and grow on in the greenhouse. Pot on when necessary. Plants should flower in about three years. Sow seeds of *C. formosus* into individual pots in February at the same temperature. Pot on without any root disturbance as soon as big enough. Grow on in large pots or baskets.

Uses: As spectacular wall or basket plants for the more experienced gardener.

Shrubs: Ballalheannagh, Brackenwood, Hilliers, Marchant, Meare Close, Notcutts, St. Bridget, Stonehouse, Treasure, Wyevale.

Seeds: Chiltern, Thompson and Morgan.

COBAEA — Cathedral Bells, Cup and Saucer Plant

(Cobaeaceae, Polemoniaceae). This plant was named after the Jesuit priest, father B. Cobo (1572-1659), a Spanish missionary and naturalist who lived and worked in Mexico and Peru.

The Cobaea is a really beautiful Jack's beanstalk of a creeper to grow from seed. It germinates quickly and keeps right on growing until it has occupied most of the greenhouse roof-space (it is tender in origin but not in behaviour) and then it will grow backwards and forwards and sideways and through all the other terrified plants, engulfing them in a green tide which if not seen to will drown them completely. This is what happens when you are too busy to really notice, but of course it is a fascinating process to watch because it happens so quickly. The pelargoniums, pale shadows of themselves, should be rescued first and then the creeper cut back until the other plants can see the sun — after all, whoever heard of a one-plant greenhouse, which is what can happen. Cobaea can also be grown (more sensibly) as an annual climber out of doors for pergolas, arches, trellis and walls though it will not flower as well unless the summer is a hot one. The whole flowering sequence is delightful — first the small heart-shaped buds are seen, which quickly (everything this plant does it does quickly) enlarge. These grow into pouched buds of a pleasing pale green, which get longer and larger, like a Canterbury Bell just before it opens. The next day the bell-shaped flower (still pale green) opens, and then it gradually (this takes all of 4-5 hours) turns to a rich violet-purple which remains on the vine for a day only and then falls off to lie sadly on the floor. The flowers, on opening, smell rather unpleasant but as they age they become more fragrant. The seedlings for garden plants should be potted on into larger pots so that they are not checked, and a six-foot cane given to each to climb. This will keep them out of mischief for a few weeks only, and then the main stem will have to be temporarily looped into a circle. If the pot is placed outside too soon the plant will not flower so well: it is a tropical heat-seeking creature. One single Cobaea is far too big for the average

eight-foot greenhouse (and I speak from experience). When the seed heads develop they are most interesting, following the form of the flower, though they look as if they have been carved out of wood. They are rare objects and would enhance an autumnal arrangement of dried fruits and seed heads.

C. scandens — Cup and Saucer plant (or vine), Cathedral Bells (1787) grows to 24ft (7.4m) with interesting flowers of green-to-purple from July to October. A vigorous but tender climber from Central S. America for a large greenhouse or conservatory or outside as an annual for sunny pergolas, porches and trellis. There is a white variety, 'Alba', though this looks as if it has forgotten to change colour.

Requirements: Any good soil (not too rich) and best in the greenhouse border. A frost-free greenhouse (min. temperature 5-8°C (41-46°F) if plant is to be permanent. If grown as an annual, a sunny sheltered (not draughty) corner and a strong support up which it will climb by means of tendrils. Water well in dry spells.

Propagation: Cobaeas grow quickly from seed sown in February in a propagator set at 18°C (64°F). Sow large seeds singly in John Innes No.1 and pot on as necessary. Give a cane for support as soon as seedling is 4″ (10cm) high. Decide whether plants are to remain under glass or go outside. If the latter, harden off in the usual way but do not put outside until June.

Uses: As a tremendously quick growing vine in the greenhouse where shade is needed; as beautiful climbers. Whole stems with buds and flowers for short-lived flower arrangements.

Seeds: Chiltern, Suttons, Thompson and Morgan, Unwin.

COLLETIA

(Rhamnaceae). The Colletia was named after a French botanist Philibert Collet (1643-1718). These uncommon spiny plants are not often seen in Northern European gardens, though two species *C. armata* and *C. cruciata* have a usefully late flowering season. They are among the spiniest of garden shrubs, and I have known friendlier cactus plants then these — they out-gorse gorse any time. One has to be careful to keep the label at a readable height lest, when bending down to see it, one gets a very sharp reminder to take more care. This is not a plant to have in a garden where there are young children, nor should it be planted near the edge of any path. Having said this as a warning, I can commend it for covering itself with small white or pale pink scented flowers in very late summer — my own is often still in bloom as late as November. *C. cruciata* is well named. Even as a small plant it will stop visitors in their tracks because of its unique appearance. It has pairs of flat triangular spines which proceed up the stems, with each succeeding pair set at right angles to the ones below. The plant is as rigid as a steel sculpture and would not look out of place in a space-fiction film-set. When covered with its tiny flowers its appearance is even stranger, though frac-

tionally softer. This plant has adapted itself to life in an unfriendly environment and no browsing animal would ever take a second bite. Curiously enough it seems quite happy in the warmer parts of the British Isles and flowers well if planted in a sunny and sheltered situation. It needs some protection in severe winters.

C. armata (1882) grows to 10ft (3m) with small hawthorn-scented white flowers (or pink-tinted in var. rosea) from October onwards. A very spiny shrub from Chile for a hot border.

C. cruciata (1824) grows to 10ft (3m) with even deadlier spiny branches and a mass of scented cream flowers from September onwards. A formidably armed shrub from Uruguay and Brazil for a sunny place.

Requirements: Ordinary well drained garden soil and full sun.

Propagation: Heel cuttings of half-ripened wood can be taken in July or August and set in a rooting compost of peat and sand. Put the pots into a cold frame until rooted then grow on in the usual way. Cuttings do not root easily (mist propagation is used by commercial nurserymen). Ripe seeds are sometimes obtainable, sow these in spring and autumn (in separately labelled pots) and leave in a cold frame until germination takes place, which may be many months.

Uses: *C. cruciata* as one of the most interesting shrubs to grow for its formidable appearance — branches from mature shrubs for arrangements. As a people-proof hedge in warm areas. Useful for late autumn flowers in the garden, and appreciated by bees and late butterflies

Shrubs: Hilliers, Kershaw, Knoll Gardens, Marchant, Otter, Scotts, Sherrard, Stonehouse, Treasure, Treseder.

COLUTEA — Bladder Senna *(Leguminosae)*. Colutea has

rather sparse racemes of yellow pea flowers which are set off by the small leaved light green foliage. This in itself is a pleasing foil to darker greens or conifers, particularly when the inflated 3″ (7.5cm) seed-vessels turn red in late summer: it is for these very decorative pods that the plant is generally grown, though it remains in flower for several months. If the pods are pressed (on dry days) they will explode with a loud 'pop', which is amusing for children though not for flower arrangers. At one time Bladder Senna was said to be the only plant growing in the crater of Vesuvius. As it was once common on railway embankments near London it seems to enjoy cinders. The 'Bladder' part of its common name refers to the pods and the 'Senna' is because the leaves are a gentle purgative and are still used in Europe instead of the true Senna — *Cassia acutifolia, C. Fistula* and *C. obovata*. Keep a watch for earwigs and other garden pests which will eat their way into the seed pods and destroy them.

C. arborescens (16th century) grows to 12ft (3.7m) with racemes of yellow pea flowers from June until September, with the pods forming and colouring to red at the same time. A deciduous shrub from S. Europe and the Mediterranean

area for a sunny sheltered position.

Requirements: Thrives in ordinary well drained soil and full sun.

Propagation: Take heel cuttings of ripened lateral shoots in September and insert in a rooting compost of sand and peat. Leave in a cold frame for the winter and pot up into John Innes No.2 in spring. Sow seeds in August if ripe or in March singly in pots of seed compost in a cold frame.

Pruning: Cut away spindly growth in March, cut back all branches to good buds. Shrub need not be pruned at all if plenty of space is available, but it can get attenuated if left.

Uses: Shrub as an unusual garden feature. Branches of bronze, red or dried pods very interesting in arrangements.

Shrubs: Brackenwood, Hilliers, Kershaw, Knaphill, Marchant, Notcutts, Roger, Sherrard, St. Bridget, Woodland.

Seeds: Chiltern

CONVOLVULUS *(Convolvulaceae)*. Most members of this

genus have climbing or twining (though strangling is a better word) tendencies. The delicate silver-leaved small shrub *C. Cneorum* with its white trumpets and ladylike behaviour is, therefore, a pleasant change. This shrub is not hardy and a severe winter may carry it off, so it should be protected as much as possible, this is difficult because the leaves are ever-grey and should not come into contact with anything wet such as protective bracken or straw. A low fence of large-mesh wire netting, interwoven with straw or bracken is the only method because the plant is too big for a cloche after two years. All this effort may seem tedious, but it is well worth it when one sees one's own small, neat, silver-leaved bush covered in white trumpets that have a pale rose reverse. The rich purple of *Lavendula stoechas* is a good companion to the Convolvulus, with some annuals such as the unusual blue *Phacelia campanularia* and a colony of purple violas. For further interest the rose *Mutabilis* can be planted nearby where one can watch the changing colours of the petals, and a potato-vine — *Solanum crispum* — with pendant clusters of yellow-anthered mauve or white flowers to scramble up and over the wall behind. All these flower at the same time and grow thus in my own garden — for the moment; the best-laid plans of better gardeners than I are often ruined by wet and freezing weather, which is the killing combination. In cold areas this shrub with its pleasing metallic-looking leaves (which are silky-hairy to the touch) is perhaps best grown in a large tub that can be pulled under cover in winter. It is advisable to take cuttings each year to replace fatalities.

C. Cneorum (1640) grows to 3ft (91.5cm) with soft silver ever-grey leaves and white flowers with the divisions marked in pink on the reverse, from May to September. A tender shrub from S. Europe for a hot sheltered position.

Requirements: A sheltered situation in full sun with ordinary well-drained soil. In particularly wet areas protect with a cloche when small and a plastic tent when larger, or as described.

Propagation: Take heel cuttings of lateral shoots in July or August; insert in a rooting compost of peat and sand in a cold frame until rooted. Pot on into John Innes No.2 when rooted and keep in a cold frame for the winter.

Pruning: None needed.

Uses: As very striking silver-leaved plants with a very long flowering season. Foliage for arrangements.

Shrubs: Ballalheannagh, Peter Chappell, Daisy Hill, Dobbies, Goatcher, Great Dixter, Hilliers, Hopleys, Hyden, Kaye, Marchant, Marten's Hall, Notcutts, Otter, Potterton and Martin, Reuthe, Rosemoor, Russell, Scotts, Shepton, Sherrard, St. Bridget, Stonehouse, Toynbee, Treasure, Treseder.

CORNUS — Cornel, Dogwood, Cornelian Cherry *(Cornaceae).* The name 'Cornus' is derived from both the Greek and Latin words for a horn, because the wood is so hard that the Romans made it into spear shafts; it is said that Cornelwood was used to build the Trojan horse. Legend also has it that when Romulus (who, with his twin Remus, was suckled by a she-wolf) was working out the intended boundaries of the city of Rome, he flung his Cornel-wood spear as far as it would go. It took root and grew, forming branches and leaves and flowers and thereafter became a sacred plant that was cared for and watered during the hot summers. *Cornus mas,* the Cornelian Cherry, has puffs of yellow flowers on bare branches from February to March. Later some shrubs (in favoured gardens) will produce beautiful translucent scarlet fruit in August which is very edible: formerly this shrub was grown in orchards for its fruit, but these days it seems to have forgotten how to bear.

Some species have large petal-like bracts that last for many weeks (the flowers are small and insignificant, as in Euphorbia) and the botanists have recently split up this large genus into new genera according to the arrangement of the floral parts. Catalogues are still listing the shrubs under 'Cornus' so I have given both names in the descriptions — the second name being more botanically correct.

C. canadensis (chamaepericlymenum canadense) is not really a shrub because it renews its aerial parts annually, but is here mentioned because it is usually grouped with the shrubs in nursery catalogues. This is a charming and useful ground-cover plant with large 4-petalled 'flowers' (bracts) that last for a very long time. In the autumn the leaves turn to very beautiful tones of yellow, orange, pink and crimson. It is easy to grow in the right soil (sandy and acid) but will dwindle and disappear if it doesn't like your garden. In Scotland the plant is called *Lus an Chraois,* the Plant of Gluttony, because its berries were once used to stimulate the appetite. *C. florida* (now *Benthamidia florida)* is an excellent shrub, with large long-lasting 'flowers' that are com-

posed of four white bracts. In autumn the whole shrub colours beautifully. *C. kousa* (now *Benthamia japonica)* has neat white 'flowers' with four pointed bracts that perch erectly along the branches. Later on the very ornamental scarlet fruits form (rather like strawberries) and the foliage changes to crimson and bronze.

C. alba now **Swida alba, Thelycrania alba** (1741) grows to 10ft (3m) but spreads into large thickets of scarlet-stemmed branches, beautiful with snow and cheering against winter skies. Corymbs of small white flowers in May and June, followed by white berries. There are several very lovely (less rampageous) and more modern varieties such as 'atrosanguinea', with a dwarfer habit and redder stems; 'Spaethii', with yellow variegated leaves and red winter bark; 'Kesselringii', with purple stems; and the lovely cultivar 'Elegantissima', which has grey green leaves margined with cream (this is also known as *Siberica Variegata).*

C. canadensis now **Chamaepericlymenum canadense** (1774) grows only to 10″ (25.5cm) with long lasting white 'flowers' in June, followed by red fruits and beautiful autumn colouration. A good (if sometimes difficult to please) ground cover plant from N. America, preferring moist, acid, sandy soil in sun or partial shade. Oddly enough, it is tender.

C. florida now **Benthamidia florida,** syn. **Cynoxylon floridum — Flowering Dogwood** (1730) grows to 20ft (6m) with white 'flowers' in May. A delicate, deciduous shrub or sometimes small tree from N. America. Best in the warmer southern counties. Very recognisable once seen because of the characteristic hanging leaves.

C. Kousa now **Benthamia japonica** (1875) grows to 30ft (9m) with 'flowers' consisting of four pointed creamy white bracts in rows along the branches in June. A large deciduous shrub or small tree from Japan and Korea, hardier than *C. florida.* Good autumn colouration.

C. Mas Long in cultivation: Cornelian Cherry, grows to 25ft (5.5m) with clusters of bright yellow flowers on bare branches in February and March, sometimes followed by very edible bright red fruits in August. A deciduous European shrub or small tree.

C. rugosa, now **Swida rugosa — Roundleaf Dogwood** (1784) grows to 10ft (3m) with clusters of white flowers in June. A deciduous shrub from N. America with pale blue berries and leaves with felted grey undersides.

C. sanguinea — Common Dogwood grows to 12ft (3.7m) with clusters of small scented flowers in June followed by black berries. Purple and crimson leaves in autumn. A deciduous European shrub for hedging and the wild garden.

Requirements: Any good garden soil in a sunny position. Moister for *C. canadensis* with partial shade.

Propagation: Take half-ripe cuttings with a heel in July, insert in a rooting compost of peat and sand and put into a propagator set at 16°C (61°F). When rooted transfer into individual pots of John Innes No.2, and keep in a cold frame for the winter. Transfer to a nursery area and grow on for several years before moving to final position. Low-growing branches may be layered and should be separated in about two years.

Pruning: Those species grown for their winter coloured barks should be cut down in April to within three or four inches of the ground.

Uses: Good garden subjects with 'flowers', autumn foliage and coloured bark in winter.

Shrubs: Ballalheannagh, Barcock, Bees, Bodnant, Brackenwood, Bressingham, Peter Chappell, Daisy Hill, Dobbies, Fairley's, Farall, Goatcher, Goscote, Hilliers, Hopleys, Hyden, Jackman, Kaye, Kershaw, Knaphill, Knoll Gardens, Lime Cross, Marchant, Notcutts, Otter, Reuthe, Roger, Russell, Scotts, Shepton, Sherrard, Smith, Southcombe, St. Bridget, Toynbee, Treasure, Treseder, Warley, Woodland, W.W., Wyedale.

Seeds: Chiltern.

COROKIA — Wire-netting bush *(Cornaceae).* The plant was named Korokia by the Maoris, but is more familiarly called the 'Wire-netting Bush' because its interlacing silver-stemmed new growth looks so much like galvanised chicken-wire. The bush is a dainty thing, just a mite tender even in our southern counties; it is irregularly scattered with charming little star-shaped yellow flowers in May and though classed as an evergreen one has to look twice — even in midsummer — to see the small spoon-shaped leaves. This shrub should be planted where its curious appearance can be seen at all times of the year — it looks right when set at the edge of a stone-edged pool (its own rigidity being echoed by the stone) or while it is young, it is light and interesting in a large rockery, though it may have to be moved at a later date.

C. cotoneaster — Wire-netting bush (1875) grows to 8ft (2.4m) with small yellow flowers in May. A rather tender evergreen shrub from New Zealand for a good position in a sheltered sunny place.

Requirements: Any good garden soil and a sunny site. Best and safest against a wall, though my own is out in the open (but it is the second plant in ten years).

Propagation: Take lateral cuttings with a heel in August and insert them in a rooting compost of peat and sand. Put into a propagator set at 16°C (61°F) until rooted. Put into individual pots of John Innes No.1 and keep in a cold frame for the winter, or a warm greenhouse if winter is very cold. Pot on and harden off in spring, plunge pots in a nursery area until plants are large enough to set out.

Uses: As fascinating background material for floral arrangements; as focal plants in the garden.

Shrubs: Bodnant, Hilliers, Holden Clough, Knoll Gardens, Marchant, Notcutts, Sherrard, St. Bridget, Toynbee,

Treasure, Treseder, Woodland, Wyevale.

Seeds: Chiltern.

CORONILLA *(Leguminosae).* The Coronillas are from the warmer parts of Europe, and always remind me of scrambled goose eggs, so rich a yellow are the flowers. They are tender shrubs, needing walls or cosy corners, but they have a long flowering season and are worth protecting. Blue-flowered *Clematis alpina* or *C. macropetala* goes well with them.

C. Emurus — Scorpion Senna grows to 7ft (2.1m) with golden-yellow flowers from May to October. A tender deciduous shrub from Central and Southern Europe for a sheltered place. So called because the seed-pods look like the jointed tail of a scorpion.

C. glauca (1722) grows to 9ft (2.7m) with pleasing glaucous foliage and rich golden flowers that are day-scented. A tender evergreen shrub from S. Europe for a sunny wall or large conservatory. There is a small brother 2ft high (61cm) var. pygmaea, with a plump and rounded shape that is good in small gardens or sitting in a rockery.

Requirements: Sandy, well drained soil, full sun and a protected position.

Propagation: Take lateral cuttings with a heel in August and insert them in a rooting compost of peat and sand. When rooted pot on into John Innes No.1 and protect for the first winter in a cold frame or greenhouse. Sow seeds as soon as ripe in boxes of seed compost in a cold frame.

Pruning: None needed.

Uses: As long-flowering garden shrubs and as cut flowers.

Shrubs: Brackenwood, Great Dixter, Hilliers, Hopleys, Kaye, Marchant, Notcutts, Otter, Scotts, Sherrard, St. Bridget, Stonehouse, Toynbee, Treasure, Treseder, Wyevale.

Seeds: Chiltern.

CORYLOPSIS — Winter Hazel *(Hamamelidaceae).* This is a spring flowering shrub that should be seen in gardens side by side with Witch Hazel *(Hamamelidaceae spp.)* because its cowslip-scented flowers follow on as the others fade. The yellow tassels of Corylopsis have more substance than those of the Witch Hazel 'spiders', but that is to be expected — the new year is now not so new and not quite so cold. Choose a planting position for this shrub that does not face east, and grow it in a sheltered place, with early pale-flowered Narcissi at its feet. In a good year there is so much sweetly-scented blossom that one cannot see through the shrub.

C. pauciflora — Buttercup Winter Hazel (1874) grows to 6ft (1.8m) with few-flowered pendant clusters of scented yellow flowers in March and April. A rather tender deciduous shrub from Japan for a sheltered position.

C. spicata (1863) grows to 6ft (1.8m) with drooping racemes of scented yellow flowers in March and April. A deciduous shrub from Japan for a sheltered position. Not as graceful as other species.

C. Veitchiana — Winter Hazel grows to 6ft (1.8m) with short crowded racemes of fragrant yellow flowers in April. A deciduous shrub from Central China for a sheltered place in the garden.

C. Willmottiae (1909) grows to 12ft (3.7m) with 3″ (7.5cm) long crowded racemes of fragrant creamy yellow flowers in April. A deciduous shrub from western China for a sheltered wall or semi-woodland conditions (Grown by Ellen Willmott from seed sent her by E.H. Wilson).

Requirements: Corylopsis are all rather tender and their so-welcome early flowers can be spoiled by frost. Plant them where they are sheltered by other trees, or on a warm wall.

Propagation: Take heel cuttings in August and insert in a rooting compost of peat and sand in a propagator set at 16°C (61°F). When rooted pot on into individual pots of John Innes No.1 and keep in a cold frame for first winter. Plunge pots in nursery area for a year, pot on as necessary or plant in ground. Protect in winter with bracken, straw and ashes.

Pruning: None needed.

Uses: As welcome early-spring scented flowers for cutting or in the garden.

Shrubs: Ballalheannagh, Bodnant, Brackenwood, Bressingham, Peter Chappell, Daisy Hill, Dobbies, Goatcher, Goscote, Hilliers, Hopleys, Hyden, Kaye, Knaphill, Knoll Gardens, Lime Cross, Marchant, Meare Close, Notcutts, Otter, Reuthe, Roger, Russell, Scotts, Shepton, Sherrard, St. Bridget, Toynbee, Treasure, Treseder, Warley, Woodland, Wyevale.

Seeds: Chiltern.

CORYLUS — Hazel (*Corylaceae*, formerly *Betulaceae*). These shrubs are grown mainly for their nuts, but who can resist smiling at the dancing catkins — Lamb's Tails to children of all ages — which mean that spring is a thing of certainty and not merely of hope. The catkins of *C. Avellana* 'Contorta' look even more interesting when seen dangling and swinging from the corkscrew branches of 'Harry Lauder's Walking Stick': visitors to a garden with a mature specimen always gravitate to it as quickly as wasps to jam in July. Filberts — *C. maxima* — are like larger hazel or cob-nuts, and there is a fine foliage shrub, *C. maxima* var. 'Purpurea', whose leaves are richly black-purple in their colouration — even darker than those of a copper beech; matching purple catkins are produced in early spring. The catkins of *C. maxima* are much longer than the ordinary native hazel. Pick the nuts before the mice and squirrels get them or they, being more discerning and quicker off the mark, will leave you all the rotten ones. The nuts should be gathered in early autumn when the husks begin to turn brown (the squirrels will tell you when). Spread them out to

dry in an airy place for a week. Pliant hazel branches have had many uses down the centuries — as spars for thatching, as hurdles for farm use, as hoops for crates and for dowsing by water diviners.

C. Avellana — Hazel, Cob-nut grows to 20ft (6m) with 2½″ (6.3cm) male catkins in early spring and nuts in autumn. A useful hedging plant within a large garden or to edge the vegetable growing area. *C. Avellana* 'Contorta', or 'Harry Lauder's Walking Stick' or the Corkscrew Hazel, has contorted branches in ringlets from which swing the catkins in spring. This variety occurred naturally, being found in a hedge in Gloucester in 1863. Plant in an open, winter-focal position, near stonework or water for maximum effect. It even has nuts.

C. maxima — Filbert grows to 20ft (6m) with longer male catkins — 3-4″ (7.5-10cm) in good years, and larger nuts. A deciduous shrub from W. Asia and S. Europe. *C. maxima* var. 'Purpurea' is a fine dark-leaved shrub to grow for foliage contrast.

Requirements: *Corylus Avellana* will grow anywhere but will yield better catkins and better nuts if grown in good soil and sun.

Propagation: Corylus can be grown from seed — sow the nuts in individual pots of John Innes No.1 in October or November and keep in a cold frame; or layer branches and sever when rooted — this method is best for *C. Avellana* 'Contorta' and *C. maxima atropurpurea*; or remove rooted suckers.

Pruning: For nut hedges the shrubs should be planted out when they are 18″ (46cm) high, with several stems or branches. Allow to become established for a few years then cut back previous year's growth by half. When flowering begins on these branches (this will take several years more), cut older branches back to a strong shoot in March. Do not 'tidy up' the twiggy lateral branchlets, as these will have the nuts. Strong new shoots often grow up in the centre of the bush or bushes during the summer, these should be cut out as near to ground level as is practicable.

Uses: *C. Avellana* as hedging, for catkins and for nuts. *C. Avellana* 'Contorta' as a specimen winter-interest shrub and branches for winter arrangements.

Shrubs: Ballalheannagh, Barcock, Brackenwood, Caldwell, Daisy Hill, Dobbies, Goatcher, Goscote, Hilliers, Jackman, Kent, Knaphill, Lime Cross, Marchant, Meare Close, Notcutts, Otter, Reuthe, Roger, Russell, Scotts, Shepton, Sherrard, Smith, St. Bridget, Treasure, Treseder, Warley, Woodland, Wyevale.

Seeds: Chiltern.

COTINUS — Smoke Bush, Smoke Tree, Silken Sumach, Venetian Sumach, Wig Bush, Burning Bush (*Anacardiaceae*). This interesting and lovely shrub had its name formally changed in recent years to *Cotinus coggygria*, the latter part of which is ugly and impossible to pronounce with grace.

The Smoke Tree, as it is appropriately named in English, has very beautiful veined leaves that are light green, dark red or purple according to the variety. In July long 8″ (20.5cm) panicles of small flowers appear among which are many silky hairs. These persist after the flowers are over, turning first pinkish and then grey. In autumn the green-leaved shrubs turn to shades of red and yellow, and the purple-leaved kinds turn redder with red veins. The shrub should be planted where the setting sun can shine through the leaves which are then even more beautiful. It is an undemanding plant, doing best in very average soil and needing no feeding at all — give it a soft life and it will stop flowering.

Cotinus coggygria (formerly **Rhus cotinus)** (1656) grows to 10ft (3m) and as much or more wide. Almost round, conspicuously veined leaves and long, loose hairy panicles of small flowers in June and July which turn into the striking plumy looking growths (which by this time are devoid of flowers, being merely a mass of branching thread-like stems). A deciduous shrub from S. Europe and the Caucasus for a sunny, focal position in the flower arranger's garden. *Cotinus c. atropurpurea* is an excellent purple-leaved variety, better than *C. c. purpurea.*

Requirements: Ordinary well drained soil and a sunny position — shade will tone down purple colouration and the shrub does not flower much.

Propagation: Take lateral cuttings with a heel in August and grow on as previously described. Pot on when rooted into individual pots of John Innes No.1 and protect through first winter. Grow on in a nursery area for a season and plant out in the second spring.

Pruning: None needed.

Uses: As a superb foliage shrub, with delicate inflorescence for arrangements.

Warning: Though moved out of the genus Rhus, this shrub may share their poisonous properties to a much lesser degree (see *Rhus*). Therefore take care when handling it.

Shrubs: Ballalheannagh, Caldwell, Daisy Hill, Dobbies, Fairley's, Farall, Goatcher, Highfield, Hilliers, Hopleys, Hortico, Kaye, Kent, Kershaw, Knaphill, Notcutts, Reuthe, Rosemoor, Russell, Shepton, Sherrard, Smith, St. Bridget, Stonehouse, Toynbee, Treasure, Treseder, Warley, Woodland, Wyevale.

Seeds: Chiltern, Thompson and Morgan.

COTONEASTER — Herringbone Cotoneaster, Rockspray *(Rosaceae).* The plant takes its name from *kotoneon,* quince, *aster,* similar, though I find it difficult to see where the resemblance lies.

The 'ordinary' Cotoneaster is *C. horizontalis* which is often scorned by gardeners who know more than a little but less than a lot. These gardeners are so used to this easy, undemanding shrub with its very regular cycle of bee-buzzing flowers in spring and scarlet leaves and berries in autumn (which last well into spring if the sparrows are engaged elsewhere) that they consider it to be too ordinary. They pull it up and plant a rarer shrub, twice the price and a quarter the size, and find that the new treasure is miffy and slow-growing and disinclined or unable to do its best on a draughty north-east wall under the dining-room window. This is where the Cotoneaster scores — I call it the 'Bay-window plant' because its genes have dictated that it shall not grow more than a few feet high — just to window-sill height, in fact. Apart from the evergreen Pyracantha, which will clothe the entire house wall up to the eaves, there really is nothing else that is so colourful and good-humoured. I think people are now appreciating the 'Herringbone' Cotoneaster not only for its nice nature but because all plants are more expensive; what one has paid more for is correspondingly more valued. I saw an inspired planting of *C. horizontalis* at Newby Hall in Yorkshire, where there is a fine collection of classical statuary that is interestingly eroded by the elements. The statues are set to one side of a wide, gravel walk and raised up on square plinths and backed by a hedge of mature yews, which are planted so as to form a separate enclave for each statue — thus, when studying them close to, one is not distracted by seeing all the others at the same time. The Cotoneaster grows round the base of each plinth, softening and yet harmonizing in its own angularity, and, though I saw it at the 'plain green' stage in August, I could imagine it frothing with flowers in late spring and scarlet in leaf and berry in the autumn and through the winter.

As well as bees and other insects, queen wasps are so attracted by the flowers that they can easily be caught early in the year. This is only if you have had a wasp's nest problem in house or garden — it is tiresome to have to abandon summerhouse or outside lavatory for the summer because the wasps are in residence.

There are several evergreen kinds — *C. microphyllus* was called 'The Architects' Friend' because it was planted to cover ugly but necessary walls, which it did — and does — so thickly that nothing of the offending masonry can be seen. Ivy, of course, does the same job but it has more sombre flowers and in any case most people are scared of ivy. There are deciduous and evergreen Cotoneasters for all purposes and all of them have berries, many of which stay on the shrub for much of the winter. The very useful *C. adpressa* is a most excellent plant for hiding drain covers in lawns or paving — builders and plumbers come equipped with sand and cement but not soul, and I have seen many an essential drain-cover placed conveniently to the house's vital systems but in aesthetically unforgivable places like terraces, porches, patios, paths and paving. *C. adpressa* is only a foot (30cm) or so high, but it likes to spread out sideways. It has myriads of white flowers in spring and scarlet leaves and berries in autumn. Plant Muscari to go with it in spring and Colchicums and asters for autumn. *C. dammeri* is even more prostrate, fitting itself to humps and hollows, and is excellent when planted to trail down rocky supporting walls. It, too, prefers to grow sideways rather than up.

C. salicifolius and *C. horizontalis* were introduced by Père David, *C. divaricatus* and *C. henryanus* by Henry Wilson and others by Forrest and Kingdon-Ward. All the Cotoneasters are attractive, some are useful and some of them are really beautiful in autumn, with their yellow or red leaves and matching crimson berries. A selection of those available follows, though there are many more; the catalogues will yield up all the nursery names.

C. adpressa (1895) grows no more than 18″ (40cm) but spreads to several yards (metres) high with pinkish white flowers in June and scarlet leaves and berries in autumn and winter. A deciduous shrub from China, exceedingly useful to edge drives, for and on walls, large rockeries, sunny banks and for covering things.

C. dammeri (1900) prostrate with white flowers in June and coral coloured berries. An evergreen shrub from China for rockeries, banks, edging, walls and concealing things.

C. Franchettii (1895) grows to 10ft (3m) with small clusters of unexciting flowers in May and orange fruit in autumn. An evergreen shrub from China for walls and arches with pleasing grey-green leaves.

C. horizontalis — Herringbone Cotoneaster, Fishbone plant (1879) grows low in nature but can be leaned against a wall. Has characteristic flat 'fishes skeleton'-shaped branches and stems. Thousands of pinkish white flowers in May and June with scarlet leaves in autumn and berries that usually remain through the winter. A deciduous shrub from China for many uses and situations. Does quite well on N. walls (but always better on S.)

C. lucidus (1840) grows to 9ft (2.7m) with pink and white flowers in May and June and black berries in autumn. A deciduous shrub from the Siberian Altai mountains, with fine autumn colour.

C. microphyllus (1824) prostrate and sideways-growing with bright white flowers in June. Evergreen shrubs from the Himalaya with scarlet berries in autumn. Very useful and attractive to grow as a draping plant.

C. salicifolius (1908) grows to 16ft (4.8m) with clusters of small white flowers in June and handsome red berries in autumn. An evergreen shrub from China for a sunny position.

Requirements: Easy plants, needing ordinary garden soil and a sunny position.

Propagation: Cotoneasters associate only too readily with each other so must be propagated vegetatively except for *C. horizontalis* which self sows in any case, or is bird sown, and

seems true from seed. For the evergreen species, take heel cuttings of ripe lateral shoots in August or September; for deciduous kinds, take heel cuttings in July or August. Put into a rooting compost of peat and sand in a cold frame. When rooted, transfer deciduous kinds to a nursery area and grow on for two years, and put evergreen species in pots of John Innes No.1. Pot on as needed for a year or so. Cotoneasters can be layered in October and will take a year to root. Seeds can be sown in seed compost and may take 18 months to germinate.

Pruning: Prune evergreen species in April, deciduous kinds in February. Evergreen hedges should be shaped when the berries have formed just after flowering, cutting back all unwanted growth. Prune deciduous species in late summer.

Uses: Good berrying and foliage plants, excellent for walls and banks and usefully strong when used to cover unsightly domestic features.

Diseases: Cotoneasters are subject to Fireblight, when the flowers shrivel and become blackened and the leaves wither and branches die back. Cut back beyond diseased part to try to arrest its progress — burn trimmings. If this fails, uproot and burn shrub and do not put another similar plant in its place for several years.

Shrubs: Ballalheannagh, Barcock, Bees, Bodnant, Brackenwood, Bressingham, Busheyfields, Caldwell, Peter Chappell, Crarae, Daisy Hill, Dobbies, Jack Drake, Fairley's, Goatcher, Goscote, Great Dixter, Highfield, Hilliers, Hyden, Ingwersen, Kaye, Kent, Kershaw, Knaphill, Knoll Gardens, Lime Cross, Marchant, Meare Close, Notcutts, Orchard, Otter, Reuthe, Robinsons, Roger, Rosemoor, Russell, Scotts, Shepton, Sherrard, Smith, Southcombe, St. Bridget, Stonehouse, Toynbee, Treasure, Treseder, Warley, Woodland, W.W., Wyevale.

Seeds: Chiltern, Fothergill, Thompson and Morgan, Suttons.

CRATAEGUS — Hawthorn, May, Whitethorn, Quick, Quickthorn *(Rosaceae)*. This genus takes its name from *kratos*, strength, because of the hardness and toughness of the wood.

The most well known of the species is the may or hawthorn, which was formerly used to make cattle-proof hedges. Branches of may-blossom were one of the most protective of plants during the important growing month of May, and it was always put round the maypole when this was erected — with all its significance — on May-day Eve, the 30th of April. The hawthorn or the may (it is the flowers that are called may) was always in bloom in time for May-day, May 1st, before the calendar was changed in 1732. Nowadays it can be the second week in May before the hedges are white with the curiously scented blossom which leaves a suggestion of old fish in the nostrils. Never bring hawthorn blossom indoors — it will mean a death in the house. The may blossom protected horses, cattle and flocks from all harm, it kept the milk from souring and helped in the butter-making. When woven into crowns or garlands it was even more lucky — the weaving was important, and it was even better if the branches were wet with May-day dew — this was sure to make the girls instantly beautiful though the dew-wet branches had to be picked before sunrise. The fairies used the solitary may bush or tree as a meeting place and sometimes they lived there, so the bush or tree would have had magic powers. Hurt or cut the tree and you might become ill of a wasting sickness, or die. But you would be quite safe from lightning if you sheltered there because the may would protect you. This was one of the reasons for the hawthorn hedges — in addition to their practicality, they protected the stock within from lightning.

All the genus Crataegus will grow in any soil, though they must have sun to do well. The haws of species shrubs (particularly *C. monogyna*, the native hawthorn) take many months to germinate, usually in the second spring, sometimes the third and even the fourth spring from ripening. Unlike most seed, the ripe haws must not be stored in a dry place: they can be heaped up outside with some sandy soil and left through two winters before sowing. For smaller quantities than that for a ducal estate, the haws can be sown in pots of seed compost which are left plunged in a shaded place for two winters. In the second spring the pots can be taken up and put in a cold frame and they are then likely to germinate.

C. monogyna — Common Hawthorn, Quickthorn, May grows to a tree of 35ft (10.5m) when allowed to do so, but is also a hedging shrub. Scented white flowers in May with crimson haws in autumn. A deciduous thorny European shrub (or larger tree) for field or wild garden hedges.

Requirements: Any soil, an open position and sun.

Propagation: Heel cuttings can be taken in July or August, or seed can be sown, see text.

Pruning: Trim hedges during late autumn or before March.

Uses: As traditional hedging, often with a mixture including Holly, Beech, Sycamore, Dogwood, Field Maple and Elder.

Shrubs: Goscote, Hilliers, Jackman, Knaphill, Marchant, Notcutts, Otter, Reuthe, Roger, Russell, Sherrard, Smith, St. Bridget, Toynbee, Treasure, Warley.

Seeds: Chiltern.

CRINODENDRON (Tricuspidaria) — Chilean Lantern Tree *(Elaeocarpaceae)*.

This is a beautiful and rather unreal-looking shrub, with coral-red 'lanterns' dangling from its branches like so many Christmas-tree decorations. It is a tender thing from Chile and is worth taking care of in winter, as it will only grow in the warmer southern and south-western counties and even then the one-off exceptionally bad winter is likely to kill it. This lovely thing comes from the Andes, and therefore should be used to cold but it is the winter wet *and* the cold that finishes such treasures

off. It was introduced into Britain in 1848 for the great firm of Messrs. Veitch by William Lobb the plant hunter, who had a rambling moss rose named after him. Once the Crinodendron has settled down in your garden it will begin producing its flower buds in late autumn, much like the Paulownia does.

C. Hookeranium syn. **Tricuspidaria lanceolata** (1848) grows to 30ft (9m) in its native country but not in the British Isles, usually 10ft (3m) is the maximum height. Coral-red lantern-shaped flowers appear as buds in the preceding autumn and enlarge and turn colour the following April to June. An evergreen shrub from Chile for a semi-shaded sheltered position. Protect in winter. Underplant with London Pride which flowers at the same time.

Requirements: a peaty soil that is quite lime-free, wall-shelter, and semi-shade. Top dress annually with leafmould. Make a circular wire netting cage slightly larger than shrub and weave bracken through holes, in bad weather cover top with bracken but remove when weather improves.

Propagation: Take heel cuttings in July or August; put in a rooting compost of peat and sand. When rooted, pot up in a compost of 3 parts lime free garden soil, 1 part sand, 1 part peat and 1 part leafmould. Protect in a frame for first winter, pot on as necessary and protect again during second winter.

Uses: As a very striking garden shrub for a sheltered focal position.

Shrubs: Ballalheannagh, Bodnant, Brackenwood, Peter Chappell, Daisy Hill, Dobbies, Goscote, Hilliers, Knaphill, Knoll Gardens, Otter, Reuthe, Roger, Rosemoor, Scotts, Sherrard, St. Bridget, Stonehouse, Toynbee, Treseder, Wyevale.

Seeds: Chiltern.

CYTISUS — Broom, Pineapple Tree *(Leguminosae)*.

The familiar yellow flowered shrub that lines roadside verges is indeed broom, and was at one time in the genus Cytisus. Botanists have decreed that it should now be called Sarothamnus and that other look-alikes are to be classed as Genista and Spartium (see index for these).

Brooms have been appreciated for centuries, so much so that they were at one time — and still are — grafted on to laburnum stocks to make standards. Their naturally graceful, weeping habit must have made them very beautiful when in flower, so much so that when the white Spanish broom was in flower it was described by Phillips as being 'clad like a virgin bride in pearls' and again 'rather studded with flakes of snow thus bedecked by Flora's hand... while its graceful waving bend so well accords with the chastity of its colour' which descriptions must have caused a sell-out in the nurseries of those times.

This grafting to make standards was continued until late in the 19th century and Robinson, who detested artificiality, said that it (in this instance, *C. purpureus*) belonged in the rock garden around the boulders there (rock gardens were the size of a small Alp in those days) and not 'grafted mop-fashion on Laburnum stems'. There is room for both kinds of gardening — one formal and the other wild (almost) as nature intended.

There are very many species and hybrid Cytisus: a reasonably representative selection is as follows:

C. Ardoinii (1866) grows only to 8″ (20.5cm) with yellow flowers in April and May. A tiny shrub from the Maritime Alps for the rock garden in full sun.

C. glabrescens syn. **C. emeriflorus** (about 1890) (sometimes included in Genista) grows to 1ft (30cm) with yellow flowers in May and June. A low, rounded deciduous bush from Central Europe, very suitable for rockeries or at the edge of paths in full sun.

C. x kewensis (1900) grows only to 18″ (46cm) but spreads sideways and preferably downwards. Masses of cream flowers in May and June. A glorious shrub for an elevated position such as a wall or bank where it can trail floriferously. Full sun.

C. multiflorus syn. **C. albus — White Spanish broom** (1752) grows to 12ft (3.7m) with white flowers in May and June. A deciduous shrub from Spain and Portugal for a sunny position.

C. nigricans (1730) grows to 6ft (1.8m) with yellow flowers from July-August. An erect deciduous later-flowering shrub from central and S.E. Europe for a sunny place.

C. purpureus — Purple Broom (1792) grows to 2ft (60cm) with flowers in shades of purple in May and June. A deciduous shrub from S. Europe and Central Spain for a sunny place.

C. scoparius — Common Broom (see *Sarothamnus*).

Requirements: Brooms are said to prefer acid soil, but oddly enough if the soil is too much so, they will not thrive. They like very ordinary (verging on poor) well drained garden soil, in full sun. They do not do well on chalk.

Propagation: Brooms should be grown from cuttings or seed (which will not come true with modern hybrid varieties) and, when large enough, planted out where they are to grow. They dislike being moved at any time in the year and will usually die. A skilful and careful gardener can move the small ones during their dormant period, taking up as much soil as possible with the shrub, but the broom will undoubtedly wake up from its winter sleep, look around crossly and thereafter it may not try so hard. I know people who have moved brooms, but they are usually new to the gardening game and can break all the rules and get away with it. They soon learn. This is an odd fact — the more you know, the less rules you break and the more plants seem to sense your doubt and fear. Or so it seems.

Take lateral heel cuttings in August and insert in a rooting compost of peat and sand. When rooted, pot on in a compost without lime (made up as for Crinodendron but leaving out the leafmould). Plunge the pots in a nursery area and grow on until the autumn. Think before you plant and remember that they really hate being moved. Sow large seeds singly in pots of lime-free seed compost in April (or when ripe), place in a cold frame and grow on, re-potting carefully as necessary.

Pruning: Prune those which flower on the previous year's growth. After flowering, cut away two-thirds of all growth. Species flowering on current year's shoots can be cut hard back in February. Pruning should not really be necessary, it destroys the characteristic airy delicacy of the shrub.

Uses: As permanent garden shrubs. For cutting. For besoms (with the prunings or with dead shrubs).

Shrubs: Ballalheannagh, Barcock, Bees, Bodnant, Brackenwood, Bressingham, Busheyfields, Caldwell, Peter Chappell, Daisy Hill, Dobbies, Jack Drake, Farall, Goatcher, Goscote, Highfield, Hilliers, Ingwersen, Jackman, Kaye, Kershaw, Knaphill, Knoll Gardens, Lime Cross, Marchant, Marten's Hall, Meare Close, Notcutts, Old Rectory, Orchard, Otter, Potterton and Martin, Reuthe, Roger, Rosemoor, Russell, Scotts, Shepton, Sherrard, Smith, St. Bridget, Stonehouse, Toynbee, Treasure, Treseder, Warley, Weald, Woodland, Wyevale.

Seeds: Chiltern, Suttons, Thompson and Morgan.

DABOECIA — St. Dabeoc's Heath, Irish Whorts (*Ericaceae*). Daboecias are really heathers with large flowers which are most colourful when they are in bloom, though when the flower is done it drops to the ground, unlike those of the heather which remain on the stem. When planning a group of heathers, plant Daboecias of different colours to flower with other heathers at the same time, so that all the colour comes together. Of course, because of their size and attractiveness, your visitors will notice and comment on the Daboecia first and may not even notice your other ericaceous treasures. If you have a large rockery (and, of course, you must have acid soil) plant a group of similarly coloured Daboecias where their very beautiful rose-purple bells will show to advantage against the stone behind them.

Edward Lhuyd, the Welsh botanist who first discovered the plant growing wild in Ireland, said that the Irish women used to carry sprigs of it wherever they went in the firm belief that this would prevent incontinency. St. Dabeoc himself (note the different spelling — it was the great Linnaeus who first mis-spelled it, and it has never been changed since) was one of Ireland's great saints who was given the care of a cave called St. Patrick's Purgatory where those penitent enough, and brave enough, could pass directly into Hell.

D. cantabrica syn. **Menziesia polifolia — St. Dabeoc's Heath** (1800) grows to 3ft (90cm) with rose, purple or white bell-shaped flowers from June-September. An evergreen shrub from S.W. Europe, Ireland and the Azores for borders, large rockeries and in association with shrubs.

For requirements, propagation, pruning and uses, see *Erica*.

Shrubs: Daisy Hill, Dobbies, Drake, Farall, Goatcher, Hilliers, Ingwersen, Otter, Russell, Scotts, Sherrard, Smith, Speyside, St. Bridget, Toynbee, Treasure, Treseder, Ward, Warley, Woodland, Wyevale.

Seeds: Thompson and Morgan.

DAPHNE *(Thymelaeacea)*. All the daphnes are as lovely as is their name, though none are really easy plants to grow. They do well for some folk who neglect them, and fail without seeming to try at all for other gardeners who do their utmost to introduce happiness into their lives. I know a house in the country where *D. Mezereum* grows everywhere — in sun or shade, out of the foundations, up out of the paving and it particularly thrives in the drive: just about anywhere in this garden; I can only suppose that this particular clone is of strong constitution and am grateful for the small plant that was thrust upon me (which is not so small now and is doing well and happily). I once grew *D. Laureola* from a cutting, and the little shrub throve until one year it suddenly died for no apparent reason, which bears out my remarks — they are contrary plants. They really have no claim to the name of Daphne, who was a nymph of radiant beauty. Indeed, so beautiful was she that she excited the jaded appetite of the Sun-god Apollo, who was used to having his own way in everything. But the nymph Daphne did not want anything to do with Apollo and was changed into the flower so as to escape his attentions. When reading about the carryings-on in Ancient Greece I wonder sometimes at the lack of grit in the gods — they seem to give up so easily — after all, if someone could get changed into a daphne, or a narcissus or a dead bluebell, one would have thought that the gods, being all-powerful, could have just as quickly changed them back again. But the stories are great fun as they are, of course.

D. Mezereum is deciduous and does not seem to mind being moved (or at least not with me) during its very brief dormant period after the leaves have fallen and before the flower buds can be seen. *D. Laureola* is called the Spurge Laurel, because it was once used as a purge (as was anything named 'spurge') and as one of the many plants used, dangerously, to procure abortions. *D. Laureola* is evergreen, and looks slightly more sinister in February (with its neat bunches of scented green flowers peeping out from beneath the glossy laurel-like leaves) than *D. Mezereum* whose bare twigs are wreathed and clustered with innocent pink or white blossom. But it is *D. Mezereum* which is the more dangerous. Sturdy Russian peasants in Czarist times would use thirty of its berries as a purgative — (thirty-one would be one too many) and French apothecaries gave fifteen as a

dangerous dose — their patients' constitutions were probably not as strong: Linnaeus said that six berries were enough to kill a wolf. The name Mezereum is derived from the Arabic *mazaryun,* which means 'destroyer of life' because of the poisonous nature of the plant. In those days it was used to alleviate the miseries of dropsy, rheumatism, scrofula and syphilis. *D. odora* is as pretty as its name, with clusters of scented pink flowers and stylish-looking evergreen leaves. The variety 'Aureomarginata' is hardier, and has cream-edged leaves and the same heavily perfumed pink or crimson and white flowers. *D. Cneorum* ('cneorum' means resembling an olive) is small and beautiful, though not so small sideways — it will spread for 2ft (60cm) to spill between rocks or drip sweetly down steps, each spray of flowers a miniature posy. Alas, it is not easily pleased, but is worth every effort. With Daphnes it really is a case of getting to know each kind and hoping that they will like your garden. On the whole they need good garden soil with the difficult combination of good drainage and plenty of moisture. Flat stones laid over their roots are usually a help in establishing them. Most like a sheltered situation in full sun, and all of them hate to be moved. It is said that most do better in limestone areas, though the reference sources do not agree on this.

D. Blagayana (1875) grows to 1ft (30cm) but can sprawl to 6ft (1.8m) with tufts of scented creamy flowers in April and May. An evergreen shrub from E. Europe for a sheltered place in semi-shade. Layer previous season's branches with flat stones and a little earth, add leaf mould and peat to soil.

D. Cneorum — Garland Flower (1752) grows to 1ft (30cm) and spreads to 3ft (90cm) with scented pink flowers in May and June. An evergreen shrub from Central Europe for a sheltered situation in sun, with moist, limy soil. Layer some of the outer shoots as for *D. Blagayana*.

D. Laureola — Spurge Laurel grows to 4ft (1.2m) with a similar spread, with scented green flowers in February and March. A European evergreen shrub for a semi-shaded position.

D. Mezereum — Mezereon (before 1561) grows to 5ft (1.5m) with a similar spread, with scented flowers of white, pink, mauve-pink and violet-crimson from February to April. A deciduous shrub of Europe and Asia Minor with poisonous red berries. One of the easiest of the Daphnes (but none is really easy) for a sheltered place in semi-shade.

D. odora (1771) grows to 6ft (1.8m) with neat, pointed evergreen leaves and very fragrant clusters of pink or pink and white flowers from January to March. A rather tender evergreen from China and Japan for a warm place.

D. retusa (1901) grows to 3ft (90cm) with scented pink flowers in May and June. An 'easier' evergreen Daphne from W. China for a sheltered place.

Requirements: Daphnes should not be allowed to dry out at the roots, and though most of them need a place in the sun, the soil should be moisture retentive but not too wet. Plants in limestone areas generally do better. Daphnes are slow-growing and the better kinds are grafted on to stocks of the more vigorous *D. Laureola* and *D. Mezereum*. It is better not to buy these as they are apt to die inexplicably.

Propagation: Daphnes such as *D. Mezereum* and *D. Laureola* come fairly easily from fresh seed sown in September, or heel cuttings of lateral non-flowering shoots should be taken in July and August, and inserted in a rooting compost of sand and peat and the pots placed in a cold frame. When rooted (usually by the following spring) pot on into John Innes No.1 and plunge the pots in a nursery area. Pot on as necessary, taking care not to disturb the roots.

Uses: As sweetly-scented cut flowers (when abundant enough — Daphnes are slow-growing). Many as pleasing evergreens.

Warning: Berries of all Daphnes are very poisonous as are all parts of the plant to a lesser degree.

Pruning: Do not. Daphnes don't like it.

Shrubs: Ballalheannagh, Barcock, Bees, Bodnant, Brackenwood, Caldwell, Peter Chappell, Daisy Hill, Dobbies, Farall, Goatcher, Goscote, Highfield, Hilliers, Hopleys, Hortico, Hyden, Jackman, Kaye, Kent, Kershaw, Knaphill, Knoll Gardens, Lime Cross, Marchant, Marten's Hall, Meare Close, Notcutts, Otter, Potterton and Martin, Reuthe, Roger, Rosemoor, Russell, Scotts, Shepton, Sherrard, Smith, St. Bridget, Stonehouse, Toynbee, Treasure, Treseder, Warley, Woodland, Wye.

Seeds: Chiltern, Thompson and Morgan.

DATURA — Angel's Trumpets, Death Angel, Thorn-Apple, Apple of Peru *(Solanaceae)*.

Many legends surround these strange plants with their beautiful flowers. Those of the tropical kinds hang indolently during the day, only opening and giving off their heavy and exotic perfume during the evening and night.

Ancient Greek legends tell of the Delphic priests who were believed to be gifted with divinatory powers, often accompanied by apparent convulsions as the oracle spoke through them. It is supposed that the priests used Datura to induce hallucinatory visions, and this practice was also employed by the priests of the ancient Peruvian civilisations. In areas where Daturas are indigenous it is widely believed that to sleep beneath them is to invite certain death — hence the name 'Death Angel'. The shrubs are not hardy in Northern Europe except in the Scilly Islands and must be grown under glass, but their tubs can be stood outside during June, July and August if the summer is a warm one, though they do not like cold nights. Large plants produce large, felted leaves.

D. sanguinea syn. **Brugmansia sanguinea** grows to 6ft (1.8m) and spreads to about 5ft (1.5m) with huge (8″) (20.5cm) long orange-red dangling trumpets in July and August. A tropical evergreen shrub from Peru for a heated greenhouse

or conservatory and for large tubs out of doors after June.

D. suaveolens — Angel's Trumpets grows to 15ft (4.5m) with a spread of about 7ft (2m) 10″ (25.5cm) white single or (more usually) double flowers in August. A tropical evergreen shrub from Brazil for a heated greenhouse or conservatory and for large tubs out of doors after June.

Requirements: Best planted in a border in the greenhouse, or in pots of John Innes No.2 according to their size. In winter reduce watering with a minimum temperature of 7°C (45°F). In spring and summer they need plenty of ventilation and water. Shade the plants if greenhouse is a sunny one and syringe leaves in prolonged hot periods. Give fortnightly feeds of liquid manure during the summer months, or plant in well manured soil.

Propagation: Take heel cuttings in May and insert in a rooting compost of peat and sand in a propagator set at 15-18°C (59-64°F). When rooted transfer into pots of John Innes No.2 and thereafter pot on as needed, finishing up with 10″ (25.5cm) pots. Re-pot annually.

Pruning: Prune to a 'standard' shape (to show off the flowers) by allowing the trunk or main stem to reach the required height before pinching out the growing tip. Prune to shape annually in February or March. If a shrubby shape is desired, cut all stems back to 6″ (15cm) in February or March, leaving suitable cutting material available for striking in May.

Uses: As exceedingly handsome greenhouse and patio tub plants.

Warning: Daturas are poisonous.

Shrubs: Hilliers, Knoll Gardens, Treseder.

Seeds: Chiltern, Thompson and Morgan, Unwin.

DESFONTAINEA (Potaliaceae) *(Loganiaceae)*.

This is a beautiful shrub that looks like a small-leaved holly until such time as the tubular red-orange flowers appear and open. It is a tender thing and needs a really favoured place in order to survive, let alone do well. It is named after the French botanist R.L. Desfontaines (1752-1833), and was discovered in South America by William Lobb on his first plant hunting expedition for the great firm of Veitch. The shrub grows slowly and needs a good wall-corner with some shade, and a soil enriched with leafmould and peat.

D. spinosa (1843) grows to 10ft (3m) though only in ideal circumstances. Tubular scarlet flowers lined with yellow appear in June and July. A tender evergreen shrub from Chile and Peru for a very sheltered situation and woodland conditions.

Requirements: Shelter, semi-shade (wall-protection), a moisture retentive soil with the addition of peat and leafmould.

Propagation: Take heel cuttings between June and August and insert in a rooting compost of peat and sand in a propagator set at 16-18°C (61-64°F). When rooted transfer into pots of John Innes No.1 and keep in a warm (frost free) greenhouse for the winter. During the following spring pot on and plunge in a nursery area.

Uses: As a very handsome wall shrub when it begins to flower.

Shrubs: Ballalheannagh, Barcock, Brackenwood, Peter Chappell, Crarae, Daisy Hill, Glendoick, Goatcher, Hilliers, Kaye, Knoll Gardens, Marchant, Meare Close, Notcutts, Reuthe, Roger, Scotts, Sherrard, St. Bridget, Toynbee, Treseder, Wyevale.

DEUTZIA — *(Philadelphaceae) (Saxifragaceae)*. This genus was named by Thunberg after Johann van der Deutz (1743-1784), a respected town councillor of Amsterdam who helped to pay for Thunberg's plant collecting expedition to Japan.

These shrubs are a recent introduction to the British Isles, by comparison to those of earlier centuries. Deutzias are quite hardy during long spells of unbroken cold (doing well in northern counties and Scotland) because they know where they are with the sort of definite weather that freezes the ground and makes the frosted leaves of evergreens rattle in the wind. But when this is interspersed with a kindly spell of warm weather that makes the tulips open to the sun like water-lilies, followed by another cold snap, it is this that kills the flowers within their buds. Deutzias come from China and Japan and the Himalayas, where the winters are real winters and when they go they are replaced in the natural order of things by spring and then summer. Not like our curious climate which teases our plants into movement, as a cat does with a mouse, only to bite off its head.

When choosing Deutzias it is best, perhaps, to select those that are June flowering, because the flower buds will have developed after the last of the frosts. For those gardeners with a protectable environment such as a conservatory, *D. gracilis* can be grown in large pots to flower most beautifully under glass. The tubs should go outside after flowering.

D. compacta (1905) grows to 6ft (1.8m) with white flowers in July. A deciduous shrub from China for a sheltered, sunny place.

D. gracilis (1840) grows to 4ft (1.2m) with many panicles of pure white flowers in June. A deciduous shrub from Japan for a sheltered sunny place.

D. mollis (1901) grows to 6ft (1.8m) with corymbs of white flowers in June. A deciduous shrub from China for a similar position.

D. scabra (1822) grows to an erect 10ft (3m) with white or pink-tinged flowers in June and July. A deciduous shrub from China and Japan. Var. *candidissima* has pure white double flowers.

D. x rosea (D. gracilis x D. purpurascens) (1896) grows to a neat 3ft (90cm) with soft rose-pink flowers in June and July. One of the many hybrid Deutzias raised by Lemoines of Nancy, in France. A deciduous shrub for a good sheltered position.

Requirements: Ordinary good well-drained soil suits Deutzias well enough, they need no feeding. They must have sheltered positions out of draughts, not east facing, and do well in sun, though the pink and crimson varieties keep their colour better in woodland conditions. The flowers will not develop fully if the buds have been frosted.

Propagation: Take lateral unflowered cuttings with a heel from July to August; insert in a rooting compost of peat and sand in pots in a shaded cold frame. During the following spring the rooted cuttings may be planted out in a nursery area to grow on.

Pruning: Not really necessary, though if you feel that you are neglecting them the flowering stems can be removed at ground level in July or when bloom has faded. Pruning not necessary with *D. scabra*.

Uses: As a good garden shrub, for cutting and for growing under glass.

Shrubs: Barcock, Daisy Hill, Dobbies, Fairley's, Farall, Goscote, Hilliers, Hyden, Jackman, Kaye, Kent, Kershaw, Marchant, Meare Close, Notcutts, Otter, Reuthe, Roger, Russell, Scotts, Shepton, Sherrard, Smith, St. Bridget, Stonehouse, Toynbee, Treasure, Warley, Woodland, Wyevale.

DIERVILLA *(Caprifoliaciaea)*. The genus was at one time much larger. Weigela, formerly *D. florida,* has been designated a genus by the taxonomists and this has reduced the number of garden plants very considerably. The genus was named after Dr Dierville who discovered *D. lonicera* when travelling in Canada in 1699-1700.

D. lonicera is not generally grown but can still be obtained — its leaves colour pleasantly in autumn as do those of *D. rivularis*.

D. florida — (see index for *Weigela*).

D. lonicera (1734) grows to 4ft (1.2m) with yellow funnel-shaped flowers in June and July. A deciduous shrub from E. North America for an open position. Good autumn tints.

D. rivularis (1902) grows to 4ft (1.2m) with panicles of yellow flowers in July and August. A deciduous shrub for a sunny position. Good autumn colour.

Requirements: Ordinary soil and a reasonably open and sunny position.

Propagation: Take heel cuttings in July and August or detach rooted suckers in early spring.

Pruning: Not necessary, though stems can be shortened back after flowering or before growth begins in spring.

Shrubs: Marchant, Roger, Scotts, Sherrard, Smith.

DORYCNIUM *(Leguminosae)*. Dorycniums are subtle shrubs, sitting comfortably on walls or on hot, dry banks, where their soft rounded grey-green hummocks provide contrast to other more definite leaf shapes such as sisyrinchiums, grasses, bergenias, alchemillas, dianthus and so on. Their pea flowers are inconspicuous, one could even say dull, on an uncharitable day when things are going wrong, but their seeds are slightly more definite, being a rusty crimson which harmonizes pleasingly with the soft colour of the leaves, though they are not exciting enough to need guarding from the more unscrupulous of your flower-arranging friends. That knowledgeable gardener, the late Margery Fish, loved her Dorycniums and it is from reading her informative books that I came to know and grow the one species that is still generally available. They do best in hot, dry soils and are, therefore, to be counted on where other things might fail. I had a fine clump of Eschscholzias last year whose bright orange flowers looked very pleasing against the soft neutrality of the Dorycniums, and both were happy in a corner of a border whose hot poor soil has hitherto been something of a problem (other larger and greedier plants take all the nourishment). Their foliage remains on the branches throughout most of the winter, rather surprisingly surviving regular periods of sub-zero temperatures (the leaves do not look happy, but they are still there, whereas those of many other true evergreens fall off in a sad circle.

D. hirsutum (1683) grows to 2ft (60cm) with softly hairy silver-green leafy branches and unexciting pink-toned white pea flowers from June to September. Rust-red seed pods contrast well. A usually deciduous semi-shrub from S. Europe for hot, dry positions.

Requirements: Any soil, even poor. Full sun and good drainage.

Propagation: Best by sowing ripened seeds in August or the following spring.

Uses: As an excellent and gently pleasing foliage plant.

Shrubs: Margery Fish, Hilliers, Hopleys, Ingwersen, Marten's Hall, Rampart, Shepton, Sherrard, Southcombe, Stonehouse.

DRIMYS — *(Winteraceae)* (formerly *Magnoliaceae*). This beautiful evergreen and uncommon shrub is doubly welcome in sheltered gardens, because one variety, *D. lanceolata* has fine coloured stems, evergreen leaves and jasmine-scented flowers, coming early enough in the year to be really appreciated.

The bark of *D. Winteri* or Winter's Bark was first used as a cure for scurvy by Captain William Winter (after whom it was named), who discovered it in the 17th century near the Straits of Magellan. He described it as a shrub, but in the right conditions it will grow to a 50ft (15m) tree. It was not introduced into cultivation until very much later (1827) and it has since been discovered that the bark is indeed anti-scorbutic.

Though not considered hardy, *D. lanceolata* has been used as a hedging plant in southern Ireland; its glossy, aromatic leaves and creamy white flowers must make a most unusual and beautiful boundary.

D. aromatica syn. **D. lanceolata — Mountain Pepper** (1843) grows to 15ft (4.5m) with very aromatic peppery-smelling leaves and bark. Scented white flowers from April-May. A rather delicate evergreen shrub in Northern Europe from Tasmania.

D. Winteri — Winter's Bark (1827) grows to 25ft (7.5m) or more in sheltered places, with clusters of fragrant white flowers in May. A delicate evergreen shrub (seldom attaining tree size), from S. America and worth one of the best and most sheltered places in the garden.

Requirements: A warm sandy soil, and a wall-protected site.

Propagation: Take heel cuttings from August to September and insert in a rooting compost of peat and sand. Put into a cold frame for the winter. Pot on into John Innes No.1 when rooted. Or propagate by layers.

Pruning: If you have a Drimys large enough to need pruning you do indeed possess a treasure. In mild areas the branches of *D. Winteri* may need shortening, which should be done immediately after flowering.

Uses: As excellent flowering shrubs, worthy of a focal wall position where the coloured stems and young growth of *D. lanceolata* may be seen.

Shrubs: Ballalheannagh, Bodnant, Brackenwood, Daisy Hill, Glendoick, Goatcher, Hilliers, Knoll Gardens, Marchant, Otter, Rosemoor, Sherrard, St. Bridget, Stonehouse, Treseder, Wyevale.

Seeds: Chiltern.

DRYAS — Mountain Avens *(Rosaceae)*. Usually classed as an 'Alpine' and found in nursery catalogues under that heading, Dryas (inappropriately, from the Greek for wood-nymph) is generally found sunning itself in an open rocky situation in limestone areas. Bean says that it is 'of easy cultivation' but nobody that I know who has tried to grow it would agree with this statement. It certainly does grow for some folk but it is shy flowering — perhaps because their soil is not quite right. Also — they may be impatient — Dryas does take more time to get into the habit of flowering than, say, a lupin. About five years from seed, by all accounts. This is often the best way to propagate plants which would otherwise just sit there doing nothing much except putting out a new leaf or so each year; it will be found that seedlings will establish themselves and grow away and begin to look as they should much more quickly than purchased nursery plants, which will have been having regular care and looking-over, but by a different-thinking person. Perhaps this is what is needed — the seedlings are so keen to grow that they take you for granted, much as a new kitten would after a few days. I read that this lovely plant flourishes in the Burren in Co. Clare, Ireland, where it may be seen in the latter part of May, hanging and dripping and flowing over the edges of the limestone rocks there, acres and acres of white and gold flowers set among their own handsome dark green oak-shaped leaves. If I should ever get to Co. Clare in late spring and see this lovely sight — on a good blue day when sky and sea are in harmony — I might indeed come back and take to growing lupins instead.

D. octopetala — Mountain Avens is an evergreen, mat-forming sub-shrub having white flowers with golden-orange stamens from May to July. Silky seed heads like *Clematis vitalba* or *Pulsatilla* develop in autumn. A rare European wild flower, rescued by reason of its beauty from any possibility of extinction.

Requirements: A sunny position, and (ideally) limestone soil and rocks. Ordinary soil if growing your own seedlings.

Propagation: Take heel-cuttings from a good flowering plant in March or August and put into a pot of damp sand in a cold frame. When rooted, carefully pot on into John Innes No.1 or John Innes seed compost. Grow on in a frame where their progress (or not) can be regularly observed. Or sow fresh seed in September in seed compost in a cold frame. Space whiskery seeds out in a seed tray so as to allow them to get well established.

Uses: As a very beautiful rockery plant.

Shrubs: Ballalheannagh, Broadwell, Cunnington, Daisy Hill, Jack Drake, Glenview, Oak Cottage, Scotts, Sherrard.

Seeds: Chiltern.

ECCREMOCARPUS — Chilean Glory Flower *(Bignoniaceae)*. Eccremocarpus takes its name from the Greek *ekkremes,* pendant, and *karpos,* fruit, and is a very easy and unusual-looking climber to grow. It is tender, and is usually treated as an annual when grown outside, though there are a few favoured localities in the British Isles where it survives the winters out of doors, notably at Brodick House in the Isle of Arran. If there is space for a colourful climber such as this in a warm greenhouse or conservatory it is worth planting it to go on cheerfully flowering well into autumn, as long as the seed-pods are picked off. It twines up and round anything it can, and from then on it will help itself upwards by means of the tendrils at the ends of the leaf-stalks. It has interesting orange or yellow foxglove-like flowers and these look even better when seen growing up through or over yew hedging, though the plants should not be set out until after the hedge has had its summer clip. The orange variety is delightful when planted to flower with blue or white flowered Group 2 Clematis, or the yellow *C. tangutica* or *C. orientalis.* This is an uncommon plant that should be seen more often. It is a good thing to grow because it looks so exotic but is almost as easy as a Nasturtium.

E. scaber — Chilean Glory Flower (1824) grows to 15ft (4.5m) with racemes of red, orange or yellow flowers from June onward. A tender twining evergreen climber from Chile with determined tendrils for trellis, posts, pergolas and in conjunction with other plants, or for a frost-free greenhouse or conservatory. Var. aureus has yellow flowers, var. ruber is flame-red.

Requirements: Ordinary well drained soil, a warm south or south west wall. Plenty of water while growing.

Propagation: Seedlings may be started off as soon as seeds are ripe: sow singly in 3″ (7.5cm) pots of seed compost, if plant is for greenhouse. If for out of doors, sow in February in seed compost in a propagator set at 13-16°C (55-61°F) put seedlings in small groups of three or four to a 5″ (12.5cm) pot, provide a cane or twiggy stick for them to climb up and grow on until they can be hardened off in May. If growth is rapid, as it usually is, pot on one more size and give them a taller support. Plant out where they are to grow and provide string, wire, trellis or other plants for them to grasp — which they will. A group of seedlings makes a better show than a single plant, and if one damps off it is not missed as much. If grown against a wall in a warm area they may well survive mild winters outside but this is the exception rather than the norm. Pick off seed pods as soon as they form to prolong flowering.

Uses: As excellent and interesting cut flowers; as quick-growing through delicate-looking wall or pergola climbers.

Shrubs: Ballalheannagh, Hilliers, Notcutts, Sherrard, St. Bridget, Stonehouse, Toynbee.

Seeds: Butcher, Chiltern, Unwin.

ELAEAGNUS *(Elaeagnaceae).* This is a wholly elegant but sturdy family of shrubs, much appreciated for their beauty of leaf which is very resistant to frosty weather, though prolonged spells of alternating wet and zero temperatures may cause some damage which the plant will repair during the following season. The best known is the subtly-coloured *E. pungens* of which there are several varieties with soft gold or cream marked or margined leaves. Branches of these seem to last forever — like fossils — when cut as background material for flower arrangements. The variety *E. pungens* 'Maculata' is particularly valuable in the garden because not only are its leaves beautiful throughout the year but it will lighten a dull corner, though it is not tolerant of deep and permanent shade as are Aucubas. It is a lovely, rather slow growing shrub which is often better than things that shoot up too quickly and change the garden landscape while doing so. If one has put a slow growing plant in exactly the right place there is then plenty of time for a bit of rare self-congratulation, which one is careful not to indulge in too often lest pestilence or a plague of grasshoppers descends on the garden. The sun-splashed *E. pungens* 'variegata' was discovered in Japan by that Russian botanist with the uneasy name of Carl Maximowicz, after whom and because of whom so many of our garden plants are named. He spent several years collecting and was successful in training others to collect for him in areas prohibited to foreigners. He

seems to have escaped most of the perils and misfortunes that are recorded about the other plant hunters of the time, and took back to Russia several hundred living plants, as many kinds of different seeds and seventy-two chests of dried specimens. During his stay in Japan he was collecting, amongst other things, as many indigenous lily bulbs as he could get, but, as is recorded, these were eaten by some pigs.

The deciduous *E. commutata*, or Silver Berry, is a lovely thing with silver-green leaves, flowers and even berries that give it an air of quiet distinction. It is slow growing and needs a reasonably sheltered place in full sun, where the light can shimmer among the leaves. It looks even better when planted near shrubs with contrasting leaves, or with a white-flowered climbing rose nearby or the gentle pink ones of *Jasminum x stephanense*.

I had *E. pungens* 'Maculata' var. *Fredericii* under my bedroom window and it eventually obscured my view of the garden, so I moved it. Large evergreen forms can be moved in November, though they will retaliate by shedding all their leaves in a rattling shower. Leave them alone and, some time during the next summer, small leaves will appear to re-clothe the scarecrow branches. I moved *E. pungens* thus and carefully, and the move was followed by a mild, wet spring and the Elaeagnus survived, though I did not really deserve it. (I should point out that I live in a single-storey thatched cottage, so the Elaeagnus was not of an exceptional size, but it had grown larger and more quickly than I had expected of a nursery description — 'slower-growing than the species').

E. angustifolia — Oleaster, Russian Olive (16th century) grows to 15ft+ (4.5m+) with silver-green leaves and silvery flowers in June, followed by amber-coloured berries. A large deciduous shrub or small tree from S. Europe for a spacious sunny position.

E. commutata syn. **E. argentea — Silver Berry** (1813) grows to 10ft (3m) with silver leaves and small yellow and silver flowers, followed by silver berries. A deciduous shrub of great elegance from the United States, for a sunny place.

E. pungens (1830) grows to 15ft (4.5m) and 8ft (2.4m) with olive green and dull gold leaves and small (usually unnoticed), fragrant silvery white flowers in October and November. Var. aurea has leaves edged with golden yellow, var. aureo-variegata has a large irregular central zone of brilliant yellow on each leaf (good in winter) and var. 'Variegata' has leaves edged with pale yellow. An evergreen shrub from Japan for a sunny position.

E. umbellata (1829) grows to 18ft (5.5m) with a wide-spreading crown. Silvery green leaves, creamy white flowers with soft red berries. A very handsome, usually deciduous, large shrub from the Far East for a specimen position on a lawn.

Requirements: Any soil, not too rich. Full or mostly sunny position, good for seaside hedging.

Propagation: The evergreen species should be propagated by heel cuttings taken in August. Insert these in a rooting compost of sand and peat and place in a cold frame. Pot on rooted cuttings in spring into John Innes No.1 and keep in an open frame or plunged in a nursery area. Deciduous species should be propagated by ripe seed sown the same year into boxes or pots of seed compost. Space seeds out when planting, and set them into a cold frame for the winter. Transplant into individual pots in spring and treat as for cuttings.

Pruning: None needed — too regular an outline spoils the characteristic shape of these lovely shrubs. Cut off plain green branches if these should appear on variegated kinds. Where Elaeagnus is grown as hedging or screening in coastal areas, prune in June or September.

Uses: Excellent evergreen shrubs; the very beautiful silver-leaved and berried forms for arrangements; as hedging in coastal and seaside gardens. As background and contrast shrubs. *E. aureo-variegata* should be planted where it can cheer in winter — it is as yellow as a daffodil.

Shrubs: Ballalheannagh, Barcock, Bees, Bodnant, Brackenwood, Bressingham, Peter Chappell, Daisy Hill, Dobbies, Goatcher, Goscote, Great Dixter, Highfield, Hilliers, Hyden, Jackman, Kaye, Kershaw, Knaphill, Knoll Gardens, Lime Cross, Marchant, Meare Close, Notcutts, Otter, Reuthe, Roger, Russell, Scotts, Shepton, Sherrard, Smith, Southcombe, St. Bridget, Stonehouse, Toynbee, Treasure, Treseder, Warley, Woodland, W.W., Wyevale.

Seeds: Chiltern.

ENKIANTHUS *(Ericaceae)*. These shrubs are grown for their spectacular autumn foliage of red and yellow. There are no half measures about them, they can be relied on always to colour well. There are two schools of opinion on autumn colour: one is to group the shrubs more or less together, the other option is to place each plant, shrub or tree where it will look best against the various backgrounds of other shrubs, evergreens, trees and walls. The first is fairly easy and, in any case, autumn colouration is never the same two years running, depending as it does on the presence or absence of frost, rain and dry or wet summer months. The second takes longer and the job is never really finished, which is fun. Enkianthus can be entirely counted on for its flaming colour so its placement is easy, providing you have acid (best) or really neutral soil and the protection of other trees and shrubs nearby.

E. campanulatus — Red-vein Enkianthus (1880) grows to 8ft (2.4m) with a similar spread. Racemes of red-veined and red-tipped yellow heather bell-shaped flowers appear in May, eventually followed by glorious autumn colouration. A deciduous shrub from Japan for a woodland setting, or as part of an autumn colour scheme.

Requirements: Acid soil, sun and a reasonably sheltered

position.

Propagation: Take heel cuttings in August and insert in a rooting compost of peat and sand and put in a cold frame for the winter. In spring, pot on rooted cuttings or plant them in a nursery bed to grow on.

Pruning: None needed.

Uses: Flowering and autumn branches for arrangements. A good shrub for autumn colouration.

Shrubs: Ballalheannagh, Bodnant, Daisy Hill, Dobbies, Fairley's, Glendoick, Goatcher, Goscote, Hilliers, Jackman, Knaphill, Knoll Gardens, Marchant, Meare Close, Otter, Reuthe, Roger, Russcll, Scotts, Sherrard, St. Bridget, Treseder, Woodland, Wyevale.

Seeds: Chiltern, Thompson and Morgan.

ERICA — Heather *(Ericaceae).* In our rather insular way, we British are inclined to think that we invented heather, or at least the Scottish kind that empurples mile upon mile of grouse-moorland. But there are more heathers, or Ericas, as they are called by the afficionados, in South Africa than one would have believed of such a hot, dry area, and therefore these species need the most careful greenhouse culture. Since this book is primarily about what can be grown in gardens, with only the occasional excursion into the greenhouse or conservatory, I shall not be discussing these for reasons of space.

Hardy Ericas have a very devoted following and it is easy to see why they are so popular. They are evergreen, colourful at all times of the year, weed suppressing, and they can be had in all sizes from pygmies to the giant *E. arborea* which can reach a height of 20ft (6m). This is *la bruyère,* the plant from whose roots briar pipes are made. Early in this century briar pipe making was an important industry in the poorer parts of southern France, Sicily and Corsica. The large roots were dug out of moorland bogs and kept in damp sheds until needed — it was important to use green wood. Then they were cut into blocks which were boiled for ten hours so as to prevent them from cracking. After they had cooled they were cut into a rough pipe-shape by dangerous mechanical saws. The men working on these saws got higher wages, and at the time, of course, there were no safety regulations and many of the workmen had mangled hands. This was not always accidental — in areas of southern Italy such as Calabria there was little work and much debt; the Italian government paid compensation for injuries and it was known that some men had deliberately sawn off their fingers in order to get this blood-stained benefit.

The flowers remain colourful on the plants for a very long time, and the foliage often changes colour with the seasons. Ericas are often grown with dwarf conifers — they seem to associate well together and the conifers fill in the blue-grey tones lacking in the Erica colour spectrum. Ericas

grow on you, and before you realise it the lawn is only half the size that it was a year or so ago, but no matter, less to mow. And there's another thing: Ericas can be left to get on with their lives but a lawn cannot — go to the Greek Islands for a month and the lawn will be two feet high when you come back, telling all the neighbourhood that you are not about. Burglars look for these tell-tale signs, so there is another reason for planting more Ericas and perhaps a few of those low, spreading conifers in the other half of the lawn, and then all you need is a casual sort of paved or gravelled path so that you and your visitors don't sink ankle-deep in autumn and winter mud. A grass path *is* nicer, and very natural-looking, but unless you are willing to import Cumberland turf (which only grows 2″ (5cm) high) you are back to worrying about grass while you are away.

Contrary to popular belief, not all Ericas demand acid soil, though if you have it you can collect indiscriminately without having to stop to check if your chosen plant is lime-tolerant. Some Ericas have reddish, yellow, orange, bronze or grey foliage which looks interesting even when the plants are not in flower. These colours intensify or change in winter and should be remembered so as not to plant a magenta-flowering Erica next to orange or yellow-foliaged plants. It is possible to have Ericas in flower throughout the year, though perhaps better to have one good and more or less simultaneous flush of bloom in the main bed or the main part of it. Because the hardy Ericas have such a satisfyingly long flowering season, and there are so many foliage and similar flower colours to choose from, another suggested planting scheme is to have the wave of colour beginning at one end of the bed, border, garden or rockery, so that as the flowers age the next plant or group of plants is about to come into flower. Ericas will spread out considerably once established, and the temptation to plant too close is very strong — the empty spaces look so very empty and the new plants so very small. But do resist the temptation to pop in a few foxgloves — these would look better at the back or side of an Erica bed, perhaps near a steely-blue conifer. The Ericas really do need all that space to grow into. The winter-flowering kinds such as *E. carnea* and varieties and *E. mediterranea* and its varieties will do well in neutral soils, though some of the varieties of *E. mediterranea* are slightly tender. *E. terminalis,* the Corsican Heath, and *E. vagans,* the Cornish Heath, will even tolerate a little lime but it is kinder not to ask it of them.

Assuming that you live in an area of acid soil and that you are about to plan a heather garden, however small — here's the first nice problem — what to leave out? You cannot have them all. Space, or the lack of it, may partly solve this one — some of the Ericas are quite tall and will reach 6ft (1.8m) in time, so perhaps it would be better to include only one or, at the most, two of these to break the flatness. Heathers look happiest when associated with rocks, as in their natural homes, and they will sit or perch or hug or drip according to their characteristics. If you have a large rockery with a collection of alpines and small bulbs, it might be an idea to make another exclusively for Ericas and closely associated genera such as Calluna, Daboecia and Cassiope. At any rate you have allocated part of the garden to the Ericas. It must be in a sunny and open position with shelter from cold winds. The soil should have been cleared of weeds and the shape of the bed marked out, try not to have any straight lines. Plan the bed, border or new rockery on paper first, it really does save moving things about afterwards. The bed should be prepared by digging, then add 4oz (115g) of bonemeal per square yard, fork this in, and a layer of peat about two or three inches thick should be laid on the surface. If the bed is wide then arrange some stepping stones or make narrow paths of these — it will save the effort of forking up your own footprints and will also save you from treading on the smaller plants. If the bed is laid out on the flat, decide whether to include any conifers — choose some slow-growing ones so that everything will all grow gradually together. Try to add one or two really big boulders — they are convenient to sit on as well as being aesthetically pleasing (do not get limestone rock).

If you are really in a hurry to have a quickly established heather garden then get three of each plant and discard two later on if necessary. Container plants can be put in at any time. When planting the Ericas, set them deeply in the ground so that they do not stick up — the stem should sit on the ground, even if you have to plant them a little deeper than their original level. Make sure that the ground is moist and that they are watered in well, rearrange the top dressing of peat around them, and make sure that this is also damp. If the first summer is a dry one then water well, also during dry winters. Use rain water whenever possible. Space the smaller plants out at about 1ft (30cm) apart, but check their spread first. Taller, larger kinds should be planted at a distance of at least 18" (46cm) apart.

E. arborea — Tree Heath (1658) grows to 15ft + (4.5m +) in a sheltered place in mild areas. Scented white urn-shaped flowers from January until April. A tender evergreen shrub from S. Europe, the Caucasus and N. Africa for a sheltered sunny position. Var. 'alpina' is less tall, has brighter green leaves and is hardier.

E. australis — Spanish Heath (1769) grows to 8ft (2.4m) with rose-pink urn-shaped flowers from April to June. A rather tender evergreen shrub from Spain and Portugal. Can be killed in hard winters, good against a wall where it will grow even taller. Var. 'Mr Robert' is white, smaller, and hardier.

E. carnea syn. **E. herbaceae** (1763) grows to 12" (30cm) and species flowers are rosy-mauve from December to April. An evergreen shrub from Central and S. Europe for the heather garden. Leaves usually green but varieties have leaves of bronze or yellow. This is the only species which will do on chalk, better on neutral and very much better on acid soils. Modern and older varieties may be had in shades of pale and deep pink, rosy-mauve and crimson, and many have a prostrate habit of growth.

E. ciliaris — Dorset Heath (1773) grows to 12" (30cm) with pale green leaves and rosy-mauve urn-shaped flowers from July to November. Older and modern varieties have flowers in all shades of rose, mauve, crimson, pale pink and white.

E. cinerea — Bell Heather, Scotch Heather grows to 2ft (60cm) with (in species) purple-rose urn-shaped flowers from June to September. A popular European wild flower, with varieties in shell pink, bright pink, red, ruby, lavender, purple and white.

E. lusitanica, syn. **E. codonodes — Portuguese Heath** (around 1800) grows to 12ft (3.55m) with a spread of 3ft (90cm) or so. Pink buds opening to white urn-shaped flowers from late February until May. A tender evergreen shrub from Spain and S. France with pale green leaves for a sheltered sunny place.

E. Tetralix — Cross-leaved Heath grows to 21" (51cm) and spreads as much with pink urn-shaped flowers from June to August. A European evergreen shrub for the heather garden or rockery. Varieties have apricot, white or pink flowers. Species plants like damp soil, varieties are all right in ordinary neutral to acid soils.

E. umbellata grows to 3ft (90cm) with pink or red urn-shaped flowers in May and June (a time when most Ericas are resting). A tender evergreen shrub from S.W. Europe and N. Africa for a sheltered garden.

E. vagans — Cornish Heath grows to 3ft (90cm) with a loose, straggling habit and purplish pink bell-flowers from July to November. A rather tender evergreen shrub from S.W. Europe and Cornwall. Varieties are in pink, rose and white, and an interesting variety 'Viridiflora' has pale green flowers.

Requirements: Ideally, Ericas do best in a light sandy peat with added leafmould. Make sure new plants are watered in, and in succeeding dry spells do not allow to dry out during first season. Brush off fallen leaves in late autumn. Very rich garden soil is not suitable for Ericas, they will make too much growth, often at the expense of flowers. See notes on pruning. Ericas should never be given animal manure.

Propagation: Is best with cuttings in a mist unit, but if unavailable take 2" (5cm) long lateral non-flowering cuttings from July to September. Take off lower leaves with a sharp knife or a razor. Insert in a moistened rooting compost of 2 parts sand to 1 part peat. Enclose each pot of cuttings in a plastic bag — close this round the pot with a rubber band. When cuttings have rooted they should be grown on in a cold frame or greenhouse. Or layering is effective with larger plants — bend down outer stems over a pot of peaty soil and hold in place with a stone or wire hoops. The shoot should be buried into the pot and can be severed after a year.

Pruning: After flowering cut off the dead flower stems of winter and spring flowering species. Cut off the flowering stems of autumn flowering types in spring.

Uses: As seasonal flowering shrubs in the garden and as long-lasting cut flowers. As ground cover. Many as contrasting foliage plants.

Shrubs: Barcock, Bodnant, Daisy Hill, Dobbies, Jack Drake, Everett, Frye, Glendoick, Goatcher, Goscote, Highfield, Hilliers, Hyden, Ingwersen, Jackman, Kent, Knaphill, Knoll Gardens, Lime Cross, Marchant, Meare Close, Notcutts, Orchard, Otter, Potterton and Martin, Reuthe, Robinsons, Roger, Russell, Scotts, Shepton, Sherrard, Smith, Southcombe, Speyside, St. Bridget, Toynbee, Treasure, Treseder, Ward, Warley, Woodland, Wyevale.

Seeds: Chiltern, Thompson and Morgan.

ESCALLONIA *(Escalloniaceae) (Saxifragaceae).* The genus Escallonia was named after Antonio José Escallon y Flores, a favourite pupil of a then famous Spanish botanist José Celestino Mutis, whose dates (1732-1808) are known. Mutis travelled to Colombia (then called New Granada) as physician to the Viceroy. Mutis became a professor of Natural History at the University at Bogota, and Escallon, formerly the Viceroy's page, became Mutis's pupil. Later on Mutis left the University to found a school of botanical collectors, which was financed by the Spanish Government. At this time Mutis was writing to Linnaeus (about 1776, until the latter's death) and sent plant specimens to him and afterwards to his son. It was suggested that a new plant discovery should be named after Mutis's pupil, but it was later found that it had already been named, and so the first Escallonia, *E. myrtilloides* was chosen to commemorate this obscure young man of whom nothing more is known, and *E. myrtilloides* itself is no longer in cultivation.

Escallonia hedges and wind screens are so much a part of the West Country scene that they have become invisible (except as regards their boy-proof efficacy) to local people, though not to the visitors. As a Cornish expatriate I instantly planted the hardiest kind, var. 'C.F. Ball', because I had read and was told that these handsome evergreen shrubs with the sticky leaves are tender here, though only in colder areas and never by the sea. The adhesive quality of the leaves is the plant's only drawback, because it means that the lower part of a roadside hedge often gets very dusty in the summer. The stickiness is resin which is exuded from glands on the leaves and twigs, but there are less of these glands in the 'garden' varieties and, in any case, the problem of dusty roads does not arise with a cherished species plant. I think of Escallonia as the West Country equivalent of Bougainvillea — it is so amiable a plant (in the right place) that it can be used as a substantial hedge or gale-proof screen, it can be clipped into neat and flower-scattered arch-

ways, it can clothe walls, with apertures for doors and windows and its shining dark green leaves always look as if they had been freshly varnished. I am speaking of childhood memories of *E. macrantha* which grew everywhere in Cornwall at that time and undoubtedly still does. The broader-leaved varieties of Escallonia are less hardy than the smaller and narrower leaved kinds, and *E. virgata*, being the only deciduous species, is the hardiest of all.

E. illinita (1830) grows to 10ft (3m) with panicles of white flowers from June to August. A rather odiferous evergreen shrub from Chile for a sunny place.

E. macrantha (1848) grows to 10ft (3m) with racemes of pink to crimson flowers from June to September. A strong evergreen shrub from the island of Chiloe (S. America) for hedges, windbreaks in coastal areas, and as wall shrubs inland. Parent or grandparent of many of the modern hybrid varieties.

E. organensis syn. **E. laevis** (1844) grows to 6ft (1.8m) with panicles of rose-pink flowers from June onwards. An evergreen shrub from the Organ Mountains in Brazil.

E. rubra (1827) grows to 15ft (4.5m) with panicles of red flowers in July and August. An evergreen shrub from Chile for a sunny place. *E. pygmaea* grows to 2ft (60cm) but spreads widely. Good on large rockeries, sunny banks and borders.

Requirements: Ordinary well-drained soil. In colder midland or northern areas Escallonias are best grown against a sunny south-facing wall.

Propagation: Take lateral heel cuttings in August or September and insert in a rooting compost of peat and sand. Set pots in a cold frame, but they will root more readily in a propagator set at 13-16°C (55-61°F). When rooted pot into John Innes No.1 and keep in a cold frame through the winter. For hedges, plant bushy plants of about 12" (30cm) high 18" (46cm) apart. Set out in autumn or spring and trim off about 3" (7.5cm) to encourage basal growth. Remember to make hedge wider at base than at top.

Pruning: None really necessary if specimen plants are being grown, though flowered shoots may be taken off. Hedges flower better if only lightly trimmed.

Uses: As fine wall shrubs, hedging, windbreaks and screens in coastal areas, and as cut flowers.

Shrubs: Barcock, Brackenwood, Daisy Hill, Dobbies, Farall, Goatcher, Goscote, Hilliers, Knaphill, Lime Cross, Marchant, Meare Close, Notcutts, Orchard, Otter, Reuthe, Roger, Russell, Scotts, Shepton, Sherrard, Smith, St. Bridget, Treasure, Treseder, Warley, Woodlands, Wyevale.

EUCRYPHIA *(Eucryphiaceae).* The name of this small genus is taken from the Greek *eu*, well, *kryphios*, covered, alluding to the brown cap-shape made by the sepals before the flowers open.

Eucryphias are just about the most beautiful of the summer flowering shrubs, growing to a considerable height when they have the right conditions. The hardiest shrub species is *E. glutinosa,* which has large — about 2½" (6cm) — white four-petalled flowers with their centres crowded with stamens. When the petals fall the stamens are still interesting, as in the case of the rose 'Mermaid', and the leaves turn to fine shades of orange in autumn.

There is something about a well-grown Eucryphia that absolutely commands respect and admiration — and envy. They are treated as wall-shrubs in this country, needing acid soil for the happiest results, though cultivars such as *E. Nymansay (E. x nymanensis* is the proposed name for hybrids between *E. cordifolia* and *E. glutinosa)* (1915) will grow in chalky areas. The first Eucryphia was discovered by one of the plant hunters employed by the great firm of Veitch. Richard Pearce came from Devon and started work for the firm as a gardener; he made two trips to South America with instructions to search for new varieties of conifer, hardy plants, flowering shrubs, trees, tender exotics suitable for stove and greenhouse and, of course, orchids. In short almost anything that was new and interesting. He was a successful collector and brought back much that we are still growing today, or that has since been used to breed from. He made two trips for Veitch and must then have become dissatisfied with some aspect of his employment, because in 1868 he left Veitch's and began working for the rival firm of William Bull who, in that year, sent him back to South America, where he contracted yellow fever from which he died after only a very short illness.

E. cordifolia (1851) grows to 40ft (12m) or more, though in the British Isles it is considered to be, and grown as, a large shrub. Large white flowers in August and September. An evergreen shrub or tree from Chile for warm southern or south-western gardens. Will tolerate chalk soil.

E. glutinosa (1859) grows to 15ft (4.5m) with large white flowers in July and August. A deciduous or sometimes partly evergreen shrub from Chile for a south or west wall. Will not grow in chalky areas.

Requirements: All Eucryphias prefer acid soil and most are quite definite about this. The soil should be moist but not wet, and other small shrubs should be grown so as to shade the roots. Eucryphias need a wall position in the British Isles, except perhaps in the Isles of Scilly. Protect young shrubs in winter with straw, bracken or sacking.

Propagation: Take heel cuttings of lateral non-flowering shoots in August or September. Insert these in a rooting compost of peat and sand and put into a propagator set at 16-18°C (61-64°F). When rooted transfer into individual pots of John Innes No.1 and keep in a frost-free greenhouse or conservatory for the winter. In late spring harden off and plunge the pots in the ground for the summer, transferring into a size larger pot at this time. Protect in a cold frame for the second winter and plant out in late spring. Eucryphias do not flower on young plants, they will do so when ready

and not before, and they grow very slowly.

Pruning: None needed though, if young plants seem to be going straight up, the leading shoot can be pinched out so as to encourage early branching.

Uses: As magnificent wall shrubs.

Shrubs: Ballalheannagh, Bodnant, Brackenwood, Caldwell, Peter Chappell, Crarae, Daisy Hill, Dobbies, Goatcher, Great Dixter, Hilliers, Knaphill, Meare Close, Notcutts, Orchard, Otter, Reuthe, Roger, Rosemoor, Russell, Scotts, Sherrard, Southcombe, St. Bridget, Stonehouse, Toynbee, Treasure, Treseder, Wyevale.

Seeds: Chiltern.

EUONYMUS — Spindle *(Celastraceae).* The best known member of this genus is, of course, the Spindle tree, *E. europaeus,* which will be dealt with in a later volume, with its bright, biretta-shaped autumn fruits of shocking pink enclosed by orange arils. Many of the other species are evergreen shrubs, some of which have pleasing foliage that is variegated in green, cream, yellow and white. Most of these are slow-growing and, though their leaves are excellent and long-lasting in arrangements, a small bush cannot spare too much as it takes so long to produce. Several of the plain green-leaved species of Euonymus are almost anonymous — they live at the back of a flower bed or the back of a mixed shrub border, and because their flowers are unexciting (and come at a busy time of year in May and June) they pass unnoticed. One usually inherits these rather stolid shrubs — I am thinking of the green-leaved *E. japonicus* in particular, so useful in coastal areas as a plump and solid screening shrub. But who can name it when asked? On the other hand, its variegated progeny are delightful garden plants, immensely useful for contrast-planting and as cut foliage. These can be small leaved shrubs that gently ascend a wall or fence, or they may be planted to plump out a rockery where they will creep slowly over the rock ledges, or down over a sunny bank like an attractive stream of bright and living lava. The genus seems to be very popular with the Lesser Ermine-moth whose caterpillars will munch their way right through a hedge of *E. japonicus.* Gardeners have a distrust of the whole genus, accusing the Spindle Tree, *E. europaeus,* of encouraging the black bean-aphis to settle down and produce its myriad progeny to decimate all the broad beans or the Nasturtiums of the neighbourhood (most of which will get black-fly in any case, if it is that kind of year) or they will mutter gloomily that this tree can start an awful epidemic of the black bootlaces of Honey fungus, *Armillaria mellea. E. japonicus* is accused of harbouring the spores of mildew, to which it is prone, but so are roses, phlox and solidago.

E. alatus is described as having 'cork-winged' branches which make this a stiff shrub, interesting to plant near others that have a softer or more graceful habit. This

Euonymus has small unmemorable green flowers in May and June, but the shrub colours beautifully in autumn. *E. fortunei* comes in all kinds of colours and sizes, and is useful as a background plant in all its many forms, one of which can climb (if firmly attached to its support) to a height of 20ft (6m) or more, though it will just as soon creep along the ground to the same length — a most useful thing, though like all good natured plants inclined to be abused. The colourful varieties of *E. japonicus* are many, as are their permutations of green and cream, green and white, green and yellow and green and gold, as well as almost all yellow. A collection of these is delightful when placed in focal points about the garden, but if put all together they become visually indigestible. One cannot call such colouration 'evergreen' because evergreen they are not in actuality, though they retain their attractive leaves throughout the year and in a mild winter a group of one kind, such as *E. variegata* (or a larger mature plant), makes a garden look well-furnished when planted near conifers or other dark-leaved evergreens, and the golden-leaved *E. japonicus* var. aureus is interesting in association with a fastigiate yew.

E. alatus — Winged Spindle, Corkbush (1860) grows to 8ft (2.4m) with stiff branches and conspicuous corky wings, especially in winter. Unmemorable small green flowers in May and June, followed by purplish fruits (a group of plants should be grown to ensure these) and excellent rose-pink or scarlet autumn colouration. A deciduous shrub from China and Japan for a position in semi-shade.

E. fortunei syn. **E. radicans** (1863) grows to 20ft (6m) if support is available. Behaves in the same way as ivy, the climbing or creeping stems do not have flowers and fruit until they reach their maximum height, when they will produce erect branches with somewhat larger leaves. In due course the plant will have green-white flowers (when it decides that it is time) in May and June, followed by bright pink and orange berries. A very useful and interesting evergreen plant from Japan for many places — as a self clinging wall climber and for old trees; as trailing ground cover, as a hummocky rockery plant and as path-edging, all in sun or shade. Varieties include: 'Carrierii' (the adult form, does not climb) with pink and orange 'fruits' in autumn; 'Coloratus' climbs to 24ft (8m) if it has strong support. Grown for its rich wine-purple leaves in winter, which (in mild seasons) change back to green again in spring, *Kewensis* syn. *minimus* has tiny pale-veined leaves and climbs, creeps or forms interesting bumps in the rockery; *Variegatus* ('Gracilis') climbs, creeps, trails or drips with grey-green leaves edged with white, sometimes pink-tinged.

E. japonicus (1804) grows to 15ft (4.5m) more if 'climbing', with small clusters of green white flowers in May and June. An evergreen shrub with handsome, shiny leaves, from Japan for hedging in coastal areas and as a background shrub. Varieties include: 'Aureus' (Aureopictus) with broad yellow

centres to leaves, edged green (can revert — cut out green branches immediately when seen); 'ovatus aureus' with wide gold edges; 'Latifolius variegatus' syn. 'Macrophyllus Albus' has white-margined green leaves.

Requirements: Any good garden soil in sun or semi-shade. Evergreen kinds will grow in deeper shade, variegated species and varieties do best in sun in a sheltered position. Provide strong support for climbers.

Propagation: Take lateral heel cuttings in August or September insert in a rooting compost of sand and peat in a cold frame. When rooted, plant out in a nursery area for two years before moving to final position. Move evergreen species in autumn and deciduous and variegated kinds in spring. *E. fortunei* can be pulled apart and replanted in November or spring. Creeping varieties often root as they go — these pieces may be detached.

For hedging: use 12″ (30cm) high evergreen plants and set out 18″ (46cm) apart. Nip out growing tips when planting, and in six months pinch out the tips of the upper shoots to make plants bushy.

Pruning: None really necessary. Hedges of *E. japonicus* should be shaped in April and tidied up in late summer.

Uses: As hedging, specimens, contrast and background shrubs, rockery and trailing plants, as edging and as climbers in sun or shade. Excellent foliage for arrangements. Small evergreen plants for tubs.

Pests and Diseases: A watch should be kept for Honey fungus. Caterpillars and scale insects are very partial to Euonymus, especially *E. japonicus*. Certain fungi and mildew also affect the plants, which need a medicine chest in the potting shed all to themselves.

Shrubs: Ballalheannagh, Bodnant, Brackenwood, Bressingham, Caldwell, Daisy Hill, Dobbies, Goatcher, Goscote, Highfield, Hilliers, Jackman, Knoll Gardens, Lime Cross, Marchant, Meare Close, Notcutts, Orchard, Otter, Reuthe, Roger, Russell, Scotts, Shepton, Sherrard, Smith, Toynbee, Treasure, Treseder, Warley, Woodland, Wyevale.

Seeds: Thompson and Morgan.

EUPHORBIA *(Euphorbiaceae)*. This enormous genus of trees, shrubs, 'cacti', succulents, annual and herbaceous plants is so diverse in its appearance as to require an entire book to itself. The handsome plants that are hardy in the British Isles are rather similar in their appearance — one gets one's eye in, so to speak — and their curious inflorescence becomes instantly recognisable. They have an unusual reproductive system called a cyathium that is unique to Euphorbias. A single female flower with a long stalked ovary, together with the male flowers which are each reduced to one stamen, is surrounded by the involucre or whorl of bracts. This is called a cyathium and is subtended or enfolded by a pair of opposite bracts in the case of *E. Wulfenii* which is described as being a sub-shrubby evergreen plant, and is therefore rather a borderline case for inclusion in this book.

But, like many people who are attracted by odd-looking plants, I love Euphorbias and am quite pleased that they are even more different when it comes to reproducing their own kind. A species such as *E. Wulfenii* growing in an isolated position is a very commanding sight when in full flower. It will have a long season of interest — spring into summer, with the uncurling of the flower-stems in spring (those with flowers hang their heads like shepherds' crooks: the erect stems are flowerless) and the subsequent colour harmonies of the lime-yellow inflorescence with the blue-green leaves and red-brown stems. Where possible they should be planted against a plain background of stone, old brick, whitewashed or pebble-dashed wall or evergreen hedge, so that one is not distracted in any way when looking at them. *E. Wulfenii* is best planted against a sunny wall in any case, as a really hard winter can kill a mature plant if it is exposed to cutting east winds. The stems will weep white tears if they are cut — this is a latex which is highly irritant to skin and eyes. When cutting for arrangements the ends of the stems should be sealed by being dipped in crushed charcoal or by scalding.

E. pulcherrima, the Poinsettia, is really classed as a shrub. Recipients of this colourful pot plant will be somewhat startled to read that in its native Mexico it grows to a height of 10ft (3m). The elegant white 'flowered' variety 'alba' is not so vigorous but all of them — crimson, scarlet, pink or white — need particular care if they are to be kept going for another season. Poinsettia-petals are, in reality, bracts, which change colour gradually to flower-shop brilliance just in time for Christmas. It will be noticed that the leaves and the petal-like bracts are very similar in shape, venation and texture, differing only in colouration when in flower.

E. pulcherrima — Poinsettia (1834) grows to 5ft (1.5m) in cultivation with scarlet, crimson, pink or white 'flowers' in winter (November to February). A deciduous shrub from Mexico for greenhouse or conservatory but usually as a house plant.

E. splendens, syn. **E. millii, — Crown of Thorns** (1828) grows to 3ft (90cm) with scarlet 'flowers' usually in winter. A colourful greenhouse shrub with spiny stems, from Madagascar. A sparsely leaved evergreen having spiteful spines instead.

E. Wulfenii, syn. **E. veneta** (about or before 1837) grows from 4-6ft (1.2-1.8m) and as much through with a yellow inflorescence from May to July. A sculpturally handsome subshrub from Southern Europe for a sheltered place in full sun.

Requirements: Hardy species need full sun, a sheltered position and ordinary well drained soil — the poorer it is the better is the leaf colour.

E. splendens and *E. pulcherrima* need to be grown in pots of John Innes No.2 with an even winter temperature of 13-16°C (55-61°F). Though they are shrubs these plants are generally treated as annuals. In summer they need a maximum greenhouse temperature of 18°C (64°F) with shade and humidity for *E. pulcherrima*. Plenty of water is needed at this time, reduce watering after flowering. Give fortnightly liquid feeds from June to September and then monthly. In very hot weather these plants need good ventilation, so the pots of *E. pulcherrima* can be stood outside (in shade) but should be brought in when nights are cold. *E. splendens* needs to be drier and hotter and needs no shade, though it should be watered well from May to August, with fortnightly feeds of weak liquid manure from June to August. If grown in pots and not the greenhouse border it will need repotting every two years.

Propagation: Take cuttings of basal shoots of *E. Wulfenii* in April or May, put into a rooting compost of peat and sand. When well rooted pot into 4 or 5″ (10-12cm) pots of John Innes No.1 and grow on; plunge pots or keep in an open cold frame. For *E. pulcherrima* take young shoots off in April and May, sealing stems, put into separate pots of a rooting compost of sand and peat. Keep in a propagator set at 18-21°C (64-70°F). When rooted and growing, pot on as necessary into John Innes No.1 and then into John Innes No.2 and the next pot size up. *E. pulcherrima* needs a constant temperature of 18°C (64°F) or warmer during the summer months. When this plant flowers it can be brought into the house but the minimum temperature should be a constant 13°C (55°F). Gradually dry off after flowering. Take unflowered tip cuttings of *E. splendens* and allow to dry off for two days. Put into the usual peat and sand rooting compost and place in an open, shaded propagator set at 16-18°C (61-64°F). When rooted pot on into John Innes No.1.

Pruning: *E. splendens* should not be pruned. Cut away old stems of *E. Wulfenii* to ground level. Cut *E. pulcherrima* down to within 6″ (15cm) of the soil level after flowering, use cuttings as cuttings.

Uses: Garden plants as focal interest, *E. pulcherrima* as greenhouse, conservatory and house plant, *E. splendens* as greenhouse and tub plant.

Shrubs: Marchant, Marten's Hall, Rosemoor, Russell, Scotts, Sherrard, Treasure, Treseder, W.W., Wyevale.

Seeds: Chiltern, Thompson and Morgan.

x FATSHEDERA *(Araliaceae).* This is an exceedingly beautiful and useful bigeneric hybrid climber (actually, it is a heavy 'leaner' needing strong support) that will grow and be as beautiful in shaded positions as if it were in a choice sunny corner. It has large lustrous ivy-shaped leathery evergreen leaves (best not put in the compost heap, as they take too long to rot down) that furnish difficult corners superbly, and in late summer it produces large panicles of greenish flowers that look like a cross, as indeed they are, between an ivy and a Fatsia. The plant is an excellent one for walls or fences in shady town gardens, or indeed anywhere that needs clothing in shining, healthy-looking green. Some exposed leaves do get damaged by bad frosts but the plant quickly produces replacements when the weather warms up. If one has only space for one evergreen 'climber' then this is the one to have, though when it gets into its stride it will be found to be an exceedingly vigorous plant which should be checked every so often to make sure that its flopping leafy branches are attached or supported, because they will break off in summer or winter gales. x Fatshedera is said to be a hybrid between *Hedera helix* 'Hibernica' and *Fatsia japonica* 'Moseri' produced by a firm of French nurserymen at Nantes called Lizé Frères.

x Fatshedera Lizei, Fatsia japonica 'Moseri' x **Hedera helix** 'Hibernica' — Fat-headed Lizzie (1910) grows to 10ft (3m) and as much sideways, with large 10″ (25cm) long panicles of greenish flowers from September to November. A very useful and vigorous wall plant of hybrid descent, good also for ground cover and for cascading down banks.

Requirements: Any soil or position — does better in better soil, but will get broken branches and frost-burnt leaves in winter if in an exposed place. Superb as a wall plant in shaded areas, or can be used as sprawling ground cover or as a house plant.

Propagation: Take tip or lateral cuttings in July and August put in rooting compost of peat and sand and set in a cold frame. When rooted (in the spring) pot into 4″ (10cm) pots of John Innes No.2 and pot on as the plants grow. Plant into permanent position in spring in cold areas and autumn in the southern counties. Peg down for ground cover.

Pruning: None needed if plant is grown to cover large areas. Nip off superfluous branches in spring when necessary.

Uses: Excellent permanent green cover for walls or archways. As ground cover, as house plants and as foliage for arrangements.

Shrubs: Ballalheannagh, Brackenwood, Beth Chatto, Goscote, Hilliers, Kaye, Lime Cross, Reuthe, Roger, Scotts, Sherrard, Treasure, Treseder, W.W., Wyevale.

FATSIA — Fig-leaf Palm *(Araliaceae)*. This is a popular and handsome evergreen shrub for town gardens, courtyards and very difficult shady corners that receive no sun at all. It has large, shining palmate leaves with from seven to nine 'fingers', and spikes of greenish-white umbels of ivy-like flowers very late in the year — often so late that they never open. It is rather taken for granted by city gardeners, who are tired of seeing it about, but they forget how good-tempered and long-suffering it is. Until they try to move it. In the southern part of the British Isles it is fairly hardy, providing it is in a sheltered place, but in the more north-erly parts of the country it will get badly damaged by frost (it has the largest leaves of any evergreen — about 16″ (40cm) across in mature plants) to be grown outside in the British Isles, except, of course, in the unfairly uncharacteristic Scilly Islands.

It does grow large and this must be remembered when choosing its position, but it is so very green and shining in midwinter when all about it is sere and brown that it is worth planting in a favoured corner with sufficient sunlight to encourage those hard, greenish white flower balls to open. It was one of Thunberg's Japanese discoveries and was at first called *Aralia japonica:* when the botanists gave it a genus all to itself they called it by a name closely resembling the original native Japanese one, then translated as 'Fatsi' or, phonetically, *Iats' de*.

Fatsia japonica (1838) grows to 15ft (4.5m) and about 8ft (2.4m) wide, depending on site and pruning or lack of this; bobbles of white green flowers in 1ft (30cm) racemes from October onwards. An evergreen shrub from Japan for a sheltered position in sun, partial shade or shade. A very sculptural and good-looking shrub all year through for difficult areas.

Requirements: Any reasonable garden soil, and shelter from cold winds. In cold and northern counties it will need to be grown against a warm wall.

Propagation: Sow seeds in spring in seed compost in pots in a propagator set at 10-13°C (50-55°F). When seedlings are large enough to prick out into individual 3″ (7.5cm) pots of seed compost. Grow on, repotting as necessary. Suckers can be detached in spring and treated as cuttings, potting into John Innes No.1 and growing on in a cold frame.

Uses: As handsome pot or tub plants for house, greenhouse or conservatory. As equally handsome evergreen garden shrubs for difficult or focal positions.

Shrubs: Ballalheannagh, Brackenwood, Caldwell, Dobbies, Goatcher, Great Dixter, Hilliers, Jackman, Kaye, Knoll Gardens, Lime Cross, Marchant, Notcutts, Otter, Reuthe, Russell, Scotts, Shepton, Sherrard, St. Bridget, Toynbee, Treseder, W.W., Wyevale.

Seeds: Chiltern, Thompson and Morgan.

FORSYTHIA — Golden Bell *(Oleaceae)*. In most old gardens the Forsythia bushes, if well-sited, have been there for some time, though the genus is not much more than a hundred years old. It was named after William Forsyth (1737-1804) who first served his apprenticeship, as it were, by being a pupil of Phillip Miller at the Chelsea Physic Garden. Forsyth later succeeded Miller in this post and then became superintendent of the Royal Gardens at St. James' and Kensington. He is chiefly remembered for the product 'Forsyth's Plaister', which was a secret compound that he claimed to have invented. This mixture was said to heal the 'wounds' of damaged trees so well that the tree would recover fully and grow into sound, straight timber which was much needed at the time for the Navy. Parliament granted him a huge fee (for those times) of £1,500 for the formula of the 'Plaister' so that all landowners could benefit from the knowledge; there was to be a further and similar grant when the results of the more general applications were known after tests. But there are no records of this further payment having been made, or, indeed of the 'Plaister' becoming generally used in forestry management, which was just as well because it was an interesting though almost useless mixture of lime-rubble, wood-ash, cow-dung, urine, soapsuds and sand. The brew was known about at the time, much as are most folk remedies so even the compound was not original to Forsyth, who was a very good gardener in all other respects. He wrote an excellent book on the growing of fruit trees but, to quote Shakespeare, 'the good is oft interred with their bones' and it is for the slightly fraudulent 'Plaister' that he will be remembered — and for the cheerful yellow-flowered bushes that bear his name.

F. suspensa is an attractive shrub with amiable ways; if it is planted against a taller shrub or tree its very long 'weeping' branches will grow through and among those of its neighbour without any assistance, and it seems to like to lean against more substantial trees, even evergreens. It is not a tidy-growing shrub at all and cannot be pruned into neatness, but this is part of its charm. The long branches hang down to touch the ground and will root at the tips if left to do so, which is most useful if more plants are needed. It has a more graceful appearance than the solid yellow block of the modern cultivars but this is, of course, only a personal preference engendered by the shrubs that I have inherited along with this old garden.

F. suspensa — Golden Bell (1850) grows to 10ft (3m) or much more against a wall or taller tree, with yellow flowers in March and April along previous years' growths. An easy deciduous shrub from China to grow with Chaenomeles spp.

F. viridissima (1844) grows to 8ft (2.4m) with a more rigid habit than *F. suspensa* and yellow flowers from April to May (associating pleasingly with dark-leaved Prunus or the earliest Ceanothus). A deciduous shrub from China.

Requirements: Forsythias will grow in any soil but do better if it is free-draining. They do best in full sun. *F. suspensa* will grow to an unrecognisable 30ft (9m) against a warm wall.

Propagation: Take cuttings of new season's growth in October and set out in a nursery drill. The rooted tips of *F. suspensa* can be separated in October and potted up or grown on in a nursery area until large enough. Or layer branches in October and detach a year later.

Pruning: Cut at least 4ft (1.2m) off the weeping branches of *F. suspensa* (and its varieties) immediately after flowering, cut back old wood and shorten any lateral branches that need it.

Uses: As an open and rather tall, airy hedge, as a wall shrub and

for cutting.

Shrubs: Bodnant, Brackenwood, Busheyfields, Caldwell, Dobbies, Goatcher, Hilliers, Jackman, Kaye, Knaphill, Lime Cross, Marchant, Meare Close, Notcutts, Roger, Russell, Scotts, Shepton, Sherrard, Smith, Southcombe, Toynbee, Treasure, Woodland.

FOTHERGILLA *(Hamamelidaceae)*. This Hazel cousin is a real chameleon of the plant world. It has interesting flowers in spring (*F. monticola*'s look like little white dish-mops) and then all goes quiet for the summer and the bush is so dull as to be quite invisible. But in autumn it is a very different story — this quiet-looking shrub gets ready for the ball, like one of the twelve dancing princesses, and changes her clothes for a gown of yellow, orange, red and crimson, though still touched with green as though to remind you that it is a bush and not a bonfire.

F. major (1780) grows to 8ft (2.4m) and as much through with cylindrical spikes of fragrant brushy 'flowers' in May*. A deciduous shrub from the Allegheny Mountains E. North America, chiefly grown for its autumn colouration.

Requirements: Fothergillas need neutral or lime-free soil, ideally, a moist but free draining peaty, sandy mixture, in a sunny or partly shaded situation.

Propagation: They can be grown from seed; this may take two years to germinate. Or heel cuttings can be taken in July, inserted in a peat and sand rooting compost and put in a propagator set at 16-18°C (61-64°F).

Uses: As excellent autumn colour. Site against a suitable background or in a group of other colourful shrubs.

Shrubs: Bodnant, Brackenwood, Caldwell, Peter Chappell, Goscote, Hilliers, Hyden, Jackman, Kent, Knaphill, Lime Cross, Marchant, Meare Close, Notcutts, Reuthe, Rosemoor, Russell, Sherrard, St. Bridget, Treasure, Treseder, Warley, Woodland, Wyevale.

FREMONTODENDRON — Fremontia, Californian Glory *(Sterculiaceae)*. This is a delicate-souled though lustily-growing wall shrub, with cup-shaped flowers rather like some of the flat flowered varieties of Campanula. Fremontias are rigid shrubs with attractive mid-green leathery palmate leaves. The flowers are abundant in good hot years but the angularity of the shrub may need a little softening, and a twining annual such as *Tropaeolum peregrinum* — Canary creeper, or *Thunbergia* — Black-eyed Susan, or even an *Eccremocarpus scaber* will fill in the gaps, as would a not-too-rampant Clematis which can be chosen to harmonize with the Fremontia and its background. It is tender and should be grown against a warm south or west-facing wall, the higher the better because, as is the nature of some contrary plants, it will bear its flowers on the upper parts of the plant which wave stiffly well above the wall, instead of having them at a convenient and comfortable

the 'flowers' are stamens, there are no petals. They appear before the leaves.

level lower down. Stem and branches are covered with a furry looking slightly sticky brown down, as are the undersides of the semi-evergreen leaves: gloves should be worn when handling the plant as this 'down' can cause skin irritation to some gardeners. Fremontias, or Fremontodendrons as they are now called, are surprisingly resistant to cold winters considering their origin. If they are well sited they can achieve a height of some 20ft (6m) or more, so this should be taken into account when planting them. They do not like being moved at any time and will usually die if transplanted. The plant was first discovered in 1846 and a small one was brought to the then Horticultural Society's garden at Chiswick, where it flowered for the first time some eight years later. After some five years, in 1859 it was for some reason sold to a nursery but, disliking the move, it died shortly after. William Lobb had in the meantime rediscovered it and it has been grown in the British Isles ever since. It is still called Fremontia by some gardeners and nurserymen though this is incorrect owing to the rule of precedence in nomenclature; the ponderous name of Fremontodendron has been its proper title since 1893. It is named after Captain John Charles Fremont who first found it in western North America.

F. californica syn. **Fremontia californica — Flannel Bush, Californian Glory** (1851) grows to 30ft (9m) though more usually to 12ft (3.7m) with golden yellow cup-shaped flowers from May onwards. A tall and tender semi-evergreen shrub from California for warm walls (not east-facing).

Requirements: Sandy, poorish, free-draining soil. Strong fixings to avoid damage to the bark — frost entering cracks in the bark will kill it. Protect main stem with a hessian 'bandage' in bad winters.

Propagation: From seed sown in John Innes seed compost in spring at a temperature of 16°C (61°F). Prick out into 3″ (7.5cm) pots of John Innes No.1 when large enough to handle, and grow on, potting on as necessary. Protect in a frame or cold greenhouse for first winter.

Pruning: None needed, tidy up winter damage in April

Uses: As unusual, evergreen wall shrubs (branches are best not picked).

Shrubs: Brackenwood, Dobbies, Hilliers, Hyden, Knaphill, Marchant, Notcutts, Otter, Read, Rosemoor, Russell, Sherrard, Stonehouse, Treasure, Treseder, Wyevale.

FUCHSIA — Lady's Eardrops *(Onagraceae).* This popular, pretty and easy species needs no description. The species Fuchsias are still grown, often as hedging plants in the mild south-west parts of England and Ireland, and were it not that I live in Dorset (which is not as warm as Cornwall) I would have such a hedge even though it is deciduous, because I have early memories of white-walled cottages and gossip-height Fuchsia hedges. As most gardeners know the

genus is named after Leonard (Leonhardt) Fuchs (1501-1566), a German botanist who wrote *De Historia Stirpium* (1542) a very beautifully illustrated early herbal. The first Fuchsia was discovered by Father Charles Plumier (1646-1706), who was another of that rather strange breed of priest, missionary and botanist to whom our gardens owe so much. Father Plumier will always be remembered for his interest in plants rather than for his devotional vocation and became King's Botanist to Louis XIV. He made several voyages to the West Indies and wrote *Nova Plantarum Americanarum Genera* in 1703, and it is in this book that the first Fuchsia is described and pictured. He named it *Fuchsia triphylla flore coccinea* and seeds of this were sent to Philip Miller at the Chelsea Physic Garden some time before 1744, though it was not long in cultivation at that time and was not seen or grown again for nearly a century. Later on, in around 1788, the first plant of *F. magellanica* was discovered — in the front window of a house in Wapping. The story goes that a prominent nurseryman called James Lee was showing a customer around his nursery. The visitor was mightily impressed, but as is the way of visitors, murmured that he had recently seen a plant that was even better than anything of its kind in the nursery. When pressed as to where he had seen this marvellous plant, the visitor said that it was to be seen in the front window of a house in Wapping. James Lee was so excited by this that he called for a coach and went immediately to look for it and indeed found a new Fuchsia quite unlike any of the few that were then in cultivation. The woman to whom this plant belonged did not wish to sell it as it had been given to her by her husband, a sailor who had recently returned from the West Indies and who was once again at sea. Lee had come out in an almighty hurry and had not thought to bring money with him, but he emptied his pockets of all that he had and managed to find the sum of eight guineas, which was a great deal of money then. The sailor's wife reluctantly agreed to part with the Fuchsia and Lee carried his treasure back to the nursery, where he propagated every smallest cutting during that season, until, as a result of his care and effort, he had some three hundred plants for sale. (So much for all the good gardening advice as to exactly when to take Fuchsia, or indeed any other, cuttings. Good gardeners, in extremis, seem to be able to will a cutting to grow even though it is not the best time of year for its first struggle as a separate entity.) Part of the bargain that Lee struck with the sailor's wife was that she should have two of the first cuttings, and this gives the story something of a happy ending. Lee sold all his cuttings at a guinea each — an excellent return on his original outlay. New introductions came in very slowly until 1824, but fourteen more were discovered in the next twenty years, including the delightful and very different *F. fulgens*. The hybridists, like so many selective bees, got busily to work and when the first botanical monograph was written in 1848, the author, a Frenchman called Félix Porcher, was able to list approximately 520 kinds of Fuchsia. Later on, round about 1880, this number had grown to 1500 named species or varieties and it was clear that a new cult had been born; records show that at Covent Garden some ten thousand plants a day were sold during their season. Fuchsias were the newest thing: they were used to decorate the pillars of the Crystal Palace, and enormous plants, often 10ft (3m) high were proudly exhibited in flower shows. They must have been an astonishing sight — those too large to be transported by cart had to travel by boat on the canals. The fashion for Fuchsias continued for a while, though it had lost its momentum towards 1900 and only some few of the most popular varieties were grown and sold — how fickle is fashion, as has been seen with tulips, auriculas, pinks and carnations.

The fruits of Fuchsias are quite edible and were there more of them they might be used in preserves because they are very sweet (though that famous gardener Shirley Hibberd describes them as being 'flat, green and somewhat poverty-stricken' and needing to be 'assisted with lemon juice and sugar'). At least they do have a definite flavour, unlike the American pumpkin which can be cooked either as a sweet or as a vegetable — unflavoured and with one's eyes shut, it has no recognisable flavour whatsoever. The same goes for watermelon, which is merely decorative and nothing else.

F. fulgens grows to 6ft (1.8m) with (in the species) long, usually single-colour flowers in shades of red or orange red; this Fuchsia from Mexico is the parent of several very characteristic modern hybrids.

F. magellanica, syn. **macrostemma** (1823) grows to 12ft (3.7m) with (in the species) red calyx and blue petals in summer through to autumn. A deciduous, mostly hardy shrub which is the parent of most of the hardier Fuchsias from S. America. Used as hedging in Cornwall and Southern Ireland and as a specimen shrub elsewhere. Plant at above eye level, where possible — one cannot keep lying down all the time to peer up at it, especially with advancing years.

F. procumbens (about 1854) trailing habit with (in the species) pale orange (or yellow) and violet 'flowers' (this species has no petals but has red and blue stamens and is altogether subtly colourful). A prostrate shrub from New Zealand with long shoots, very suitable for baskets. The 1" (2.5cm) long red fruits are a distinctive and very attractive feature of this Fuchsia.

Requirements: In southern parts of the British Isles several kinds of Fuchsia are hardy, though this should never be taken for granted. These are *F. magellanica* and its well-known hybrid *F.m.* 'Riccartonii'; also *F.m.* 'Gracilis' and *F.m.* 'Versicolor' with leaves variegated in grey-green, white and pink; *F.m.* 'pumila' grows only 6" (15cm) high and is very suitable for rockeries or raised beds.

These and similar 'garden' Fuchsias need sunny, sheltered positions and ordinary well drained soil with the addition of some peat and an annual fillip of bonemeal. Leaf mould is very much appreciated but is not essential. Water well during dry weather. In cold areas cut plants grown as shrubs down to ground level in November and mound up the roots with a protective heap of ashes, peat, straw or bracken. Keep straw or bracken from blowing away, with a small piece of wire netting. In warmer counties leave them be to grow as large as wanted, taking off winter-damaged shoots in March or April. Plants overwintered in greenhouse or conservatory should be kept almost dry (only watering occasionally) and in a minimum temperature of from 4-7°C (39-45°F). Start them into growth in March by increasing temperature and beginning to water. If plants are to be kept growing throughout the winter they will need a temperature of 13°C (55°F). Permanent greenhouse residents need a cool, shaded, humid temperature with plenty of ventilation.

Propagation: In the greenhouse take tip or lateral cuttings off in March, put into small individual pots of a rooting compost of peat and sand and keep at a temperature of 16°C (61°F). Grow on when rooted in larger pots of John Innes No.1, potting on a size at a time into John Innes No.2 until they are in 5 or 6" (12.5-15cm) pots of John Innes No.3. Pinch out leading shoots to keep plants bushy and turn pots regularly to keep a symmetrical shape. To propagate from hardy Fuchsias, take lateral cuttings with a heel from June onwards and treat as described. Protect for first winter.

Pruning: In warm areas hardy Fuchsias can be grown as deciduous shrubs (which in nature they are not) in the garden; winter-damaged shoots and branches can be taken off in March or April when the plant begins to grow. Greenhouse species and varieties can be trimmed lightly in March (use trimmings as cuttings).

For standard plants (best in large conservatory or greenhouse) allow plant to grow to desired height, making sure that it has a straight stem; leave on some short lateral branches (to feed plant and make a thicker stem more quickly) these shoots can be carefully taken off later. Pinch out leading shoot. Turn plant regularly if light is from one side.

Uses: Hardy kinds as hedges and specimen shrubs. As greenhouse shrubs and as pot plants; excellent in baskets and planted out in containers of all kinds; as standard plants and for rockeries. Always best when planted at a raised level.

Pests: Red spider and whitefly are a nuisance in greenhouses — fumigate regularly; clearing out of greenhouse litter in late summer and spraying with a pesticide will help to eliminate them.

Shrubs: Ballalheannagh, Baker, Brackenwood, Beth Chatto, Church, Dobbies, Goscote, Great Dixter, Highfield,

Hilliers, Ingwersen, Jackman, Kaye, Kershaw, Knaphill, Marchant, Marten's Hall, Meare Close, Notcutts, Otter, Potterton and Martin, Reuthe, Roger, Russell, Scotts, Shepton, Sherrard, St. Bridget, Stonehouse, Toynbee, Treasure, Warley, Woodland, Wyevale.

Seeds: Chiltern.

GARDENIA — Cape Jasmine *(Rubiaceae).* The Gardenia is named after Dr. Alexander Garden (1730-1791), a friend and correspondent of Linnaeus. The shrubs were to be found as a matter of course in every large and overheated Victorian conservatory and the richly fragrant flowers were a fashionable and permissible adornment in the hair and on the bosoms of the very proper young ladies of the time. However wealthy their families were it was not the thing to wear jewellery before marriage and a white Gardenia indicated innocence, fragility (the petals bruise very easily), simplicity and good taste, and in the Language of Flowers the Gardenia meant 'refinement'.

The flowers need to be cut from the bush just as they are about to open and will last quite a while in water. The blooms are very like Camellias in appearance except, of course, for the delicious scent. They are really hot or warm-house plants and need quite a deal of careful and regular attention.

Plants should be discarded after three or four years when grown under glass; this does not apply when they are grown in the ground in their native tropics.

G. jasminoides — Gardenia (1754) grows to 6ft (1.8m) with richly scented single or double white flowers from June onwards. A tender evergreen shrub from China and Japan for a heated greenhouse or conservatory.

Requirements: Gardenias are most particular plants, as well as being greedy. They need semi-shade and plenty of heat, humidity and moisture while growing and, specifically, the temperature from March to September should be kept at from 15-28°C (60-85°F) though it may be allowed to drop to between 10-15°C (50-60°F) during the winter, with correspondingly less water. Their growing medium should consist of equal parts of sandy peat, fibrous loam and well decayed dung. This may be substituted by John Innes No.2 or the equivalent, but I would rather use the real thing — the flower scent is that much richer. They should always be watered with rain water, they need plenty of water but they should not be allowed to stand in it and the watering programme needs to be consistent or the flower buds will drop off. Pot on annually in spring. In long periods of hot weather the pots may be plunged outside but beware of cool night temperatures.

Propagation: Take lateral cuttings with a heel in January, February or March (the earlier the better — they may well flower the same year) and put in pots of a rooting compost of peat and sand in a propagator set at 18-21°C (64-70°F).

When well rooted plant the little cuttings into the growing compost. If John Innes No.2 is used, water with a liquid feed once a fortnight after the first month. Stand them in the shade of another climbing plant or shade them in some other way, they do not like direct sunlight. Pinch out the tips to encourage a bushy shape.

Pruning: After flowering shorten all growths by half.

Pests: Gardenias are very prone to attack from all greenhouse pests such as scale insects, red spider, aphis and mealy bugs.

Uses: As exquisite cut flowers and (better) as handsome greenhouse plants which can be stood outside for special occasions if there is a prolonged warm spell.

Seeds: Butcher, Chiltern.

GARRYA — Silk Tassel Bush, Quinine Bush *(Garryaceae).* This is a subtly elegant shrub for a sheltered wall, particularly if other winter flowering plants and flowers can be grouped near it so as to make this part of the garden come alive at this time. Suggestions are: the earliest Crocus (often needing a cloche for protection) Hellebores, Jasminum nudiflorum, Galanthus, Leucojum and Bergenia. Its long pale green suede catkins look very special when seen against the dark evergreen leaves, though these may be discoloured by frosts in a hard winter. But — you win some and you lose some and a hard winter brings comfort in the knowledge that it will kill a lot of garden pests. This is an American shrub, discovered first by Archibald Menzies on one of his expeditions (some time during 1790-1795) but he did not name it and it was not until later that it was found by David Douglas, in 1827, who sent it back to the Horticultural Society. It flowered for the first time in 1834 and created a great deal of excitement among the learned botanists, who like to dot their i's and cross their t's more than most folk apart from mathematicians. It seems that this plant slotted very neatly into a hitherto unfilled gap between two other great plant families and therefore it became a new genus as well as a new Natural Order.

The plant commemorates Nicholas Garry, the Deputy-Governor of the Hudson Bay Trading Company during the time that Douglas went on his expeditions. It was through the help of the Company that Douglas was well accommodated, and he was able to send back his plant collections and use its guides and interpreters.

There are several other species in this family, but only this one is generally grown: most of the time it is the male form; the female has shorter catkins and has greenish purple fruits. Both plants are needed for these, but since an adult Garrya can grow very large there is seldom space for academically interesting plants that take up 10ft (3m) of wall at the very least (one is enough of anything in most average-sized gardens). Garryas can look superb in midwinter when grown as isolated free-standing shrubs but they must have a sheltered situation.

G. elliptica (1828) grows to 12ft (3.7m), though in eventual maturity it will be larger, with 6″ (15cm) long (often longer) silvery green catkins from November to February. A vigorous evergreen from California for most wall positions (not east-facing). Male form only stocked by most nurseries.

Requirements: Any good free-draining garden soil. Do not allow to dry out during hot summers — wall-shrubs get very dry. The leaves of Garryas get badly frost-burnt in cold winters which spoils the appearance of the delicately coloured catkins, so plant in as sheltered a position as possible. Do not attempt to move except in infancy. (I am on my third Garrya, having made all these mistakes.) Protect in first winter in your garden. They flower better in sun in spite of having a reputation as a good wall-shrub for north-facing positions.

Propagation: Take heel cuttings in August and put into a rooting compost of peat and sand in a cold frame. In spring pot up the rooted cuttings in John Innes No.2 and plunge the pots in a nursery area. Pot on as needed without disturbing the roots.

Pruning: Don't. Or if you must, just take away the oldest growths immediately after flowering.

Uses: As handsome winter flowering shrubs. Catkins for long lasting arrangements. As large-growing wall shrubs.

Shrubs: Ballalheannagh, Barcock, Bees, Bodnant, Brackenwood, Busheyfields, Peter Chappell, Daisy Hill, Dobbies, Goatcher, Goscote, Highfield, Hilliers, Hopleys, Hyden, Jackman, Kershaw, Knaphill, Lime Cross, Marchant, Meare Close, Notcutts, Otter, Reuthe, Roger, Rosemoor, Russell, Scotts, Shepton, Sherrard, Smith, St. Bridget, Toynbee, Treasure, Treseder, Warley, Woodland, W.W., Wyevale.

GENISTA — Broom (*Leguminosae*). A stylized representation of broom was adopted as an heraldic device at a very early period, particularly in France. There is an old story that, in the 12th century, as Geoffrey of Anjou was about to go into battle he plucked a spray of flowers from a broom bush whose roots were holding back a steep bank. Legend relates that as he thrust the blossoms into his helmet he is reputed to have said '. . . this golden plant, rooted firmly amid rock, yet upholding what is ready to fail, shall be my cognizance*. I will maintain it on the field, in the tourney and in the court of justice'. His troops were able to see the yellow flowers during the battle and the spray of broom flowers became the emblem of the great Plantagenet family; the medieval name for broom was 'Planta genista' (though now it has been re-named *Sarothamnus scoparius*). This story appears to be slightly apocryphal because it was a spray of broom *pods* that Geoffrey's son, Henry II, later wore as his badge, but the second recorded event was probably later in the season when there were no flowers to be had, so Henry obviously did the best he could with what there was. I have told the tale here when writing about 'Genista' — legend

takes precedence, for once, over the put-and-take of the botanists.

Genistas are very like Cytisus (also called broom where applicable, just to confuse the poor gardener) and some of them flower at the same time. Many have yellow flowers.

G. aetnensis syns. **G. aethnensis, Spartium aethnense — Mt. Etna Broom** (about 1826) grows to 15ft+ (4.5m+) with showers of yellow flowers in July and August. A graceful shrub, but almost leafless, with rushlike branches that become pendulous with flowers, from Sicily for a sunny, sheltered place. Cold winters will kill the branches.

G. hispanica — Spanish Gorse (1759) grows to a prickly cushion 1½ft (46cm) high by 10ft (3m) wide with (in mature plants) thousands of golden yellow flowers from late May to end of June. A deciduous spiny shrub from S.W. Europe for a position in full sun in ordinary to poor well-drained soil. Allow plenty of room for sideways spread.

G. pilosa (about 1790) grows from very low 3″ (7.5cm) to 2ft (61cm) high and spreads to 2ft+ (61cm) with yellow flowers from May to July. A rather variable shrub from S.W. Europe which can either be almost prostrate or, alternatively, a bush with, in both cases, a tangled mass of whiplike shoots. Suitable for sunny walls, banks, large rockery ledges and terraced gardens.

G. saggitalis (1588) prostrate, spreads to several feet in maturity, yellow flowers in June and July, with curious 'winged' jointed branches. Best grown to drip over large ledges or down walls. A shrub with wide evergreen stems and few leaves from Central and S.E. Europe for a hot well-drained place as edging for borders and for walls. As its stems are flattened, they look as though they have been stepped on, which is sometimes a reminder to later garden visitors to tread more carefully.

Requirements: Most Genistas like hot sunny banks with exceedingly 'ordinary' soil which must have good drainage. No feeding is necessary. *G. saggitalis* is said to do in semi-shade but mine did not — it died, so now I grow this interesting-looking plant on a hot rock ledge.

Propagation: Take heel cuttings in August and put into a rooting compost of peat and sand in a cold frame. Pot on rooted cuttings in spring into individual pots of John Innes No.1 and plunge in a sheltered nursery area. Pot on as necessary until ready to plant, taking care to disturb the roots as little as possible.

Pruning: *G. hispanica* is apt to die off in patches in bad winters or centrally in old age. Cut dead portions away as soon as these can be distinguished from the new season's growth.

None needed for other species except to tidy up winter-damaged shoots in late March or early April.

Uses: As exuberant and colourful garden and rockery shrubs.

Shrubs: Ballalheannagh, Barcock, Bees, Bodnant, Brackenwood, Bressingham, Peter Chappell, Beth Chatto, Daisy Hill, Dobbies, Fairley's, Farall, Glenview, Goatcher, Goscote,

*Note: *how I am recognised, or known*

Great Dixter, Highfield, Hilliers, Hopleys, Hyden, Ingwersen, Jackman, Kaye, Kershaw, Knap, Lime Cross, Marchant, Marten's Hall, Meare Close, Notcutts, Otter, Potterton and Martin, Reuthe, Robinsons, Roger, Rosemoor, Russell, Scotts, Shepton, Sherrard, Smoth, Southcombe, St. Bridget, Toynbee, Treasure, Treseder, Warley, Woodland, Wyevale.

Seeds: Chiltern, Thompson and Morgan.

GREVILLEA *(Proteaceae).* These fascinating shrubs originate from the antipodes and have an excitingly unusual look to them. They need, as may be imagined, a little more care than usual, but will more than repay the extra work by their exotic appearance. The genus was named after Charles F. Greville (1749-1809), who was a founder member of the Royal Horticultural Society. Grevilleas have no petals, but the tubular perianth or calyx has an opening through which the long style or styles protrude, and it is these which give the plant its characteristically different appearance. They look rather like exotic honeysuckles. The plants can be grown in large pots to stand outside in summer, or the pots can be plunged for the summer in the border and then lifted in autumn to return to the shelter of greenhouse or conservatory. It is asking too much to expect them to be safe outside in the British Isles, except in the Paradise Islands of Scilly, when they really need the year long pleasantness of Californian or Mediterranean temperatures.

G. alpina (1854) grows to 4ft (1.2m) and as much through with curious red and yellow flowers in April and May or longer. An evergreen shrub from Australia, good in tubs.

G. ornithopoda (1850) grows to 4ft (1.2m) with pendulous branches, and attractive pale green leaves. Clusters of cream and pink flowers appear in April. An evergreen shrub from W. Australia for the conservatory.

G. sulphurea grows to 6ft (1.8m) with yellow flowers from May to August. This is the hardiest of the species and can be grown outside in sheltered sunny places in Devon, Cornwall and other S.W. sea-coast areas. A tender evergreen shrub from New South Wales for conservatory, greenhouse, tubs or warm gardens.

Requirements: Frost-free or warm winter shelter according to species, neutral or acid soil enriched with peat and leafmould. Never chalk.

Propagation: Take heel cuttings in July, put into a rooting compost of peat and sand and put into a propagator set at 15-18°C (59-64°F). Cuttings do not always strike easily. When rooted transfer into pots of John Innes No.2 and pot on as the plants grow. Greenhouse shrubs can be potted on until the larger kinds are in 9-12" (23-30cm) pots or tubs, repot every other year and feed with weak liquid manure during the summer months.

Pruning: None needed.

Uses: As beautiful greenhouse or tub plants.

Shrubs: Ballalheannagh, Bodnant, Brackenwood, Great Dixter, Hilliers, Knoll Gardens, Marchant, Otter, St. Bridget, Stonehouse, Treseder, Wyevale.

Seeds: Chiltern.

GRISELINIA *(Cornaceae).* Though it often passes unnoticed by visitors to coastal towns, this shrub is as much a part of those same towns as the floral clock, the Punch and Judy or donkey rides on the sands. Griselinia is even more appreciated when you realise that you are living in an area where it is barely hardy. Flower arrangers like its fresh apple-green leaves, and it should be grown more often as a contrast shrub because of this pleasant colouration. It can be and usually is kept clipped into neat shape by seaside 'Parks and Gardens' departments, but this destroys its character completely. Griselinias are planted as windbreaks and screens, calmly enduring salt-laden gales. This they do not seem to mind, whereas they often succumb in cold wet winters inland. The genus was named after the Italian botanist, Franc. Griselini (1717-1783). They will grow to tree-proportions in mild coastal areas, so this should be taken into consideration when planting them, though up to about 6ft + (1.8m +) high they can be moved in damp weather in November if one is careful and quick. After that one must cut one's losses. The plants are dioecious and their flowers are inconspicuous, though where both sexes are grown there will be plenty of self-sown seedlings.

G. littoralis (1872) reaches to 20ft (6m) in time, and is grown for its attractive light green leathery leaves. An evergreen shrub from New Zealand for sunny sites in any soil for hedges, screens and as specimens.

Requirements: Any soil and sun. Established plants will withstand exposed positions in maritime areas but are liable to frost damage inland, so plant in a sheltered place. Protect young shrubs in winter with bracken or straw in a wire netting tube.

Propagation: In August take cuttings with a heel of half ripe lateral shoots; insert into a rooting compost of peat and sand and put into a cold frame or a propagator with gentle bottom heat. Remove rooted cuttings from the propagator and protect through the winter, leave others in frame until spring. Pot up all cuttings individually into John Innes No.2 and plunge in a semi-shaded nursery area for the summer. Protect in a frame for the following winter and plant out in the second spring. For hedges set plants 18" (46cm) apart and for screening they should be planted at intervals of 2 to 3ft (60-90cm).

Uses: As specimen shrubs for the foliage-conscious gardener (they are beautiful near Yew, Hollies, Rhus coggygria and shrubs or climbers with yellow leaves). As hedging and screens for windy seaside gardens. As foliage for arrangements.

Shrubs: Ballalheannagh, Bodnant, Brackenwood, Caldwell, Peter Chappell, Crarae, Daisy Hill, Dobbies, Goatcher, Great

Dixter, Hillier, Kaye, Kershaw, Knaphill, Knoll Gardens, Lime Cross, Marchant, Meare Close, Notcutts, Orchard, Otter, Reuthe, Roger, Russell, Scotts, Sherrard Smith, St. Bridget, Stonehouse, Toynbee, Treseder, Warley, Woodland.

HAKEA *(Proteaceae)*. This genus of interesting shrubs from Australia is named after the Baron von Hake (1745-1818) who was a patron of botany. The shrubs are all tender in the British Isles, except in the south west counties, but they can be grown in cold greenhouses elsewhere or as tub plants until they get too large. Never be deluded into thinking that they will be really safe outside; they may endure the changing rigours of our milder winters with fortitude for a short cycle of years, and then there will come one of the always-expected bad ones, like a seventh wave, which causes wholesale destruction and even kills the wallflowers. I speak from experience, and you cannot turn round in my greenhouse in the winter, so full is it of seasonal refugees.

However, do not let me deter you from trying to grow these rare and interesting shrubs. While they last they are lovely, and you may just get away with it with the help of St. Phocas* and the help of a sheltered garden with an arid, south-facing bank (grow Cistus and Rosemary there too — they will love it).

H. acicularis syn. **H. sericea — Needlebush** grows to 15ft (4.5m) or more with pinkish-white flowers in axillary clusters from May to July and hard woody fruits in due course. An interesting evergreen from Australia and Tasmania for an arid south-facing bank or large tub in a large greenhouse.

H. microcarpa grows to 6ft (1.8m) with fragrant creamy flowers in axillary clusters in May, followed by woody Beech-like seeds. A tender evergreen shrub from Australia and Tasmania for similar conditions or against a warm south-west wall.

Requirements: Hakeas need acid or neutral soils and will not do on chalk. When grown in containers in the greenhouse they need a compost of sieved loam, silver sand and peat in equal parts. They need plenty of water in summer while growing and flowering but very little in winter (this is what causes their demise outside, not cold but wet and cold together). Water well when growing outside and contrive a 'roof' over them in winter to shed water, this may prolong their lives.

Propagation: Take ripened cuttings with a heel in July and place in a rooting compost of sand and peat. Leave for a week and then put in a ventilated propagator over gentle bottom heat. Sometimes seed can be obtained, sow this in the usual way in a soilless seed compost with extra silver sand.

Uses: As fascinating greenhouse or tub shrubs. Seed stems for arrangements.

Shrubs: Hilliers.

Seeds: Chiltern, Thompson and Morgan.

Patron saint of gardeners.

HAMAMELIS — Witch Hazel, Winterbloom *(Hamamelidaceae)*. Witch hazels have curious spidery flowers in winter and early spring, which are yellow and very sweet-scented, and a good-sized shrub is a joy in any garden. Most witch hazels grow large — to 10ft (3m) or more — and are rather dull to look at in summer; they must have a sheltered, sunny site, best near evergreens or an Ivy-clad wall against which the bright flowers will show up most handsomely. Treat this as a patch of early spring, with winter-flowering pansies, the earliest cyclamen and Crocus and a few Polyanthus raised in shelter and planted out when the witch hazel comes into bloom. The strap-shaped flower petals become limp in frost temperatures but recover amazingly as soon as the day warms up. The leaves of *H. mollis* turn to a good yellow in autumn, which is another reason for planting it against an evergreen background.

Witch hazel is a familiar and benign medication that soothes the pain or irritation of insect bites and stings. Earlier herbalists used it for poultices or decoctions, infusions, extracts and ointments to cure inflammations, swellings, haemorrhoids, ophthalmic problems, menorrhagia, bleeding of the bowels, the treating of varicose veins and for bruises, burns and scalds. The leaves and bark of *H. virginiana*, the American Witch Hazel, were used, and this is the plant that was known to Indian medicine-men long before the advent of the first settlers. *H. virginiana*, though most useful medicinally, is not a shrub of great beauty; rather, it is used as a stock plant for the grafting of more ornamental species, much as briars are used for rose-growing.

H. mollis was discovered in 1879 by Charles Maries, who was collecting plants for Veitch. The shrubs were sent back to England from China and were at first thought to be another form of the irritatingly variable *H. japonica*, and were planted out in the nursery and allowed to grow virtually unseen by anybody except the gardeners for over twenty years. Early in this century the then Curator of Kew Gardens was touring the nursery and recognised the shrub (then in bloom) as a new and beautiful species. The shrubs were propagated (by grafting) as quickly as possible and were ready for sale by the following year.

H. japonica — Japanese Witch Hazel (1862) grows to 8ft (2.4m) with characteristic horizontal branches bearing faintly perfumed deep yellow flowers from February to March. Yellow leaves in autumn. A deciduous shrub from Japan for a sunny, sheltered place.

H. mollis (1879) grows to about 10ft+ (3m+) with fragrant yellow flowers on leafless branches from December to February. Yellow foliage in autumn. A deciduous shrub from China for a sheltered part of the garden.

Requirements: These shrubs need neutral to acid soil, not chalk, with leaf-mould and peat added. Fork in a little well-decayed manure or rich compost before planting. They should be planted with sufficient room to grow in a sunny position, sheltered from cold winds.

Propagation: Can be by layering; the branches will take about two years to root. Or take heel cuttings in September and insert in a rooting compost of peat and sand. Keep in a cold frame for winter. This is not always successful; cuttings are really best propagated under mist in July and August. Pot on in a soilless or lime-free potting compost and plunge pots for the summer.

Pruning: None needed in large gardens. Cut back too-long branches after flowering if necessary.

Uses: A good winter-flowering shrub; branches as sweetly scented cut flowers.

Shrubs: Ballalheannagh, Brackenwood, Bressingham, Caldwell, Peter Chappell, Daisy Hill, Dobbies, Goatcher, Goscote, Highfield, Hilliers, Hyden, Jackman, Kent, Kershaw, Knaphill, Lime Cross, Marchant, Meare Close, Notcutts, Otter, Reuthe, Roger, Rosemoor, Russell, Scotts, Shepton, Sherrard, Smith, St. Bridget, Toynbee, Treasure, Treseder, Warley, Woodland, Wyevale.

Seeds: Chiltern, Thompson and Morgan.

HEBE (formerly Veronica) *(Scrophulariaceae).* The botanists have split off almost all of what were formerly called 'The Shrubby Veronicas' into the genus Hebe, though the Royal Horticultural Society's Dictionary of Gardening — 2nd Edn, 1973, surprisingly still groups all the Veronicas (confusingly) together. Bean gives both names, which is something of a comfort in this taxonomic jungle, though saying 'The genus *Hebe* is closely allied to Veronica, a genus of herbs mainly confined to the northern hemisphere and, though long included in it is treated as distinct in all modern works'. Gardening catalogues will be an exception to this latter statement, you may be sure.

Most of the Hebes — or shrubby veronicas — are tender if not actually delicate and even in woody maturity their presence should never be taken for granted. Heave a sigh of relief in June when they are (usually) flowering, offer up a prayer of thankfulness and quickly take some cuttings in July. Many are maritime shrubs, and do not mind wind or salt-laden air but will succumb to frost. They do best in the southern and south-west parts of the British Isles. Hebes are Antipodean in origin and about two-thirds of the species originate in New Zealand. They are as promiscuous as asters and in a garden collection there may well be some interesting seedlings. Alice Coats tells of a New Zealand gardener, very learned as to his native flora, being shown a collection of veronicas (Hebes) in a British west-country garden — not one of which had he ever seen before.

H. 'Pagei' is a charming plant, with low cushions of grey leaves and white flowers in midsummer. It looks excellent as an edging, or it sits well in a rockery. It will spread to several feet sideways, though never growing higher than 1ft (30cm) or so, but in old age it gets bare in the middle and

will need to be replaced when this happens. *H. Armstrongii* is a most attractive plant for those gardeners who appreciate the slightly odd. *H. Armstrongii* syn. *H. ochracea* is one of the 'whipcord' hebes, whose branches look like those of a Cypress. These are golden-yellow at their tips, and in time the plant will form a striking-looking bush. When sited in a warm and cosy corner where it feels safe it will begin to produce small white flowers in June. *H. Hulkeana* is a very beautiful, but very tender, wall shrub (for safety) with dark shining leaves and long, loose sprays of lavender or lilac flowers. This really must be protected in winter, but is well worth it. *H. speciosa* and its crosses are what I call the 'seaside hebes' — an ignored bush in public or street planting and in hotel gardens, with its utterly reliable annually occurring spikes of purple, lilac, pink or crimson flowers. It is not until you try to grow it other than on the south coast that you realise how nice a bush it is, and how very useful are its abundant flowers for arrangements.

Many south-coast nurseries specialising in shrubs will have a number of hebes in their catalogues. If your main reason for having this plumptious plant is for flowers of white, lilac, purple, pink or crimson, then life is easy — pick them out by colour. But if you really want a particular species Hebe then a trip to the nursery of your choice at flowering time is almost a necessity — the tangle of nomenclature, latinised names and varietal names of plants of 'uncertain parentage' is too complicated to deal with by post.

H. Armstrongii syns. **H. ochracea, Veronica Armstrongii** grows to 3ft (90cm) with scale-like golden green leaves and white flowers from June to August. An evergreen shrub from New Zealand for a sunny, sheltered position.

H. brachysiphon syns. **V. brachysiphon** and, wrongly, as **V. traversii** grows to 6ft+ (1.8m+) and more wide, with white or lilac flowers in July. An evergreen shrub from New Zealand for sunny positions and seaside planting. Hardiest of the species.

H. Hulkeana syn. **V. Hulkeana** (1860) grows to 4ft+ (1.2m+) with 18″ (46cm) long sprays of lilac-lavender flowers in May and June. A tender evergreen shrub from New Zealand needing wall and winter protection.

H. ochracea (about 1900) grows to 2ft (61cm) with characteristic old-gold or copper- brown 'whipcord' stems and white flowers in July and August. An evergreen shrub from New Zealand for a warm sheltered but focal position. (Often confused and sold as *H. Armstrongii*).

H. Pagei syns. **V. pageana, V. pinguifolia** grows to 1ft (30cm) but may spread to 3ft (90cm) with pleasing blue-grey leaves throughout the year and white flowers in May and June. A low evergreen shrub from New Zealand for edges, ground cover, rockeries and banks, needing full sun and well-drained soil.

H. speciosa syn. **V. speciosa** (1835) grows to 5ft (1.5m) and as much wide and (in the species) red-purple flowers from July to September. An evergreen shrub from New Zealand and parent of very many beautiful cultivars which grow well in coastal resorts.

Requirements: Hebes are best in south or south-west coastal areas where they do very well. They need good drainage, sheltered, sunny positions (when grown in inland gardens) but are not fussy as to soil type. Wall and winter protection are recommended in colder areas. Dead head all kinds immediately after flowering. In tubs in greenhouse or conservatory they need a minimum temperature of from 5-7°C (40-45°F) and should be grown in John Innes No.2 or its equivalent.

Propagation: Take heel cuttings in July or August and put into a rooting compost of peat and sand. Keep in a cold frame or greenhouse for the winter. Cuttings of *H. speciosa* need frost-free winter conditions. In spring, transfer rooted cuttings into John Innes No.1. Depending on locality, young plants can be planted out in September or, in cold areas, the tender kinds need another winter under glass.

Pruning: Very little needed — these shrubs have tidy natures except for *H. Hulkeana* which has a lax (but very beautiful) habit.

Uses: As seaside screens and hedges. Inland, as specimen or rockery shrubs in warm sites or against walls. For arrangements and for foliage.

Shrubs: Ballalheannagh, Bodnant, Bressingham, Caldwell, Peter Chappell, Beth Chatto, Dobbies, Farall, Glenview, Goatcher, Goscote, Great Dixter, Highfield, Hilliers, Hyden, Ingwersen, Jackman, Knaphill, Knoll Gardens, Lime Cross, Marten's Hall, Notcutts, Orchard, Otter, Potterton and Martin, Reuthe, Roger, Rosemoor, Russell, Sherrard, Smith, Southcombe, St. Bridget, Stonehouse, Toynbee, Treasure, Treseder, Warley, Woodland, W.W., Wyevale.

Seeds: Chiltern.

HEDERA — Ivy *(Araliaceae).* The word 'ivy' often strikes fear into a gardener's heart. he may well have memories of neglected buildings rendered shapeless by the luxuriance of this plant, or he might know of fine but neglected woodland trees that are asphyxiating in the ivy's evergreen embrace. These are but two examples and are occasioned by man's neglect or lack of proper management — nature abhors any vacuum and will do something about it with the next perching bird or passing breeze. I am an admirer of ivy in all its many forms, all of which (and this cannot be said for many species) are beautiful with their ever-present leaves that shine with health (if they do not it can generally be attributed to wrong planting or the pollution of the atmosphere). The many variegated-leaved kinds are a constant blessing — easy to grow and needing very little attention while they get on with it, and a delight in winter when all about them is sere and brown. There are several reliable species and their

cultivars that can be counted on to soften new walls in sun or shade, climb pillars, posts, pergolas, archways and old tree-stumps, or even do duty as house plants. The most popular and well-known is *Hedera canariensis* — the Canary Island Ivy, whose cultivar 'Gloire de Marengo' has fine large leaves of deep green, grey-green and ivory, often pink-edged in winter. This grows quickly and looks very handsome, though it is a little tender and should not be planted in exposed positions. *H. helix,* the Common Ivy, has many named varieties which are quite different in colour and form from the well known typical plant. This can be used as ground cover beneath trees where nothing else will grow, though it must be prevented from climbing. In certain northern American states this plant, which Americans call 'English Ivy', is much appreciated (though in actuality it is probably the cultivar *H. hibernica* — Irish Ivy). It is planted in narrow formal borders of brick, stone, or concrete which it rapidly fills, forming a ribbon of living, shining green in urban planting, or in grander gardens where I have seen it growing in borders on the shady side of buildings which it fills to the exclusion of all weeds. Far better to have this vigorous and vital plant than bare and neglected flower beds. It needs regular clipping to keep it neat and, once planted, that is all. When it is used by landscape gardeners to fill long, low walled beds that are often part of a handsome garden design, it looks absolutely beautiful, and I am surprised that we do not use it more in this way in the British Isles. Of course, it must be regularly and firmly controlled and I suppose that may be a drawback, though clipping is easier than hand weeding. I am trying to find a corner of my own garden that I can 'formalize' in this way; fortunately, ivy does well in semi-shade, so if I move the laburnum, a large Aruncus, a Fatsia and a flight of steps then I shall have the very place.

Hedera helix is a very interesting plant in any case. While it is scrambling about on the ground or beginning to climb walls or trees the plant has the characteristic five-lobed ivy-shaped leaf. This it retains until it reaches the top of its support, when it sends out bushy branches of entire glossy leaves that bear flowers and berries. Cuttings taken from the creeping stems with their aerial roots will continue to creep and climb. Cuttings of the aerial branches will never climb, though they will grow into interesting low bushes with flowers and fruit.

Ivy has many legends and quite a number of uses. It was a plant of magical protection and was plaited with Honeysuckle to make protective circlets to hang over the cattle in their byres and to put round the milk pans. Thick old ivy stems were made into cups, and children drinking milk from these were, so it was believed, cured of whooping cough. In the taverns of old, wooden cups or goblets of ivy wood were used to serve wine, which dated back to an older belief that ivy prevented drunkenness; at one time Bacchus was pictured with a wreath of ivy leaves and not those of the grape. Before the days of inn-signs, taverns had a bush of ivy over the door to tell travellers that their wines and ales were of the best — hence the saying 'good wine needs no bush'. In medieval times the black ivy berries were infused in white wine as a protective drink against the plague, and the leaves were used as poultices to heal sores or wounds. Though ivy was at one time much used by herbalists it has since been discovered that the plant is capable of destroying red blood corpuscles when taken internally. Used externally, however, it is quite safe and was and still is used as a fresh poultice or as a compress to alleviate phlebitis, neuritis and sciatica. In the Language of Flowers it meant fidelity and at one time Greek priests presented an ivy wreath to newly-married couples.

H. helix — Common Ivy, English Ivy grows up to 100ft (30m) with lobed leaves when at ground level and when climbing and almost ovate leaves on the flowering branches. Flowers from October followed by black fruits. Ivy clings to almost any surface by means of flattened sucker-pads at the tips of the aerial rootlets which are seen all along the stems and branches. Uppermost growth should be kept clear of guttering and tiles. Its well-mannered presence on a house wall will keep this warmer and dryer than would otherwise be the case, though old brickwork with poor pointing should be attended to before the ivy is given its head.

Requirements: All ivies will grow in any soil and most of them in any aspect: the variegated ones do better in sunnier positions; not all of these are absolutely hardy. Therefore choice plants should not be grown on cold, draughty north-east facing walls, though *H. helix* will do well anywhere, regrowing from frost-damage very quickly. Frost, wet and cold winds may kill *H. canariensis* 'Gloire de Marengo' which should never be planted in an exposed position. Green-leaved ivies do well in semi-shade, and many are quite happy in sunless areas such as city basements, small back-yards or on north-facing walls, or in the ground beneath them.

Propagation: Take short — about 5" (12.5cm) — tip cuttings in July and August and insert in a rooting compost of peat and sand and leave in a closed frame until rooted. When rooted (about six weeks-two months) repot into John Innes No.1 and give each plant an 18" (46cm) cane so as to avoid root damage when it begins to grow; plunge the pots for the first winter and protect with bracken or straw or take into a cold greenhouse for shelter. Take cuttings from the aerial, adult growth if non-climbing bushes are wanted; if climbers are needed, take cuttings from the runners. Runners touching the ground invariably root and can be potted up and eventually detached.

Pruning: This is very important with ivies to maintain attractive and beautiful-looking plants and avoid neglected overgrown ones. For ivies on walls, cut hard back to their support in March, thin out overcrowded runners and branches and brush out dead leaves and sparrows' nests, unless you love sparrows. In which case, spring clean in April, by which time the brood will have hatched and flown. The ivy will not look as neat for the summer but your choice of priorities is your own.

Prune lightly in summer to maintain a shapely appearance. Check that, even where the ivy is being allowed to grow at will, it is well secured at the top; though the aerial roots are strong they are not always strong enough to hold the heavy foliage of the upper part of an ivy, which may break away in summer or winter gales. Wear gloves when handling the leaves — there are minute hairs on the stems which can irritate sensitive skins. Cut out reverting green stems on variegated kinds as soon as seen.

Uses: Endless. As clothing for chain-link or plastic wire-mesh fencing; as eternal wall-covering for ugly buildings; special varieties as wall, tree stump, arch, posts, trellis, pergola or fence covering; as excellent ground cover in shade; as pot plants; as low, fruiting bushes; as nectar plants for late bees and butterflies; as cover and shelter for many forms of wild life; for topiary; foliage for arrangements, Christmas decoration and as house plants.

Shrubs: Bees, Bressingham, Busheyfields, Caldwell, Peter Chappell, Jack Drake, Fairley's, Margery Fish, Goatcher, Goscote, Great Dixter, Highfield, Hilliers, Hopleys, Hortico, Hyden, Ingwersen, Jackman, Kaye, Kershaw, Knaphill, Knoll Gardens, Lime Cross, Marchant, Meare Close, Notcutts, Orchard, Otter, Potterton and Martin, Reuthe, Roger, Russell, Shepton, Sherrard, Smith, Southcombe, St. Bridget, Warley, Weald, Whitehouse Ivies, Woodland, W.W., Wyevale.

Seeds: Chiltern.

HELIANTHEMUM — Sun Rose, Rock Rose *(Cistaceae)*.

Rock Roses come in a gay multitude of colours with toning or yellow-contrasting centres to their crinkled paper petals, and pleasing more-or-less evergreen or evergrey foliage. They look best grown in companionable groups of different colours and there are so many to choose from that it is pleasantly possible to have them from white through cream, buff, apricot, orange, chestnut, red, crimson, pink and, of course, yellow, which is the colour of the native British wild flower *H. nummularium*. They look very attractive when planted in contrived chinks in paving — their roots enjoy the coolness under the stones and their aerial parts can bask in the reflected warmth. They should not be planted in a general thoroughfare because they will make quite large plants which can be a trap for the unwary, especially at night. They look and are excellent when planted so as to spill over wide paths, and a pink-flowered variety is charming in front of annuals such as love-in-a-mist *(Nigella)*, with pink and blue cornflowers *(Centaurea)* behind to complement the theme. The plants that are grown today are the progeny of crosses between *H. nummularium, H. appeninum* and *H. glaucum.* A Scottish gardener called John Nicoll of Monifieth, near Dundee, specialised in Rock Roses and bred a number of differently-coloured varieties which he named after Scottish mountains — 'Ben Nevis', 'Ben Afflick', 'Ben Lawers', 'Ben Vorlich' and so on. But Rock or Sun Roses do not open on dull days, and in any case their flowers close in the afternoon, so much work went into trying to breed varieties that were a trifle more courageous and not so sleepy.

H. appeninum, syn. **H. polifolium — White Rock Rose** grows to 18″ (46cm) with yellow-centred white flowers from May-July and grey leaves. A European wild flower, doubtfully native in Devon and Somerset, for a hot rockery, raised bed or sunny border.

H. nummularium syns. **H. chamaecistus, H. vulgare —** Rock Rose, grows to 6″ (15cm) with (in the species) yellow flowers in June and July. A native British and European wild flower with evergreen leaves, always best in full sun. A parent of many of the modern Helianthemums with single or double flowers. Not always hardy in cold, wet winters.

Requirements: Full sun, very free draining soil; they will do best on chalk or lime-stone walls but are not really fussy so long as they can sun-bathe. Protect in very cold, wet winters.

Propagation: Take short heel cuttings from non-flowering shoots from June to August and insert in a rooting compost of sand and peat. Put into a cold frame until rooted, then pot on into John Innes No.1 and grow on. Protect in the frame for the first winter. When growing well, pinch out the growing tips to make bushy plants. Set out in the following spring.

Uses: As delightful rockery, edging, wall or paving plants.

Shrubs: Beth Chatto, Jack Drake, Farall, Glenview, Highfield, Hilliers, Hopleys, Ingwersen, Kaye, Robinsons, Scotts, Sherrard, Stonehouse.

Seeds: Chiltern.

HELICHRYSUM *(Compositae).* The name of these plants comes from *helios,* sun, and *chrysos,* golden. Most of the shrubby members of this large genus have yellow, cream or white flowers and silver-grey (often woolly) foliage which is sometimes pleasantly aromatic. There is a tender species, *H. petiolatum,* which is becoming increasingly popular for flower arrangements; it has long (often very long) trailing branches set with small white-felt leaves. The effect of this plant when seen trailing out of large urns, old horse-troughs or other suitable vessels is quite delightful especially when it is grown with white Petunias and Pelargoniums. It is most tender, however, and must be taken up and put in a pot in a warm dry greenhouse or conservatory for the winter, where it should be given a position in full light and great aridity. It does not like humidity, so there are always logistical problems in trying to keep everything at least

alive, if not exactly happy, and as I count the corpses during a bad winter I reflect that the space they took up means that everything else can move up one on the survival-ladder.

H. splendidum is a fine grey-leaved shrub with yellow flowers (often nipped off by purists with white and silver gardens). It makes a good round hummock if pruned hard in early April (as Blue Rue should be) and lightly snipped over in July; the trimmings can be used for cuttings. The silver branches make an excellent background for other flowers both in the garden and indoors in a vase, and it is then that one appreciates such a plant which will make peace between the warring colours of magenta and yellow, and its flowers should be allowed to bloom so as to join things up, as it were.

H. angustifolium is called 'The Curry Plant' because its foliage smells of curry-powder. It is often grown in herb gardens because of this, though the leaves have no real culinary use. It has the characteristic yellow flowers in summer. Grown in breezy sea-side gardens it is even more aromatic because the wind is constantly rubbing the branches together.

H. angustifolium — The Curry Plant grows to 15″ (38cm) high with downy white-leaved branches and yellow flowers from June-August. An 'evergrey' from Southern Europe for a hot sheltered place with poor soil and good drainage. Good for hot sea-coast gardens.

H. lanatum grows to 2ft (60cm) high with silver-grey flannelly leaves and long-stalked flat yellow corymbs of yellow flowers in July and August. A very striking and sculptural plant from South Africa for a hot, terraced garden, or any other warm, south-facing sheltered spot. Needs protection in winter.

H. petiolatum syns. **H. alveolatum, H. triliniatum** trails to 4ft (1.2m) or so, or can be tied to a thin stake to grow upwards, which is not its natural desire. Felted white leaves and yellowish flowers in late summer. A trailing tender shrub from S. Africa for large raised containers or steep banks. Pot up and take into a dry south-facing conservatory, sunny windowsill or a greenhouse that is not humid for the winter.

H. splendidum grows to 5ft (1.5m) if unchecked by secateurs, with grey-white downy leaves and yellow flowers in July and August. A very white South African shrub — on hot, dry days, less so on wet ones as are most silver plants. Needs a position in full sun.

Requirements: Full sun, a sheltered site, hot, poor free-draining soil and protection in wet winters.

Propagation: Take short, lateral heel cuttings of all from April to July; insert into a rooting compost of one part silver sand to two parts sharp or coarse sand and one part peat in a shaded cold frame. When rooted pot on into a growing compost of one part grit or coarse sand to two parts of John Innes No.1. Grow on in frame and leave there for the winter, with plenty of ventilation on cold, bright days.

Pruning: Cut *H. splendidum* hard back in April if a neat shape is wanted. Tidy it up again in July. Cut *H. lanatum* hard back after flowering to keep it neat, unless dried flower-heads are wanted for winter decor.

Uses: As 'contrast' plants, foliage for arrangements, dried flower heads of *H. lanatum* for winter decor.

Shrubs: Margery Fish, Notcutts, Oak Cottage, Old Rectory, Parkinsons, Rampart, Scotts, Sherrard, Stoke Lacy, Stonehouse, Toynbee, Treseder.

HELIOTROPIUM — Cherry Pie, Turnsole *(Boraginaceae).*

This sweetly-perfumed old-fashioned shrub is named Heliotrope because at one time it was believed that the flowers turned round with the sun (hence also 'Turnsole'). The Language of Flowers, which is often based on very accurate observation, gives the meaning as 'devotion' or 'I turn to thee'.

Heliotrope is a very tender plant, and I think if you whispered the unkind word 'frost' to it in midsummer it would shrivel in terror and its flowers would drop off. It *must* be kept in a frost free greenhouse from September until June, with a constant minimum winter temperature of not less than 13°C (55°F) which is essential to its survival, not to say well being. Two main species are grown, *H. peruvianum* and *H. corymbosum* with, logically, *H. x hybridum* which may sometimes be more easily obtainable.

Heliotrope was grown very much more in·Victorian times, perhaps because there were more hothouses and cheaper coal. But *H. peruvianum* has been grown in this country since 1757 so its requirements would have been well known. All three can be easily grown from seed, which is often the easiest way to have the plants (always remembering that they need a heated greenhouse or propagator in which to start life).

If you have a heated lean-to greenhouse or conservatory heliotrope can be planted against the (usually warmer) back wall, where it will grow quite large and produce clusters of heavily-scented flowers. Once it was grown for the perfume industry, but now, alas, the characteristic fragrance has been synthesized. I have always associated this perfume with Great-aunt Maude, who wore mauve satin and tight stays which creaked alarmingly. Once she came to stay and there was a domestic crisis of some kind in the small hours; Aunt Maude appeared quite quickly in the circumstances, still creaking and, as always, surrounded by eddies of heliotrope. I was named after her (Maude is the second of my four Christian names) and, though I do not really care for the colour mauve, I dearly love the scent of heliotrope which really does smell as delicious as Cherry Pie.

Large greenhouse shrubs can be used as stock plants to yield cuttings which will make neat little summer plants for tubs (too nice to use en-masse for bedding out, except per-

haps around a sundial in an old herb-garden). They are best planted in tubs at waist level or higher, so as to minimise the effort needed in order to sniff their delicious scent. The flowers are like two-toned mauve forget-me-nots; those for the garden should not go outside until June and will need to come back into the safety of the greenhouse (if they are being kept) at the beginning of September. Heliotrope is an amiable plant and can be brought to or kept flowering at any time of year by increasing the temperature. Standard shrubs can be grown by allowing the centre stems to grow to about 4ft (1.2m) or the desired height, when the growing point or points should be stopped. The new branches that will quickly grow can be stopped again to form a round ball-shaped head. The plant must be turned round regularly if it is being grown where the light-source is one-sided.

H. corymbosum (1808) grows to 4ft (1.2m) with fragrant lilac flowers (larger than *H. peruvianum)* from May to September. A tender evergreen shrub from Peru for warm greenhouse and summer planting.

H. peruvianum — Heliotrope, Cherry Pie (1757) grows to 6ft (1.8m) with heavily-scented purple and mauve flowers from May to September. A tender shrub from Peru for the warm greenhouse and for summer planting.

Requirements: Heliotrope should be grown in pots of John Innes No.2 or the equivalent. Large plants must be kept in the greenhouse and can be planted in a suitably enriched border. Standards should be stood outside from mid-June until the end of August to ripen their wood, and these can be kept flowering during winter if the temperature is above a constant 16°C (61°F). For greenhouse-dwellers, whether in the border or in pots, the temperature should be kept on the humid side by damping down the floor in very hot weather. Water well while growing and flowering, decreasing in winter to bare necessity for those plants that are being kept for a further season. For any that are to be kept flowering, the temperature needs to be higher; these can be watered as normal. Feed flowering plants with weak liquid manure from May to September. Tie or stake large shrubs adequately. Young plants flower better, so discard those grown for pots when over two or three years old.

Propagation: Take heel cuttings in September or February; insert in a rooting compost of peat and sand in a propagator set at 16-18°C (61-64°F). When rooted pot into John Innes No.1 and grow on in the warm greenhouse. Seeds can be sown in February in seed compost at a temperature of 16-18°C (61-64°F). When large enough, prick out into individual pots of John Innes No.1. The plants do not care for disturbance once established. Pinch out growing tips to make bushy plants. Harden off with circumspection, whisking them back into the warm if cold nights are forecast.

Pruning: Cut back large greenhouse shrubs by half in February. Grow standards as described, but stop leader a little higher than height required. Stop growing shoots at five leaves or

Plate 1 SPRING *Chaenomeles lagenaria* — Japanese Quince; *Magnolia stellata; Daphne mezereum* — Mezereon; *Syringa vulgaris* — Lilac; *Wisteria floribunda.*

Plate 2 SUMMER *Nerium oleander* — Oleander; *Cistus ladanifer; Buddleia davidii* — Butterfly bush; *Bougainvillea glabra; Fuchsia magellanica.*

Plate 3 AUTUMN *Ceratostigma Willmottianum; Vitis coignetiae* — Glory-vine; *Vaccinium Myrsinites; Parrotia persica; Thelicrania sanguinea* — Dogwood.

Plate 4 — WINTER *Jasminum nudiflorum* — Winter Jasmine; *Garrya elliptica* — Silk Tassel-bush; *Corylus maxima* — Filbert; *Viburnum fragrans; Chimonanthus praecox* — Wintersweet.

Plate 5 CLIMBERS *Akebia quinata; Clematis macropetala; Lonicera periclymenum* — Honeysuckle; *Plumbago capensis.*

Plate 6 ROSES *Rosa officinalis; Rosa alba maxima* — The Jacobite Rose; *Rosa gallica versicolor* — 'Rosa Mundi'; *Rosa moyesii; Rosa Willmottiae.*

Plate 7 FOLIAGE *Cornus alba; Hedera canariensis* — Canary Island Ivy; *Rhus cotinus coggygria* — the Smoke Bush; *Artemisia absinthium* — Wormwood; *Elaeagnus maculata*.

Plate 8 EVERGREENS *Camellia japonica* 'Adolphe Audusson'; *Daphne laureola* — Spurge Laurel; *Vinca major* — Periwinkle; *Mahonia Bealei; Escallonia* 'C.F. Ball'.

so and laterals again similarly. Standards should last well for several years if all top growth is cut back by half when re-potting; this is best done in October. Pinch out growing shoots in the following spring.

Uses: As delightful old-world tub and container plants; as spec-tacular standards for bedding out in special areas; as green-house shrubs and pot plants; as very fragrant cut flowers and for pot-pourri.

Shrubs: Old Rectory, Weald.

Seeds: Chiltern, Suttons, Thompson and Morgan, Unwin.

HIBISCUS *(Malvaceae)*. There is no use trying to deceive oneself or (more difficult) the plant — Hibiscus, as a tribe, are the most glorious of tropical flowers, happiest in a humid, steamy jungle environment or behind the ear of a Tahitian girl. It certainly is possible to grow Hibiscus in the British Isles in stove-house, warm greenhouse or conserva-tory and in the Scilly Islands but the plants seem to be pining for warmer climes, or so it appears to me. Hibiscus belong where there is no twilight and where the sun dips suddenly into the ocean at night and as quickly rises in the early morning — one moment dark, the next bright day, with just a trail or so of morning mist. I took the photo-graph of *Hibiscus rosa-sinensis* in Lagos just before dark, when the heat and humidity were almost too enervating. But the moisture gleamed on the healthy leaves of the many flowers — they, unlike myself, belonged in that place and were happy.

We English have been striving to grow *H. syriacus* with varying degrees of success since 1597, when Gerard wrote that he was expecting success with some seeds that he had sown. Parkinson was growing it by 1629 and observed that it was tender and '... it would not be suffered to be uncovered in the Winter time, or yet abroad in the garden, but kept in a large pot or tubbe in the house or in a warme cellar, if you would have them to thrive'. Later on it seemed that gardeners had learned to care for the species sufficien-tly well for it to be recorded by Cobbett in 1833 as being a fine plant '... before the door of the farmhouse at the Duke of Devonshire's estate at Chiswick, that is full twelve feet high (3.7 metres), and that blooms regularly every year'. Even in the 17th century the plant was being hybridised and further species of different colours were being intro-duced. It is interesting to note that old named varieties such as 'Coeleste' (Coelestis) and 'Duc de Brabant' are still obtainable today; another variety called 'Totus Albus' may still be found by diligent searching in the catalogues, though it has been replaced (horrid but only too exact phrase) by 'Snowdrift' which is described as being 'scarcely different'. It depends on your point of view here — if you have an old garden and want old flowers and plants to match, I would most certainly attempt to get 'Totus Albus' (to use this as an example) but if you just like beautiful

flowers and wish to save yourself the cost of 'phone calls, postage, carriage or petrol, then plump for 'Snowdrift'. Nobody but you will know the difference, and the chromosome count may well be similar.

H. syriacus is pretty hardy in southern England, making fine large bushes in sheltered sunny places. It flowers late in the year, and because of this it is a great enlivener in the late summer garden when everything appears to be coming up yellow. This Hibiscus has pink, mauve, white or blue flow-ers, some being double. The double-flowered kinds were being generally grown in the first half of the 19th century; these do not open properly late in the year if the weather is cold or wet, or both — and, after all, can you blame them?

H. rosa-sinensis is called 'Shoe Flower' in Jamaica, where the petals are, or were, used to clean shoes; *H. esculenta* is Okra or Gumbo, used to flavour the strange, spiced dishes of the Carolinas and the Deep South. (Being an adventurous eater, with complete faith in my own diges-tion, I once made the mistake when in New Orleans of ordering File Gumbo and Soft-Shelled Crab. I gave up very quickly — the crab won, even in death and upside-down in a dish).

H. Rosa-sinensis — Hibiscus grows to 8ft (2.4m) — it is a tree in the wild, with bright rose-red flowers in the species and single or double flowered varieties in cultivation. A warm-house evergreen shrub from China and the sub-tropics.

H. syriacus formerly **Althaea fruticosa** or **Althaea frutex — Shrubby Hollyhock** (1596) grows to 6ft+ (1.8m+) with single or double flowers in white, pink, blue, rose and purple usually with a dark centre, or yellow in some white varieties. A deciduous rather tender shrub originally from the Far East, though introduced into Syria very early on. For a sheltered and warm place in the garden, often best against a wall.

Requirements: Greenhouse species need to be grown in John Innes No.2 or No.3, in large — 8-12″ (20.5-30.5cm) — pots or in the border. They need a minimum winter temperature of 7-10°C (45-50°F). If colder than this the plants may not die but will probably lose their leaves. During winter if a warmer temperature can be constantly maintained — 16°C (61°F) — they will keep their leaves. They should be watered with care, keeping the soil just damp, but when spring comes and growth recommences more water can be given. The plants should be kept in a well-lit part of the greenhouse or conservatory but should be shaded lightly — a vigorous climbing plant such as an Ipomoea or Cobaea is ideal, since these can be cut to size, so to speak. On very hot days — 21°C (70°F) — ventilate the house. Give weak liquid feeds fortnightly in summer and re-pot each spring. *H. syriacus* needs a sunny, rather sheltered place and any well-drained light, rich soil. Does well in sandy areas and is better as a wall-shrub in cold gardens.

Propagation: Take heel cuttings of *H. Rosa-sinensis* at any time during summer (April-August). Insert in a rooting compost of peat and sand and put into a propagator set at 18°C (64°F). When rooted transfer to pots of John Innes No.2 and grow on, pinching out growing tips to keep plants bushy.

For *H. syriacus* take half-ripe lateral heel-cuttings in July and insert in a rooting compost of peat and sand in a propagator set at 16°C (61°F). When rooted, transfer into pots of John Innes No.1 and grow on. Protect in a cold frame or greenhouse for the winter. In the spring pot on and plunge pots in a warm, sheltered place until autumn, when they can be set out in their permanent position.

Pruning: Cut back warm-house shrubs to within 3" (7.5cm) of the old wood and take away one third of the new spring growth. *H. syriacus* is not generally pruned in the British Isles, except to cut back an extra-long branch or so immediately after flowering.

Uses: *H. syriacus* as a sumptuously flowering late-summer garden shrub (group other late perennial plants of toning colours near it) and *H. Rosa-sinensis* as a stove-house exotic.

Shrubs: Goatcher, Notcutts, Orchard, Reuthe, Russell, Scotts, Shepton, Sherrard, St. Bridget, Toynbee, Treasure, Woodland, Wyevale.

Seeds: Chiltern, Thompson and Morgan.

HIPPOPHAE — Sea Buckthorn *(Elaeagnaceae)*. The name
of this genus is taken from *Hippophaës*, an old name for a prickly type of spurge. The shrubs are usually spiny and make an excellent and very beautiful hedge because of the rather willow-like leaves which are silvery when young; the fruits or berries (too sour for any bird, however hungry) are orange-yellow and occur as thick clusters along the branches from September to February. This is a plant which needs two of a kind, though one male plant should be allowed to about six females. The flowers are inconspicuous and forgettable. Sea Buckthorn is an easy tempered shrub and will grow in almost any soil including beach sand. If only two plants are grown make sure that they are close together (the pollen is wind borne), though they will take up quite a bit of space. Try to plant them where the setting sun can illuminate the orange-yellow berries — this is a lovely sight. Though called a Buckthorn, it is not, and though the fruit is not poisonous it is seldom eaten — except by the Tartars who made jelly out of it and by Bothnian fishermen who used it to flavour their catch.

H. rhamnoides grows to 10ft+ (3m+) in normal circumstances though it may reach 40ft (12m) in a sheltered position. Grown for its thick, long-lasting clusters of berries. A spiny deciduous native and European shrub for seaside hedging, windbreaks or as (two) specimen shrubs which should be planted close together.

Requirements: A sandy or ordinary but free-draining soil, and an open sunny position.

Propagation: By layering or seed, though the first method will take about eighteen months. If numbers of plants are wanted for hedging or windbreaks then they can be grown from seed which should be planted in October in seed compost. Put boxes in a cold frame. In spring prick out the seedlings into deeper boxes or individual pots and grow on until they can be planted into nursery rows. Move to permanent positions in late autumn. It will not be possible to differentiate between male and female plants until they (all) flower. For a good hedge set the young shrubs about 2ft (60cm) apart in a staggered double row. For windbreaks plant about 4ft (1.2m) apart.

Pruning: None really necessary except to cut off about a third of hedge and windbreak growth.

Uses: As (paired) specimen trees, as boundary hedges or windbreaks and branches of berries for arrangements; silvery young growth very attractive also.

Shrubs: Barcock, Bodnant, Brackenwood, Caldwell, Dobbies, Goatcher, Hilliers, Jackman, Knaphill, Marchant, Notcutts, Roger, Russell, Scotts, Shepton Sherrard, St. Bridget, Toynbee, Treasure.

Seeds: Chiltern.

HOHERIA — Lacebark *(Malvaceae)*. This very beautiful
small genus of flowering shrubs, whose name comes from the original Maori, *Hoihere*, is not generally hardy in the British Isles, except in the southern counties and, even better, in the south-west. These shrubs are grown for their abundant scented flowers which come in mid or late summer when there is often a dearth of interest in the garden. (Also there is a degree of one-upmanship in the possession of a flourishing specimen.)

Many of these beautiful Antipodean plants and shrubs are almost too tender for the British Isles. I remember being told in school geography lessons that the climate of New Zealand is 'almost the same as ours' which is not true — it is wetter, hotter, higher and colder (Mt Cook is 12,349ft (3,702m) high), and in addition there are hot springs and glaciers. So it is no wonder that some of our importations are a bit restless. *Hoheria Lyallii* was discovered by Dr. Andrew Sinclair who, with Julian van Haast, was one of the few collectors (apart from the Cornishman William Colenso) to send back plants that are still being grown today. There has never been a tide of fashion for the flora of New Zealand as there has for that of other countries, and the very many plants, shrubs and trees native to that country have, so to speak, crept in by degrees. No large firm of nurserymen — such as Messrs. Veitch — sent collectors to New Zealand, possibly because it was too far even for them and it may have been thought that there was not much there of interest. Which brings us back to the Hoherias — a group of shrubs having exquisite flowers with almost translucent petals rather like cherry-blossom, a similarity which is accentuated by the toothed, veined leaves.

H. glabrata syns. **Gaya Pyallii, Plagianthus Lyallii** grows to 15ft (4.5m) spread about 10ft (3m) with scented white flowers in June and July. A deciduous shrub from New Zealand for a sheltered garden or wall position.

H. Lyallii (1871) grows to 15ft (4.5m) with a spread of 10ft (3m) and more in sheltered areas, with scented white flowers in July and August. A deciduous shrub from New Zealand for a wall or very sheltered position.

Requirements: Any good, well-drained garden soil in sun or semi-shade. A site against a south, west or south-west facing wall is advantageous.

Propagation: Best by seeds sown in spring in seed compost at a temperature of 13-16°C (55-61°F). Wher large enough transfer into individual pots of John Innes No.1 and grow on. Protect for first winter. Long shoots may be layered in September and will take a year to root.

Pruning: Very little needed except for cutting out winter-damaged shoots and branches, and a little judicious thinning out of wall shrubs.

Uses: As rather special and uncommon garden shrubs.

Shrubs: Ballalheannagh, Daisy Hill, Hilliers, Knoll Gardens, Marchant, Notcutts, Scotts, Sherrard, St. Bridget, Treasure, Treseder.

HOLBOELLIA (sometimes called **Stauntonia**) *(Lardizabalaceae)*. This genus of evergreen twining climbers is named after Frederick Louis Holboell (1765-1829). The plants are vigorous, once they get started and if they can have both a good growing season and a mild winter. They have dangling corymbs of scented flowers early in the year and are well worth giving a special place on a sunny wall where they will begin to flower in a few years. These rather special climbers, such as Akebia, Aristolochia and so on, do need time to settle into your garden but, as they say, once established there will be no holding them. I am planning to do dark things to my Akebia once I see how one of its layers is doing on another wall where, I tell myself, it will be far happier; in the meantime I have a bad conscience about it, particularly as I write this, because it seems to have more flower buds than at any time previously and I may well have to forgive it for strangling two other creepers and choking three roses to death. Even the Bindweed has a hard time of it in this bed, and my *Clematis orientalis* actually retreated and is climbing along a nearby wall as fast as it can in the opposite direction. So, as I was saying, give it everything that you think it wants and then go away and re-make another bit of the garden; when you come back the rather tender, special, allegedly delicate creeper will have climbed a street lamp using a full-grown apple tree to practise on en route.

H. coreacea (1907) grows to 20ft (6m) with purplish male flowers in terminal clusters and green-white female flowers in axillary clusters in April and May. A strong growing evergreen climber from China with trilobed leathery leaflets, for a sheltered sunny wall or to clothe an old tree.

H. latifolia syn. **Stauntonia latifolia** (1840) grows to 20ft (6m) with racemes of fragrant green-white (male) and purple (female) flowers in March. A more tender evergreen from the Himalaya for similar wall or garden positions. Best in a large conservatory or cold greenhouse.

Requirements: Any good free-draining garden soil, sun and a sheltered growing position.

Propagation: Layer lower growth in spring or September and sever in a year. Or take half-ripe cuttings with a heel in August, insert in a rooting compost of peat and sand and put into a propagator with gentle bottom heat or a closed frame. Or sow seeds in spring in seed compost and place in a propagator set at 13-16°C (55-61°F). When seedlings are large enough transfer into pots of John Innes No.1 and grow on (with cane for support). Protect for first winter.

Uses: As unusual twining plants for a conservatory or warm wall.

Shrubs: Marchant, Sherrard, St. Bridget.

HOYA — Wax Flower, Porcelain Flower *(Asclepiadaceae)*. The genus is named after Thomas Hoy, gardener to the Duke of Buckingham. Hoyas are very special greenhouse climbing plants with waxy, artificial-looking flowers, certain specific requirements and rather odd ways. The unreal-looking star-shaped flowers are scented and were much in favour as buttonholes in Victorian times. They manufacture so much nectar that they positively drip with it, and this stickiness should be taken into account when deciding on their home. Hoyas are excellent plants because they climb by means of their own aerial rootlets and this is always more pleasing than stakes, netting, string or wires. The entirely naked stems of the new season's growths develop to their full length before any leaves appear, and this can at times be disconcerting to the anxious gardener. But just forget them and do something useful elsewhere and before you know it the leaves will have developed. Flowers do not generally appear on young plants — Hoyas need to be at least two or three seasons old before they bloom. In addition to the green-leaved form there are two variegated kinds, sometimes harder to find but well worth having if there is the space. Hoyas can be grown as house plants, but they really prefer the humidity of a warm greenhouse or conservatory, and they like warm, damp walls best of all. There are several other species but they are not easy to obtain, so are not listed here.

H. bella (1847) grows to 12″ (30cm) and spreads to 18″ (46cm) with pendulous branches and purple or crimson centred white flowers during the summer — between May and September, but not for this whole period. A tender plant from India very suitable for hanging baskets.

H. carnosa — Wax flower (1802) grows to 20ft (6m) with fragrant, rather sticky umbels of perfectly-formed star-shaped waxy flowers from May to September. A tender but vigorous climber from Queensland for the warm greenhouse.

Requirements: Hoyas need peaty compost such as an ericaceous mix or John Innes No.2. They need a minimum winter temperature of 10°C (50°F) but would do better at 13°C (55°F). Both species need a minimum growing temperature in spring and summer of 16°C (61°F). *H. carnosa* needs some shaded glass, *H. bella* should hang beneath a roof-climbing deciduous creeper or be beneath heavier shading. In winter they need no shade. Humidity is essential during spring and summer, though ventilation and regular leaf-syringing is beneficial. They need very little water during winter but need much more in the growing seasons and regular feeding with liquid manure. *H. carnosa* can be grown in a 10″ (25.5cm) pot, re-potting every other year but is best planted in the greenhouse border, and is better when kept cooler and lower down than when allowed to grow up to the roof glass.

Propagation: Hoyas layer well, in April or May, and will soon root. (Remove some of the leaves.) Or take cuttings of stems of *H. carnosa* and shoots of *H. bella* in June and insert in a rooting compost of peat and sand in a closed propagator with some bottom heat. When rooted grow on and use to replace older plants. Pinch out some of the growing tips of the new plants.

Pruning: The flowers of *H. carnosa* form on old flower-stems as well as on new wood so it is best not touched.

Uses: As sweetly scented flowers very suitable for formal arrangements; as rather special greenhouse climbers and basket plants.

Shrubs: Roger.

Seeds: Butcher.

HUMULUS — Hop *(Urticaceae)*. The familiar and beautiful hop, seen so characteristically twiddling about among other climbers or up through large shrubs, takes its name from *humus,* the ground, because if this climber was not supported by other plants it would just lie down and make an untidy heaving mass. Some climbers can be allowed or even encouraged not to climb and it is like suddenly discovering a new plant, but the hop is not one of these. This is a particularly easy and pleasing plant to grow over arbours, summer-houses, large pergolas and tall or long (or both) walls and fences, where its attractive 'hop-bells' will dangle from late summer onwards. Planted in association with strong-growing rambler roses such as 'American Pillar', 'Albertine' or 'Alberic Barbier' it will just be getting into its stride as these are flowering. Then when they are over the hop-bells take their place in interest, and later on the bright hips will contrast with the sprays of autumn-brown hops. The roses can be chosen to flower early before the vine really·gets going, or to flower later so that sprays of flowers grow through a curtain of leaves and juvenile hop-bells. It should be remembered that the hop will strangle the rose or roses unless governed firmly, and that the rose needs sun on its stems to ripen them. Plant them apart and feed the rose well. The hop needs no feeding but will probably steal as much of the rose's nourishment as it can get. I have *H. Lupulus* var. 'aureus' which encompasses a vigorous climbing modern rose called 'Morning Jewel'. The rose has excellent dark green shiny foliage, very different from the yellow foliage of the hop, and the clear pink flowers are lovely among all the yellow leaves. However, as no garden ever stays the same for long, I have moved the hop (which was at least seven years old and quite filled a wheelbarrow) to a new wall which I want it to swarm up and over and along. To keep it company I have planted the climbing rose 'Golden Showers' and the species rose 'Serascarpa' and I hope for a symphony of yellow and white in due course. Mature hops do not like being moved, they have very long, brown shreddy roots that hang on tightly, but the moving was done in March, during the last of the hop's dormant and resting period. Soon it will send up its twining stems and, suddenly, the new wall will be covered with a tracery of pleasingly shaped leaves in a delicious shade of lime-yellow — very cool against the new brick which will be fine in about eighty years or so. This climber is good on its own but is even finer when grown with large-flowered Clematis or late flowering honeysuckles such as *Lonicera belgica* or *L. halliana* (which it might help to keep down a bit) or up through summer-flowering Ceanothus (but keep an eye on this association).

Hops are used in the brewing of beer and are grown in great plantations for this purpose. Before this use for them was discovered, all kinds of wild plants were used such as Ground Ivy (called Ale-hoof in former times), Yarrow, Sage, Alecost (*Chrysanthemum balsamita*) and Bog Myrtle; and because country folk brewed their own beer there would have been many others. Hops are as English as the hedges that they live in, and their young shoots can be cooked as a vegetable which is not as tasty to eat as its cousin the Stinging Nettle. There is an annual-growing hop that is sold as such; this has pleasantly variegated leaves and will whizz up a trellis in no time. Mine, as expected, dwindled and vanished in late autumn but it may be that grown under glass or in warmer climes this plant might and should be a perennial. It did not appear to be *H. japonicus variegatus* which is green and gold and rampant; my seedling plants were green and white and grew so far and no further.

H. japonicus (1898) grows to 20ft + (6m +) with pleasing palmately-lobed but uncharacteristic green leaves and the usual dioecious green flower panicles in summer. Var. *lutescens* (1898) has bronze-gold leaves, *variegatus* has gold-spotted green leaves. A vigorous climber from Japan for walls, fences, old trees, ugly buildings, pergolas and floral arrangements.

H. Lupulus — Hop grows to 20ft + (6m +) with rougher typical leaves and graceful panicles of hop-bells in summer. Var. *aureus* (syn. *H. luteus*) has golden leaves that even on their own are very beautiful. A native and European climber, needing strong support, for similar situations. Best in sun where the variety's yellow variegated leaves are yellower.

Requirements: Any good free-draining garden soil, full sun and strong supports.

Propagation: Divide established clumps in late March or early April, or sow seed in spring in seed compost. Grow on in the usual way, prick out into individual pots with a cane to each. Plant out with little disturbance or grow on until large enough.

Uses: As graceful but vigorous clothing-climbers for almost any situation except real shade. Foliage and sprays of hop-bells for arrangements.

Shrubs: Beth Chatto, Hilliers, Kaye, Notcutts, Read, Roger, Shepton, Sherrard, Stonehouse, Toynbee, Weald.

HYDRANGEA *(Saxifragaceae) (Hydrangeaceae)*. There are many types and kinds of Hydrangea — named from *hydro*, water, *aggeion*, vessel, because of the cup-shaped fruit and not because the plant likes to grow beside water, though this it certainly does. This is a misconception because if ordinary *H. Hortensia* grows in damp places, or beside a waterfall (or, as I have observed, a choked gutter which has a similar cascading effect) the corymbs of flowers will grow as large as dinner-plates. But, as I was saying, this genus has flowers which last in interest and beauty from early summer until their desiccated remains are blown away by winter gales; in a sheltered place they may well last until the new leaves are apparent and should, indeed, be left on the plant.

Other species Hydrangeas that should be seen more often are *H. petiolaris* the self-clinging Hydrangea which climbs, as does Ivy, by means of aerial rootlets. It is quite happy on a north-facing wall but will flower better on one of a south or west-facing aspect. Its leaves have a rounded shape with toothed edges and are a pleasing acid green all summer, turning almost simultaneously to a good yellow in autumn. The white flowers are characteristically Hydrangea-like with large (sterile) flowers set round the edge of the corymb and small fertile ones in the centre. But be warned: *H. petiolaris* can and does grow to 60 or 70ft (18-21m). I have it on my studio in the garden, a puny building measuring some 16ftx10ft (4.8mx3m) and the Hydrangea is doing very handsomely on its north side. So far. I shall encourage it at each end but at that point I shall have to be firm unless I want to be squeezed to death (I have no room on the south side because of the greenhouse). But it is early days yet — the Hydrangea is only seven years old.

Another interesting species for large gardens (which

mine is not) is *H. quercifolia* — the Oak-leaved Hydrangea. This is a fine substantial shrub with handsome (*almost* oak-like) leaves that colour wonderfully in autumn. The flower panicles are pointed, like lilac (Syringa), and are large to match the bush — some 12″ (30cm) or so in an established plant. They are white to begin with, gradually turning purplish, and the fine red leaves and dark flowers are an arresting sight in autumn. I was so arrested when visiting a favourite nurseryman called Charlie Marchant, whose establishment is not far away from my garden. Walking down a wet path last autumn being dripped on by his wet laurels, I came out into sunlight and there was this magnificent spectacle — *H. quercifolia* in all its autumn glory. So I bought a little one and shall watch it grow.

H. paniculata could be mistaken for a small lilac except for the fact that the inflorescence is much bigger — up to 18″ (46cm) — in mature shrubs. This is another plant that can grow very large (30ft (9m) in its native China and Japan) but do not be afraid — it does not seem to want to try so hard in our climate. A most useful species to have in shady gardens is *H. Sargentiana* which actually quite likes shade. It is not an arresting sight when in full flower or autumn plumage, like *H. quercifolia*, but its shade toleration makes it a very useful shrub for larger gardens with too many trees. It is sometimes rather an ungainly shrub, but interesting because of its bristly-furry flower stems (see description for cultural note). A delicately pretty species is *H. arborescens* which, despite its name, does not try to emulate a tree. It is a graceful shrub with many white flowers on slender stems in late summer that appear to be heavy (but are not) because after rain the plant needs a gentle shake to release the water from the saturated flower heads which will then perk up once more. The foliage is light green and the shrub has an elegance not shared by the plump and rather matronly Hortensias. It is quite happy in semi-shade, and looks particularly nice against the darkness of evergreens or, as in my garden, against a fine brick wall.

I do not denigrate *H. Hortensia* (or *H. macrophylla*, or *H. opuloides* — depending on which catalogue you will read next); it is an excellent, reliable, pleasing, substantial and easy (though dull) shrub — there is little challenge and not much excitement about it, except during one week in autumn when the leaves turn to a pale yellow that is stained with violet — the colour of passion and love-letter ink. The blue flowers will have faded to turquoise tinged and changing to wine and crimson, indigo and prussian blue — and then it is an interesting plant and it is then that I painted it for the fun of it and to record its rainbow-range of subtleties. In addition to being (generally) dull it is infuriating — sometimes pink varieties turn blue and blue ones turn pink. In my garden I have a pink variety, which is fine, but further along there is a blue variety which is pink. On the other side of the garden, in totally unsuitable soil, there was a large and blousy shrub which had fine blue flowers. When moved because the shed fell down on top of it, it turned pink (this may have been from delayed shock, of course). I am fed up with *H. Hortensia,* as you can see. It is small consolation to know that in other gardens a Hydrangea may change from blue flowers to red in successive years, or the other way about. Hydrangeas were first introduced in 1736 by Peter Collinson, who discovered *H. arborescens.* (Later on, in 1860, *H.a.* 'grandiflora' was found in Pennsylvania; it is this particular variety which has large white flower heads that seem too heavy for the delicate, bending stems.) After this first discovery, many Hydrangeas were found in quick succession in North America and in the Far East. *H. Hortensia* was known to botanists under several names, such as *Sambucus aquatica, Viburnum macrophyllum,* and finally as *Hortensia opuloides.* Since none of these introductions produced fertile flowers and subsequent seeds the botanists could not place them in a genus of their own. Eventually, matters were sorted out in 1959 by a Mr. Haworth-Booth who made an exhaustive and comprehensive study of the genus, including the parentage of the many cultivars. This was essential because the different species (and varieties) have different requirements.

Before launching into the description of the various species, here is an interesting note: in Japan the leaves of *H. thunbergii* were dried and used to make a sacred infusion which was called Celestial Tea. This was used to bath all the statues and effigies of Buddha on his birthday — April 8th. And, lastly, Hydrangea should, I am told, be pronounced Hy-drain-gea. But old, bad habits die hard and it is a free world still in the garden.

H. arborescens (1736) grows to 4ft (1.2m) with rather flat corymbs of at first green then white flowers in July and August. A deciduous shrub from E. North America. Var. *H.a.* 'grandiflora' has larger flowers of a more rounded shape. Both do well in semi-shade.

H. macrophylla (syns. **H. Hortensia, H. opuloides**) — **Mophead Hydrangea** (1790) grows to 12ft (3.7m) and as much through, when contented. Rounded corymbs of (usually) sterile flowers — these are the large, showy ones — in all shades of pink, mauve and blue from July to September. 'Lacecaps' are a separate variety in which the small fertile florets are surrounded by a neat circle of the showy sterile flowers. The blue kinds can turn pink and vice versa but the white ones, depending on parentage, do not generally change colour. A deciduous shrub (species originally from Japan) for many garden situations in sun or semi-shade and by the seaside; it is a thirsty plant needing much watering in summer. Not always hardy in colder areas.

H. paniculata (1861) grows to 15ft (4.5m) by as much through, with pointed panicles of white aging to pink or purple flowers in August and September. A deciduous shrub from China and Japan for many garden situations in sun or semi-

shade. *H.p.* 'grandiflora' has much larger panicles (up to 18″ (46cm) long).

H. petiolaris — Climbing Hydrangea (1878) grows to 60ft + (18m +) with white corymbs of flowers in June. Pleasing bright, light green leaves with yellow autumn colour. A very vigorous self-clinging deciduous climber from Japan for high, north, or any sheltered walls or for tree-climbing. Can be grown as a bush in the open where it will flower well and not be uncontrollably rampant.

H. quercifolia — Oak-leaved Hydrangea (1803) grows to 6ft (1.8m) and as much through with handsome oak-shaped leaves (*H. platanifolia* has larger ones) that colour well in autumn. Panicles of white flowers in July, aging to purple. A substantial shrub for a focal garden position.

H. Sargentiana (1908) grows to 10ft (3m) and as much through with brown, bristly-stemmed corymbs of white flowers in July and August. A very large growing deciduous shrub from China needing an isolated position in sheltered woodland conditions to do well. If not too cramped by roots or the too-close presence of other shrubs or trees it makes a handsome plant. Tender when young. Because it likes shade it is often given a rather thankless position.

H. villosa (1908) grows to 9ft (2.7m) with delicate lace-cap-like corymbs of mauve or purplish flowers in August. A deciduous shrub from China, valuable for its late flowers and delightful when grown with small-flowered late Clematis.

Requirements: Generally all Hydrangeas do well in ordinary free-draining soil and a position in sun or semi-shade. They must all have plenty of water during the summer and their leaves will droop miserably as a reminder if you do not attend to this need. They should be planted in an initial compost of well decayed manure and peat or garden compost, bonemeal and peat. Do not site them facing east, as new growth can be damaged by late spring frosts. *H. petiolaris* will take several years to establish itself, during which time it should be mulched each April with well-decayed manure or garden compost. When planted as a wall or tree-climber in north-facing situations do not forget to water. *H. villosa* needs semi-shade with some sun. *H. Hortensia* likes constant moisture such as the side of a natural pond, water-course or ditch.

Blue varieties will (though not always) turn pink on alkaline soils. If blue colouration is to be retained they should be planted in a compost containing aluminium sulphate in the proportion of 2½lbs (1.15kg) of crystals to 1cwt (50.4kg) of soil or, for top-dressing, ¾oz (20g) for the surface of a 5″ (12.5cm) pot, 1½oz (40g) for a 6″ (15cm) pot. Existing plants should be dressed in November with from 1 to 2lbs (450-900g) per plant depending on size, up to 10lbs (4.5kg) for a large specimen. This must be done every year to keep the colour. Pink kinds should have an annual application of 2oz (50g) of ground limestone per square yard (0.84 sq.m).

Propagation: Hydrangeas are somewhat unkindly called the gardener's pet by Shirley Hibberd, because they are so easy to grow. For shrubby species and varieties take non-flowering cuttings in August or September and insert in a rooting medium of peat and sand in a propagator set at 13-16°C (55-61°F). They can be rooted in a closed cold frame but will take longer. When rooted pot on into John Innes No.2 and protect for the winter. To grow for containers pinch out growing tips after three pairs of leaves have been produced. For climbing species take short non-flowering lateral cuttings in June and July. When rooted grow on, plunge pots outside in a sheltered place until they can be planted in final positions.

Pruning: Leave flower heads on until March, then take off and at the same time cut away weak and winter damaged shoots (depending on seasonal temperature: do not do this in freezing weather). Cut back the flowering branches of *H. arborescens* by one-third and *H. paniculata* by one-half. Cut out three year-old flowered shoots of *H. Hortensia* at ground level.

Uses: As one of the most useful and long-lasting in flower of all garden shrubs; for pots, tubs and containers (water copiously for these); *H. Hortensia* for seaside gardens in full sun and, conversely, for shady and moist gardens. As spectacular wall covering. Summer flowers for short-lived arrangements. Immature flowers (best from white varieties) excellent for green arrangements. Dried flowers for winter decor. Shrub flowers when left on help to 'furnish' barren winter gardens.

Shrubs: Ballalheannagh, Barcock, Bees, Bodnant, Brackenwood, Busheyfields, Caldwell, Chappell, Crarae, Daisy Hill, Dobbies, Fairley's, Farall, Goatcher, Goscote, Great Dixter, Highfield, Hilliers, Hortico, Hyden, Jackman, Kaye, Kent, Kershaw, Knaphill, Knoll Gardens, Lime Cross, Marchant, Meare Close, Notcutts, Otter, Reuthe, Roger, Rosemoor, Russell, Scotts, Shepton, Sherrard, Smith, St. Bridget, Stonehouse, Toynbee, Treasure, Treseder, Warley, Woodland, Wyevale.

Seeds: Chiltern.

HYPERICUM — St. John's Wort, Tutsan, Rose of Sharon, Aaron's Beard *(Guttiferae)*.

The 'Rose of Sharon' or *Hypericum calycinum* has become debased and even scorned because of its wide, no-trouble use as ground cover in town planting. Its cheerful — and very beautiful — large yellow flowers are almost ignored in these circumstances because of its hapless juxtaposition with urban litter that is trapped by the strong, wiry stems of this useful and, I always feel, courageous plant. But visit a large country garden where it has been planted intelligently and rightly on a sunny drive-bank; there the flowers are many and bright, the leaves are healthy and the plant does a fine job — it is all a matter of care and maintenance, though this last is minimal. This particular species, because of its strong rhizomatous roots, is good for holding up banks and slopes where the soil is loose.

H. patulum is an old species which is seldom grown today, having been replaced by admittedly better and therefore younger cultivars.

The smaller and delightful *H. olympicum* is a good plant for a sunny corner or in a rockery because it has, so to speak, full-size Hypericum flowers on very small plants. It is tender and once established it should be left alone — it detests being moved and will usually die.

There are many legends about the wild Hypericum — *H. perforatum* — called so from the apparent prick-holes in the leaves, which are best seen when the leaf is held up to the light. The holes are said to have been made by the Devil who busily pricked them all over and through and through in an attempt to spoil their virtues and usefulness, because at one time the plant was used as a herb of healing and was always associated with protection against lightning, demons and all evil spirits. It is the wild plant that is called St. John's Wort, and this herb is one of several that were picked just before dawn (when the magic dew was still on them) on the 23rd June, which is St. John's Eve. The dew was potent in its efficacy, as was the smoke of the fires kindled on the evening of the 23rd. The herbs of St. John were 'smoked' to strengthen their virtues, after which they were either used medicinally or for magic or for protection. St. John's Eve was a time for somewhat fearful revelry — men and girls jumped across the fires for more powerful protection against evil in the year to come. In France, these beliefs were just as strong — live cats (the Devil's creatures) were burnt on the St. John's Eve fires in medieval times, and the plant bore the name of *chasse-diable;* in Latin it was called *fuga daemonum.*

H. Androsaemum — Tutsan (from the medieval *Tout-sain* or *Tota-Sana* because 'it helith all') (before 1600) grows to 3ft (90cm) with cymes of yellow flowers followed by red and black berries; flowers and berries appear together from midsummer onwards. A European deciduous shrub at one time much in use medicinally. Good in shade but better in sun. Colourful for poor corners, any soil.

H. calycinum — Rose of Sharon, Aaron's Beard (1676) grows only to 1ft (30cm) with fine large — 3¼" (8cm) — yellow flowers continuously from June to September. An excellent and vigorous stoloniferous semi-evergreen shrub for any garden position. Good in dry places under large trees but better out in the open. Needs a firm hand but you cannot have vigorous, enduring plants *and* beautiful flowers *and* mild manners.

H. elatum grows to 5ft (1.5m) with yellow flowers from July to October followed by crimson leaves and berries. A tender shrub from Madeira and the Canary Islands for a sheltered position. Red-stemmed berried branches good for arrangements.

H. x Moserianum (about 1887) grows to about 18" (46cm) with yellow flowers from July to October. A deciduous shrub for a sheltered sunny position. *H. x* 'tricolour' has leaves variegated in green, white and pink or red. For a sheltered hot spot.

H. patulum (1862) grows to 3ft (90cm) in the species with yellow flowers from July to October. An evergreen shrub from China and Japan. This is a tender plant that has been replaced by hardier kinds such as *H.p.* 'Forrestii' and *H.p.* 'Henryi' and the famous modern var. *H.p.* 'Hidcote'.

Requirements: Any well-drained garden soil; most species need full sun, *H. calycinum* does very well in shade (but plant a comparable group in a better, sunnier place and see the difference). Set out plants of *H. olympicum* in spring, protect those you have in winter — they are not truly hardy, but will not tolerate being lifted and 'framed' for the winter. Just keep taking replacement cuttings. Keep an eye on *H. calycinum* and restrain its impetuosity.

Propagation: For *H. olympicum* and other small species take short cuttings of softish basal growth in May or June and root in a compost of peat and sand in a cold frame. When rooted pot up individually in John Innes No.1 and grow on. Keep in a frost-free greenhouse or conservatory for the winter. Divide *H. calycinum* in winter. For taller species, take lateral heel cuttings in August or September and insert in a rooting compost of peat and sand. Treat as described for other species. *H. patulum* can be divided when well established.

Pruning: Be ruthless with *H. calycinum* and shear it over in March to within two or three inches (5-7.5cm) of the ground. Do this every three years or so. At other times give it a close clipping and spring-tidy in March. Prune *H. elatum* to within 6" (15cm) of the ground every second year. *H. patulum* and varieties may have many winter damaged shoots to cut away (do not do this before April). Prune to within two or three leaf buds of the old wood in mid-April.

Uses: As colourful (almost always golden yellow, though) mid to late summer flowering shrubs. Small species as rockery or raised bed shrubs. Not long-lasting as cut flowers, though berried branches of *H. elatum* good for arrangements.

Shrubs: Ballalheannagh, Barcock, Bees, Brackenwood, Bressingham, Caldwell, Peter Chappell, Beth Chatto, Daisy Hill, Dobbies, Jack Drake, Goatcher, Goscote, Great Dixter, Highfield, Hilliers, Hyden, Ingwersen, Jackman, Kershaw, Knaphill, Lime Cross, Marchant, Meare Close, Notcutts, Orchard, Otter, Potterton and Martin, Reuthe, Robinsons, Roger, Rosemoor, Russell, Scotts, Shepton, Sherrard, Smith, Southcombe, St. Bridget, Stonehouse, Toynbee, Treasure, Warley, Weald, Woodland, Wyevale.

Seeds: Butcher, Chiltern.

INDIGOFERA (*Leguminosae*). This is a large group of plants (some 700 species) though only a few are grown in gardens and of these *I. gerardiana* is the best known and most easily obtained. The shrubs have characteristic ferny foliage with racemes of 'pea-flowers' which spring from the leaf-axils successively throughout mid or late summer. *I. gerardiana* is a rather tender shrub, sensibly late coming into leaf and needing a sheltered position against a warm south-facing wall. Once established it puts down deep roots and will not tolerate being moved. It prefers hot-to-drought conditions and flowers much better; in cold, wet summers there will not be as many flowers, though the foliage has an elegance that always arouses interest. The name 'Indigofera' is from *Indigo*, the blue dye, and *fero*, to bear, because several of the species, particularly *I. tinctoria*, produce the dark-blue Indigo dye.

I. gerardiana syn. **I. heterantha** (1840) grows to 8ft (2.4m) with masses of delicate light green foliage and rose-purple flowers from June to September. A tender deciduous shrub from the Himalaya best grown against a wall except in Cornwall or Devon. (It is not deciduous in warmer countries and will grow much larger.)

I. Potaninii (1911) grows to 6ft (1.8m) with 5" (12.5cm) racemes of rose-pink flowers in June and July. A hardier and deciduous shrub from China for a sheltered position in full sun.

Requirements: Ordinary free-draining garden soil — not clay — and a sheltered, sunny position. Grow among herbaceous plants or other shrubs (best against a wall) so that its late leafing is not too apparent.

Propagation: Sow seed in spring in seed compost in a cold frame (soak seed overnight in warm water). When seeds germinate and are large enough, prick off into individual pots of John Innes No.1 and plunge in an open cold frame (cover if late frosts threaten, protect frame if winter is extra cold or bring seedlings in to a conservatory or warm greenhouse). Plant out in May. Protect young plants in following winter with heaped ashes and bracken or straw.

Pruning: Cut previous season's stems of *I. gerardiana* back to within 4" (10cm) of ground in April.

Cut back strong stems of other species by half in April and remove winter-damaged shoots.

Uses: As elegant though tender wall shrubs and as foliage plants.

Shrubs: Bodnant, Brackenwood, Goscote, Hilliers, Hyden, Jackman, Kaye, Marchant, Notcutts, Reuthe, Roger, Sherrard, Southcombe, St. Bridget, Stonehouse, Toynbee, Treasure, Woodland, W.W.

ITEA (*Saxifragaceae*). This genus takes it name from *Itea*, the Greek name for a willow.

I. ilicifolia is a handsome, though tender, evergreen shrub for a sheltered, sunny corner, best grown against a wall in colder gardens. When established it may attain a height of some 10ft (3m) with flat, Holly-shaped leaves (though without the solidity of Holly) and later on, when settled in and growing well, it will produce long — up to 14" (35cm) — racemes of scented green-white 'catkins' which are spectacular in a mature specimen. In America the deciduous *I. virginiana* is called 'Sweet-spires' because its scented panicles of flowers are erect (rather like those of Hebe).

I. ilicifolia (1895) grows to 8ft (2.4m) with long arching 6-14" (15-35cm) catkins of scented flowers in August, and flat dark green Holly-like leaves. An evergreen shrub from W. China for a sheltered corner in sun or partial shade.

I. virginiana, syn. **I. virginica** (1744) grows to 6ft (1.8m) with erect racemes of creamy, scented flowers in July. A deciduous shrub from the E. United States for a place in semi-shade.

Requirements: Any good garden soil for *I. ilicifolia* and a wall or sheltered position. Both species do better in partial shade and moist soil. *I. virginiana* likes it really damp.

Propagation: Take heel cuttings in July or August of both species and insert in a rooting compost of peat and sand in a propagator set at 13°C (55°F). When rooted pot into John Innes No.1 and plunge pots in a frame for the winter. Large clumps of *I. virginiana* can be divided in early spring.

Pruning: None needed for *I. ilicifolia;* take away some older flowered stems of *I. virginiana* which will send up new shoots from the ground.

Uses: *I. ilicifolia* as a very focal plant for a sheltered corner — foliage and flowers for arrangements.

Shrubs: Bodnant, Peter Chappell, Great Dixter, Hilliers, Hopleys, Knoll Gardens, Marchant, Marten's Hall, Notcutts, Otter, Reuthe, Rosemoor, Shepton, Sherrard, St. Bridget, Stonehouse, Treasure, Treseder, W.W., Wyevale.

JASMINUM — Jasmin, Jasmine, Jessamine, Jessamy

(Oleaceae). This is as much a flower of the Middle East and the Seraglio as it is of the English cottage garden. I am, of course, thinking of the deliciously perfumed summer-flowering shrub whose many white stars glow luminously in the dark. The scent is stronger at that time and the structure of the flower, with its deep carolla-tubeful of nectar, causes it to be visited by appreciative day-flying moths such as the rare Humming-Bird Hawk-moth, which I have seen hanging and vibrating in front of the curtain of white blossom that my old *Jasminum officinale* produces each year. Loudon said that 'Jasmine and potato are the food-plants of the larvae of . . . that very remarkable lepidopterous insect, the Death's-Head Hawk-moth'. It is very possible that this famous gardener had observed a Death's Head feeding on Jasmine flowers (which it is structurally quite able to do) and he was right about the potato, though wrong in stating that the larvae fed on Jasmine leaves. It has black berries in good, hot years, and Bean says '. . . Fruits not regularly or freely produced' so my old shrub which has been there for forty-odd years must be quite happy. I wish I could say that

it is in a good position, but it is not — it is rather crammed up against a T-shaped piece of wall near one of the single gates; one end of the plant gets reasonable (not good) sunlight, ventilation and rainfall, and that only in the last year or so since a boundary-wall was demolished. The other end of the shrub produces just as many flowers which are much enjoyed by the passers-by. Jasmine perfume is very old. Dioscorides knew of it and described the method by which 'oil of Jasme' was made. The Persians steeped the flowers in sesame-oil; florets were pressed into layers of fat, these were thrown away and replaced by fresh flowers each day until the fat had absorbed the perfume. (This process is called effleurage from the French *effleurer* — to touch lightly.) Today this is distilled, adding a refinement which the Greeks would have appreciated.

In the seventeenth century 'Jessamy gloves' were very fashionable, and the oil, or 'butter' to renew the scent could be bought at the glovers for a few pence. In earlier centuries poisoned gloves (favoured, I believe, by the Borgias) made deadly gifts; the wearer would absorb a slow-acting poison and die at a conveniently later time when remedy or antidote would have been too late.

The tender greenhouse species *J. polyanthum* will do on a sheltered warm wall in the south and south-west counties, but is liable to be badly cut back or killed by frosts. It is too vigorous a twiner for most greenhouses or small conservatories, but is an excellent plant for large ones, making dense shade in the roof under which many equally tender plants are content in the summer. The perfume given off by the large many-flowered panicles of white flowers (rose-tinged outside and pure white within) is powerfully sweet and the flowers come at a rather barren time of year from November to March or April (at least, they do so with me in my too-small warm greenhouse, in which I should never have planted the jasmine that I grew from a cutting taken at the wrong time of year). However, a Cymbidium lives under it and they flower together. The jasmine leaves that are close to the upper glass get badly browned in bad winters but these will protect those beneath and can easily be tidied away later. In any case this jasmine needs to be curtailed in its growth a bit, be it by the gardener's scissors or by the elements. The books say that this will grow to 20ft (6m). I am quite sure that it would be much larger in an ideal growing condition which is not Northern Europe.

Jasminum nudiflorum is the green-stemmed deciduous 'leaner' that begins to produce clear yellow flowers in November. In mild years the shrub will go on flowering until March which is a real joy throughout the dark days of winter. The stems of buds can be picked (just before a frost warning) and they will then open indoors. The rush-like branches are bright green during winter, making this plant seem as if only briefly sleeping.

J. revolutum should be more often grown, though it

shares the scandent habit of most jasmines which can be anathema to a too-tidy-minded gardener. It has scented yellow flowers in summer, thus combining the virtues of the scentless *J. nudiflorum* and the perfumed *J. officinale*.

J. humile — Italian Jasmine (1656) grows only to 4ft (1.2m) with yellow flowers in June and July. A semi-evergreen rather variable scandent shrub from South East Europe for a warm shrub border.

J. nudiflorum — Winter Jasmine (1844) grows to 12ft (3.7m) with yellow flowers from November to February. A deciduous hardy shrub for winter flowers, best in sun.

J. officinale — Common Jasmine grows to 40ft (12m) if trained, pruned and fed. A wall-leaner with deliciously scented white flowers (best in evening) from June to September. A deciduous shrub from China, north India and what was formerly Persia.

J. polyanthum (1891) a very vigorous twiner up to 20ft + (6m +) having heavily scented panicles of pink-flushed white flowers from November to April in a warm greenhouse or conservatory, and May until July or later outside, depending on situation and winter-damage.

Requirements: Jasmine will do in ordinary good well-drained garden soil. *J. nudiflorum* will flower better in full sun but is uncomplaining in partial shade or even on a north wall. The others need sun. *J. polyanthum*, because of its vigour, should be planted in the greenhouse border. It needs a minimum winter temperature of 5°C (41°F) though warmer will pursuade it into flower earlier, also everything else besides. It needs to be watered well while growing and flowering, with plenty of ventilation in the summer months. Provide strong wires or trellis, it is strong enough to lift the panes of glass.

Propagation: Take semi-ripe nodal cuttings (sever stem just below a node or joint) in August or September; insert in a rooting compost of peat and sand and put in a cold frame, except for *J. polyanthum* which should have heel cuttings taken at the same time and put into a propagator set at 16°C (61°F). When all are rooted pot into John Innes No.2. Protect hardier species in a frame for the winter. Or layer shoots into pots in September or October. Trailing shoots of *J. officinale* will root of their own accord at any time and can be discovered and potted up.

Pruning: *J. officinate* is a 'leaner' and is never tidy and this should be accepted. Take off winter-damaged shoots only and visualize the cascading summer foliage and flowers when tying in. Cut back flowered shoots of *J. nudiflorum* to within a few inches of the base. Take out older growth and tie in young shoots. This is another 'leaner' which will need unobtrusive but strong support. Thin out a little after flowering if necessary, but it is not the character of this shrub to be anything else but leafy and vigorous.

Prune *J. polyanthum* after flowering by taking out flowered shoots. If there is limited space (in the greenhouse

or conservatory) the jasmine can be cut back accordingly.

Uses: *J. nudiflorum* as excellent winter flowers — scented flowers of *J. polyanthum* also when grown in a warm greenhouse. *J. officinale* near a traditional arbour or summer seat, for its scent.

Shrubs: Ballalheannagh, Barcock, Bodnant, Brackenwood, Busheyfields, Peter Chappell, Fairley's, Goatcher, Goscote, Great Dixter, Highfield, Hilliers, Hopleys, Hortico, Hyden, Ingwersen, Jackman, Kaye, Kent, Kershaw, Knaphill, Knoll Gardens, Lime Cross, Marchant, Marten's Hall, Meare Close, Oak Cottage, Orchard, Otter, Read, Reuthe, Roger, Russell, Scotts, Shepton, Sherrards, Smith, St. Bridget, Stonehouse, Toynbee, Treasure, Treseder, Warley, Woodland, Wyevale.

Seeds: Chiltern.

KERRIA — Batchelor's Buttons, Jew's Mallow *(Rosaceae).* This cheerfully golden spring-flowering shrub is almost as ubiquitous as Forsythia or Chaenomeles, with which it is often grown. It is the double-flowered cultivar, *K. japonica* 'Pleniflora' or 'flore pleno' that is most often seen, with its bright yellow pom-poms that sometimes appear very early on the still winter-bare green stems that are so characteristic of this shrub. The flowers are completely different to those of the species plant, *K. japonica*, which has delicate buttercup-like single blossoms on slender twigs. Both types of Kerria have similar leaves that are dark green, toothed, deeply veined and neatly attractive. *K.j.* 'Pleni-flora' is taller and stouter with surprisingly bright green stems throughout the winter. An old bush left unthinned will become greedy of new ground and will spread into an untidy-looking thicket which is incapable of standing up without the support of a taller, stronger shrub like a Buddleia. I had just such an association, which was fine until the Buddleia died of old age, creating a very large disaster-area. The dead branches of the Buddleia became even more brittle than they normally are and ceased to serve any more as a support for the flopping, graceless tangle of the Kerria stems which, in desperation, had to be bound up with a spare length of linen-line until autumn came and, with it, decision time. The interwoven roots of Kerria and Buddleia were gradually removed by younger muscles than mine, and I still miss this very ordinary screen which once gave me such excellent privacy.

The species Kerria, on the other hand, never becomes a real nuisance because it does not grow as tall. It also blooms later, and the slender, flower-bedecked branches are a delight for many weeks.

The Kerria was named after the plant collector William Kerr (d.1814), who was sent to China to find new plants for Kew. The shrub is still (wrongly) called Jew's Mallow because the first introduced plants, being double-flowered, were difficult to identify and were thought to belong to the

Corchorus family; *C. olitorus* was called Jew's Mallow from 1640 onwards because this yellow-flowered shrub had leaves that were 'a favourite sallad with these people, and they boil them and eat them with their meat'. So the common name was assigned to the Kerria along with the wrong classification and, even when its family was correctly identified in 1817, the incorrect name of Jew's Mallow has persisted into the catalogues of today. The double-flowered variety was introduced into Britain before the species plant and perhaps this is why the double kind is the more often seen — it had a start of about thirty years. Certainly, both are equally hardy.

K. japonica (sometimes called 'simplex') (1834) grows to 6ft (1.8m) with single golden-yellow flowers in April and May. An elegant deciduous shrub from China and Japan for a focal place in full sun. *K.j.* 'Pleniflora' or 'flore pleno' (1804) grows to 12ft (3.7m) with thicker green stems and very double golden-yellow flowers which sometimes begin to open from February onwards in mild seasons. A spreading rather floppy plant for a large shrub border.

Requirements: Sun, any soil. Some kind of supporting companion shrub for *K.j.* 'Pleniflora'.

Propagation: Take short lateral cuttings in August or September and insert into a rooting compost of equal parts peat and sand. Keep in a cold frame through the winter. Large shrubs will never miss a good-sized wedge of rooted stems, smaller shrubs can be lifted and divided any time during the dormant period.

Pruning: Kerrias can be allowed to grow as they will or the flowered shoots can be cut back. *K.j.* 'Pleniflora' can be encouraged to stand up for itself by purposeful thinning.

Uses: Green stems of *K.j.* 'Pleniflora' very attractive and vital in mid-winter; flowers of both good for arrangements.

Shrubs: Bees, Brackenwood, Busheyfields, Daisy Hill, Dobbies, Fairley's, Goatcher, Goscote, Great Dixter, Highfield, Hilliers, Hortico, Jackman, Kaye, Kent, Kershaw, Knaphill, Knoll Gardens, Lime Cross, Marchant, Meare Close, Notcutts, Oak Cottage, Orchard, Otter, Reuthe, Roger, Russell, Scotts, Shepton, Sherrard, Smith, St. Bridget, Stonehouse, Toynbee, Treasure, Warley, Woodland, Wyevale.

Seeds: Chiltern.

KOLKWITZIA — Beauty Bush *(Caprifoliaceae)*.

There is only one species of Kolkwitzia, which is very rare in the wild. Fortunately it grows well from seed and cuttings strike easily, otherwise our gardens might not know this easy-to-grow and very floriferous summer shrub. The Kolkwitzia was unattractively named after R. Kolkwitz, a German professor of botany. The bushes look well when grown in isolation on a lawn or grassy bank, or against a dark hedge where their flower-laden branches will show to better advantage than in a mixed shrub border.

K. amabilis — Beauty Bush (1901) grows to 6ft (1.8m) with a sideways spread of from 5-10ft (1.5-3m) and pink, bell-shaped flowers in May and June. A deciduous shrub from China for a good position in the garden. Older bushes flower better.

Requirements: Ordinary soil, full sun and winter protection in cold areas.

Propagation: Take non-flowering cuttings in the usual way in July and August and grow on in a cold frame for the winter. Or sow ripe seeds in September and in spring if a quantity of plants are needed.

Pruning: Kolkwitzias do not really need pruning but some of the older branches can be cut away after flowering to promote healthy new growth. Tidy winter-damaged shoots away in spring.

Uses: Excellent for cut flowers.

Shrubs: Barcock, Bees, Brackenwood, Caldwell, Daisy Hill, Dobbies, Farall, Goatcher, Goscote, Highfield, Hilliers, Hyden, Jackman, Kaye, Lime Cross, Marchant, Meare Close, Notcutts, Otter, Reuthe, Roger, Russell, Scotts, Shepton, Sherrard, Smith, St. Bridget, Stonehouse, Toynbee, Treasure, Treseder, Warley, Woodlands, W.W., Wyevale.

Seeds: Chiltern, Thompson and Morgan.

LAGERSTROEMERIA — Crape or Crêpe Myrtle, Pride of India *(Lythraceae)*.

The Crape Myrtle, *L. indica*, is not often seen in the British Isles; this is surprising because it grows and flowers as far north as Washington in the United States. Of course, Washington has hotter summers which ripen the wood well, so enabling the shrub (which can grow into a small tree) to withstand the long, cold winters. The flowers are well named, having frilly edges just like those that we once made of crêpe paper. In sub-tropical climes the shrubs should be cut back almost to the main trunk in winter. In more temperate areas they will not grow so large but will colour well in autumn. Curiously, one can get seeds and the plants produced can be grown as annuals, flowering in their first season, and they can then be treated as tub or pot-plants until they grow too large. Truly a versatile species.

Lagerstroemeria was named after Magnus Lagerstroem (1691-1759), who was a friend of Linnaeus, and the plant was introduced to American gardeners by André Michaux sometime after the year 1789, when this assiduous but impoverished plant-hunter was attempting to start a nursery of his own in order to make ends meet. The seeds of *L. indica* came from China along with the fabled Gingko and the beautiful *Albizzia julibrissin*. It is interesting to note that the plant hunters of former times were almost invariably destitute, often hungry, ill, injured or utterly exhausted. They were seldom adequately paid for their privations and feats of endurance, and often died, thousands of miles from their families, in desperate circumstances.

L. indica — Crape or **Crêpe Myrtle** (1759) grows to 30ft (9m) though usually treated as a shrub. A deciduous plant from China for the extreme south west of the British Isles or for the greenhouse.

Requirements: Sub-tropical conditions or a warm greenhouse. Ordinary, good garden soil.

Propagation: Take unflowered cuttings in August or September and place in a rooting compost of peat and sand and grow on in the usual way. Or sow seed in February in a temperature of 21°C (70°F). (These seeds are generally of a modern dwarf variety bred for bedding out.)

Pruning: Lagerstroemerias flower on new season's growth and so can be pruned hard back each winter when grown in a greenhouse or conservatory.

Uses: As unusual (in the UK) flowering shrubs for a large, heated greenhouse.

Shrubs: Hilliers, Treseder.

Seeds: Chiltern, Suttons, Thompson and Morgan.

LANTANA *(Verbenaceae)*. Lantana is the old name for Viburnum and this most attractive plant when grown in the British Isles is admired for its good foliage and brightly coloured posy-flowers. But say 'Lantana' to an Australian* whose home is in the bush and watch him react: the word seems to have the same bad connotations as Ground Elder has with the average British gardener. *L. camara* is the villain here; it seeds itself most effectively, though only in tropical countries, and its spiny stems make it a painful plant to contend with and to walk through. What an incongruity this is — my youngest son lives in a hilly area in New South Wales. Before he could begin to build his house he had to clear the land of Lantana with a machete. However, this is an unlikely event for the British gardener, because in these islands Lantana is grown as a cheerful though tender bedding out plant or as a conservatory shrub — what a difference latitude makes to the size, strength and even general spitefulness of some plants.

L. camara (1692) grows to 10ft (3m) (in the tropics) with rounded heads of pink or yellow flowers that change to orange and red. A tropical evergreen shrub from Jamaica, for bedding and as a rather special border or tub plant and as a conservatory shrub. Regarded as a pernicious weed in other parts of the world.

Requirements: Good soil, full sun and a sheltered situation when grown outside; when planted in tubs, pots and troughs, soil should be enriched for better flowers: use a compost of two parts loam to one of leaf-mould and one of well-rotted manure, or John Innes No.3. Lantanas need a minimum temperature of 7°C (45°F) in northern latitudes, which should be increased to 10-13°C (50-55°F) to start them into growth in the spring. They need good sunlight, and if grown under glass they should have ventilation,

damped-down floors, as for orchids, and regular fortnightly feeds.

Propagation: Take cuttings of unflowered shoots in August or September and insert in a rooting compost of peat and sand in a propagator set at 16-18°C (61-64°F). When rooted transfer to individual pots of John Innes No.1 and grow on for the winter. Re-pot into John Innes No.2 in spring. Nip off leading shoots in spring to promote bushy plants. Or sow seeds in February in a temperature of 16°C (61°F) in a good seed compost (soak for a day in warm water before sowing) Grow on in the usual way. These plants may be planted out in late June but must be brought back under glass in mid-September.

Pruning: Lantanas grow very vigorously and can be pruned according to the requirement and situation. Greenhouse shrubs flower better when kept cut back. Standards may be trained and can be kept in flower for six months with a judicious balance of warmth, light, humidity, ventilation, feeding and nipping off too-exuberant new growths. Hedges are attractive (and thorny) in warmer Mediterranean areas, where the plant is much used for edging. Pruning should be done in February in northern latitudes.

Uses: As interesting and very attractive pot, tub and trough plants and shrubs for warm greenhouse or conservatory and for planting or standing out in summer. For arrangements, though scent is not pleasant and stems are thorny.

Seeds: Chiltern, Thompson and Morgan.

LAPÁGERIA — Chilean Bell Flower, Copihue *(Liliaceae)*. This lovely climber was named after the Empress Josephine, whose maiden name was Tascher de la Pagerie. If one has a large enough conservatory or greenhouse there is one plant that should be grown and that is Lapageria. It has but one species — *L. rosea,* with beautiful dangling pink bells of flowers that have an almost edible deliciousness. There is an equally lovely white variety and the two should be grown together. The flowers are exquisite and when they bloom the contemplation of their form and beauty compensates for many of the petty irritations of life.

The plant was first discovered in Chile by William Lobb (commemorated by the moss rose that bears his name) some time between the years 1845 and 1848, though the Royal Horticultural Society's Dictionary of Gardening (2nd Edn.) gives the date as 1897. Somehow this does not matter to the dedicated gardener, what matters is that this beautiful plant (like a beautiful woman) is very precise as to her requirements.

L. rosea — Chilean Bell Flower (1847) grows to 15ft (4.5m) with 3″ (7.5cm) long waxy, crimson-pink bell-shaped flowers from July to October. 'Albiflora' has white flowers. An evergreen climber or twiner from Chile for a large warm greenhouse or conservatory or against a warm wall in the southern counties. (It is listed by Bean as being hardy in the

In Queensland, New South Wales and Victoria.

British Isles.)

Requirements: Acid to neutral well-drained soil with plenty of humus such as leaf-mould. When grown under glass a compost of one part loam to three parts fibrous peat, with plenty of sharp sand and some crushed charcoal. The foliage on its own is attractive but not remarkable, and everything should be done to encourage the plant to flower.

Some shade in the middle of the day, strong supports for the shoots to twine round. Plenty of water during the growing season, syringing or humidity if grown under glass. Protection from slugs, greenfly, mealy bug, thrips and scale insects to which the shoots are as caviar. Winter protection of straw or bracken if grown outside. A minimum winter temperature of 7°C (45°F) is needed when grown under glass, and shade above the Lapageria, such as a taller growing climber like *Jasminum polyanthum*, *Cobaea*, *Ipomoea learii*, etc.

Propagation: Sow seeds as fresh as can be got in March or April in seed compost at a temperature of 16-19°C (61-66°F). It is also recommended by one seed merchant that a germinating temperature of 21-24°C (70-75°F) be maintained, so try two separate batches, though this should be done simultaneously so as not to miss the season. Soak seeds for three days before sowing, changing water several times a day (and during the night if you should happen to be awake). Germination may take from one to three months. Do not allow compost to dry out and do not soak it unduly. Remove forming algae or moss, spray with a fungicide. When seeds have germinated, grow on in the usual way and transfer them into a lime-free compost and shade them during the summer. Stop the young plants when they are growing well to encourage branching. Or take cuttings of side shoots in August and insert in a rooting compost of peat and sand. Put into a propagator set at 16-18°C (61-64°F) and when they have rooted grow on and pot into a lime-free compost with extra nourishment. Or layer pegged-down shoots which can be detached after a year. When Lapagerias are grown under glass their root run should be somewhat restricted by a brick or slate wall otherwise shoots will begin to appear all along the bed.

Pruning: Thin out weakly growth after flowering.

Uses: You do not 'use' such a plant — you gaze at its pendulous blooms and are grateful.

Shrubs: Ballalheannagh, Hilliers, Marchant, Meare Close, St. Bridget.

Seeds: Chiltern, Thompson and Morgan.

LAVANDULA — Lavender *(Labiatae)*. The name 'Lavender' evokes a sunlit herb garden and low hedges a-hum with bees. This is a plant long in cultivation for its scented oil and the species plants grow wild in Mediterranean countries. Lavenders were once separated into *L. vera* which was grown for the excellence of its oil and *L. spica* which yields

more oil though of lesser quality. Nowadays a form of the plant called Dutch Lavender is grown, which is considered to combine the virtues of *L. vera* and *L. spica*, though the intricacies of botanical nomenclature are very complex for any but the true botanist. It is thought that the term 'Dutch' was used in a rather derogatory sense to denote oil of an inferior quality or a tendency to flower too late in the season. Lavender was once called 'Nardus' by the Greeks because it was grown near the Syrian city of Naada; many people called the plant 'Nard' at that time, and it is probably the origin of the Biblical Spikenard. However, Nard (or lavender) was called 'Asarum' by the Romans, who never used it in their garlands because they thought that the plant was often the home of the small but deadly asp.

L. stoechas, the French lavender, is a tender species from the Mediterranean and more particularly from the island of Hyères which the Romans called 'Stoechades' because of the plant, which was gathered and dried to be used as a perfume for the bath; the plant's Latin name is derived from Lava or *Lavare* — to wash.

The essential oil for which the plant is so famous is found mainly in the calyces, though the whole shrub is similarly perfumed to a lesser degree.

L. spica syn. **L. officinalis — Lavender** (1568) grows to 4ft (1.2m) and as much through with grey-blue 'lavender'-coloured flower spikes from July to September. An ever-grey shrub for a sheltered sunny position. (There is a white variety *L.s.* 'Alba'.)

L. Stoechas — French Lavender grows to 2ft (60cm) with strikingly different looking flower spikes with purple tufts or bracts at the top, from May to July. A more tender shrub from the south west Mediterranean for a sunny corner, or against a warm wall. There is a white variety *L.s.* 'Albiflora'.

Requirements: All lavenders need an open free-draining soil and a sheltered place in full sun. All are rather tender and a hard, wet winter will usually kill some of them. Rich soil does not suit lavenders, they will be greener-leaved in such conditions with less volatile oil. Remember the growing conditions of the lavender in its wild habitat — bare stony soil and full sun — and do not try to cosset it. Conversely, too hot a situation in tropical climates will rob the plant of its fragrance.

Propagation: Take heel cuttings at any time of the year from June until September and insert in a sandy compost in a cold frame and grow on, or larger cuttings — 6″ (15cm) — may be inserted in a prepared sandy bed out of doors in September. Place cloches over these if worse winter weather than usual is forecast.

Pruning: Clip hedges to a neat shape after flowering and again in spring. Do not cut right back to the woody main stem once the plants have become top heavy and leggy, discard them, they will never really recover the trim neatness of their youth. Pets and small children make short-cuts through establishing hedges and these routes will become wider with time and such use. Decide which is the more important — the hedge, the hound or the heir and act accordingly. Single bushes grown as 'full-stops' at the ends of beds or as foliage contrast shrubs can be allowed to loosen their corsets with age, but even these will eventually have to be replaced. Buy compact bushy shrubs at this time — the difference between a 5ft (1.5m) wide hummock and a 10″ (25.5cm) twig is too much of a visual shock, though the newly-gained space will be marvellous for fresh plants. For a while.

Uses: Too numerous and well-known to enumerate here in full. Pick lavender stalks *before* the flowers are fully open to obtain the maximum fragrance. Hang up the bunches of flower stems to dry in a cool, airy place, not in sun. Mature bushes are excellent as grey-blue foliage plants throughout the year, dwarf types are very pleasing for similar furnishing in the rockery.

Shrubs: Barcock, Dobbies, Margery Fish, Goscote, Hilliers, Hopleys, Ingwersen, Jackman, Knaphill, Lime Cross, Meare Close, Notcutts, Oak Cottage, Old Rectory, Orchard, Otter, Parkinsons, Rampart, Reuthe, Roger, Russell, Scotts, Shepton, Sherrard, Smith, St. Bridget, Stoke Lacy, Stonehouse, Toynbee, Treasure, Warley, Weald, Woodland, Wyevale.

Seeds: Chiltern, Suttons, Thompson and Morgan, Unwin.

LEPTOSPERMUM (*Myrtaceae*). Leptospermums are almost always tender, but can be carefully sited so as to survive all but the most dreadful winters. They are very beautiful when in flower with their delicate small-leaved branches so crowded with tiny blossom that they are well worth the extra care. Never plant them facing east, and do not get to love them too much. It is said that Captain Cook (who was of an experimental turn of mind when it came to comestibles) brewed what he described as 'tea' from the small leaves of this shrub, and ever since the species *L. scoparium* has been called 'Tea-tree'.

L. humifusum syn. **L. scoparium prostratum** grows to 9″ (23cm) high with a prostrate speading habit of about 3ft (90cm) and with white flowers in May and June. The hardiest of the Leptospermums. An evergreen shrub from Tasmania for a sheltered sunny position, best sprawling over rock work. Good for sea-coast gardens.

L. scoparium — Tea-tree (1772) grows to 10ft (3m) and more against a wall in a sheltered corner. White flowers in the species in May and June. An evergreen shrub from New Zealand. Many modern varieties have red, pink or crimson single or double flowers.

Requirements: Sunny sheltered corners, light soil and the gardener's fatalistic acceptance of winter mortality.

Propagation: Take short heel cuttings in June or July and insert them in a rooting compost of peat and sand. Put pots in a propagator set at 16°C (61°F) until rooted, then transfer into individual pots of John Innes No.1. Keep in a frost-free conservatory or greenhouse for the first winter.

Pruning: None needed except to tidy away winter-killed shoots in spring.

Uses: Branches of flowers very beautiful in arrangements. Foliage of grey-leaved types most attractive against brick walls and in small arrangements.

Shrubs: Ballalheannagh, Bodnant, Hilliers, Hyden, Jackman, Kaye, Knoll Gardens, Marchant, Meare Close, Notcutts, Otter, Potterton and Martin, Russell, Scotts, Sherrard, Southcombe, St. Bridget, Stonehouse, Toynbee, Treseder.

Seeds: Chiltern, Thompson and Morgan.

LEYCESTERIA — **Himalayan Honeysuckle, Flowering Nutmeg, Elisha's Tears, Lace Hysteria** (*Caprifoliaceae*). This handsome shrub with its tassels of crimson and white 'flowers' is very easy to grow in most parts of the British Isles. It is, like so many accommodating plants, so good-natured as to be often abused and is planted in odd corners or squeezed up between two other shrubs in a space that was perfectly adequate when all were small but which now is not. (Such is the case with my own shrub and I find myself apologising to it as I clear away the Ground Elder from between its toes. However, its situation on one side is a good one, as it is planted in a raised position so that one can look up into its interesting dangling inflorescence.) A young Leycesteria is a nice thing to give new gardeners with new gardens, because it is unfussy and enduring by nature and begins producing its flowers early on.

The plant's proper name honours William Leycester, a Chief Justice in Bengal in the early nineteenth century, who was a zealous gardener and collector in Hindustan. 'Elisha's Tears' is a corruption of Leycesteria, and I know of several people who refer to their shrubs as 'Lace Hysteria' which is much easier to remember though not as apposite.

The shrub has pointed, blue-green stems which make it look rather like a leafless Bamboo in winter. The purplish fruits are enjoyed by birds, and the shrub has been planted as an exotic addition in game-coverts because pheasants like the berries.

L. formosa — (1824) grows to 8ft (2.4m) with long — 4″ (10cm) — racemes of white flowers and crimson bracts from July to September. A deciduous shrub from the Himalaya for a good garden position in full sun, best when at a higher than eye level, and very good in coastal gardens.

Requirements: Full sun (they will grow quite well in partial shade but will not flower as profusely); any ordinary garden soil and some winter protection.

Propagation: Take woody cuttings in October and line them out in a prepared nursery bed. Or sow seeds in spring in the usual way if a quantity of shrubs is required.

Pruning: Take off the old flowers shoots at ground level in

March.

Uses: A pleasing shrub for raised positions, branches of flowers and bracts, or purplish-black berries and bracts for arrangements.

Shrubs: Bees, Bodnant, Brackenwood, Bressingham, Caldwell, Dobbies, Hillier, Jackman, Kaye, Knaphill, Knoll Gardens, Lime Cross, Marchant, Notcutts, Otter, Roger, Russell, Scotts, Shepton, Sherrard, Southcombe, St. Bridget, Toynbee, Treasure, Wyevale.

Seeds: Chiltern, Thompson and Morgan.

LIGUSTRUM — Privet *(Oleaceae).* Privet is almost too easy to grow and can be clipped into submissiveness but it is inclined to escape at the first opportunity, as well as possessing greedy roots that extract all nourishment from the ground on both sides of any hedge. It is, of course, always associated with hedges, though there are other species that are sometimes seen as specimen shrubs. The Victorians loved privet for its tractability and because labour was cheap, privet hedges abounded. But given the choice between a hedge of 'Leylandii' and one of privet, I would choose the latter (I have the former) because a privet hedge can only grow to a maximum height of about 15ft (4.5m) whereas *Cupressus x chamaecyparis* 'Leylandii' can rocket up to 50ft (15m) in almost as many years. Left unchecked, of course; I am therefore frightened of my 'Leylandii' hedge and I think it knows it.

Privet has been esteemed for centuries as a hedging plant and in 1629 Parkinson said that it was used for hedging and for arbours 'whereunto it is so apt, that no other can be like unto it, to bee cut, lead, and drawne into what forme one will, either of beasts, birds or men armed, or otherwise; I could not forget it, although it be so well knowne unto all'.

Privet will stand being clipped twice a year, with tidyups in between for special occasions, but it is pretty when in flower in July, especially if a perpetual-flowering pink rose can be persuaded to grow beside, along, near or through it. The rose will need much extra feeding, and this association should be planned so that a 2ft (60cm) square pit can be dug for the rose, with slate, brick or slabs of paving cemented in place to form a receptacle for some good loam, compost and well-rotted manure. The greedy privet roots will try to get at this richness, so the cementing should be thorough on three sides of the pit. The old-fashioned rose 'Dorothy Perkins' flowers late and the two together are charming.

The native privet, *L. vulgare,* grows as a wild plant throughout Europe. It is not an exciting shrub, nor very floriferous and has long been superseded by *L. ovalifolium* which has more substance and larger flowers followed by (poisonous) black berries. The golden privet so much beloved by flower-arrangers is *L. ovalifolium var.* 'aureum' or *L.o.* 'aureo-marginatum' which retains its yellow colouration well, though it will grow green if planted in shade.

The flowers have a strong scent if one is being kind and an unpleasant rather fishy smell if one is not. Bees love it, but bee-keepers try to site their hives well away from known flowering hedges because privet-nectar taints and discolours the honey. When first sniffed, privet flowers smell sweetish but the presence of trimethylamine gives them an ammonia undertone that makes one think of doubtful fish. There are several other privet-species that are both easy to obtain and to grow, and these have flowers resembling lilac *(syringa)* in form and size, thus making a useful contribution to the late-summer garden.

L. japonicum — Japanese Privet (1845) grows to 20ft (6m) with large — up to 8″ (20cm) — panicles of white flowers from July to September. A slow-growing evergreen shrub from Japan, Korea and for a good position where its large, shining leaves can be appreciated. Not for hedges.

L. ovalifolium — Oval-leaved Privet (1842) grows to 15ft (4.5m) with 4″ (10cm) panicles of white strong-smelling flowers in July, followed by black berries. A semi-evergreen that will grow in very poor corners or under trees; most useful for this purpose.

L. Quihoui (1862) grows to 12ft (3.7m) with 8″ (20cm) long panicles of whiter white flowers than most of the other privets, in September, followed by purplish berries. A deciduous shrub of some elegance for a sunny position.

L. sinense — Chinese Privet (1852) grows to 20ft (6m) with 4″ (10cm) panicles of good white flowers in July. A deciduous shrub from China for a 'specimen' position in sun. A very floriferous shrub with winter interest, the purple-black berries remaining until spring.

L. vulgare — Common Privet. Grows to 10ft (3m) with strong-smelling creamy flowers in June and July. A native evergreen that does well on chalk.

Requirements: Any good garden soil and best in a sunny position, particularly *L. japonicum, L. Quihoui* and *L. sinense.* Soil should be prepared for hedging by adding well-rotted manure or a general fertiliser before planting.

Propagation: Take woody cuttings of *L. japonicum* in September and insert in a rooting compost of peat and sand and place in a cold frame. Plant out in a sheltered nursery bed in late spring and grow on until the following spring. For hedge plants, take woody cuttings of *L. ovalifolium* in October and plant in a nursery row in ordinary garden soil in a sheltered position. Grow on until the following winter, when the cuttings can be planted in their final places. For hedging, take bushy plants and set them in a staggered double row 12-18″ (30-46cm) apart. Cut back to one half of their height in April to promote strong lower growth. Do not be in a hurry for height, this will happen all too soon.

Pruning: Clip hedges twice annually, in May and September and slope the hedge so that it is narrower at the top than at the bottom, to enable rain, sun and wind to get to the lower branches. Be strong-minded and prevent your hedge from swallowing up the border, which it will the minute your back is turned. The best thing to do is to route a path beside it — this way you will notice when you cannot get through. No pruning is necessary for the more ornamental species, except to trim away winter-damaged shoots.

Uses: *L. ovalifolium* and *L.o.* 'aureum' for hedges. The latter is more slow-growing, and can be used in town window-boxes and tubs for some years. Feed annually. Excellent as background foliage for contrast and for arrangements. For topiary. The other species as specimen shrubs, though flowers best not picked except for *L. Quihoui* which are pleasantly fragrant. Black berries interesting in arrangements, especially in association with the white ones of *Symphoricarpos*.

Note: Berries are poisonous.

Shrubs: Barcock, Brackenwood, Daisy Hill, Dobbies, Margery Fish, Goscote, Hilliers, Hopleys, Hortico, Jackman, Kent, Knaphill, Knoll Gardens, Marchant, Marten's Hall, Notcutts, Oak Cottage, Otter, Roger, Russell, Scotts, Sherrard, Smith, Southcombe, St. Bridget, Toynbee, Treasure, Treseder, W.W., Wyevale.

Seeds: Chiltern.

LIPPIA — Lemon Verbena, Sweet-scented Verbena, Lemon-scented Verbena, Aloysia, Herb Louisa

(Verbenaceae). An unexciting plant to look at, with its small, neat leaves and its small, neat panicles of tiny pale mauve flowers. But this is one of the most deliciously scented of all the foliage plants and for this reason it has been cherished for centuries. It was grown by cottagers outside their front doors as one of a pair of scented-leaved plants, the other being rosemary, southernwood or myrtle. The shrub (in its native Chile it grows into a small tree) was named after August Lippi, an Italian botanist who was born in Paris in 1678. It is not hardy in the British Isles, except in Cornwall, where I first encountered it as a fine large bush outside the sunny front door of the retired petty officer who taught me to row and to sail. He was a fascinating man who had a small fleet of boats collected from all over the world whose only thing in common was that they were all painted red. He also had a cat called Lobengula who used to come fishing with us on one of the boats; she regularly swam ashore on our return if we took too long clearing up on the mooring. I called my teacher Uncle Bill, and remember him for his kindliness, his patience, his bush of lemon verbena and because he always had to hatch out his duck eggs himself (carefully placing them all round his waist inside his shirt). Their mother was not particularly conscientious and could not be relied upon to stay on the nest. One year he got fed up with having to walk around with all those eggs, so he borrowed a broody hen who finished off the job of hatching the eggs most satisfactorily. The ducklings thought they were chickens for a few days and did not attempt to swim in

the creek nearby, but instinct prevailed in the end and I shall always remember the sight of that frantic hen, flapping and squawking and ankle deep in the incoming tide, trying to call in her brood who were bobbing happily about just out of reach of her beak.

The Lippia was first discovered in the 18th century by a French botanist, and from South America it was sent to Spain where it became very popular. For years it was called *Aloysia citriodora* to honour Luis Antonio de Bourbon, Prince of Asturias and brother to Carlos III of Spain. (Aloys is the Provencal form of the name 'Luis' and 'Aloisio' is the Spanish.) In those days titles were often bestowed at a very early age so as to keep things tidy, and Prince Luis was made Archbishop of Toledo when he was only eight. Lippia (or Aloysia) was grown all over Spain, being also called *Yerba Luisa,* and it soon found its way to England where it was much grown by market gardeners for 'bouquet-work' from 1784 onwards.

L. citriodora syns. **Aloysia citriodora, Verbena triphylla** grows to about 5ft (1.5m) high in the British Isles with a spread of 4ft (1.2m). Panicles of tiny lilac flowers from August until October. Leaves deliciously lemon-scented. A tender deciduous shrub from Chile for a warm place against a wall in the south-west of England or in a large pot that can be stood out in the summer months and kept in a frost-free greenhouse during the winter.

Requirements: Full sun and a sheltered site, or a large pot that can be taken into a frost-free greenhouse for the winter and stood out in the summer. Any well-drained soil. If grown in pots use John Innes No.2 as the potting medium. Protect shrubs outside in winter.

Propagation: Take short lateral cuttings and insert in a rooting compost of peat and sand in July, and put in a propagator set at 16-18°C (61-64°F). When the cuttings have rooted, transfer to John Innes No.1 and protect as described for first winter.

Pruning: Cut back pot-growing shrubs by half in April to keep them bushy. Take off winter-killed branches in April, if plant appears dead do not despair, it may spring up from the roots in early summer. Always keep a cutting in a warm place as insurance.

Uses: As a fragrant-leaved shrub for herb gardens; foliage for pot-pourri (gather at flowering time — scent will remain for years if leaves are dried carefully); in herbal medicine for dyspepsia, indigestion and flatulence.

Shrubs: Bodnant, Brackenwood, Great Dixter, Hillier, Hopleys, Marchant, Meare Close, Notcutts, Oak Cottage, Old Rectory, Roger, Rosemoor, Shepton, Sherrard, St. Bridget, Stonehouse, Toynbee, Treseder, Wyevale.

LITHOSPERMUM *(Boraginaceae)*. This is quite a large genus

but only one kind is generally grown. The most popular kind is the mat-forming, lime-hating *L. diffusum* which has gentian-blue flowers that can form a startling carpet of brilliant colour (in the right conditions) which will stop the beholder in his tracks. Alas, I cannot grow it well, it prefers really acid soil and so I go and admire it in friends' gardens up the hill from me where Foxgloves, Camellias and Rhododendrons all flourish. The other types are lime-tolerant but are taller-growing and very tender and therefore more suited to an alpine house, except in Cornwall.

L. diffusum syn. **L. prostratum** (1825) grows only 6" (15cm) but may form mats about 2ft (61cm) across. Brilliant blue flowers from June to October. An evergreen sub-shrub from the Mediterranean area for sunny places, not on chalk or limestone. The named varieties are 'Heavenly Blue' which lives up to its name and which spreads rapidly, and the neater-growing 'Grace Ward' (1930s) which has larger, slightly paler flowers. 'Album' has white flowers and is for those who collect albinos of everything. The blue-flowered kinds look beautiful with some dwarf heaths.

Requirements: A sandy-peaty or acid soil with leaf-mould, very well-drained — Lithospermums do not care for boggy conditions. A position in full sun or a bank or in a rock garden (not any kind of limestone rocks).

Propagation: Take heel cuttings in July or early August and insert in a rooting compost of peat and sand and place in a shaded cold frame. Water well until rooted and then pot on into John Innes No.1. Protect in frame for the first winter.

Uses: As beautiful late-summer flowering, carpeting plants among heaths and heathers and planted to clothe sunny banks.

Shrubs: Bodnant, Farall, Hilliers, Marchant, Marten's Hall, Potterton and Martin, Robinsons, Stonehouse, Treasure.

Seeds: Chiltern.

LONICERA — Honeysuckle, Woodbine, Eglantine *(Caprifoliaceae)*.

The wild honeysuckle of Shakespeare's verses is too well-known and loved to need any description. In former times gypsies believed that all kinds of illnesses could be cured by passing the sick person nine times through a 'girth' or garland of honeysuckle, which had to be made from the still-growing plant.

A Scottish ballad tells of a darker use, where an evil witch tried to prevent the birth of a child by planting a 'bush o' woodbine' between her hovel and the lady's couch.

In any case, the wild honeysuckle — *L. Periclymenum* is a powerful plant, quite capable of killing its own host tree by squeezing it to death — a veritable vegetable anaconda. Look at the taller hedgerow trees next time you are out for a walk and those that support a honeysuckle will usually have trunks that are constricted by the spiralling stems of the honeysuckle which will, in time, kill them. I have a Ceanothus in the garden which bears these wounds, which hurt me just as much and which are a permanent reproaching reminder of a summer when, owing to pressure of work, I allowed the garden to revert to jungle.

There are quite a number of Loniceras that have differing requirements and habits. *L. pileata* for example, doesn't look like a Lonicera at all at first glance, as it forms a neat-leaved mounding bush that is quite content in shade. It has small, sweet-scented flowers though these are very inconspicuous and its chief asset is its willingness to look as if it were enjoying life in the fairly dense shade under deciduous trees. I can thoroughly recommend *L. pileata*.

The winter-flowering honeysuckle, *L. fragrantissima*, has heavily scented flowers during the dark days of winter. The shrub is never very elegant, being partially evergreen in our climate and thus it is neither one thing nor the other and consequently looks like a half-plucked fowl. But the scent of the small, paired flowers is piercingly sweet, and a large bush will generally yield some reasonable-looking twigs which, like some others of the tribe, flower along the stem and not at the ends of the branches. This is a shrub for an out-of-the-way corner where it can be forgotten for most of the year, though it needs a sunny place. *L. tragophylla* is a twiner with fine yellow flower trusses which, alas, are scentless, but it is very beautiful when well grown. It likes to have its roots in shade and these should not be allowed to dry out in hot summers. Another species for a shady wall is *L. Henryi* which is most valuable because it is evergreen and does well in semi-shade. Its flowers are not striking, being a rather subdued shade of red, but it does flower quite well and does not (when grown in shady conditions) attract aphids as most other species do. *L. japonica* is a usefully rampant almost evergreen which has heavily-scented, creamy flowers along the stem for several months in the summer. It must be prevented from growing into old apple trees because the foliage is so dense that it will stifle that of the apple, though blackbirds much appreciate this tangle for their nests. I use it in difficult corners for its greenness, *almost* sure in the knowledge that giving it a rather uncomfortable situation will slow it down a bit. But forget it at your peril, it is a natural-born colonizer. The varieties of our own native *L. Periclymenum* are deliciously scented and can be had to flower in succession. *L. Periclymenum* 'belgica' has flowers of deep pink and crimson, followed by very handsome scarlet berries that will usually yield a fine crop of seedlings. *L. Periclymenum* 'serotina' comes in to flower as 'belgica' finishes, and the pink and yellow flowers are just as sweetly perfumed. *L. x Brownii* has brilliant orange-scarlet (but scentless) flowers twice a year — in spring and again in late summer — and is a beautiful climber to grow through dark-leaved evergreens or with white, blue or yellow-flowered Clematis. *L. nitida* is inestimably useful as a small hedging plant or for clothing walls.

L. x Brownii — Scarlet Trumpet Honeysuckle (before 1858) grows to 15ft (4.5m) with orange-scarlet, scentless flowers either in late spring and again in autumn (August to October), or continuously from June to September or later. Can be badly affected by aphis. (There are several named modern varieties.)

L. fragrantissima (1845) grows to 6ft (1.8m) with a similar spread. Heavily perfumed white flowers from December to March. A semi-evergreen shrub from China for a sheltered position, out of a draught.

L. Henryi (1908) grows to 30ft (9m) in good soil if unchecked, with dull pinkish red unscented flowers in June. A vigorous evergreen twiner from China for a shaded wall or into other shrubs.

L. japonica (1806) grows to 30ft (9m) with sweetly scented cream-yellow flowers from July onwards. Species very rampant, a useful evergreen cover-up, from China, Japan and Korea. (The modern variety 'Halliana' is generally grown.)

L. nitida (1908) grows to 6ft (1.8m) and as much through. This species is generally grown for its foliage or as a hedge and will do quite well in shade. Tiny evergreen leaves and unnoticed flowers in May. (The modern variety 'Baggesen's Gold' has yellow leaves and needs a place in full sun.)

L. Periclymenum — Woodbine, Honeysuckle, Eglantine, grows to 20ft (6m) with scented creamy-pink flowers in July and August. A much-loved European wild plant for old gardens.

L. pileata (1900) grows to a neat, rounded bush 3ft (90cm) high and as much wide. Inconspicuous but scented flowers in May. A semi-evergreen shrub from China for ground cover under trees and as a foliage contrast shrub that looks well with Bergenia, *Iris foetidissima* and *Geranium macrorrhizum*.

L. tragophylla — Chinese Woodbine (1900) grows to 20ft (6m) with yellow, scentless flowers in June and July. A twiner from China for a position where its roots are in shade in a moisture-retentive soil.

Requirements: Most honeysuckles should be grown with their roots in shade and so that their tops can climb into the sun. The exceptions to this are *L. nitida, tragophylla, pileata* and *Henryi* which can be grown in quite shaded places. All benefit from being grown in good soil enriched with leaf-mould, with an annual dressing of well-rotted compost in March, though a light hand with the pastry is what is required or there will be too many leaves and less flowers.

Propagation: In July or August take short — 4-5″ (10-12.5cm) — stem sections of climbing species and insert them, the right way up, in a rooting compost of peat and sand. When they have rooted transfer into individual pots of John Innes No.2 and grow on until the following year. Take heel cuttings of shrub species in July or August. When rooted transfer into John Innes No.2. Stems of climbers may be layered between August and October. They can be detached and potted up after fifteen months (ie. two springs later). Seeds of *L. Periclymenum* should be sown into seed compost in September or October, or when ripe. Place boxes or pots in a cold frame for the winter; the plants will take two or three years to come to flowering.

Pruning: Tidy up tangled stems of old wood on climbing species every few years; this should be done after flowering. *L. japonica* 'Halliana' never stops until Christmas in my garden, so do this one in early spring. Tidy shoots of winter damaged shrubs in late spring. Trim *L. nitida* two or three times a year, or as necessary.

Pests: Aphids are a real nuisance in some years, and the climbing species in sunny positions should be regularly sprayed or the flowers will not form properly.

Uses: Scented climbing species for posts and pergolas and round, up and over summer-houses and arbours. Evergreen climbing species very useful in shaded places, as is *L. pileata* and *L. nitida*. Foliage of the latter very good in arrangements.

Shrubs: Barcock, Bodnant, Brackenwood, Busheyfields, Peter Chappell, Beth Chatto, Daisy Hill, Dobbies, Fairley's, Farall, Margery Fish, Goscote, Great Dixter, Highfield, Hilliers, Hopleys, Ingwersen, Jackman, Kaye, Kent, Knaphill, Knoll Gardens, Lime Cross, Marchant, Marten's Hall, Meare Close, Notcutts, Orchard, Otter, Read, Reuthe, Roger, Rosemoor, Russell, Scotts, Shepton, Sherrard, Smith, Southcombe, St. Bridget, Stonehouse, Toynbee, Treasure, Treseder, Warley, Woodland, W.W., Wyevale.

Seeds: Chiltern.

LUPINUS — Tree Lupin, Lupine *(Leguminosae)*. Most of the lupins are annual or herbaceous plants but there are a number of shrubby types and of these the wild Tree Lupin is the best known. It is a handsome plant with typical lupin-like leaves that are a pleasing soft pale green. The scented flowers are almost always creamy-yellow. It likes a sunny position and can be seen growing on sand dunes and railway banks where it seems to thrive in these very arid conditions. It came originally from California and from 1930 onwards it has colonised certain areas of the south and east coasts of England. It looks well when grown in groups, particularly against a plain or dark background where the flower spikes can be seen to advantage. It is particularly useful when used to clothe areas of dry, poor soil where its evergreen leaves are pleasing throughout the year. It seldom lives longer than a few years, so a constant succession of seedlings should be brought on as replacement plants.

Lupinus arboreus (1793) grows to 6ft+ (1.8m+) with scented, typical lupin-like cream-yellow flowers (sometimes white or blue) from June to September. A short-lived evergreen shrub from California that has naturalised itself in some coastal and some inland areas of the British Isles. Good in seaside gardens.

Requirements: Full sun and free-draining sandy soil. Grows well in acid conditions though not essential.

Propagation: Sow seeds as soon as ripe in a sandy seed compost (soak seeds first), prick out and grow on in individual pots. Plant out as soon as large enough and set out in casual groups where they are to flower. They do not transplant well after the first year.

After flowering: Remove seed heads unless these are needed for propagation.

Uses: Excellent for windy cliffside gardens where the soil is thin.

Warning: Lupin seeds are toxic but are bitter enough to prevent any over-indulgence.

Shrubs: Farall, Hilliers, Meare Close, Scotts, Shepton, Sherrard, Woodland, Wyevale.

Seeds: Butcher, Chiltern, Thompson and Morgan.

MAGNOLIA — Yulan, Lily-tree *(Magnoliaceae).* For over a hundred years the descriptive phrase 'Magnolia-skinned' has evoked an instant image of southern belles and perfect feminine beauty, for the trees and shrubs belonging to this genus have some of the most beautiful flowers in the world. Our somewhat hypocritical ancestors drew a parallel between the ivory-blushed petals of the one and the cherished complexions of the other.

Many species of Magnolias ultimately become large trees when well grown in the right site and the right soil, but some of them begin to flower when only about 2ft (60cm) tall (eg. *M.* 'stellata'); these, for the purposes of this book, are classed as shrubs.

Magnolias come from North America and also from the Far East, where they have been known and grown since the seventh century. Loudon said that in China they have always been esteemed so much so 'that a plant in flower, presented to the Emperor, is thought a handsome present, even from the governor of a province'. Another quotation of that time describes an Asiatic species, *M. denudata* as 'a naked Walnut Tree with a lily at the end of every branch' which, of course, is not strictly accurate, though this is the plant that is called the Yulan (it is classed as a tree, so does not properly belong in this book). The best known species is the deciduous *M. x Soulangiana* which is the happy result of a natural association of the two plants *M. denudata* and *M. liliflora* at a château belonging to a M. Soulange-Bodin who lived at Fromont near Paris. The new Magnolia was being distributed throughout the British Isles as early as 1828 and it quickly became deservedly popular. Most of the early introductions had sumptuous white flowers, except for *M. denudata* whose blossoms are purple outside and white within. The flowers of the even more popular *M. x Soulangiana* 'nigra'* are crimson-purple, and the plant is slightly hardier. (The very beautiful but more tender pink-flowered Magnolias, such as *M. Campbellii* and *M. Sargentiana* are classed as trees and they do not usually flower for twenty years or so, by which time they are as many feet high.) Linnaeus named this genus after a physician Pierre Magnol (1638-1715) who was a Protestant botanist living in Mont-

pellier. At that time some universities closed their doors to Protestants and Mr. Magnol had to take his degree elsewhere than at Montpellier; though nominated for a professorship, he was not able to advance his career further until he changed his religion some 27 years later.

Most Magnolias have flowers like upward-facing goblets, but those of *M. Wilsonii* and *M. Sieboldii* hang downwards and are thus fairly well protected against the cruelties of the British climate. When the shrubs are young one has to lie prostrate on the muddy ground to get beneath them to look up into the flowers, which is no fun in middle years and in the average British spring.

M. denudata — classed as a tree.

M. grandiflora — Bull Bay in the US (1737) grows to an 80ft (24m) tree in its native habitat but is generally treated as a large wall shrub in the British Isles. Huge, fragrant, waxy cream-white cup-shaped flowers, 10″ (25.5cm) across, from July to September. Very large — 10″ long (25.5cm) — evergreen leaves. A beautiful plant from the eastern USA for a sheltered position, good against a large wall.

M. liliflora (1790) grows to 12ft (3.7m) having purple flowers that are white inside, from April to June. *M. liliflora* 'nigra' has dark claret-purple flowers; this is sometimes called *M. x Soulangeana* 'nigra'. Deciduous shrub from China and Japan for a sheltered corner.

M. salicifolia — generally classed as a tree.

M. Sieboldii (1865?) grown as a large shrub or small tree, with fragrant cup-shaped hanging white flowers from May to August. A deciduous large shrub or small tree from Korea and Japan for a sheltered position.

M. x Soulangiana syn. **M. Soulangeana** grows to 15ft (4.5m). White 'shuttlecocks' with a purple streak in the centre of each petal appear on bare branches in April, and as the leaves open the flowers continue until June. A deciduous large shrub for a focal but sheltered position.

M. stellata (1877) (dwarf form of *M. Kobus* which is a 30ft (9m) tree) grows to 10ft (3m) with a similar spread. Fragrant, white, star-like flowers on bare branches in March and April. A deciduous shrub from Japan for a sheltered focal position, good against a dark background, such as Yew, Holly or conifers. There is a pink flowered variety, *M. stellata* 'rosea'.

M. Wilsonii (1908) grows to 25ft (7.5m), with fragrant, nodding cup-shaped white flowers in May and June. A fairly hardy deciduous shrub or small tree from China for a sheltered position.

Requirements: Magnolias do best in a prepared soil of leafmould, peat and compost. They all need positions sheltered from the east and are happy in partial shade — in full sun the flowers open and go over too quickly. Young shrubs should be firmly staked when planted, leave the stakes in for about two years and inspect the ties regularly. Magnolias do not like being moved as they have fleshy roots that are very

*See note under species list

easily damaged. Most shrubs do not even notice if they are moved in dormancy, but the deciduous forms of Magnolia may never waken from their winter sleep if they have been carelessly treated, so move them carefully in May, when new growth is beginning. All like moisture-retentive (though never sour) soil and plenty of water is essential in the growing season of their first few years. Gardeners with rather poor soil should prepare a large area (equal in width to the final width of the shrub or tree) and excavate a 2-3ft (61-90cm) hole. Half of the excavated soil should be replaced by equal quantities of leaf-mould, peat and well-decayed compost, and an annual dressing of the same mixture is, as they say, beneficial.

Propagation: Is by sowing very fresh seed — this does not remain viable for long. Sow in October of the same year in a peaty seed compost and set the pots or boxes out in a cold frame. Germination can take from one to two years. When the seedlings are large enough, transplant carefully into individual pots of John Innes No.1 and grow on, plunging the pots in a nursery area or in the frame. Or heel-cuttings can be taken in July; insert these in pots of sand in a propagator set at 21°C (70°F). When they have rooted, grow on in individual pots potting on as necessary. They may be planted out, but great care must be taken when the small shrub is to be moved.

Uses: As focal shrubs (often trees: this should be remembered when siting them). Beautiful as branches of cut flowers.

Shrubs: Ballalheannagh, Barcock, Bees, Bodnant, Brackenwood, Bressingham, Caldwell, Peter Chappell, Daisy Hill, Dobbies, Fairley's, Farall Goscote, Highfield, Hilliers, Hortico, Hyden, Jackman, Kaye, Kent, Kershaw, Knaphill, Knoll Gardens, Lime Cross, Marchant, Meare Close, Notcutts, Otter, Reuthe, Roger, Rosemoor, Russell, Scotts, Shepton, Sherrard, Smith, Southcombe, St. Bridget, Stonehouse, Toynbee, Treasure, Trehane, Treseder, Warley, Woodland, Wyevale.

Seeds: Chiltern, Thompson and Morgan.

MAHONIA *(Berberidaceae)*. All Mahonias are easy to grow and some are very striking-looking shrubs with glossy, spiny evergreen leaves. There is often much confusion as to nomenclature because the Asiatic species *M. japonica* and *M. Bealei* are very alike when not in bloom. They were discovered at about the same time (around 1843-1850) and were at first thought to be similar though geographically different plants. Nurserymen have been mis-calling them ever since, and in some catalogues they may be seen as *M. japonica 'Bealei'*, or *M. Bealei 'japonica'* which solves the nurseryman's problem, but not that of the serious gardener. When the shrubs bloom they may be told apart by the habit of the flower-spikes: those of *M. Bealei* are erect yellow tufts and those of *M. japonica* have drooping racemes with a definite Lily-of-the-Valley scent. Seen side by side the ever-

green leaflets are quite different, those of *M. Bealei* having a broader base and greyish-green colour, while those of *M. japonica* are darker, glossier and more spiny. Just to confuse matters, the plants have (in the past) frequently hybridised, so some that are sold under one name or the other may have the characteristics of both parents. The moral of all this is if you want pedigree plants go to a pedigree nursery, but if you have inherited an established garden you take what you get and identify the contents later.

M. Aquifolium — Oregon Grape (1823) grows to 5ft (1.5m) with thin holly-like leaves and scented yellow flowers in March and April, followed by clusters of blue-black edible berries. A useful evergreen from the E. United States to plant in shady places, though it will do better in partial sunshine.

M. Bealei (1850) grows to 8ft (2.4m) with a spread of 4ft (1.2m) and yellow flowers from December to February. An evergreen shrub from China for winter flowers for a place in sun or partial shade.

M. japonica grows to 10ft (3m) with pendulous racemes of scented yellow flowers from January to March. An evergreen shrub from Japan for a similar situation to *M. Bealei*.

M. napaulensis (before 1850) grows to 20ft (6m) with yellow flowers from March to April. A handsome, large-leaved species for the larger garden.

Requirements: Mahonias should be planted in good garden soil, with the addition of peat and leaf-mould if soil is on the poor side. Most of them quite like semi-shade, where their leaves are the characteristic glossy dark green. However, when sited in a sunny position, the leaves turn to spectacular shades of crimson in summer and early autumn, though for the other parts of the year, if the position is too dry, the leaves will have a dull and pale appearance. They take a little time to settle down if moved and they may die, as they definitely resent clumsiness on the part of the gardener. They are best bought as container plants. Move established plants in damp weather in October or November or after flowering if you have to.

Propagation: Can be by seed, sow when ripe (when they fall off) in pots or boxes of seed compost. Leave in a cold frame for the winter; germination takes about six months. Transplant carefully into individual pots or into open ground and grow on for two years, potting on into John Innes No.1 as necessary. Mahonias hybridise easily, so if named species are required (in a garden where several types are growing) take lateral cuttings in July or leaf-cuttings of the larger-leaved sorts in October or November. Insert in a compost of peat and sand in a propagator set at 16-18°C (61-64°F) until rooted. Transfer into individual pots of John Innes No.2 and keep in a frost-free greenhouse for the winter. Grow on for a further season before setting out.

Pruning: Seldom needed. Larger Mahonias grow tall and 'leggy' and need something plump and leafy in front of them. They cannot be 'cut back' to promote bushiness lower down, though *M. Aquifolium* can be kept low, as ground cover, by pruning hard after flowering. Do this with secateurs to avoid damaging leaves.

Uses: As sculptural shrubs for a year-round focal position. For shady places and for scented winter flowers.

Shrubs: Ballalheannagh, Bees, Brackenwood, Bressingham, Caldwell, Daisy Hill, Dobbies, Fairley's, Goscote, Hilliers, Hyden, Jackman, Kaye, Kent, Kershaw, Knaphill, Knoll Gardens, Lime Cross, Marchant, Meare Close, Notcutts, Otter, Reuthe, Roger, Rosemoor, Russell, Scotts, Shepton, Sherrard, Smith, St. Bridget, Stonehouse, Toynbee, Treasure, Treseder, Warley, Woodland, W.W., Wyevale.

Seeds: Chiltern, Thompson and Morgan, Unwin.

MENZIESIA *(Ericaceae)*. These very beautiful shrubs are rather like giant heathers and, like them, they should be grown on acid soil; and for those people with heather gardens these plants will add extra interest and height. They are slightly tender and should always be planted in a position protected from late frosts which will scorch the forming flowers. The roots of the shrubs should be planted so as to be in the shade and this can be done by siting them carefully in a large rockery or by utilising the shade of other plants. The genus is named after Archibald Menzies (1754-1842), the botanist and surgeon who accompanied George Vancouver on his survey voyage of 1790-1805.

M. ferruginea (1811) grows to 6ft (1.8m) with white urn-shaped flowers in May. A deciduous shrub from western N. America.

M. pilosa (1806) grows to 6ft (1.8m) with creamy-bell-shaped flowers in May. A deciduous shrub from eastern N. America to grow in association with heathers. (Best increased by seed.)

Requirements: Menziesias are slightly tender and should be sited with some care so as not to catch cold in late spring. They need a moisture-retentive acid soil incorporating leaf-mould, and a mulch of this should be given in April. **Note:** for lime-haters like these, take care not to include the leaf-mould that comes from leaves collected from paved paths.

Propagation: Sow seeds in February in small pans of a moist sand and peat mixture. Set a propagator to a temperature of 13°C (54°F) and allow the pans to reach the same temperature before planting the seeds. After germination remove from the propagator and grow on in a frost-free greenhouse; when large enough to handle, prick out into a seedling compost of equal parts of lime-free loam, peat and sand. Keep in a cold frame for the following winter and pot on as necessary or plant out in a nursery bed. Or take heel cuttings of unflowered shoots in July and insert them in a rooting compost of peat and sand in a propagator set at 16°C (61°F). When rooted grow on as for seedlings.

Pruning: None needed.

Uses: As unusual shrubs to grow in association with Ericas, Rhododendrons and Cytisus. (There are other members of this genus that were introduced after 1914. of these, *M. ciliicalyx* and *M. purpurea* are very fine.)

Shrubs: Ballalheannagh, Jack Drake, Glendoick, Hilliers, Scotts, Smith.

MYRTUS — Myrtle *(Myrtaceae)*. The myrtle is an aromatic and tender shrub that is best grown against a warm south-facing wall. When in flower, which usually last until the first frosts, it buzzes with happy bees. When looking at a myrtle one is always aware that it has many classical legends associated with it and it is, of course, mentioned in the Bible (Zechariah, 1, v.8-11). It is a tree of peace — the Romans crowned their generals with myrtle when they had won a bloodless victory because Venus, to whom the myrtle belongs, was much averse to war. It is very likely that the Roman legions would have brought some small slips of myrtle with them when they came to British shores, and I like to think of those long-dead gardeners among the cohorts who marched their fine straight roads. The myrtle was well known before 1597, and six varieties were being grown even at that time. These tender shrubs were cared for as well as could be managed then and must have been ported in and out at the appropriate seasons, much as we do with our Pelargoniums today. In 1722 there is a record of myrtles being sent to the nursery-gardens 'to be taken Care of for the Winter at the Usual Price'.

Myrtles were very much in demand in the 18th century and vast quantities of foliage and potted plants were grown for the flower-markets. There is a note about a variety called the 'Jew's Myrtle' which had three leaves at each joint instead of two, 'by which particular circumstance this species is in universal estimate among the Jews in their religious ceremonies, particularly in decorating their tabernacles, and for which purpose many gardeners about London cultivate this variety with particular care, to sell to the above people, who are often obliged to purchase it at the rate of sixpence or a shilling for a small branch; for the true sort, having the leaves exactly by threes, is very scarce, and is a curiosity'. Shakespeare might have made something of this opportunism on the part of the Gentiles, I feel.

There is a great deal of sentiment surrounding the Myrtle, and the saying 'No lady would be without her myrtle' originated in 1851. It was said by the same author, George Glenny, that 'slips of this will root any-where and anyhow'. But this is not always true, as any gardener will know of any plant, and superstition decreed that the cuttings would not strike if she who plants was destined never to marry. A sprig of Myrtle was always included in a bride's bouquet, but it was thought to be very unlucky if the bride herself planted the Myrtle-sprig, though, oddly enough, it was safe for the bridesmaids to do it. One would have thought that a bride, having caught a husband, could plant her Myrtle-sprig with impunity, whereas the bridesmaids had plenty of time in which to become old maids. Another old country tradition bade the maiden (or wife?) to 'spread the tail of one's dress and *look proud*'. Now, just try doing this in your dressing-gown one morning — it will give the milkman quite a turn and will very likely start the whole neighbourhood talking. The Myrtle was Venus's plant and, therefore, it had a reputation as an aphrodisiac and, in the 18th century, a lotion called 'Angel-water' was made by the Portuguese from the flowers.

The Myrtle got its name from a Greek legend about a nymph called Myrsine who was particularly good at all athletic sports. She was Minerva's favourite hand-maiden and it was her duty to crown the winners at the Games. But, as with all games, the losers grumbled and in the end they got together and killed her. Minerva was very annoyed about this and caused a new tree to spring up, which she named 'Myrsine' after the girl. It is said that she loved this tree as much as she had loved the maiden.

M. communis — Common Myrtle (before 1597) grows to 15ft (4.5m) against a wall in the southern counties of the British Isles. In very bad winters it will be killed back but a mature specimen will generally cling to life, though it may take two years to refurbish itself. A tender evergreen shrub from Southern Europe and W. Asia for a sheltered site against a wall.

Requirements: A warm, sunny and sheltered site and ordinary good garden soil.

Propagation: (Do it this way and don't look proud until they've rooted.) Take short lateral heel cuttings of non-flowering shoots in June or July. Insert in a rooting compost of peat and sand in a propagator set at 16°C (61°F). When they have rooted, pot on into individual containers of John Innes No.1. Keep in a cold frame for the winter. It is amazing that those bridesmaids had any success at all with the wedding-bouquet sprays, which would often have been in flower.

Pruning: Take off winter-damaged shoots in April.

Uses: Leaves and flowers as an aromatic addition to pot-pourri. Cut flower branches for their fragrance. As a bee plant.

Shrubs: Ballalheannagh, Brackenwood, Great Dixter, Hilliers, Knaphill, Knoll Gardens, Marchant, Meare Close, Notcutts, Oak Cottage, Otter, Reuthe, Rosemoor, Russell, Scotts, Sherrard, St. Bridget, Stoke Lacy, Stonehouse, Toynbee, Treseder, Warley, Wyevale.

Seeds: Chiltern, Thompson and Morgan.

NANDINA — 'Chinese Sacred Bamboo' *(Berberidaceae)*. This plant has been known to gardeners since the early years of the 19th century, though it has only recently become popular because of the surge of interest in foliage plants. In spring when new leaves form they are red, and in autumn they turn to beautiful shades of crimson and purple with long-lasting scarlet berries. In China the shrub was used for decoration and branches of the leaves and berries were sold in the streets. The shrub sometimes colours well after a hot summer, but it is unlikely to fruit as well as it would in its native home. The Japanese planted Nandina close to their garden doors and treated it with great respect; they believed that if anyone in the house was afflicted with a nightmare or a bad dream, that person had but to tell the 'home shrub' and all would be well. The leaves do not really look like those of Bamboo.

N. domestica — Nandina, Chinese Sacred Bamboo (1804) grows to a height of 8ft (2.4m) with panicles of cream-white flowers in June and July. A tender evergreen of historical interest from China for a warm and sheltered spot.

Requirements: A very sheltered, warm and sunny spot, deep, rich moisture-retentive soil; or can be grown in a large tub in the warm greenhouse and stood out in the summer months.

Propagation: Sow seeds in October in a cold greenhouse. They will take some months to germinate. When seedlings are large enough, transfer into individual pots of John Innes No.1 and grow on until the following autumn when, in mild areas, they can be planted out in a nursery area. When large enough (they make slow progress) they can be transferred to their permanent position. Or take lateral heel cuttings in September and insert into a rooting compost of sand and peat. Put into a cold frame for the winter and then transfer to a nursery area for a couple of seasons.

Uses: As rich autumn colour in a good season.

Shrubs: Brackenwood, Bressingham, Hilliers, Hopleys, Kaye, Knaphill, Knoll Gardens, Marchant, Notcutts, Otter, Roger, Sherrard, St. Bridget, Treseder, Wyevale.

Seeds: Chiltern, Fothergill.

NEILLIA *(Rosaceae)*. Neillias are not often seen in gardens, but as they are perfectly hardy this situation is easily remedied. *N. longiracemosa* is the best and has interesting and attractive rose-pink flowers (rather like a shrimp-plant) which are most unusual and unguessable in arrangements.

N. longiracemosa grows to 6ft (1.8m) with racemes of pink flowers in May and June. A deciduous shrub from China for a sunny or partially shaded place.

Requirements: Any good moisture-retentive soil and a sunny, sheltered position. It will grow in dappled shade but may not flower as freely.

Propagation: Take lateral heel cuttings in August or September and insert in a rooting compost of peat and sand.

Uses: As an unusual and rather delicate flowering shrub; branches of flowers for arrangements.

Shrubs: Hilliers, Marchant, Notcutts, Roger, Sherrard, Smith, Southcombe, St. Bridget, Treasure.

NERIUM — Oleander, Rose-Laurel, Rose-Bay *(Apocyn-aceae)*. All along the Mediterranean plazas and promenades the Oleanders are there, as one would expect, with Bougain-villea, 'Angels' Trumpets', Palms and Orange-trees to keep them company. And very fine Oleanders they are too, with good thick trunks in many cases. How different are these sturdy, leafy shrubs from our cherished pot-dwellers, that have to be trundled in and out of conservatories and green-houses at the appropriate season. But with typical British obstinacy, we go on doing exactly the same as Gerard did because the Oleander is a very beautiful (though very deadly) shrub, with attractive single or double flowers in shades of pale pink, rose, red, cream and occasionally white. It is interesting to note that varieties with striped flowers were available in the middle of the 18th century, though these are now lost to us.

The Borgias also liked Oleanders, but for a different purpose — legend has it that they had charming little drink-ing cups turned from the wood which they presented to their associates (with the Borgias, the word 'friend' is not really applicable). Since all parts of the plant are equally deadly, any person drinking from such a cup would be imbi-bing poison from the plant along with the best vintage of the year. The perfume is supposed to be equally noxious and you may be sure that I had all the windows — and the doors as well — open when I was painting the flowers. I'm still here.

Oleanders are remarkably good-natured shrubs. They will (just about) tolerate extreme cold, as long as the frost does not actually get to them; I have seen some very fine specimens that survived the dreadful winters and springs of 1985 and 1986 in an outdoor shelter, their only protection being a roof and three walls, the fourth being open. This I do not recommend, but these were too big to be brought inside, and they survived. What they really like in this country is to be kept cosily in a warm greenhouse for the winter. In spring they need a treat and they should be re-potted early and fed, with a gradually increasing temperature and they will then begin to form their flower buds sooner. When they are stood out, the best position is close against a light-painted south-facing wall which will reflect the heat. Oleanders can be cut hard back (after flowering) if they are growing too tall for their accommodation. Mine has, but I have not as yet taken this drastic step though I shall be forced into it next year. Most greenhouse-dwellers are afflicted with mealy-bug or scale insects, as can be seen by the unsightly and disfiguring 'honeydew'. The only remedy is to wipe each leaf with cotton-wool moistened with warm water, giving extra attention to the undersides of the leaves. Gloves should be worn for this job, and it should be done in the open air. I always want to add the appropriate pest killer to the water but do not wish to inhale any fumes over a period of time, so

I spray very thoroughly afterwards, again giving particular attention to the undersides of the leaves where the 'crawlers' lurk.

In the 18th century this shrub was propagated by layer-ing, and it was a fairly common practice in some gardens for the gardeners to do this and sell the surplus plants. One can only assume that the owner of the garden was seldom at home or he would have seen this going on; layering can take a year or more. In 1706 Liger says 'Most hir'd Gard'ners are apt to lay these Branches of Rose Bays to make a Penny of them: Preferring their own Advantage to their Master's Pleasure, who would delight in seeing a Rose Bay-tree adorned with Branches at the Foot; whereas if 'tis naked there it loses half its beauty; for which reason Gentlemen should look after their Gard'ners, and see they don't serve their Rose Bay-trees so for their own Interest'.

N. oleander — Oleander (1596) grows to 15ft+ (4.5m+) and as much wide, with pink, rose or red single or double fragrant flowers from June to October. A tender evergreen shrub from the Mediterranean region for large tubs in the green-house.

Requirements: A warm, or at any rate a frost-free, glasshouse during winter. (Pots or tubs can be stood out in summer.) Good light during winter months. Grow in John Innes No.2 with regular fortnightly liquid feeds from May until end of August, then at three weeks until end of September. Watch for pests and deal with these before they get too numerous.

Propagation: Take half-ripe cuttings in June or July, insert in a rooting compost of peat and sand and put pots into a propa-gator set at 16-18°C (61-64°F). When rooted, transfer into individual pots of John Innes No.1 and grow on. Keep winter temperature above 13-16°C (55-61°F). Re-pot annu-ally or as necessary into John Innes No.2. Or sow seeds in April and place pans or boxes in a propagator set at 18-21°C (64-70°F). When large enough prick out into individual pots of John Innes No.1 and grow on.

Pruning: To keep plants bushy, shorten lateral shoots or branches after flowering, to about 6″ (15cm) away from base of shoot and cut back flowered shoots.

Uses: As very ornamental tub plants, though flowers not for picking.

Note: All parts of the Oleander are poisonous.

Shrubs: Knoll Gardens, Treseder.

Seeds: Chiltern.

OLEARIA — Daisy Bush, Muskwood *(Compositae)*. The Daisy Bush is very well named because each branch ends in a myriad of daisy-flowers. Being evergreen the shrub is most useful during the winter months, though it is tender in all but the south and south-west counties. It is particularly good for seaside gardens where it rigidly manages to with-stand gale-force winds. The hardiest member of this

Antipodean genus is *O. Haastii* which is often seen in town gardens because this one can also endure the pollution of urban life. In fact, it has now become so rare in the river-gorges of its native New Zealand home that there are undoubtedly more plants now in gardens than there are in the wild. This is not the most attractive member of the family, however, as its scented flowers are not a good white, but its usefulness outweighs this. *O. Gunniana* has the typical white flowers but a diligent search of the catalogues will yield nurseries that stock the much rarer varieties which have pink, lavender blue and mauve flowers which make an unexpected sight when coming upon them suddenly, because they look exactly like Michaelmas Daisies in May. Olearias can grow very large in the right conditions and this should be remembered, but as their leaves are very attractive (particularly the silver-grey ones of *O. macrodonta*) they get 'pruned' into vases throughout the year.

O. Gunniana syn. **O. stellulata** (1848) grows to 5ft (1.5m) with a similar spread. A tender evergreen shrub from Tasmania for a very sheltered sunny place. Pure white flowers in June. There are mauve, pink, blue, purple and lavender-flowered varieties.

O. x Haastii (1858) grows to 8ft (2.4m) and as much through, with scented off-white daisies in July and August. An evergreen shrub from New Zealand for a sunny place. Good in town and coastal gardens; it is the hardiest of the genus.

O. macrodonta (1896) grows to 20ft (6m) in its native New Zealand, but there is little likelihood of this happening in the British Isles. White daisies in July, and very attractive toothed leaves of silvery-green. Needs a sheltered, sunny place and room to spread sideways.

O. semidentata (1910) grows to 9ft (2.7m) and as much through. Pale mauve flowers with a deeper purple centre in June and July. A very tender and beautiful evergreen shrub from the Chatham Islands for the mildest parts of the British Isles; best in a large cold greenhouse.

Requirements: Ordinary soil with the addition of a little peat; and a sheltered position in full sun.

Propagation: Take woody lateral cuttings in August and insert in a rooting compost of two parts of sand to one of peat, and put into a cold frame. When rooted, transfer into John Innes No.1 and keep in the cold frame for the winter. Plant out in a nursery area for the summer and transfer to flowering position in October. For *O. semidentata* take cuttings in July and put into a sandy rooting compost in a propagator set at 16°C (61°F). When these have rooted, transfer to pots of John Innes No.1 and keep in a warm greenhouse (minimum winter temperatures 7-10°C (40-45°F).

Pruning: Tidy away winter damaged shoots.

Uses: As excellent seaside screening shrubs, and foliage and flowers for decorations.

Shrubs: Ballalheannagh, Bodnant, Brackenwood, Daisy Hill, Dobbies, Goscote, Great Dixter, Highfield, Hilliers, Hyden, Jackman, Kent, Kershaw, Knaphill, Knoll Gardens, Lime Cross, Marchant, Meare Close, Notcutts, Orchard, Otter, Reuthe, Roger, Rosemoor, Russell, Scotts, Shepton, Sherrard, St. Bridget, Stonehouse, Toynbee, Treasure, Treseder, Woodland, Wyevale.

Seeds: Thompson and Morgan.

OSMANTHUS — Sweet Olive *(Oleaceae).* These rather tender evergreen shrubs have attractive toothed leaves like hollies in some species, and very fragrant clusters of small flowers. Some have blue berries in late summer, thus prolonging their season of interest, though it has to be a very hot summer for this. Osmanthus come from the Far East except for an American cousin, *O. americanus,* whose common name is 'Devil-Wood'.

The leaves of the sweetly-perfumed *O. fragrans* are rather like finely-toothed Bay leaves. In former times the Chinese grew the plant in temple courtyards, where it was convenient for its use in their religious ceremonies. Nowadays the flowers are used to perfume tea. This shrub needs to be grown in a warm greenhouse if it is to survive and blossom well and a small plant, with but a few flowers, will scent the whole greenhouse or, better still, a warm conservatory that is large enough to dine in.

Others of the genus, such as *O. Delavayi* and *O. heterophyllus* are hardier, especially in the warm southern counties, but are best grown in a choice position against a warm wall. *O. Delavayi* was first seen in 1890 by the Jesuit Père Jean Marie Delavay, the botanist priest who discovered some 1,500 new plant species when he was plant collecting in Yunnan. Because of the long voyages, seeds were collected wherever possible, and therefore the seeds of this new plant were sent back to France where they were distributed carefully. Of this batch, only one seed germinated (grown by the Paris School of Arboriculture) from which came all the other plants in cultivation for many years.

O. Delavayi syn. **Siphonosmanthus Delavayi** (1890) grows to 10ft (3m) and as much through, with small white perfumed flowers in April. An evergreen shrub from China for a sheltered partly shaded position.

O. fragrans syn. **Olea fragrans — Sweet Olive** (1771) grows to 6ft (1.8m) with small, heavily perfumed white flowers from June to August. A very tender evergreen shrub from the S.E. United States for a place against warm walls in Cornwall. Should be grown in a greenhouse or conservatory elsewhere.

O. ilicifolius syn. **O. heterophyllus, O. Aquifolium** (1856) grows to 20ft (6m) though usually much less in the British Isles. Fragrant white flowers in September and October. An evergreen shrub from Japan for the warmer parts of the British Isles. Leaves holly-like or smooth, both kinds on one shrub. Can be used for hedging in the southern counties but there will be few flowers. Blue berries (rarely).

Requirements: Osmanthus need a partly shaded and very sheltered place in the garden and are best against a wall. Ordinary well-drained soil. *O. fragrans* should be grown in a warm conservatory to be certain of the deliciously fragrant flowers.

Propagation: Take woody cuttings in July and insert in a rooting compost of peat and sand in a propagator set at 18°C (64°F). When rooted, transfer into individual pots of John Innes No.1 and keep in a cold frame for the winter. The small plants can be set out in a protected nursery area for some two years as they are very slow growing, before planting out in their final positions. Or layer branches of mature shrubs in September. These will take two years, at least, to root safely before they can be severed.

Uses: *O. heterophyllus* can be used as a hedge-plant in sheltered places; *O. Delavayi* to grow for its scented flowers and *O. fragrans* as a conservatory shrub.

Pruning: None needed except for the hedge-clipping of *O. heterophyllus*.

Shrubs: Ballalheannagh, Barcock, Bodnant, Brackenwood, Caldwell, Crarae, Daisy Hill, Dobbies, Great Dixter, Hilliers, Hyden, Jackman, Kaye, Knaphill, Lime Cross, Marchant, Notcutts, Otter, Reuthe, Roger, Russell, Scotts, Shepton, Sherrard, St. Bridget, Toynbee, Treasure, Warley, Woodland, Wyevale.

PAEONIA — Peony *(Paeoniaceae)*.

The tree-peonies are fine plants to have in the right kind of border because most them have very handsome leaves, particularly in the early part of the season. In those bad years when there are few (or no) flowers, the leaves are a minor compensation. Tree-peonies have always had a reputation for being difficult, miffy, choosy or just hard to establish, but in reality they are not. Just give them *exactly* what they need and, like a beautiful woman, they will reward you (briefly) and depart, leaving you with unforgettable memories. One could almost fall in love with a tree-peony — it is a plant of stature and substance, with beautifully-wrapped buds that gradually grow larger and larger until they are ready to open; it is no wonder that the Chinese called it the King of Flowers.

To quote Lyte the plant is named after 'that good old man, Paeon, a very ancient Physition who first taught the knowledge of this Hearbe'. It is said that he used the roots of the peony to cure the injured god Pluto who was wounded by Hercules.

Peonies have been lovingly cultivated for many centuries — indeed, records show that the herbacious kinds were grown five centuries before the birth of Christ. The tree-peony, on the other hand, seems to be 'one of the newer fellas' whose pedigree seems only to go back to the 8th century A.D. The Chinese cherished peonies above all other flowers and had festivals in their honour, and there is an early monograph on the species that dates back to the eleventh century. The peony was the inspiration for designs, both stylized and naturalistic, on silks and ceramics, and there seems to have been a Far-Eastern form of 'Peonimania' which may almost have rivalled the European craze for tulips. The grafted plants were sold for large sums of money and one Chinese variety was called 'A Hundred Ounces of Gold', which gives an indication of the value set on this special flower. A Chinese poet called Po Chu-i (who lived from A.D. 772-846) wrote on the price of peonies in the flower-market as follows:

'. . . The cost of the plant depends on the number of blossoms
For the fine flower — a hundred pieces of damask
For the cheap flower — five bits of silk . . .'

With all this history, and with the existence of exquisite china and embroideries portraying the flowers, it is no wonder that western gardeners knew about the peony and were anxious to acquire it for their gardens. But peonies do not care for travel and, though many attempts were made, almost all the plants died during the long sea-voyages of the times. One of the first to survive was given to Kew in 1789, though it perished soon after its arrival. A little later (in 1794), an East Indiaman called the 'Triton' arrived with a cargo of horticultural treasures from the Far East. After a difficult voyage, culminating by being dismasted in the English Channel (see the entry on Chimonanthus) the ship finally tied up at Tilbury with much of her delicate deck-cargo in a shattered condition. There were seven tree-peonies on board, two of which died, but the other five lived to become the first peonies in the British Isles. A few more plants survived the passage in the early 19th century, but it was not until Robert Fortune was sent to China in 1834 by the Horticultural Society that more peonies were discovered. Fortune had been instructed to search for a 'blue' peony in particular, as well as new and different herbaceous and tree-types; he found that each district visited had its own kinds, and he was able to buy young plants of tree-peonies (grafted on to wild stock) at local nurseries. It was the custom to do this and then to force the peony into producing one huge and lovely flower, after which the plant was discarded. Fortune acquired about thirty or forty kinds to send back, among which were several 'new' colours — very dark crimson, mauve, a very double purple (which might have been the so-called 'blue') and a white bloom with a yellow centre.

The Japanese had also fallen in love with peonies (esteeming them almost as much as their sacred Chrysanthemums), but their species were quite different to the Chinese kinds. In 1844 Dr. Philippe van Siebold brought a large collection of these Japanese peonies to Europe, and the French nurseries began a programme of hybridisation that has resulted in most of the varieties that we grow today, though the species plants such as *P. lutea*, with its pendulous yellow flowers, *P. suffruticosa* and *P. Delavayi* are still easily obtainable. The Japanese peonies generally have fewer petals than those of Chinese origin and are therefore less likely to hang their heads. Try to see several kinds of tree-peony in flower before you make your choice. These beautiful plants can be seriously damaged in spring; this susceptibility of the emerging shoots and buds to frost being the cause of the tree-peony's reputation, not winter cold which will not harm it. It grows best and most safely when planted in a slightly shaded north-facing aspect without any overhanging branches, and in an open position not closed in with other shrubs. If it is planted in a warm and sheltered corner, which may seem the obvious thing with such a particular plant, it will, as Bean says, get excited into early growth with the probability of having flowers and foliage ruined by late frosts. It should not be planted too close to anything else because it needs a continuous current of air around it which will help to prevent the onset of *Botrytis paeonia,* the dreaded peony blight that can kill even mature and well-grown specimens. If infected shoots or buds are noticed they must be cut away and burned, and the plant should be sprayed with a systemic fungicide. Peonies are greedy plants and they should be mulched annually after flowering, with a rich mixture of leaf-mould and well-rotted manure (*never* fresh).

P. Delavayi (1892) grows to 5ft (1.5m) with dark red flowers in May. A deciduous shrub with handsome leaves from China for a carefully chosen position.

P. lutea (1900) grows to 5ft (1.5m) and as much through, with fragrant yellow flowers in June. A deciduous shrub from China and Tibet for a focal position. (Has been superseded by *P.l. ludlowii* which does not hide its larger flowers among the pale green leaves as *P. lutea* does.)

P. suffruticosa — Moutan Peony (1787) grows to 6ft (1.8m) and as much through, with single or double flowers in shades of pink, rose, crimson, scarlet, rose-violet, bright pink or white. (The species has white flowers with a maroon central blotch or it may be in various shades of red. The species plant is fragrant, some of the newer garden kinds are not, and some may not smell nice at all.)

Requirements: Tree-peonies are quite definite about their requirements and they should be planted in a north-facing border in an airy position with space between themselves and other plants and no overhanging branches. They prefer shade for part of the day and need well-drained but moist soil that has been very deeply dug and previously enriched with peat, leaf-mould and vintage horse-manure. They do not mind either acid or slightly calcareous soil. Their performance will be improved with an annual mulch after flowering and, if an artificial fertiliser is used, it should have a high content of phosphate and potash. For protection in spring a 'tent' can be made with bamboos or other stakes in the form of a tripod and covered with hessian; this should

be erected round the peony at dusk, or before, on cold days, and should be removed the following day. This may seem like a lot of work but peonies have the unfortunate characteristic of leafing and flowering too early for their own good where the British weather is concerned, and gardeners have been covering up their peonies for centuries.

Propagation: Not easy. It is best done by fresh seed sown in autumn in seed compost; pots should be kept in a cold frame and they will probably, though not always, germinate in the following spring. If purchased seed is used, keep in a cool (but not cold) place until the early summer, and sow in seed compost as before; it will germinate in the following spring if it is going to do anything at all, but do not throw out the pots if nothing has happened, keep in a shaded well ventilated frame and care for them in the normal way. Branches may be layered and this should be done in March. The new roots will take about two years to form.

Cuttings are seldom successful, but a green-fingered gardener may like the challenge of taking a hardwood cutting in October or November, which should be inserted into a rooting compost of peat and sand and placed in a cold frame. Purchased cultivars have (usually) been grafted and must, like roses, be planted to the same depth as in their pot, the union should be covered with soil to a depth of from 2-3" (5-7.5cm).

Uses: As stately focal plants, with beautiful foliage which is subtly coloured in spring. Foliage and flowers for arrangements.

Shrubs: Ballalheannagh, Peter Chappell, Hilliers, Holden Clough, Kelways, Russell, Scotts, Sherrard, Treasure, Treseder, Woodland, Wyevale.

Seeds: Chiltern, Thompson and Morgan.

PARROTIA (*Hamamelidaceae*). This is a Cinderella shrub, dressed in quiet and respectable green all through the summer and therefore quite unremarkable. But in the autumn, and depending on the weather during the summer, the soil in its part of the garden, the aspect and whether you, the gardener, have been sufficiently humble, why, then it will get ready to go to the ball. Of course, this dressing-up is not a definite event each year, which is why the shrub is such fun to have. Some years it will end up as one over-all tone of yellow, which is nice enough, especially when it is growing in front of a scarlet-leaved Acer that is doing its stuff in the proper way. But in other years, it is quite wonderful with Joseph's-coat leaves of pink, orange, lemon, amber, gold, scarlet, crimson, brown, bronze, black and green. Each year it can be different, according to the summer that it has enjoyed — or endured — and usually it improves with age. The genus is not named after the bird as one might think, but after F.W. Parrot, a German naturalist, who made the first recorded ascent of Mount Ararat in 1829. In its natural home the Parrotia can grow to 80ft (24m), which might be something of a surprise in a carefully-planned shrub border. However, it is very slow-growing so, even in conditions that may resemble its native home, it will be many years before you need to sharpen the saw and the Parrotia is more likely to grow wide rather than high in any case.

P. persica — Iron Tree grows (in nature) to 80ft (24m) but rarely to more than 20ft (6m) in cultivation, with a similar spread. Small flowers with conspicuous red stamens in spring but (usually) outstanding foliage colouration in autumn. A deciduous shrub or small tree from northern Persia (Iran) and the Caucasus for a focal position in a sunny place. (Plan surrounding trees and shrubs to harmonize or contrast.)

Requirements: Any good well-drained garden soil in sun. Equally tolerant of chalk or acid soil.

Propagation: Is by layering or seed. Layer suitable lower branches in September. They will take about two years to root. Sow seeds when ripe in late autumn in seed compost. Place in a cold frame for the winter. Germination may take as long as 18 months. When the seedlings are large enough, transfer into individual pots of John Innes No.1 and grow on. Pot on as necessary and plunge pots in a nursery area. Parrotias are slow growing and it will be about five years before you have a reasonable-sized shrub. Commercial plants are sometimes grafted on to *Hamamelis mollis,* the Witch Hazel, and a watch should be kept for plain-leaved suckering branches (these would also turn yellow in autumn, so they may be difficult to identify).

Uses: As an autumn colouring shrub for a focal position.

Shrubs: Ballalheannagh, Bodnant, Brackenwood, Daisy Hill, Dobbies, Goscote, Hilliers, Jackman, Knaphill, Lime Cross, Marchant, Meare Close, Notcutts, Otter, Rosemoor, Russell, Scotts, St. Bridget, Treasure, Treseder, Woodland, Wyevale.

PARTHENOCISSUS — Virginia Creeper, Japanese Creeper, Boston Ivy *(Vitaceae).* There are several all too vigorous climbers that are called 'Virginia Creeper' because the tidy-minded botanists have moved them from genus to genus over the centuries. This keeps *them* happy but makes life difficult for nurserymen and gardeners who, on the whole, are simple souls though far from simple-minded. In fact, the complexities of botanical nomenclature would tax the intelligence of an Einstein at times.

I will deal first with that giant green blanket whose shining leaves are guaranteed to quickly cover all and everything without apparent effort. This is the true Virginia Creeper, *P. quinquefolia* discovered in North America early in the 17th century. At that time it was classed as an 'Ivie' and called *Hedera quinquefolia* until the latter part of the 18th century, when it was place in the Vine genus to become *Vitis quinquefolia.* In 1803 it was transferred to the new genus of Ampelopsis, though not all botanists agreed

with this classification, continuing to call the plant Vitis, a vine. In 1887 the new genus of Ampelopsis was divided into two and the Virginia Creeper became *P. quinquefolia.* It may, therefore, be found under several synonyms in the catalogues and a list of these is given with the description of the plant.

Virginia Creeper climbs well and quickly by means of its clasping disks at the ends of the tendrils, and Liger, who wrote 'The Retir'd Gardener' said that 'it will shoot up so high, that whatever Height the Ridge of the House may be of 'twill soon surpass it'; and it was therefore used to garland (or cloak, depending on the beholder's point of view) large, tall and often unsightly town buildings because it seemed to be impervious to the urban pollution of earlier times. I like the account of a London residence that was clothed by this creeper until the owner cut it down 'to prevent having his house indicted as a nuisance for harbouring sparrows, whose twittering commenced too early in the morning for those whose evening parties began at midnight'.

The original Virginia Creeper is now accompanied in the catalogues by *P. tricuspidata* with a formidable number of synonyms to make confusion thoroughly confounded) which is correctly called the Boston Ivy, though as it comes from the Far East it is equally correctly (though seldom) called the Japanese Creeper. This grows lustily in the same manner, but it may be distinguished from *P. quinquefolia* by its three kinds of leaf-shapes, best seen in an adult plant. The reference books describe the leaves as 'variable' which is the coward's way out; a help to correct identification will be to examine the leaves at the base of this beanstalk-plant; these will be very large, as much as 8″ (20.5cm) or more across. It goes without saying that the leaves of both creepers turn to glorious shades of red, purple and crimson in autumn. *V. Henryana,* on the other hand, is a most elegant and dignified plant, with very beautiful dark green leaves clearly veined in white. In late summer and early autumn they begin to change to an interesting dark red and finally to crimson, still retaining the white venation. The leaves of all stay on the vine for some weeks, though in some years there can be a sudden drop in temperature and one can come out to find knee-high drifts of scarlet as if the creeper has just shrugged off its clothes.

P. vitacea is also called Virginia Creeper by nurserymen (it comes from N. America) and, though its leaves are similar to those of *P. quinquefolia,* the tendrils have no sticky pads and the plant climbs by means of the grasp of these same tendrils which behave in the same way as those of a Sweet Pea.

Just to make the gardener's life even more interesting, natural hybrids between this species and *P. quinquefolia* sometimes occur, with the inevitable characteristics of both. But this climber is very useful when a self-clinging plant is not needed, as it is in many ways better than either of its parents.

P. Henryana (1900) can grow as tall as its support, with handsome white-veined dark green leaves changing to crimson in autumn. A deciduous rather tender climber from China for a sheltered north-facing wall. Leaves are variegated with white along veins, this only developing well when climber is grown in a shaded site.

P. inserta (syns. **P. vitacea, Ampelopsis vitacea**) — **'Common' Virginia Creeper** (before 1824) grows vigorously with similar leaves changing to brilliant tones of red in autumn. A deciduous tendrilled climber from N. America for climbing large old trees or evergreens.

P. quinquefolia syns. **Vitis quinquefolia, Hedera quinquefolia, Vitis hederacea, Ampelopsis hederacea — True Virginia Creeper** (1629) grows to any height, being supported by pads on the ends of each branched tendril. A deciduous climber from eastern N. America for lofty buildings, tall walls, the concealment of unsightly buildings or fences and for growing into trees.

P. tricuspidata syns. **Ampelopsis tricuspidata, Ampelopsis Veitchii** and **Vitis inconstans — Boston Ivy, Japanese Creeper, Virginia Creeper** (1862) grows to any height, being similarly equipped with adhesive pads on each branched tendril. A deciduous climber from China and Japan for similar situations. Good autumn colour.

Requirements: This genus will grow in almost any soil, but it is best to prepare a planting hole 2ft (60cm) wide and 18″ (46cm) deep. Mix well rotted compost and manure with some of the soil taken from the hole. All this strong-growing family need an equally strong and large support so check this before planting; Virginia Creepers are not for bungalows.

Propagation: Take short half-ripe nodal cuttings in August and insert in a rooting compost of two parts sand to one of peat; put into a propagator set at 13-16°C (55-61°F) until rooted. Transfer into a frame or cold greenhouse for the first winter, potting on as necessary or in the spring. Ripe seeds may be sown in October in seed compost, then place pots or boxes in a cold frame. When the seedlings are large enough, transfer into individual pots of John Innes No.1 and grow on. In spring plunge all pots into a nursery area and stake well until they are needed. Shoots can be layered in October and will take a year to root. It is best to leave these in position until the following spring before severing and potting up or planting out.

Pruning: Take away growth as necessary during the summer months. Or sneak up on it from behind, so to speak, in the winter, and have at it while you can really see what you are doing. It will be sleeping soundly and will not notice you and your shears.

Uses: As an excellent cover-up for large unsightly buildings. As a handsome and rapid-growing climber for new houses (check the colour of the bricks first, sometimes the crimson glory in the autumn really clashes). To grow into large, old or dead trees — good with mature silver Birch, Scots pine, yew and runaway Leylandii.

Shrubs: Bodnant, Busheyfields, Fairley's, Goscote, Hilliers, Kent, Knaphill, Knoll Gardens, Lime Cross, Otter, Read, Reuthe, Russell, Sherrard, Smith, St. Bridget, Stonehouse, Toynbee, Warley, Wyevale.

Seeds: Chiltern.

PASSIFLORA — Passion Flower (*Passifloraceae*). The name of Passion Flower was given to this plant by the missionaries who first attempted to christianise South America. The parts of the flower and leaves were thought to symbolize the implements of the Crucifixion, therefore the leaves represent the hands of Christ's persecutors, the five anthers are the five wounds of Christ, the tendrils are the cords and whips of his tormentors, the column of the ovary is the pillar of the cross, the three styles are the nails, the stamens are the hammers that were used to make the cross, the filaments or corona are the crown of thorns, the calyx is the glory, the five sepals and the five petals are for ten of the Apostles (Peter and Judas being left out), the white petals are purity and the blue ones represent heaven.

Strangely enough, this genus is a large one, with about 500 species, almost all of which are from the tropical regions of America. *P. caerulea* is the only kind that will grow out of doors in the British Isles (always excepting the sea-girt Isles of Scilly) for any length of time, but it is not reliably hardy even against a south-facing wall. This is where the gardener has to accept reality, and after a really cruel winter he must shrug his shoulders, dig up the corpse and start all over again — the new plant will grow so quickly that it will soon occupy the same area.

The oval fruits of *P. caerulea* are very beautiful when ripe, being a soft glowing orange colour. They taste excellent and, in a good year, they can be very abundant, though for some reason not all plants produce fruit however well-grown and well situated they may be.

P. caerulea — Passion Flower (1699) grows to 30ft (9m) on a warm wall, with fragrant bluish-white flowers from June to September and very edible golden-orange fruits from August onwards. A tender evergreen climber from Brazil for a tall south or west-facing wall. The plant climbs rapidly by means of tendrils, so adequate trellis or strong wires should be placed ready for it. A hard winter will apparently kill it, but new growth may sometimes spring up from the roots. 'Constance Elliott' (1884) has whiter flowers and is hardier.

P. edulis — Granadilla (1810) grows to 20ft (6m) with purple-centred white flowers in June followed by edible purple fruits (not often seen in the Northern Hemisphere). A tropical climber from S. America for a large warm greenhouse or conservatory.

P. quadrangularis — Granadilla grows to 20ft (6m) or more, with pinkish-purple flowers followed by yellow egg-shaped fruits which are grown commercially in the tropics. A very vigorous climber for a heated greenhouse or conservatory.

Requirements: *P. caerulea* will grow in any good garden soil. Protect the young plants from autumn onwards for their first few winters. *P. edulis* and *P. quadrangularis* should be grown in the greenhouse border with a minimum winter temperature of 10°C (50°F). Water these sparingly in winter, but plentifully in the growing and flowering season. They should be grown in a shaded greenhouse or the leaves will scorch in summer. They like a humid atmosphere, so damp down the floors in hot summers, though when the temperature exceeds 21°C (70°F) the doors and ventilators should be left open. Mulch with well-rotted compost in spring.

Shrubs: Bodnant, Busheyfields, Goscote, Highfield, Hilliers, Jackman, Knaphill, Knoll Gardens, Lime Cross, Marchant, Meare Close, Orchard, Otter, Read, Reuthe, Roger, Russell, Scotts, Shepton, Sherrard, St. Bridget, Toynbee, Treseder, Warley, Woodland, Wyevale.

Seeds: Chiltern, Fothergill, Suttons, Thompson and Morgan, Unwin.

PERNETTYA *(Ericaceae)*. The Pernettya is named after Dom Antoine Joseph Pernetty, a Benedictine abbé (1716-1801) who accompanied de Bougainville on his South American voyage to the Falkland Islands in 1763. Pernetty was an enthusiastic botanist, though interested in all aspects of natural history and he spent much of his time on the voyage making drawings and water-colours of the birds and fish caught by the sailors.

These evergreen shrubs have jolly, very artificial looking berries that are most attractive and useful in the autumn garden and in arrangements, coming as they do when much is drear and sere and brown. The berries come in all the heather-colours — pink, rose, cerise, lavender, mauve, purple, crimson and white — and the shrubs look most attractive when grown to harmonize with autumn-flowering heaths and heathers. It is as well to check the flowering times of these, as the Pernettya berries will begin to turn colour in autumn and will remain gay and bright through the winter and into spring — depending on the ferocity or otherwise of winter temperatures. Birds don't like the berries and will strip Cotoneaster and Pyracantha but can be relied on not to touch the waxy-looking sprays on the Pernettya bushes. On the other hand, the flower-arrangers get pretty desperate for natural material in winter, and these last are not deterred by black cotton. When in full fruit, a Pernettya looks like a bushful of marbles.

There is an unusual Chilean species, *P. furens,* that has most attractive sprays of fat bell-shaped white flowers that are larger and better on the stem than those of *P. mucronata* which are single and axilliary, though very numerous. However, the berries or fruits of *P. furens* are rather dull, being a sombre red, whereas those of *P. mucronata* are very striking, especially when a collection of berrying plants of different colours are grown all together. But the berries of *P. furens* are dangerous to eat, causing over-excitement, delirium and mania which may lead to coma and death. Perhaps it is just as well that this more tender plant is difficult to obtain and may usually be seen only in botanic gardens. This poisonous quality in one closely associated member of the genus may be the reason why winter-hungry birds do not touch the jolly berries of *P. mucronata* — or they may just taste unpleasant.

The species *P. mucronata* should be regarded as unisexual, and a male plant should be planted among a covey of female ones to ensure cross-pollination and a good show of berries or fruits. There are hermaphrodite species; the modern variety 'Bell's Seedling' is hermaphroditic, and can be grown alone to produce its large cherry-red fruits.

P. mucronata (1828) grows to 3ft (90cm) with white flowers in May and June followed by eye-catching marble-like berries in pink, rose, lilac, mauve, purple, crimson and white. An evergreen shrub from the Magellan area of S. America.

Requirements: A sunny position and lime-free to acid soil. One certified male plant per three to five female plants in order to ensure a good show of berries.

Propagation: Take cuttings of named varieties in September or October. Insert in a rooting compost of peat and sand and keep in a cold frame. When rooted transfer into individual pots of John Innes No.1 (lime-free) and grow on. Mark each cutting taken from a male shrub or keep separately. Or sow seeds in October in a lime-free seed compost and keep in a cold frame. When large enough the seedlings can be potted up individually and grown on. Where groups of Pernettyas are grown in happy conditions they will seed themselves about. Seeds do not come true as Pernettyas hybridise very readily, but you may get some interesting berry colours in due course. When planting out in groups be sure to keep the ratio going of at least one male per three or five female plants.

Pruning: Trim away winter-damaged shoots. Mature plants get leggy and should be cut hard back in early spring; in old age they may need replacing.

Uses: As beautiful autumn and winter-berrying shrubs, and very good in association with heaths and heathers of toning colours. Berried branches good for arrangements. As excellent ground-cover for large areas.

Shrubs: Ballalheannagh, Bodnant, Brackenwood, Caldwell, Peter Chappell, Daisy Hill, Dobbies, Jack Drake, Glendoick, Goscote, Hilliers, Hyden, Ingwersen, Jackman, Kershaw, Knaphill, Marchant, Meare Close, Orchard, Otter, Reuthe, Russell, Scotts, Sherrard, Smith, St. Bridget, Toynbee,

Treasure, Treseder, Warley, Woodland, Wyevale.

PEROVSKIA — Turkish Sage *(Labiatae)*. This is a quietly elegant plant that when well-grown will excite admiration, particularly among herb-growing folk or those with sea-coast gardens. In a herbaceous border it is particularly attractive, having an airy appearance with delicate spires of blue flowers on silver-white stems and grey leaves, all of which are very aromatic. In windy seaside gardens it can be sited where the distinctive fragrance from the plant can be enjoyed — the constant breezes can be relied on to blow it about, thus causing stems and leaves to rub together and release their aromatic oils. This is even better on a hot day. I have noticed that in such situations, where gardening can often be so very difficult, there are definite rewards; an aromatic bush does not have to be touched or stroked or squeezed to give up its scent — it sits there emanating delicious scents because the eternal wind is forever ruffling it about, though at times, of course, the branches may be lashing to and fro. This has its advantages — rosemary is imediately recognisable 20ft (6m) downwind, as is lavender, rue, Cistus and many another Mediterranean plant that we grow in inland gardens and often pass by, unnoticing. There are several other species, but *P. atriplicifolia* is the one most generally grown.

P. atriplicifolia (1904) grows to 5ft (1.5m) with white-stemmed spires of violet-blue flowers from August until the frosts. A sage-scented shrub from Afghanistan for a hot, sunny border.

Requirements: Does well in ordinary free-draining garden soil, but better in chalky areas and by the coast. Needs a position in full sun. Leave on last season's growth for the winter as protection and cut down to about 18″ (46cm) from ground level in spring.

Propagation: Take woody heel-cuttings in July and place in a rooting compost of peat and sand in a cold frame. When rooted transfer into individual pots and grow on; overwinter in the frame.

Uses: As a quietly spectacular back-of-the-border plant because of the contrast between white-leaved flower stems and violet-blue flowers. For coastal and herb gardens.

Shrubs: Bressingham, Farall, Hilliers, Hopleys, Jackman, Knaphill, Marchant, Meare Close, Notcutts, Otter, Rampart, Reuthe, Roger, Russell, Scotts, Shepton, Sherrard, St. Bridget, Stonehouse, Toynbee, Treasure, Woodland, Wyevale.

Seeds: Chiltern.

PHILADELPHUS — Mock Orange and, wrongly, **Syringa** *(Philadelphaceae,* formerly *Saxifragaceae).* Of all the easy-going and easy-growing shrubs, the Philadelphus is one of the most popular. It needs little attention (which is often what it gets) and can be relied upon to produce its mountains of scented white blossom in June. The perfume from a large specimen (mine is about 17ft (5.1m) tall) is quite wonderful, stealing over the garden in gentle eddies. When the flowers are over, they fall in heaps, like snow, quite covering paving and paths all around. But after a day or so's admiration they must be swept up because summer rains make them slippery and dangerous. This fine old shrub was inherited with the garden and for years we took much pleasure in its annual wealth of blossom. But all things change, and a wall had to be built round the garden, and part of the Philadelphus was threatened. I had to stand in front of it, in an attitude of resolute protection while a bulldozer rumbled towards me. The machine stopped (or I wouldn't be writing this now) and an altercation of the usual type ensued along the lines of 'we weren't told' and 'I didn't know'. Previous meetings with all concerned had extracted a promise to bridge the roots but this would not have been done had I not popped out, just in time, like a furious rabbit. But the roots were bridged, an excellent wall was built over them and now the old shrub is safe; each year cascades of scented creamy-white flowers flow down over the wall for the delectation of the passers-by, and the cover of this book features the Philadelphus in its June glory.

Its common name of 'Mock Orange' is a good name for it because the scent is almost as good as the real thing, though hay-fever sufferers have a bad time because of the tremendous quantity of pollen. Some folk find the perfume altogether too much of a good thing, as often happens with lilies.

The confusion over the name 'Syringa', which is quite often wrongly attributed to this shrub, is because the Philadelphus and the Syringa (or lilac) were both introduced at the same time, by Ogier Ghiselin de Busbecq, that most famous Ambassador to Sulieman the Magnificent; de Busbecq will be forever remembered by gardeners because he brought back to Vienna the first tulips ever seen in Europe. Because the two shrubs came in the same saddle-bag, so to speak, confusion arose between them then and this still exists today, because at first they were classified as being of the same species, though differing so widely in their appearance. The name 'Syringa' comes from *'syrinx'*, a pan-pipe, because the Turks used the hollow-stemmed branches to make these musical instruments, beloved by Gods and goat-herds. Gerard called the lilac the 'Blew-pipe' and the Philadelphus the 'White-pipe' and by the time he wrote his great herbal he was able to say that he had the 'White Pipe' in his garden in 'very great plentie'.

The name 'Philadelphus' comes from an old Greek name meaning 'brotherly love' and not, as may be imagined, because some species were discovered in that part of North America.

There are a large number of species Philadelphus and now there are many beautiful hybrids, almost all of which are heavily scented. The first American kinds were *P. pubescens* and *P. grandiflora* (introduced in the early part of the 19th century). A little later on *P. coulteri* and *P. microphyllus* were introduced to Europe. *P. coulteri* had a purple blotch at the base of each petal, which characteristic was passed on to all the hybrids that derived from it. Its common name was 'Rose Syringa' and it was used by the famous French firm of Lemoine of Nancy as one parent of a succession of hybrids. It is not grown today.

In the late 19th century, *P. microphyllus* was discovered and in 1883 it was sent to Lemoine who crossed it with *P. coronarius*, the oldest and most familiar garden form. A number of hybrids resulted from this union, which was and still is known as the 'Lemoinei' group, best known of which is 'Lemoinei' (1888) a small shrub with very fragrant white flowers; 'Erectus' (1892) is very floriferous and is heavily scented, with small neat leaves and flowers; 'Avalanche' (1896) has so much blossom that the small, single, perfumed flowers often bend down the branches of this little shrub; 'Manteau d'Hermine' (1898) grows to about 5ft (1.5m) with scented, double creamy-white flowers.

One of the most famous names from the Lemoine nursery is 'Virginal' (1909) which is a tall-growing variety — to 10ft (3m) — having large richly-scented double flowers. Other well-known double-flowered kinds are 'Boule d'Argent' which has large clusters of double pure white flowers on a smaller bush (not as fragrant as most, therefore better for those who dislike the strength and power of Philadelphus scent); 'Enchantment' having clusters of sweet-scented double white flowers on a medium-sized shrub; 'Pyramid' with semi-double white flowers on a tall-growing bush; 'Favorite' has large single white cupped flowers with serrated petals; 'Innocence' is single white, scented and very floriferous — leaves sometimes variegated; and 'Norma' which has large — 2" (5cm) wide — single, slightly fragrant flowers on wand-like branches.

The genus of Philadelphus is difficult even for botanists to sort out because some of the species are so like each other; the advent of modern hybrids makes things even more confusing. Philadelphus seeds grow well but do not come true, so the resulting plants may be interesting but will have no respectability and therefore no pedigree.

P. coronarius — Mock Orange (1596) grows to 12ft (3.7m) with racemes of strongly scented cream-white flowers in June. A large strong-growing deciduous shrub from S.E. Europe and Asia Minor for a sunny part of the garden; does well on dry soil.

P. x Lemoinei (about 1883) (see text).

P. microphyllus (1883) grows to 5ft (1.5m) with smaller leaves and very fragrant white flowers in June. A deciduous shrub from western N. America.

P. purpurescens (1904) grows to 12ft (3.7m) with strongly scented white flowers and striking deep violet calyces in June. A deciduous shrub from China for a good garden position in sun.

Requirements: Any good garden soil and a sunny position.

Propagation: Take short half-ripened heel cuttings in June or July and insert them in a rooting compost of peat and sand in a cold frame. Alternatively, the cuttings may be rooted in a propagator set at a gentle bottom heat of 10-15°C (50-60°F). When rooted they can be potted on into John Innes No.1; they should be kept in the cold frame for the winter and can be planted out into a nursery area to grow on for the summer. When the leaves fall the cuttings can be planted out in their permanent positions, or this can be done in the following spring.

Pruning: With the large strong-growing species or hybrids old wood and flowered shoots can be cut out. New young shoots will bear flowers in the following year so do not cut these away.

Uses: As very ornamental mid-season flowering shrubs whose size can be chosen to fit the garden. Cut flower branches seldom last more than a day in water, but are very beautiful for (brief) special occasions. Where garden is large enough, site shrubs against a dark or coloured background so that the purity of the white flowers will be enhanced.

Shrubs: Ballalheannagh, Barcock, Bees, Brackenwood, Bressingham, Caldwell, Peter Chappell, Daisy Hill, Dobbies, Fairley's, Farall, Goscote, Highfield, Hilliers, Hopleys, Hortico, Hyden, Ingwersen, Jackman, Kent, Kershaw, Knaphill, Knoll Gardens, Lime Cross, Marchant, Meare Close, Notcutts, Orchard, Otter, Reuthe, Robinsons, Roger, Rosemoor, Russell, Scotts, Shepton, Sherrard, Smith, Southcombe, St. Bridget, Stonehouse, Toynbee, Treasure, Treseder, Warley, Woodland, W.W., Wyevale.

PHLOMIS — Jerusalem Sage *(Labiatae).* This shrub has attractive leaves that are ever-grey, except in really bad winters which can denude the plant and sometimes kill it. The new flower-buds sometimes begin to form in January and it is heartbreaking to see both them and their flower-stems shrivel in a cold, wet spring. But in drought years these shrubs are happy, and they should in any case be planted in a hot, dry situation on free-draining soil or on a bank. They are best not planted facing east as mine was. Note the past tense.

Phlomis takes up quite a lot of space in maturity and this should be allowed for. It is an easy plant to propagate and to grow, and is handsome at all times of the year. The name 'Phlomis' comes from *Phlogmos,* a flame, because the plant has leaves which were 'fit to make candlewicks' (rather like those of the Mullein which are truly soft if not positively furry). The botanists of the 16th century could not have been that desperate for lamp-wicks, and I wonder if any of them actually tried out these sometimes rather bizarre suggestions.

P. fruticosa — Jerusalem Sage (1596) grows to 4ft (1.2m) with a flopping spread of about the same. Whorls of soft yellow flowers in June. An ever-grey shrub from the Mediterranean area for a warm, sheltered position in full sun.

Requirements: Good, well-drained garden soil and a warm, sunny, sheltered position. Prolonged periods of cold alternating with wet may kill the plant; prune away damaged branches and wait for some months before thinking of a replacement, new shoots may spring up.

Propagation: Take short heel cuttings in August or September and insert in a rooting compost of peat and sand. When rooted, pot on into John Innes No.1 and grow on, potting on as necessary. Pots should be plunged for the first summer and some protection given during the second winter. They can be planted in their final positions in the second spring.

Pruning: Tidy away winter-damaged shoots in spring.

Uses: As a handsome all-year round shrub with unusual flowers and leaves smelling slightly of sage. Good in arrangements.

Shrubs: Ballalheannagh, Bodnant, Brackenwood, Bressingham, Daisy Hill, Margery Fish, Great Dixter, Hilliers, Hopleys, Jackman, Marchant, Meare Close, Notcutts, Old Rectory, Otter, Reuthe, Roger, Russell, Scotts, Sherrard, St. Bridget, Stoke Lacy, Stonehouse, Toynbee, Treasure, Treseder, Woodland, W.W., Wyevale.

Seeds: Chiltern.

PHOTINIA *(Rosaceae).* Photinias have a reputation for being rather special shrubs; This is another way of saying that unless your garden suits them they will not grow well, which is more or less true. There are evergreen and deciduous types, the evergreen species doing well on chalk soils and the deciduous kinds needing acid or at least neutral conditions. Photinias are grown for their spring foliage — scarlet when young, like that of Pieris — and the autumn colouration of the deciduous species. They are rather tender shrubs (or small trees) and should always be sited in a sheltered place in the garden. Their name comes from *photcinos,* meaning shining or bright which some of them are at the appropriate season.

One of the most easily obtainable species (apart from the more modern hybrids) is *P. Beauvardiana* which is perhaps the most floriferous of the genus, having very hawthorn-like flowers in spring and scarlet berries in autumn. These, set among the rich and glowing tints of the leaves, make this Photinia an excellent shrub (though it will grow to a tree-type height) if you are planning some autumn colour.

P. Beauvardiana grows to a 45ft (13.5m) tree in its native country of China, where it was considered handsome enough to be planted to surround sacred shrines. The 'instant-garden' gardener should examine specimens for signs of a union and if he sees this these plants should be rejected, they will have been grafted on to the more vigorous Crataegus (Hawthorn).

P. Beauvardiana (1900) grows to 30ft (9m) in time with clusters of white flowers in May, followed by crimson fruits in autumn, together with good autumn colouration. A deciduous shrub or small tree from China for a sheltered garden. (Hardier than most other Photinias.)

P. Davidsoniae (1901) grows to 30ft (9m) with clusters of white flowers in May. Orange-red fruits in autumn. Bronze-red spring growths. An evergreen shrub or tree from China for a sheltered garden.

P. villosa syn. **P. variabilis** (1865) grows to about 16ft (4.8m) with clusters of white Hawthorn-like flowers in May, followed by scarlet haw-like fruits and bright-coloured autumn leaves. A deciduous shrub from China, Japan and Korea to grow for its autumnal display. Needs acid soil.

Requirements: All Photinias need careful positioning because they can be killed by bad winters. Site them in a sunny position to face south, west or south-west, never east. They need a good loam, and it should be remembered that the deciduous *P. Beauvardiana* and *P. villosa* will not grow on chalk soils, while the evergreen *P. Davidsoniae* does well.

Propagation: Take half-ripe cuttings in July of the deciduous kinds and insert in a rooting compost of peat and sand in a propagator set at 16-18°C (61-64°F). When rooted transfer into larger pots of a lime free compost and grow on. Take heel cuttings of evergreen species and hybrids at the same time and treat as before until they have rooted, then transfer into John Innes No.1 and grow on.

Pruning: Very little needed except to trim away winter damage, or to restrict growth if your garden is warm and sheltered. If your Photinia is growing well, and the evergreen kinds are berrying to match, it is better to move the restriction itself. Unless it is the shed or the garage, in which case you may have to re-think that part of the garden.

Uses: Deciduous kinds for autumn colour, site accordingly. Evergreen types as pleasant evergreens, some with bright spring growth which can be a focal point.

Shrubs: Ballalheannagh, Brackenwood, Daisy Hill, Dobbies, Goscote, Hilliers, Hyden, Otter, Rosemoor, Russell, Scotts, Sherrard, St. Bridget, Toynbee, Treasure.

PHYGELIUS — Cape Figwort *(Scrophulariaceae).* Phygelius can be something of an all-things-to-all-gardeners genus and is therefore most useful and attractive in several widely differing garden positions. Two kinds are obtainable in the British Isles: *P. aequalis* which grows only to 3ft (90cm) and is most generally seen as a border plant, and *P. capensis* which is much more versatile. Their name comes from *phyga,* flight, and *helios,* the sun: which indicates that the plant shuns the light. Here is a curiosity — the genus comes from S. Africa and one would expect it to crave sun and warm conditions (which it does, and when given them it thrives) but, conversely, plant *P. capensis* against a warm north-facing wall (yes, there are such things, I have one) and it will do very well, flowering from July to October. Both will endure drought conditions as one might expect because of their origins, and are very useful in dry, quick-draining gardens. *P. capensis* can also be grown as a border plant, but it does better when grown against a hot, sunny wall. In mild areas such as Cornwall it may achieve a height of 20ft (6m), which can come as something of a surprise when most of the gardening books give 6ft (1.8m) as a maximum height. This species has branching dark-stemmed airy wands of tubular, rather foxglove-like flowers in shades of orange, salmon, rust or red. *P. aequalis* has a rather one-sided cyme of similar flowers, though these have shorter pedicels and are therefore closer together. Therefore, it would seem that with the versatile Phygelius, you can grow it either as a border plant or as a wall shrub (or even as an assisted climber) on south or north-facing walls.

P. aequalis grows to 3ft (90cm) with salmon-orange or crimson flowers from July until the frosts. A small evergreen (in its native South Africa) shrub usually treated as a border plant for a sunny position.

P. capensis — Cape Figwort (1855) grows to 7ft (2.1m) and more in suitable conditions, with yellow-throated orange-red flowers from July until the frosts — var. 'Coccineus' has really red blooms. A tender evergreen from S. Africa for a warm, sunny border in the open or against a warm wall facing south, west or north.

Requirements: Good free-draining garden soil, a sheltered wall and support for *P. capensis* and winter protection of straw, bracken or litter for both.

Propagation: Divide the roots in April or sow seeds in a cold frame in April. Or take half-ripened cuttings in July, insert into a rooting compost of peat and sand and place in a cold frame until rooted. Transfer into individual pots of John Innes No.1 and grow on. Protect in cold frame or greenhouse for first winter.

Pruning: Cut off all the winter-damaged shoots.

Uses: As border plants and wall shrubs in a range of different garden positions.

Shrubs: Ballalheannagh, Bodnant, Beth Chatto, Margery Fish, Great Dixter, Hopleys, Ingwersen, Knoll Gardens, Marchant, Notcutts, Reuthe, Robinsons, Roger, Shepton, Sherrard, Southcombe, Stonehouse, Toynbee, Treasure, Wyevale.

Seeds: Chiltern, Thompson and Morgan.

PHYSOCARPUS — 'Nine Bark' (*Rosaceae*).

Physocarpus is a little-grown genus, one of which deserves greater garden recognition. This is *P. opulifolius* 'Luteus' whose early-summer growth is a beautiful clean yellow, like newly-emerging Brimstone butterflies. The shrub looks very striking when seen against a dark leaved Prunus such as *P. cerasifera* 'Atropurpurea' (formerly and still often called Pissardii) with a Eucalyptus nearby, whose blue-grey leaves will complete the colour harmony. This association looks well until after the Physocarpus has flowered, when its leaves tend to go greener. Not actually green, but more green than their previous sun-bright yellow. Mine grows thus in full sun in the dry free-draining soil of this garden. I read that it would prefer damp soil and I pass this information on, but with the assurance that it grows with unbounded vigour without such moisture. In fact I am having to select large portions where spring reductions are to be made, as the Physocarpus has eaten a Peony and the *Euphorbia wulfenii* and has just come hard up against a very large *Phormium tenax* (which I feel needs none of my protection).

The genus Physocarpus was formerly placed with Neillia and both are closely related to Ribes, as can be seen by the similarity of the leaves. The bark peels attractively in winter, leaving shining new surfaces, hence its common name of 'Nine Bark'. None of this genus do well on chalky soil.

P. opulifolius — 'Nine Bark' (1690) grows to 6ft (1.8 + m) with neat hemispherical clusters of pale pink flowers in June. A vigorous deciduous shrub from N. America for a sunny open position with moist soil.

'Luteus' has yellow spring growth lasting until flowering time. White flowers.

Requirements: A position in full sun, in good garden soil. Will undoubtedly grow even larger in moist conditions.

Propagation: Take unflowered half-ripe cuttings in July and insert in a rooting compost of peat and sand in a cold frame or in gentle bottom heat.

Pruning: None needed where there is space.

Uses: As excellent and very striking foliage contrast with other shrubs or trees. Flower sprays attractive in arrangements.

Shrubs: Beth Chatto, Dobbies, Hilliers, Marchant, Notcutts, Otter, Reuthe, Sherrard, Smith, St. Bridget, Stonehouse, Toynbee, Treseder, Woodland.

PIERIS — Lily of the Valley Shrub (*Ericaceae*).

The name of this genus is taken from Pierides, the 'surname' of the Muses. Looking up their rather complex origins I can only find their first names, which of course one could hardly call 'Christian'. These were Calliope, Euterpe, Erato, Melpomene, Thalia, Polyhymnia (or Polymnia), Terpsichore, Clio and Urania, and these nine were afterwards joined by Arethusa. Nowhere in their geneology can I find any mention or derivation of the name Pieris, so I, along with all the other works of reference, shall have to leave my opening statement as it stands.

But to return from the slopes of Mount Olympus — the genus Pieris is beautiful all through the year, but only, alas, in those gardens with acid soil. The young growth on these evergreen shrubs is as scarlet as a Poinsettia-bush and, indeed, looks very like this from a distance, except that the new Pieris leaves are shiny and the bracts of the Poinsettia are softly matt. At about the same time the pendulous clusters of flowers open, which makes a mature specimen a very fine addition to the garden. Several of the species do not begin to flower until they have really settled down, but whilst flowerless for a few years, the scarlet spring growths, especially in *P. formosa* 'Forrestii', is a comforting spectacle and is a foretaste of the pleasure to come, though *P. taiwanensis* does begin to flower earlier than the others (this species was introduced in 1918 so a description cannot be included in this book). Next in order to flower is *P. formosa,* the species of which must be among one of the most elegantly spectacular of spring-flowering shrubs, with its scarlet new leaves and the erect panicles of white flowers that look so much like Lilies-of-the-Valley. These are, happily, slightly scented. The variety 'Forrestii' has even brighter red new growths and larger flowers. These shrubs are somewhat tender and, as the flower panicles form in the autumn and are carried through the winter, they may often be so severely frosted as to be damaged, if not entirely killed. Therefore this form of Pieris requires particular care in siting. It is named after George Forrest (1873-1932), who was one of the most intrepid of all plant hunters, braving insurrections, illness, injuries and enduring privations and hardships that make one feel faint even to read about. It is excellent that so many of our garden plants are honoured in this way, as well they should be. *Pieris formosa* 'Forrestii' was discovered on his trip to China in 1910-1911 and was grown in England from seed collected at that time.

P. floribunda syn. **Andromeda floribunda** (1800) grows to 6ft (1.8m) with panicles of white urn-shaped flowers from March to May. A handsome hardy evergreen from the eastern United States for a sheltered position not facing east.

P. formosa syn. **Andromeda formosa** grows to 12ft (3.7m) and as much and more through, spreading by suckers. *P. formosa* 'Forrestii' (1910) grows to 20ft (6m) and spreads widely in warm districts (up to 50ft (15m) in circumference). Fine scarlet new growth in the former and even better in the latter, with larger white flowers in April and May. Spectacular evergreen shrubs from China and upper Burma for a sheltered, focal place in the garden.

P. japonica syn. **Andromeda japonica** (by 1870) grows to 10ft (3m) and as much through, with drooping racemes of waxy white flowers in March and April. Copper-coloured young growth in spring. A fine evergreen shrub from Japan for a semi-shaded place.

Requirements: Pieris need acid, moisture retentive soil (they grow best in those enviable gardens with natural springs). They need to be planted in semi-shade with the protection of large trees nearby, and they should be top-dressed each year with the best leaf-mould that you have. Mulch after watering in dry weather to prevent soil drying out and water in dry and desiccating winters.

Propagation: Take half-ripened heel-cuttings in August and insert in a rooting compost of two parts of sand to one of peat. Place in a cold frame until they have rooted and keep there for the winter. In spring make up a compost of equal parts of leaf-mould, peat, lime-free loam and silver sand. Transfer the rooted cuttings to individual pots of this and grow on, potting on as necessary in the same mixture. Plant out in a nursery area in autumn and grow on for two years, do not allow to dry out in summer.

Pruning: None required except to cut off frost damaged flower sprays.

After flowering: Cut off flowered sprays.

Uses: As excellent evergreen shrubs in the right kind of garden. Flowering branches and brilliant scarlet new growth for arrangements.

Shrubs: Ballalheannagh, Barcock, Bees, Bodnant, Brackenwood, Caldwell, Peter Chappell, Crarae, Dobbies, Glendoick, Fairley's, Goscote, Hilliers, Hyden, Jackman, Kershaw, Knaphill, Knoll Gardens, Lime Cross, Marchant, Meare Close, Notcutts, Otter, Reuthe, Roger, Rosemoor, Russell, Scotts, Sherrard, Smith, St. Bridget, Toynbee, Treasure, Woodland, Wyevale.

Seeds: Chiltern.

PILEOSTEGIA *(Hydrangeaceae* syn. *Saxifragaceae).* This is a fascinating and very obliging climber that should be seen more often, as it has so many virtues which I will here list: it is evergreen, it will grow in sun or semi-shade, it is not fussy as to soil type, and it is even more interesting in bud than in flower, and last but not least it is self-clinging. With such a catalogue of useful garden virtues I am sure you will want to rush out and get one right away. The average garden centre will not have it, but be of good cheer, my usual list will take care of this problem.

Pileostegia has conspicuous, spherical creamy buds that actually look like unusual flowers at first glance; these sit there for quite a while and then unfold to reveal a boss of cream stamens that are much more visible than the petals. This climber can be grown up trees, up (or down, as the case may be) walls and cliffs, providing evergreen cover and interest throughout the year. I think that all it asks for is an annual top dressing of leaf-mould or garden compost, though it would probably survive just as well without either. I have seen it growing under a south-facing window where the proliferation of prominent cream buds were very eye-catching, and in such a situation there would be plenty of room for it to mount the walls of the house. I grow it against a sheltered shaded wall, where it is doing quite well — I would not say it is romping upwards or sideways — and I am thinking of moving it to where it would be happier (and where it might reward me with more flower-buds, of course). But as it has only been with me for two seasons, which included the appalling winters and springs of 1984/85 and '86, I cannot judge its performance fairly yet, other than that it said 'thank-you' for the protection that I gave it.

P. viburnoides (1908) grows to 20ft (6m) with interesting buds and flowers forming from late August until October. A self-clinging evergreen climber from China for trees, walls or banks in sun or partial shade.

Requirements: Does better in good soil, otherwise unfussy.

Propagation: Take half-ripened cuttings in July or August and insert in a rooting compost of peat and sand. Place in a cold frame until well rooted and then transfer into John Innes No.1 and grow on in the usual way. Protect in a cold frame for first winter.

Pruning: None required; shaping (if necessary) can be done at end of flowering season if weather is mild, otherwise leave until end of April.

Uses: As an excellent and interesting climber; branches of flowers (at unopened stage) for arrangements.

Shrubs: Bodnant, Farall, Hilliers, Marchant, Sherrard, Treseder, Wyevale.

PIPTANTHUS *(Leguminosae)*. This is a small genus of ever-green shrubs that are very good for drought conditions and dry gardens generally. They grow quickly once installed and produce jolly yellow pea-flowers in May. They do need protection in cold counties and they cannot be relied on for longevity, but in the right place in the right garden they are most attractive, and are 'different' enough to cause comment and enquiry. The species described is sometimes called the 'Evergreen Laburnum', though in hard winters it may lose its leaves or, indeed, be killed. Young plants grow quickly, so this is a good shrub for new and empty gardens, and it can be planted to occupy a space that some other more slow-growing shrub will eventually fill. The mortality-rate of Piptanthus is high, so 'natural wastage' will take care of the situation.

P. laburnifolius syn. **P. nepalensis — Nepal Laburnum** (1821) grows to 12ft (3.7m) with a similar spread; golden yellow flowers in May. An evergreen shrub from the Himalaya for a warm, dry garden.

Requirements: Full sun, dry free-draining soil and a warm, sheltered position.

Propagation: Take short woody heel cuttings in August (ensure no pith is exposed) and insert in a rooting compost of two parts of sand to one of peat. When well rooted transfer to individual pots of John Innes No.1 with extra sand added and grow on. Or sow seeds in spring in a compost of equal parts of peat and sand. When large enough to handle, transfer to individual pots of John Innes No.1. Grow on for the summer, potting on once, then transfer to a sheltered sunny nursery area. Protect in winter with bracken.

Pruning: Cut away dead branches in early spring.

Uses: As an attractive shiny-leaved evergreen shrub, very suited to dry gardens.

Shrubs: Bodnant, Brackenwood, Busheyfields, Great Dixter, Hilliers, Notcutts, Otter, Roger, Scotts, Sherrard, South-combe, St. Bridget, Stonehouse, Toynbee, Treasure.

PITTOSPORUM *(Pittosporaceae)*. Gardeners in the southern counties of the British Isles are inclined to take at least one species of Pittosporum for granted, the pale, wavy-leaved black stemmed evergreen *P. tenuifolium* beloved by florists and flower-arrangers.

This shrub (or small tree) is often popped in to fill a gap and, because it has a run of luck as regards our winters, it survives and grows well and then becomes something of an embarrassment in the garden, having invariably grown out of its space which in any case was not planned. But plant it as part of a focal foliage scheme, with small-flowered white roses or species clematis wreathing their trails of blossom through its elegant branches, or as a contrast in texture and colour to golden or crimson foliage, dark conifers and yews and then it will come into its own. It is undoubtedly tender, which is a good thing for the careless gardener, as its demise after a bad winter will teach him a lesson in appreciation. It may be grown as a hedge in mild districts, and should be planted as a pale ribbon of contrast against darker ever-greens, but it should be remembered that it will always try to be the tree that it really is.

P. Tobira is a shrub which asks for one of the best and warmest garden positions. It has particularly handsome dark-green leathery leaves that grow in a formalised way which give this species an air of distinction throughout the year, but it will in time grow very large so allow for its eventual spread.

P. tenuifolium grows to 30ft (9m) or more with inconspicuous purple flowers in May that give off a strong honey-fragrance in the evenings. A very attractive evergreen from New Zealand for a warm garden in southern counties.

P. Tobira (1804) grows to 20ft (6m) and spreads to 10ft+ (3m+) with clusters of creamy orange-blossom scented flowers from April to July. A tender evergreen from China and Japan for a focal position; best against a warm wall.

Requirements: *P. tenuifolium* does best in sheltered gardens in full sun in any good garden soil. When used for hedging it should be sited carefully, as cold winters may kill part (though never all) of it. *P. Tobira* should be given the protection of a warm wall where its dark rosettes of leaves can be admired and where the perfume from the flowers can be easily enjoyed. As this plant may eventually grow very large, siting it can be something of a problem and the path may get swallowed up under its skirts. Set out small plants of *P. tenuifolium* 18" (46cm) apart for hedging.

Propagation: Take half-ripe heel cuttings in July and insert them in a rooting compost of peat and sand in a propagator set at

16-18°C (61-64°F). When well rooted transfer to John Innes No.2 and keep in a frost free frame or cold greenhouse for their first winter. *P. Tobira* grows slowly and should be plunged in its pot in a nursery area or cold frame for another year before setting out in its final position. *P. tenuifolium* grows more rapidly and can be planted out in the spring.

Pruning: Prune hedges in spring and again in July. For a new hedge of *P. tenuifolium* cut back leading growths in the first season to encourage basal shooting; do this as necessary.

Uses: *P. tenuifolium* as a contrast shrub or as hedging in mild counties, foliage for arrangements. *P. Tobira* as a handsome focal plant, scented flowers good for cutting.

Shrubs: Brackenwood, Peter Chappell, Daisy Hill, Dobbies, Great Dixter, Hilliers, Hopleys, Hyden, Jackman, Kaye, Knaphill, Knoll Gardens, Lime Cross, Marchant, Marten's Hall, Meare Close, Notcutts, Otter, Reuthe, Roger, Rosemoor, Russell, Scotts, Shepton, Sherrard, Southcombe, St. Bridget, Stonehouse, Toynbee, Treseder, Warley, Woodland, Wyevale.

Seeds: Butcher, Chiltern, Thompson and Morgan.

PLUMBAGO *(Plumbaginensis)*.

The name Plumbago is taken from Pliny's name for the plant which in turn was derived from *plumbum,* lead; it was thought at the time that the Plumbago would cure lead poisoning.

Not many plants have flowers that are this exact shade of milky-blue. It is a very beautiful colour, particularly when the climber is healthy and happy; this, alas, is difficult to achieve in the British Isles because, however clever we may be, we cannot deceive the plant into thinking that it is back home in South Africa. Therefore it has to be grown in a warm conservatory or greenhouse for good results. The stems are angular and rather weak and will need careful tying up, or the corymbs of flowers will just lie on the floor. Or the Plumbago can be planted very close to a sturdier climber such as *Ipomoea learii,* which has twining, strangling stems. The Plumbago can be tucked behind these and both will flower together. The combination of the delicate azure Plumbago with the blue-purple of the Ipomoea is very beautiful, but you must keep a watch on this association to prevent the Plumbago from being strangled. Snip off the Ipomoea's leaves judiciously so that the Plumbago can get sufficient light. You must also keep watch on the Plumbago because, once it has settled down in the greenhouse border, it will send up suckers which might in turn suffocate the Ipomoea. There is no rest with all this 'management', which is what they call it, they'll be at each other's throats the minute you turn your back. Plumbagos can be grown in a large pot, which solves the planting question in a conservatory with a paved floor. Because of the beautiful colour of the flowers and the very long flowering season it is worth every effort to make this plant feel at home.

P. capensis — Leadwort (1818) grows to 8ft+ (2.4m+) with clusters of sky-blue flowers from April to October. A sprawling evergreen from S. Africa for the warm greenhouse. (There is a white-flowered variety appropriately named 'Alba' which looks very like a Jasmine without the scent.)

Requirements: A warm greenhouse or conservatory with a minimum winter temperature of 7°C (45°F). If a warmer temperature is maintained the flowering season will be longer. Grow in John Innes No.3 and provide trellis or wires — or another climber — to tie or tuck the Plumbago into. The greenhouse should be partly shaded in hot summers or the blue of the Plumbago will be bleached, the other climber can earn its keep as a parasol. Water well from spring onwards but keep fairly dry in winter. Feed fortnightly with liquid manure from May until September, then decrease strength and number of feeds (of course, the other climber will benefit from all this too).

Propagation: Take heel cuttings of unflowered shoots in June or July; insert in a rooting compost of sand and peat and put into a propagator set at 16-18°C (61-64°F). When rooted transfer into John Innes No.1 and, when re-potting is necessary, pot on into John Innes No.2.

Pruning: Cut back after flowering, shorten all stems by about half or two-thirds.

Uses: As very beautiful greenhouse climbers. Young plants can be grown in large pots to stand out in hot summers, remembering that full sun will fade the flowers (there is not too much likelihood of this happening in the British Isles).

Shrubs: Bodnant, Hopleys, Roger, Scotts, St. Bridget.

Seeds: Butcher, Chiltern, Thompson and Morgan, Unwin.

POLYGONUM — Russian Vine, Mile-a-minute creeper

(Polygonaceae). *P. baldschuanicum* takes its name from the town of Baldschuan, in the Bokhara area, near where the vine was first discovered by a German botanist called Albert von Regel, whose father was the director of the botanic garden of St. Petersburg, as it then was. Seed was sent to Kew and the first plant flowered in 1896. I can imagine those gardeners of long ago standing there watching this enormous plant growing before their very eyes; I wonder if they allowed it to attain its full height, or length, or coverage? And has anybody?

It is nice to be able to rely on something to do what all the legends say it will. I would be frightened of *P. baldschuanicum* in good soil because once planted it would swarm up and over everything in its path, this gardener included. I have it in my garden, but at the uncomfortable northern edge where it is overshadowed by the end of the Leylandii hedge. This is so poor a position that the vine does not get going until mid-summer, and its life is made even harder because it is cut off at the same time as the hedge has its hair-cut. But despite all this cruelty the vine sends up its annual shoots and the festoons of pinkish-white flowers look very delicate against the darkness of the hedge. People dislike this creeper because it is hard work to hold it, but it really is the best cover-up ever introduced into this country. Fortunately it is not hot enough in these northern latitudes for seed to be set, or it would be another story.

There are always places in larger gardens where *P. baldschuanicum* can be planted to cover untidy, ratty-looking sheds and outhouses, especially if funds do not permit of demolition and redevelopment of these, as is so often the case. One small plant in a pot and Hey-presto! In three years you will have a great green tablecloth dripping with lacy flowers that will hide everything beneath it. *P. baldschuanicum* usually grows as if there were no tomorrow, but it does not do too well in coastal gardens, where it behaves like a more-or-less normal creeper; it would seem that the salt-laden air, together with the continuous worrying effect of the wind, inhibits the vine's growth. The creeper drapes like crêpe and it should be grown to show off this attractive characteristic. For example, it looks very beautiful when hanging in green and white festoons from the limbs of a dead tree. The breeze will cause constant movement and the whole thing will look like a piece of living sculpture. You will have to be firm with it of course, which is why I say that the conditions prevailing in maritime gardens are just right for this sort of thing. See illustration.

P. baldschuanicum — Russian Vine, Mile-a-minute creeper (1883) grows to an almost unlimited extent — 40ft + (12m +) should be allowed (both ways). It has loose panicles of pinkish-white flowers from July until October. A rampant deciduous creeper from S. Turkistan generally used to cloak or cover or screen unsightly buildings, outhouses, fences or walls. Can be very beautiful if properly (and tirelessly) managed.

Requirements: Quite unfussy as to soil. Young plants need some shelter until their stems become woody.

Propagation: Take half-ripe heel cuttings in July or August and insert into a rooting compost of peat and sand. When rooted transfer into pots of sieved garden soil and grow on.

Pruning: Do it often.

Uses: Many — as screening cover on old and ugly fencing, as a climber (needing tying in) for buildings of all kinds. As a beautiful piece of living drapery on a large, long pergola or old dead tree, or into big evergreens such as Holm oaks (*Quercus Ilex*) or a row of yews *(Taxus baccata)* or Leylandii (x *Cupressocyparis leylandii)*. Trailing flower shoots lovely in arrangements.

Shrubs: Bodnant, Busheyfields, Fairley's, Goscote, Highfield, Hilliers, Jackman, Kaye, Kent, Kershaw, Knaphill, Lime Cross, Marchant, Meare Close, Otter, Reuthe, Roger, Russell, Scotts, Shepton, Smith, St. Bridget, Toynbee, Treseder, Warley, Woodland, Wyevale.

POTENTILLA — Shrubby Cinquefoil *(Rosaceae)*. The

shrubby Potentillas are easy, comfortable plants, sure to cover themselves with wide open flowers for at least five months of our gardening year. Give them a warm place in the sun, plant them at the right time and in the right way and then forget them. What a pleasure it is to be certain of something in the garden, and how rare. As I write this the temperature has dropped to three degrees below zero and by the very nature of things my ordinary, easy, obliging, colourful, no-trouble Potentilla may well have died, and I shall not know for several months yet. Moral: do not make rash statements about anything in the garden, particularly rash and optimistic statements, or a plague of grasshoppers will come and eat the lot.

The genus is named from the word *potens,* power, because the wild herbaceous forms were much used in ancient medicine and as good-luck plants to keep away witches and demons.

The first shrubby Potentilla was found growing wild in England in 1670 and it is nice to know that there are still some similar plants growing in inaccessible places in the Lake District and in Wales, while others may be found in Co. Clare, Galway and Mayo. This same plant has been recorded as being in cultivation ever since, though the plants that we grow today and call by the same name are very allied species and hybrids from Asia that have a tidier habit and a longer flowering season. They all hybridize very freely and are difficult (even for botanists) to tell apart. There are many modern cultivars in colours ranging from red through orange, all tones of yellow, cream, white and pink.

P. fruticosa — Shrubby Cinquefoil grows to 5ft (1.5m) with a succession of yellow flowers from May until September (in my garden). An easy, deciduous European shrub for a sunny place.

P. glabra (1822) grows to 4ft (1.2m) with white flowers from June to October. Pale green foliage and red stems. Deciduous shrub from Siberia for a sunny part of the garden.

Requirements: Full sun and free-draining soil. Good in seaside gardens.

Propagation: Take short, half-ripe heel-cuttings in September or October and insert in a rooting compost of peat and sand in a cold frame. They will have rooted by spring and can be grown on in individual pots or in a nursery area.

Pruning: Take old branches out at ground level and keep plant plump and bushy by cutting off flowered shoots. Pruning may be done in spring, but flowering will be delayed and usually lessened, so tidy the plant immediately after flowering which is often just before the frosts.

Uses: As a plump and floriferous small shrub to grow for colour and foliage contrast. Flowers for cutting.

Shrubs: Bressingham, Dobbies, Jack Drake, Farall, Goscote, Highfield, Hilliers, Hopleys, Hortico, Ingwersen, Jackman, Kershaw, Knoll Gardens, Lime Cross, Marchant, Meare

Close, Notcutts, Orchard, Otter, Robinsons, Roger, Russell, Scotts, Shepton, Sherrard, Smith, St. Bridget, Stonehouse, Toynbee, Treasure, Warley, Woodland, Wyevale.

Seeds: Chiltern.

PRUNUS — Cherry Laurel, Common Laurel, Portugal Laurel, Blackthorn, Sloe *(Rosaceae)*.

Because this book is about shrubs there can be no place in it for that large and lovely collection of cherries and plums whose blossom beautifies the spring garden. But the so-useful laurel, *P. Laurocerasus* (standby of the Victorian shrubbery and used to fill shaped beds, difficult corners and to hide things), is a member of this genus and grown as a flowering shrub. You will find it very attractive with many visitors enquiring as to what it is.

Laurel is quick growing and immensely useful as a screen or a windbreak, though where there are constant strong winds it will be slower in growth. But for screening off your neighbours it is excellent, being quicker than yew, not as frightening as Leylandii, not prickly like holly and not as tame as privet. One should remember, when considering laurel for hedging, that it will try to grow about 6ft (1.8m) wide or more and you may only want to give it 3ft (90cm) and there will therefore always be a conflict. But laurel is handsome and elegant and its shining leaves always look polished and clean. If they do not it is because urban pollution in all its nasty forms has been too much for the shrub. It is excellent as part of a big mixed hedge on a boundary where neither party is standing by with a tape-measure, also as an isolated shrub in semi-shaded places, where it will flower quite well and always look handsome. The flower spikes on *P. Laurocerasus* stand stiffly erect in bunches and by these it is easily recognised from *P. lusitanica*, the Portugal laurel, whose single flowering sprays form gracefully at the ends of the branches. *P. Laurocerasus* can be used as hedging in the same manner, but it is more often seen as a large boundary shrub, thus combining a useful function with an ornamental appearance. Laurel leaves are poisonous, containing hydrocyanic or prussic acid, which comes to the same thing. As a child during the war years of 1939-1945 I collected butterflies and quite rightly I was not allowed to have a 'grown-up' killing bottle. In the books I read that crushed laurel leaves would give off a gas that would be fatal to the butterflies, so I tried this. I mashed up some laurel leaves and put them into a jar, then popped in a Cabbage-white which I had just caught. This was a fine, newly emerged specimen, in the prime of life, and it took far too long to die, beating its wings vainly and damagingly against the glass walls of its terminal prison. Since this was unpleasant both to watch and to hear, I abandoned this method of despatch and turned to the much cleaner, quicker use of methylated spirit. It must be remembered that this

was around 1942 or 43, when there seemed limitless numbers of butterflies, as indeed there were. We are wiser now, and sadder.

P. spinosa is the Blackthorn or Sloe, so excellent in pasture hedging and for its blue-bloomed fruit. It is quite easy to tell the difference between hawthorn (*Crataegus*) and blackthorn in midwinter — the trunk and spiny branches of the latter are dark, hence the name of blackthorn, while those of the hawthorn are brown and are not so fiercely armed. Blackthorn wood is hard and enduring and was formerly used for making parts of farm tools, such as the teeth of hay-rakes.

My father had a wonderfully strong, straight and spiky blackthorn walking stick which was at least 60 years old when he came by it; this supported him very well until his death at the age of 89. I was upset when I found that somebody had stolen it during that sad time afterwards when one has to sort out all the furniture and personal possessions; I truly wish that I still had that stick because it personified my father's great strength of character.

There are superstitions about the blackthorn which has a reputation for both good and bad luck. It is bad luck to bring the white blossoming branches into the house, however welcome they may be after a hard winter. It is equally bad luck to wear them for any purpose. But luck is strong for the owner when a straight blackthorn stem is made into a stick or a shillelagh.

P. Laurocerasus — Common Laurel, Cherry Laurel, Versailles Laurel (1629) grows to 20ft (6m) with a similar spread. Erect racemes of white flowers in April. An evergreen shrub from E. Europe and Asia Minor for many garden positions. Not always hardy.

P. lusitanica — Portugal Laurel (1648) grows to 20ft (6m) with a similar spread. Racemes of cream flowers in June. An evergreen from Spain and Portugal for hedging, boundaries, screens and as a specimen shrub. Hardier than *P. Laurocerasus.*

P. spinosa — Blackthorn, Sloe grows to 10ft (3m) with creamy-white flowers in April on bare branches. A European deciduous shrub or small tree for wild-garden hedging and for fruit.

Requirements: Ordinary good garden soil for the laurels, *P. lusitanica* does quite well on chalk; any soil for *P. spinosa*. The laurels do best in sun but grow quite well in semi-shade. In deep or constant shade they will gradually become attenuated. *P. spinosa* needs sun to flower and fruit well.

Propagation: Take heel cuttings of the laurels in August or September and place in a rooting compost of peat and sand in a cold frame. When rooted transfer to individual pots of John Innes No.1 and grow on, keeping in the frame for the winter. Take half-ripe heel cuttings of *P. spinosa* in July and place in a rooting compost of peat and sand. Put into a propagator set at 16-18°C (61-64°F) and when rooted transfer to pots of John Innes No.1, to give them a good start. Keep in a cold frame for the winter and then, if a number are being propagated for hedging, plant out in a nursery row to grow on for a season.

Pruning: Laurels must be pruned with secateurs, never with shears, as the large leaves when sliced or torn in half look dreadful. Pruning of hedges can be done in April, this will prevent flowers forming, or in August for specimen shrubs. Tip shoots of young plants to promote bushiness. *P. spinosa* can be pruned at any time of the year, but hedges are best done immediately after flowering. If the fruit is wanted cut back after picking which should be done in November (frost tempers the acidity of the sloes).

Uses: Laurel makes an elegant hedge (put some wire fencing in the middle to prevent dogs and children short-cutting) and excellent boundaries, screens and specimen shrubs. The flowers are good in short term arrangements. *P. spinosa* makes an animal and people-proof hedge. Flowers and fruits of *P. spinosa* can be used medicinally and fruits for Sloe wine and gin.

Shrubs: Goatcher, Goscote, Hilliers, Hopleys, Ingwersen, Jackman, Knaphill, Knoll Gardens, Lime Cross, Notcutts, Orchard, Otter, Roger, Rosemoor, Russell, Scotts, Shepton, Sherrard, Smith, Southcombe, St. Bridget, Stonehouse, Toynbee, Treasure, Treseder, Woodland, W.W.

Seeds: Chiltern, Thompson and Morgan.

PUNICA *(Punicaceae)*. Pomegranates are evocative of caliphs and camels, palm-trees and pyramids, and one wonders why the sensible gardener attempts to grow a plant so unsuited to our latitude. But gardeners are not sensible, they are visionaries filled with coloured dreams induced by catalogue photographs or holiday memories, so they plant pomegranates for the flowers (they say) which are very colourful and they remember that every ten years there is a drought and maybe *then* there might be fruit (which there are not, normally: the pomegranate has more sense than to waste the effort). It does not matter that one can buy these exotic things (full of slippery seeds) in the greengrocer's, one can do the same with grapes, but we all keep trying to grow grapes because one's own fruit always tastes quite marvellous. But plant this Middle-Eastern tree, for this is what it is, against a warm south-facing house wall and there will be a good show of the silky scarlet flowers in late summer (in warm years). The flowers always remind me of ballet-practice skirts — the petals fall off quite quickly leaving the firmer, lobed calyx which stays colourful for some time.

The pomegranate is an important part of Middle-Eastern culture and custom, with many legends surrounding it since ancient times. For example, a newly married Turkish woman will predict the number of her children by throwing a ripe fruit to the ground and then counting the scattered seeds. Since the pomegranate has a very large number of seeds it is the Middle-Eastern equivalent of an emblem of fertility and one lifetime would not be long enough to produce similar progeny. The pulp is used to flavour drinks, ices and sherbert, and the rind produces a red dye that is used in the preparation of Moroccan leather. The pomegranate is often considered to be the original apple coveted by Eve, and fruit and flowers have appeared in stylised designs and embroideries for centuries, much as the peony and the chrysanthemum have in the Far East. The pointed sepals are thought to have inspired the shape of King Solomon's crown though they remind me of the Red Queen's in 'Alice through the Looking Glass'; the plant symbolized the ancient Babylonian god of storms and thunder, Ramman, and today its Arabic name of Rumman is much the same.

The dwarf pomegranate, *P. Granatum* 'nana', is smaller in every way but is hardier, and it makes a very attractive tub plant that can be brought under cover in winter.

P. Granatum — Pomegranate (16th century) grows to 10ft (3m) and as much wide against a wall (more in its native home) with scarlet flowers from July to September. Fruit mostly in greenhouses, or the extreme south-western parts of the United Kingdom. A deciduous shrub (or small tree) from S.E. Europe and Asia for warm walls, greenhouse or conservatory. *P.g.* 'nana' (1723) grows to 3ft (90cm) with correspondingly smaller flowers and is generally hardier and certainly more manageable.

Requirements: Sunny, sheltered wall space and good well drained loam. Protect as much of it as possible in winter. If it is to be grown in the greenhouse a planting hole should be filled with John Innes No.2 and a minimum winter temperature of 5-7°C (41-45°F) will keep it alive. A warmer temperature of 13-16°C (55-61°F) will help to produce fruit in autumn (it will be much cheaper to buy these). Water well from early spring onwards and open doors and ventilators on mild days. Plant *P.g.* 'nana' in pots of John Innes No.2 and treat similarly for winter, autumn and spring; in summer the pots can be placed on patio or terrace or can be plunged in the garden. Bring inside in September.

Propagation: Take half-ripe heel cuttings in July, insert into a rooting compost of peat and sand in a propagator set at 16-18°C (61-64°F). When rooted transfer into pots of John Innes No.2 and grow on. Or sow seeds in spring in pots (three to a pot) in a propagator set at 16°C (61°F). When large enough discard or transplant survivors into John Innes No.1 and grow on until they need re-potting, then transfer into John Innes No.2. *P.g.* 'nana' is an attractive patio or terrace plant and can be sunk, pot and all, into a rockery. Plant it against a large rock or slab and in warm years the reflected warmth may be sufficient to ripen the little fruits.

Pruning: None needed, except to tidy away winter-killed branches. Do not cast out an apparently dead plant until after midsummer, it may spring again from the roots.

Uses: As ornamental flowering shrubs, any fruit can be considered as a bonus.

Shrubs: Hilliers, Notcutts, Otter, St. Bridget.

Seeds: Butcher, Chiltern, Thompson and Morgan.

PYRACANTHA — Firethorn (*Rosaceae*).

This vigorous and beautiful shrub is so useful in the garden that it is often planted without any thought of the future. But because it is hardy and very fast-growing it will usually outgrow the space it was planted in and can then become a constant worry. The moral of this is do not put one in unless the space available measures 20ft x 20ft+ (6m x 6m+), or you will be forever chopping and clipping and losing a season's berries in the doing. I speak from experience — my wall measures 15ft+ (4.5m+) sideways but not upwards, being a fairly standard 6ft (1.8m) in height. The Pyracantha loved its position, flexed its muscles and grew apace, flowering and fruiting with abandon, much to the joy of the sparrows in January who fight and flutter and squabble over the berries until the bush looks bristly with picked-over stems, like the grapes when the visitors have gone. Pyracanthas do need sun to flower and for colouring the berries, which are such a long-lasting brightness in winter. If planted in prepared holes in yards or to grow up house walls, they will do well because their roots will be cool under paving or concrete. They need very strong support to grow to because being evergreen they present a considerable amount of windage during gales, but the stems are exceedingly strong and though they may at times creak they seldom crack. They look very handsome when grown and shaped as arches or to make symmetrical bands of living green on house walls. Being quick-growing and very vigorous the results are encouraging to the impatient gardener, though he should not turn his back for too long. I am speaking of *P. atalantioides* with which I am very familiar. If grown in semi-shade the shrub flowers well enough but does not berry much, or so I found when I planted the variety 'Aurea' of this species. The wood is very close grained and strong as well as thorny and removing a mature shrub piecemeal was hard and painful work and taught me several valuable lessons.

The flowers are beloved by bees and a hedge of Pyracantha is a nice neat surround to a collection of beehives, though it might be better to make it a mixed hedge with very late and very early-blooming flowers as well so that the bees have their food to hand, so to speak, at both ends of the season.

P. angustifolia (1889) grows to 10ft+ (3m+) with a spread of 8ft (2.4m) with creamy flowers in June and July and distinctive leaves that are grey-felted beneath. Orange-red, rather flattened berries in late autumn, lasting throughout the winter. An evergreen shrub from China for sunny walls.

P. atalantioides syn. **P. Gibbsii** (1907) grows to 20ft+ (6m+) with a similar spread and clusters of cream-white flowers in June and scarlet berries in early winter lasting (birds permitting) until March. A lusty evergreen from China for tall, wide, sunny walls as hedging or as a free-standing specimen. (This is the most vigorous species.) Var. 'Aurea' has yellow berries.

P. coccinea — Firethorn (1629) grows to 20ft+ (6m+) with clusters of white flowers in June followed by scarlet berries along the branches. A vigorous evergreen from S. Europe and Asia Minor for similar situations.

P. Rogersiana (1911) grows to 12ft (3.7m) with white flowers in June followed by red, orange or yellow berries according to the variety. (Species has orange-red berries.) A less rampageous evergreen shrub from China for smaller areas.

Requirements: Good garden loam and full sun for best berries and flowers. Less good conditions result in less berries, though flowers may still be abundant. Strong wires or trellis essential for wall shrubs. Allow maximum space for plants according to species or variety chosen.

Propagation: Take short unflowered cuttings of current season's shoots in July or August and insert them in a rooting compost of peat and sand. Put in a propagator set at 16°C (61°F). When the cuttings are well rooted transfer into individual pots of John Innes No.1 and grow on. Keep in a cold frame for the winter. Or woody cuttings may be taken in October, inserted in pots of the same rooting compost and left in a cold frame for the winter. By late spring they will have rooted. Both types of cuttings can then be potted on and plunged in a nursery area for the summer. Pyracanthas grow well from seeds — collect fresh berries in October and crush them with a piece of wood to get the seeds. Sow these immediately in boxes of moistened John Innes seed compost or equivalent and place in a cold frame for the winter. When large enough to handle Transfer into John Innes No.1 and grow on. This is an inexpensive way of producing large quantities of plants for hedging.

Pruning: Trim off winter-damaged shoots in April, before flowering to keep shrub attractive. Prune to shape between May and July, a season's berries will often be lost, so take away slightly more growth in one year so as to leave shrub free to flower abundantly the next. Hedges should be trimmed after flowering. Free-standing shrubs need no pruning. Isolated arches need strong supports.

Uses: As evergreen wall or specimen shrubs, as arches and as hedges. Berries for arrangements, can be used with holly when this lacks berries at Christmas, but Pyracantha berries do not last as long out of water as those of holly.

Shrubs: Goatcher, Goscote, Highfield, Hilliers, Hyden, Jackman, Kershaw, Knaphill, Knoll Gardens, Lime Cross, Meare Close, Notcutts, Otter, Reuthe, Roger, Scotts, Shepton, Sherrard, Smith, St. Bridget, Stonehouse, Toynbee, Treasure, Warley, Woodland, W.W., Wyevale.

Seeds: Chiltern.

RHODODENDRON (includes **AZALEA**) *(Ericaceae).* This large and complex genus now includes Azaleas, though these will generally still be listed as such in nurserymen's catalogues. The name Rhododendron comes from *Rhodon,* a rose, and *dendron,* a tree, and is very descriptive for the larger-growing kinds. The following remarks may be familiar to Rhododendron afficionados and I hope they will bear with them and with me for the sake of new gardeners thirsting to start growing the genus (which with careful selection can be chosen to flower for eight months of the year).

To make things as easy as possible 'Rhododendrons' are evergreen and 'Azaleas' are deciduous — though the 'evergreen' Azaleas actually lose some of their new season's leaves in autumn, and some semi-evergreen Azaleas keep some of their leaves (at the tips of their branches) depending on the coldness of the winter months. Otherwise there is no difference. Rhododendrons need acid soil with only one exception, *R. hirsutum.*

The genus is hardy, again, with only a few exceptions, and even these can be grown in warm, sheltered southern gardens. Most Rhododendrons prefer semi-shade or 'light woodland' conditions where this is possible and a sunscorched shrub would rather have the shade and shelter from a large Weigela, lilac or flowering cherry than none at all (though care must be taken to avoid competition from these, particularly the cherry which has surface roots), so gardeners with small gardens need not set about planning a shelter-belt for their new treasures. Frost can be a peril for early flowering species and varieties, as can cold, drying winds, hence the need for protection.

Almost all the species came from India, Burma, China, Tibet, the Himalaya, Malaysia and New Guinea, with a few species originating in N. America and Europe.

Rhododendrons are comparatively new to old and and new-world gardens because their main countries of origin were so inaccessible even to the first plant-hunters. Of course, a few species had been discovered and introduced at an early time, notably the European *R. ferrugineum* with its rose-pink flowers, which in 1583 was seen and described as being like an Oleander. Several American species were found and sent to England where they were distributed among the gardens of Tradescant, Philip Miller and others. They were slow to flower and it must be assumed that those famous gardeners, though taking every possible care, did not know that an acid soil was essential. The Rhododendron that springs most quickly to the British gardener's mind is *R. ponticum* which has taken to our islands like a duck to water, growing wild on heaths and in woodland much as it does in its native home on the shores of the Black Sea. It was named by Tournefort who discovered it whilst travelling in

that region during 1700-1702, but oddly enough the first plants to be sent to England came from Spain. This shrub quickly became very popular and was grown as a pot plant to begin with (round about 1803) and it was some time later that country landowners discovered its hardiness and began to plant it out by the thousand to embellish their estates. In the same year *R. caucasicum* was discovered on the slopes of Mount Caucasus, while *R. catawbiense* was found in great profusion on a mountain-top in North America. With these species, together with *R. maximum,* also from N. America, a breeding programme began, though the colours were not very exciting at first. Then the first scarlet-flowered Rhododendron, *R. arboreum,* was discovered by a Captain Hardwicke in 1796, who sent seeds of it from the Himalaya. These may not have germinated because there was a later introduction which flowered in 1815. This species is a rather tender one suitable only for large greenhouses or to be grown in Cornwall. These and their progeny were sufficient to arouse considerable interest in the genus and, what was more important, it was hoped that there might be others of different colours. In 1847 Dr. Joseph Hooker was commissioned by Kew to collect plants in India. He made four separate journeys and endured appalling discomforts and dangers, including starvation and imprisonment through the political machinations of the Dewar (or Prime Minister) of Sikkim who was endeavouring to keep all the British out of the kingdom, even though the ageing Rajah was himself pro-British. It is delightful to read that part of one journey was made in style on the backs of elephants, who were so intelligent that they had been trained to pluck down flowers from the trees. These journeys yielded quantities of Rhododendron-seed and, in 1851, Hooker set sail for England with these precious seeds (he had discovered over 40 new species) and had many dried specimens, with drawings and descriptions of the Rhododendrons and other plants such as the beautiful blue orchid, *Vanda caerulea.* The descriptions and drawings were sent home long before Hooker himself left India and formed the first part of the book 'Rhododendrons of the Sikkim Himalaya' which his father, Sir William Hooker published in sections. The book stimulated the interest of growers and collectors even before Joseph Hooker had left India, and the promise of botanical richness was to attract many of the famous plant-hunters such as Delavaye, Forrest, Farrer, Kingdom-Ward and E.H. Wilson.

The new Rhododendrons, when they flowered, proved to be so exciting to gardeners and nurserymen that very many hybrids were produced, most of which are still in today's catalogues. In addition to this the main flood of Rhododendron introductions did not begin to pour out of the Far East until the early part of this century and it must have seemed like a cornucopia of colour, which, of course, it is because the flowers can now be had in every shade except true blue.

There are several stories about *R. ponticum* whose unadulterated honey is poisonous. In the year 40 B.C. Xenophon's army was defeated in battle. Retreating in good order they camped at a deserted village on the shores of the Black Sea whose inhabitants had, wisely, abandoned hearth and home rather than risk possible massacre, those being violent times. The villagers had honey-bees, and the combs were full, so the licentious soldiery ate their fill. Now, you will remember that I said that *R. ponticum* was first discovered on the shores of the Black Sea; the flowers were or had been in bloom, and therefore the honey would have had a high percentage of Rhododendron nectar which made the men violently ill — so much so that had the villagers returned they could have sent in grandmothers and children to polish off the troops without the aid of the menfolk. But this did not happen, the villagers stayed away and the soldiers recovered from their symptoms which were sickness, purging, temporary madness and, for the greediest, coma. It will never be known whether the deadly nectar came from *R. ponticum*, *R. luteum* or the *Nerium Oleander*, all of which grew nearby, but this incident was told by Pliny and later botanists found that *R. luteum* had a similar reputation. The honey from the latter plant was actually used medicinally in Constantinople (Istanbul, as it now is). The Tibetans crystalise the flowers of ponticum as Europeans do violets or any flower, and the leaves of *R. chrysanthum* were sedative and narcotic. These properties were put to use by the physicians in Siberia who used the plant to relieve the pains of rheumatism and gout.

Azaleas were discovered in America, Europe, Asia, China and Japan. They are mainly deciduous, though as with most plant descriptions or statements there are notable exceptions.

In the seventeenth century the first Azalea — *R. viscosum* — was discovered in America by the Reverend John Bannister, who sent a plant to his friend the botanically-minded Bishop Compton. The same plant was again found in 1734 and was sent to England, along with *R. nudiflorum*. Soon afterwards William Bartram described *R. calendulaceum* (like a marigold in colour) as the 'Fiery Azalea' because the flowers were all shades of orange, gold, yellow and cream. This is one of the Azaleas that smothers itself with flowers so thickly that no leaves are visible. Bartram saw acres covered with this plant in North America which he described as being 'like a hillside set on fire'. He sent dried specimens to Sir Joseph Banks in 1774 but there is no record of the plant itself being in cultivation in the British Isles before 1806. The 'Pontic Azalea' or *R. luteum* had also arrived, as had seeds of several other kinds from Asia Minor, so that there was sufficient material (and many colours this time) for plant breeding to begin. In the early part of the 19th century a Belgian baker in Ghent, called

Mortier, developed his hobby extensively and began raising a new race of Azaleas by forcing or holding back early and late flowering species so that he could make crosses that were not hitherto possible. Other growers in his area followed suit and the 'Ghent Azalea' strain eventually numbered about 500, some of which were sent to England to act as parents in their turn to those already in cultivation. Other Azaleas were now being discovered — the tender *R. molle* from Japan and the hardy *R. japonicum* in 1830, and *R. occidentale* from California whose sap runs in the veins of many of the Exbury Azaleas. The 'Kurume' strain was discovered by E.H. Wilson on the Japanese island of Kyushu, where they had been grown for centuries. Wilson's 'famous 50' were selected in 1918 and are therefore outside the time-scale of this book. On the whole, the deciduous-leaved Azaleas prefer a sunny, airy situation, with the same acid soil, though if it is possible to plant them so that they are shaded by tall trees at mid-day, it will be found that the flowers do not fade or go over so quickly.

The serious gardener needs to know that the genus has been divided into four rather unequal sections or series as follows: Lepidote (those Rhododendrons with minute scales), Elepidote or Hymenanthus Rhododendrons (without scales), Azaleas and Azaleastrums. There is a Rhododendron society and there are many specialist books on this enormous, fascinating and very beautiful group of shrubs and trees. A list of species plants follows, which is made incomplete as a collection by the necessity of omitting the later introductions (ie. after 1914), but I hope that I have included foliage interest, which is of year-round importance, a representative spectrum of colour and early and later-flowering kinds. The best thing to do is to visit a specialist nursery during the main flowering months.

R. adenopodum (1901) grows to 10ft (3m) with white or palest pink, sometimes crimson-spotted bell-shaped clusters of flowers in April to May. Long, narrow dark leaves, fawn tomentum beneath. An evergreen shrub from China.

R. arboreum (1815) grows to 31ft+ (9m+) with a similar spread and should be classed as a small tree with white to blood-red flowers from March to April. An evergreen with large 8″ (20.5cm) long leaves from the Himalaya and Ceylon. Protect east-facing early flowers with other screening shrubs.

R. Augustinii (1901) grows to 10ft (3m) with a spread of 6ft (1.8m) and mauve-blue flowers in May. An evergreen shrub from China. Darkest-blue flowered shrubs are the most tender.

R. auriculatum (1900) grows to 20ft+ (6m+) with clusters of white to pink flowers in July and August. Large-leaved evergreen shrub or small tree from China. Does not flower until maturity.

R. brachyanthum (1906) grows to 5ft (1.5m) with a similar spread and pale yellow flowers in June or July. A neat evergreen shrub from China with aromatic leaves.

R. calendulaceum (Azalea calendulaceae) (1806) grows to 10ft (3m) with a similar spread. Yellow, orange, scarlet or cream flowers in May. A deciduous shrub from N. America.

R. campanulatum (1825) grows to 12ft (3.7m) with a similar spread. Clusters of rose-purple bell-shaped flowers in April. A spreading evergreen shrub from the Himalaya.

R. campylogynum (1912) grows to 4ft (1.2m) with a similar spread. Plum-purple bell-shaped flowers in May. A low cushiony evergreen shrub for the larger rock garden. Flowers when young.

R. caucasicum (1803) grows to 3ft (90cm) with a similar spread. Pale yellow flowers in May. An evergreen shrub from the Caucasus.

R. ciliatum (1850) grows to 5ft (1.5m) with a similar spread. Deep rose-coloured buds, pale pink flowers fading to white in April. An evergreen shrub from the Himalaya, much used by hybridists.

R. decorum (1889) grows to 10ft (3m) with a similar spread; shell pink flowers in May or June. An evergreen shrub from China.

R. ferrugineum — Alpine Rose (1752) grows to 4ft (1.2m) with a similar spread with deep pink or rose-scarlet flowers in June. An evergreen shrub from central Europe where it flowers in July or August, according to altitude.

R. Forrestii (1914) creeps only to 12″ (30cm) high with a spread of 5ft (1.5m) deep crimson flowers in April and May. A mat-forming evergreen creeping shrub from China, having rounded leaves. Needs semi-shade and moist conditions.

R. Fortunei (1855) grows to 12ft (3.7m) with a similar spread and pink-lilac flowers in May. An · evergreen shrub from Chekiang in E. China.

R. hirsutum — Alpine Rose (1656) grows to 4ft (1.2m) with a similar spread and deep pink flowers in June. Shoots, margins of leaves and stalks all bristly. Evergreen shrub from central Europe — the first Rhododendron to be introduced to British gardens. Grows on limestone.

R. impeditum (1911) grows only a few inches (cm) high, with scented mauve or lavender-blue flowers in May. A dwarf evergreen shrublet from China for the rock garden.

R. lutescens (1904) grows to 10ft (3m) with a similar spread and clear yellow flowers from February to April. An open evergreen shrub from Tibet, needing a very sheltered position.

R. luteum, Azalea pontica (1793) grows to 12ft (3.7m) with a similar spread. Sweetly scented yellow flowers in May. A deciduous shrub from E. Europe and Asia Minor with fine autumn colouration.

R. maximum — 'The Great Laurel' or **'Rose Bay'** of the United States (1736) grows to 10ft (3m) in cultivation, much more in its native home. Pale pink or purplish pink flowers in June and July. A fine evergreen with large — 10″ (25.5cm) long — leaves. Useful for late flowers in woodland.

R. mucronulatum (1907) grows to 8ft (2.4m) with a similar spread and bright rose-mauve flowers from December to February on naked stems. A deciduous shrub from N.E. Asia for the winter flower garden. Protect lower part of shrub from hares and rabbits.

R. neriiflorum (1906) grows to 8ft (2.4m) with a similar spread; rich red flowers in March or April. A handsome evergreen with white undersides to leaves, from China

R. obtusum, Azalea obtusa — Kirishima Azalea (1844) grows to 3ft (90cm) with a similar spread. Flowers variable: pink, red, orange, salmon, magenta, rose, crimson or white (var. 'album'). Cultivated for centuries in Japan, particularly on the island of Kyushu. (Parent of many of the 'Kurume' Azaleas introduced in 1919 by E.H. Wilson.)

R. ponticum (1763) grows to 20ft (6m) with a similar spread. Familiar flowers of rose-mauve in June. A vigorous evergreen from Asia Minor, formerly used as ornamental hedging on large estates. Now naturalised on heaths and in light woodland.

R. prostratum (1910) a prostrate shrub growing to 4″ (10cm) in the wild with rose-purple flowers in April and May. A small-leaved evergreen from China for the rock garden.

R. quinquefolium (1896) grows to 3ft+ (90cm+) with white flowers in April and May. A very beautiful deciduous shrub from Japan with purple-margined pale green young leaves, colouring well in autumn.

R. Rirei grows to 18ft (5.4m) and as much through with spotted purple-blue bell-shaped flowers in March. A large evergreen shrub from China.

R. Schlippenbachii, Azalea Schlippenbachii (1893) grows to 15ft (4.5m) with spotted pale pink flowers in April and May. A beautiful deciduous shrub from Korea with excellent autumn colouration.

R. scintillans (1913) grows to 3ft (90cm) with lavender or purple-blue flowers in April. A twiggy evergreen from China with tiny leaves, good against rocks.

R. Simsii syn. **A. indica — 'Indian Azalea'** (1808) grows to 5ft (1.5m) with flowers in scarlet, pink, crimson, magenta, violet, rose and orange. A tender evergreen from China for the greenhouse. Grown as Christmas and early spring house-plants.

R. Thomsonii (1849) grows to 12ft+ (3.7m+) with a similar spread. Blood-red flowers in March, April or May. A large evergreen shrub or small tree from the Himalaya. Needs feeding annually.

R. viscosum, Azalea viscosa — Swamp Honeysuckle (1734) grows to 8ft (2.4m) with very fragrant white flowers in July. A deciduous shrub from N. America.

R. yunnanense (1889) grows to a rounded bush 10ft x 12ft (3m x 3.7m) with white or pale pink crimson-spotted flowers in May. A very floriferous evergreen from China, appreciating feeding and mulching.

Requirements: A naturally acid soil improved by sand, well-decayed leaf-mould and peat. Do not dig in newly fallen or half-rotted leaves, the soil will shrink and the process of decay will rob the existing soil of nitrogen. Moist soil is best, remembering that in nature most (though not all) Rhododendrons grow in areas of high (incredibly high) rainfall. Dry, free-draining soil can be safely planted with Rhododendrons which should be kept well watered and mulched; large-leaved species and hybrids need particular care and attention since these come from tropical rain forests. Dappled shade from mature deciduous trees such as oaks, which are deep rooting, is the best possible situation, though the shade from almost any trees will do so long as their rooting formation is noted and compensated for. Protection as well as essential shade is given by the trees, because many species or varieties bloom early and the buds or flowers will be ruined by frosts. This also applies to the leafing of deciduous types. Rhododendrons should always be planted in a south or south-west facing aspect to avoid the rays of the sun falling on frosted plants. Greedy surface-rooting trees like sycamores, beech, birch, Prunus and large conifers will be a problem; a mature oak needs 300 gallons on a warm day in June, and other trees are as commensurately thirsty according to size. Rhododendrons need moisture at their roots (being comfortable in latitudes with 50″ (1.3m) of rain per annum). While this cannot easily be emulated it should be remembered, and in drought conditions all plants should be mulched after a thorough soaking (not tap-water if this comes from a chalk district nearby, as it does in my own area). Rhododendrons actually under trees will not get the rain that they need, so this must also be remembered, and if they are sited under trees with low branches they will grow to the lightest side and lose what may be a very characteristic shape. Rhododendrons do well in areas of high rainfall in the British Isles, such as Wales, Scotland and Ireland. The climate of Cornwall, though not as wet, is the best that we can offer them and it is here that they are happiest.

Choose later-flowering species or varieties if your garden is frosted regularly — better a bush in luxuriant blossom in May than perennially blackened hopes in April. Cold winds are equally damaging, since they dry out the moisture in the leaves which are often large and sometimes very handsome. Mulching helps here as it prevents frost getting into the ground and the deeper roots of the Rhododendron can continue their work of replacing what water is available in dry winter months.

Plant Rhododendrons very firmly and carefully, using a rounded stick or the handle of a broken tool, suitably shaped to firm the soil as it is replaced, and soak the containerised plant for an hour in a bucket first. Set the shrub and its ball of soil 2″ (5cm) deeper in the ground, finishing up with a lower soil surface, like a saucer. Future watering in dry weather will get to where it is needed immediately, instead of running off the surface, and any mulches will stay put for longer.

Rhododendrons can be easily moved when young, which is a great comfort, especially when you have made a mistake in evaluating the growth rate. Do the moving as carefully as possible on a damp day when more rain is forecast. Do not move them in hot weather or on a hot day. Give the plant a short stake, placed so as to be as inconspicuous as possible, to prevent wind rock. Move deciduous Rhododendrons (Azaleas) in autumn, after leaf-fall.

All Rhododendrons benefit from mulching and, after a good watering, fallen leaves can be collected round the stems; in areas of poor soil a nice mixed mulch of one-third peat, one-third well-rotted manure and one-third 'seasoned' leaf-mould to which has been added chopped June bracken is beneficial. Do not heap up round the stem, leave a hollow for this in the middle and add more mulch as the first lot sinks.

Mature plants will withstand drought reasonably well considering their heritage, but keep a watch on newly planted shrubs and water well.

Propagation: Is from seed, and from layering and different kinds of cuttings. Collect seed when ripe: this time will vary according to type and weather conditions. (Mixed collections of Rhododendrons will not be true to type.) Sow from January to end of February in clean clay pots of peat and silver sand, in the proportions of seven of peat to three of silver sand. Place pots in a dish of rain water so that the compost becomes evenly moist, leave to drain. Sprinkle seeds very sparingly on the surface and cover with a dusting of silver sand. Place the pots in a propagator or a warm greenhouse where a constant temperature of 13-16°C (55-61°F) can be maintained. Keep 'watering water' at the same temperature. Stand the pots on new peat and cover with a sheet of paper and glass, prop up with wire so that paper does not touch soil surface. Change the paper every day, water drying pots by standing them in the rain water. After germination, which is usually irregular, tweak out any seedlings that have damped off. Shade seedlings from bright light with paper on sunny days, remove this on dull days. In April the larger seedlings can be transferred into a seedling compost of equal parts of acidic loam, peat, sieved leaf-mould and potting grit, watering as before. Keep in the same temperature until summer, then move to a cold frame. Carefully harden off, though slow plants will need the protection of the frame for their first winter.

Layering can be done from October until early spring. Choose suitable branches that are a pleasing shape of both evergreen and deciduous species or varieties. Take off leaves and twigs at ground level and scrape away the bark on the underside of the branch. Improve the soil beneath by adding peat, sand and well-decayed leaf-mould. Peg the prepared branch firmly into the ground and cover with about 2″ (5cm) of soil and tie the upright tip to a stake. Sever from parent plant about 18 months to two years afterwards. Keep a regular check to see that pegs, wires or stakes have not been moved by wind, frosts, pets, moles, rabbits, mice, squirrels or your spouse.

Small growing pigmy-sized Rhododendrons are easier, as the same procedure is done in miniature.

Propagation by cuttings is done according to leaf size, and a propagator is almost essential.

Starting with the single-leaved types (dwarf evergreens), take short half-ripe cuttings from current season's growth in August (cut just below a leaf joint). Insert into a rooting compost of equal parts of sifted peat and sand. Place in a sheltered cold frame and keep shaded and just moist — water with rain-water as previously described. They should have rooted by the following spring.

For larger-leaved species, from August to October take 3″ (7.5cm) cuttings from lateral shoots of current season's growths. Take cuttings at a joint, cutting off the leaves. Reduce the leaf area of those left by cutting these in half; remove any terminal buds or shoots. Dip base of moistened cutting into hormone powder and follow instructions on canister, it will be found that taking off a shaving of green skin at the base of the cutting will increase the rooting area. Insert cuttings into a rooting compost of peat and sand and place in the propagator set at 19°C (65°F). They will take some time to root and present a challenge to a gardener who is good at propagating generally. Rooted cuttings should be protected from cold spring weather and can then be planted out in a nursery area.

For *R. Simsii* and all its jolly-coloured progeny, take short half-ripe cuttings in June and insert them in a rooting compost of peat and sand in a propagator set at 16°C (61°F). When they have rooted, transfer into the growing compost previously described and grow on in a frost-free environment such as a warm greenhouse or conservatory. Use a hormone rooting powder for better success, as Rhododendrons do not strike easily.

Pests and diseases: Unfortunately, Rhododendrons seem to attract specific insectivorous vermin which must be dealt with as soon as noticed or there will be no flowers. Rhododendron bug or fly — *Stephanitis rhododendri* — is specific in its likes, it likes Rhododendrons. Its sucking equipment causes brown mottling on the upper side of the leaves and a rusty appearance beneath. The leaves will then turn brown and the shrub will be considerably weakened as the pest gets into its stride in the generative game. Spray at three week intervals with malathion and look for the pests in the interval. Eggs can be found on the undersides of the succulent young growth, along the midrib.

Rhododendron Leafhopper — *Gracocephala coccinea* — appears to be the main cause of the disease called bud-blast; the leaf-hoppers are a nice bright green with red stripes, and as the adults are half an inch (1.3cm) long they can be easily seen on shrubs that are low enough to get at. The eggs are

laid in the forming buds in late summer, and the young emerge in spring to feed on the juicy sap of the bud-scales which they puncture, thus allowing the spores of the disease to enter.

Rhododendron whitefly — *Dialeurodes Chittendenii* — produces scale-like larvae which can be found on the undersides of the leaves of Azaleas from August until April. As with all scale insects, they match nicely and they excrete sticky honeydew which is unsightly. And as with all scale insects they are determined survivors. Spraying and wiping will get rid of them eventually.

The presence of the disease called bud-blast shows as brown patches on the flower buds in late autumn or early winter. These patches develop into characteristic bristles with pin-heads, which means that your favourite shrub (of Ponticum extraction) is infected. The buds should be picked off and burnt and it will be noticed that infected buds need a sharp pull to break them off, whereas frost-damaged buds, which can look very similar, are snapped off easily. There is no direct cure.

Azalea gall is caused by *Exobasidium vaccinii* and shows itself by causing the leaf to thicken and blister. When it turns white it is at the spore-bearing stage, after which the leaf shrivels. Pick off all the affected leaves and burn them.

Frost will cause buds to discolour and turn brown, after which they will rot and fall off (this is better than bud-blast).

Honey fungus — *Armillaria mellea* — strikes terror into the Rhododendron lover's heart: it is evidenced by drooping lack-lustre leaves that hang miserably without falling. It will kill the shrub, and this must be sacrificed to save the others. Change the soil to a distance of six or eight feet (1.8m to 2.4m) round and to a depth of at least two feet (60cm). If this is not possible the soil *must* be sterilised before any replanting, which is best not done for a year. Annuals can be grown temporarily to fill the space. Never, never leave stumps or roots of anything to decay in the ground, or your conscience will prick you for ever after.

Silver leaf — *Stereum purpureum* — does not turn Rhododendron leaves silver, as it obligingly does on members of the Prunus family. It causes die-back of whole branches and sometimes the whole shrub, which must be removed and burnt. There is no known cure.

Pruning: Rhododendrons do not need pruning, though some times they need a little tidying. Any dead branches should be removed as soon as seen. Large hedges of *R. ponticum* need keeping within bounds, and this can be done immediately after flowering. If a large-growing or even a medium-sized shrub has outgrown its expected space it is often better to consider moving it rather than to try to make it fit. Pick off dead flower-trusses using hairdresser's scissors, not secateurs, which will damage the new growth nestling in the same place. Or use the best tool of all, your fingers, unless you have a great many shrubs to attend to.

Uses: If they did not flower so gloriously, Rhododendrons could be used as foliage shrubs, because there are so many kinds and sizes of leaf from the impressive *sino-grande* (a tree) to a pigmy rock-shrub. Many of the evergreen kinds have a fascinating brown, cream or silver-white 'tomentum' under-surface to their leaves which is easily seen as the shrub grows in stature. The leaf-shape and habit of the bush or shrub should be seen in an adult state (especially when space is at a premium, as it so often is) because the shrub is there throughout the year while the flowers, lovely as they are, may only last for a month. Rhododendrons can be used as beautiful boundary shrubs, as contrast foliage and as specimen groups or single plants. (Check flowering times for groups.) Flowers are magnificent in arrangements.

Shrubs: Ballalheannagh, Bees, Bodnant, Brackenwood, Bressingham, Busheyfields, Caldwell, Chappell, Cunnington, Daisy Hill, Dobbies, Jack Drake, Exbury, Fairley's, Farall, Glendoick, Goatcher, Goscote, Highfield, Hilliers, Holden Clough, Hyden, Ingwersen, Jackman, Kent, Kershaw, Knaphill, Knoll Gardens, Lea, Lime Cross, Marchant, Meare Close, Notcutts, Otter, Potterton and Martin, Reuthe, Roger, Rosemoor, Russell, Scotts, Sherrard, Smith, St. Bridget, Toynbee, Treasure, Treseder, Warley, Woodland, Wyevale.

Seeds: Chiltern, Thompson and Morgan.

RIBES *(Grossulariaceae).* Most people think of the tomcat-smelling 'American Current' *R. sanguineum* when the name 'Ribes' is mentioned, but there are several other shrubs which are most interesting or ornamental. The tender *R. speciosum* looks as though it were decorating itself very early for Christmas, with swinging scarlet pendants that are quite different from anything else. *R. aureum* is the American 'Buffalo Currant' which has yellow flowers and typical leaves that turn yellow and orange in autumn. The bright yellow flowers have a pleasing spicy clove (or cinnamon) scent, and these are followed by round fruits which can be yellow, red or black — these are highly regarded by birds, bears and buffalo in the plant's native home. At one time Indians used the fruits as an addition to their pemmican by mixing dried buffalo meat with rendered fat and these berries, which made a sustaining concentrated food needing good teeth with which to eat it.

There was a tradition in the village of Mexborough (Yorkshire) that this shrub had to be grown in a bottle. Spring cuttings were put into a bottle of water standing on a window sill; these usually rooted and then the bottle was broken and the cuttings were planted properly. I do this with mint sometimes and I can vouch for the method (with mint only). Next year I will try it with some slips from *R. sanguineum* which, being of the same genus and vigorous to boot, will probably oblige me with a whole row of unwanted progeny.

A shrub that should be more often grown is *R. laurifolium* which is an interesting little plant for the winter garden. It has pendant racemes of green-yellow or green-white flowers in February, and being dioecious it needs to be planted with a male plant to produce the red then dark berries. This is unusual in the rockery and can, unlike the conifers, be absolutely guaranteed not to grow large.

R. sanguineum, despite its indoor-odiferousness, is a very attractive spring flowering shrub. I grow it behind a Eucalyptus and in spring the flowering branches of the Ribes lean casually through the grey-blue leaves, making a delightful contrast, and the dying red leaves of the gum match the crimson pink tassels almost exactly.

R. aureum syn. **R. tenuiflorum — Golden Currant, Buffalo Currant, Clove Bush** (1812). Grows to 8ft (2.4m) with a sprawl of about 5ft (1.5m). Yellow, spice-scented flowers in April, followed by edible berries and golden-orange foliage in autumn. A deciduous shrub from western N. America for a sunny place in the garden.

R. laurifolium (1908) grows to 18″ (46cm) with racemes of yellow-green or yellow-white flowers in February. A large-leaved dwarf evergreen shrub from China for rock garden interest in early spring. (Dioecious)

R. sanguineum — American Currant (1826) grows to 9ft (2.7m) with a spread of about 6ft (1.8m). Dangling racemes of deep rosy-red flowers are a herald of summer in April and May. A deciduous shrub from western N. America for any sunny position.

R. speciosum (1828) grows to 10ft (3m) with a spread of 6ft (1.8m) with dangling clusters of decorative scarlet flowers from April to June. A tender semi-deciduous (or semi-evergreen?) spiny shrub from California for a sheltered place against a warm wall in south and south-west England.

Requirements: The species described here will grow in any good well-drained garden soil in sun. All appreciate a good feed in early spring — do it at the same time as you feed the Hellebores and the Phlox (and those Roses you forgot in November).

Propagation: Take woody cuttings of the hardy kinds in October and set in a prepared nursery bed. They will root by late spring and can be transplanted during the following winter. Take cuttings of unflowered shoots of *R. speciosum* in August and insert in a rooting compost of peat and sand in a cold frame or in a propagator with gentle bottom heat. When well rooted transfer into John Innes No.1 and grow on.

Pruning: Cut out old wood in May, unless large shrubs are desired.

Uses: As ornamental spring-flowering shrubs, *R. laurifolium* interesting at a raised level. The flowers of *R. sanguineum* are odiferous, and though this is a pretty shrub it is best not used in arrangements for this reason.

Shrubs: Barcock, Daisy Hill, Dobbies, Fairley's, Goatcher,

Goscote, Hilliers, Hopleys, Jackman, Kershaw, Knaphill, Marchant, Marten's Hall, Meare Close, Notcutts, Otter, Reuthe, Roger, Russell, Scotts, Shepton, Sherrard, Smith, St. Bridget, Toynbee, Treasure, Treseder, Warley.

ROBINIA *(Leguminosae).* Robinias are named by Linnaeus after Jean Robin (1550-1629), herbalist and gardener to Henry IV of France. Robin was in charge of all the royal gardens and also had his own small area on the Ile de la Cité in the Seine, where he grew over a thousand different flowers and plants. At this time he supplied the flowers which formed the illustrations in the *Jardin du Roi* (1608) written and painted as a pattern-book by the King's embroiderer, Pierre Valet, for Queen Marie de Medicis.

Most of the Robinias are tall delicate-leaved trees but the dainty rose-coloured *R. hispida,* the Rose Acacia grows only to 8ft (2.4m) or so and is delightful against a warm wall where it looks like a pink Wisteria. It looks even better with a blue or crimson-flowered species Clematis trailing through it though the roots of the latter must be kept shaded by a small strategically placed shrub or bushy herbaceous plant. This dainty-looking shrub is very tolerant of atmospheric pollution, as are all the species, and this may be useful in a town garden, as is its pleasant habit of flowering on and off for the rest of the summer as long as the flower-sprays are nipped off immediately they are over. All Robinias have a well deserved reputation for fragility, which is borne out by a small incident in my garden. I have a young *R. pseudoacacia* 'Frisia' which, at the time, had three reasonable branches. A fat blackbird, heavy from over-indulging in Amelanchier fruits, landed on the best branch and took off again immediately with a squawk and an extra bounce because my marmalade tom was poised beneath it waiting for him. This tiny push from the frantic bird snapped the branch off, and the tree has been lop-sided ever since. So mind what you are at when you are tidying Robinias.

R. hispida — Rose Acacia (1743) grows to 8ft (2.4m) with a similar spread and has dangling racemes of pink flowers in May and June and intermittently throughout the summer. A very beautiful deciduous shrub from the S.E. United States for a sunny wall.

Requirements: Any good but not rich free-draining garden soil. Rich soil will encourage quick lush growth which will be even more fragile. A sunny, sheltered wall.

Propagation: Detach suckering growths in early spring.

Uses: As a beautiful flowering and foliage shrub for a sunny wall, made even more lovely by planting a non-vigorous small-flowered Clematis to twine up through the branches (co-ordinate the flowering times).

Shrubs: Caldwell, Farall, Goatcher, Hilliers, Marchant, Meare Close, Notcutts, Sherrard, St. Bridget, Stonehouse, Wyevale.

ROMNEYA — Tree Poppy, Matilija Poppy *(Papaveraceae).* Tree Poppies in full bloom are a wonderful sight but this phenomenon is generally only seen in a drought year when they remember their Californian heritage and cover themselves with their huge (in the case of *R. trichocalyx)* Poppy-like flowers. In other cold or rainy years they are not happy, and this must be accepted. *R. trichocalyx* has the largest flowers that open flatter and with less creases; it is also the largest and hairiest of the two species in the genus; *R. Coulteri* is best for smaller gardens but whichever one you grow needs a hot dry bed to itself, which it will occupy exclusively and greedily and will try to colonise even further. There is no moderation with Romneyas, but they are so beautiful that they are worth every foot of space. Do not be surprised if your plant (once established) begins to move itself to what it thinks is a better part of the border; underground runners will pop up, indicating its preference for left or right, and there is no stopping it. It does not care for shade or damp. My plant of *R. trichocalyx* was a glory of pure white papery petals in the drought year of '76, and after that the Eucalyptus grew too tall too quickly and the Romneya, having tried to escape through a double-flowered gorse, sadly gave up on life. Ever since, I walk round this small garden in midsummer asking myself just where I can find 10ft (3m) of sunny border and what I would have to cast out to make room for another Romneya. I shall do it one day, perhaps when the myrtle gives up on me. *R. Coulteri* might be the answer, but its flowers always seem to need more ironing.

The genus was named after an astronomer called Dr. Romney Robinson because, as often happens in botanical christenings, all the appropriate names had been already used for other plants. The first Romneya (Coulteri) was discovered in 1875 by an Irish botanist, Dr. Thomas Coulter, who travelled in Mexico, California and Arizona collecting and making a great number of herbarium specimens. Returning to Ireland Dr. Coulter began to sort and classify his finds but had not completed the task by the time of his death in 1843. When his work was being examined by his successor, Dr. W.H. Harvey, this Poppy-flower was found which proved to belong to a new genus. But as there was already a genus named 'Coulteria' another name had to be chosen and it was decided to name the plant after Coulter's great friend, Dr. Romney Robinson, astronomer-in-charge at Armagh Observatory. Since the name 'Robinsonia' had already been used, Dr. Robinson's middle name of 'Romney' was adopted.

R. Coulteri — Matilija Poppy, California Tree Poppy (1875) grows to 8ft (2.4m) with a similar spread (which it does — sideways). Large, creased, pure white fragrant flowers with a golden boss of stamens from July to September. A glaucous-leaved semi-herbaceous shrub from California for a hot dry sheltered situation. Spreads by underground runners. Good on chalk.

R. trichocalyx — Tree Poppy (1902?) grows to 6ft (1.8m) with a similar spread; larger white flowers from July to September. Takes a while to settle but can be even more far-reachingly invasive.

Requirements: A sunny, sheltered space and good-to-rich free-draining soil. Protect stems in winter with a mound of ashes, or in warmer counties wrap in hessian or bracken. Do not ever try to move an established plant.

Propagation: Is not easy. Dig up the runners or suckers in April and pot up in a rooting mixture of peat and sand. Or sow seeds very thinly in a sandy seed compost in spring and place in a propagator set at 13-16°C (55-61°F). When large enough transfer into individual pots of half sand and half John Innes No.1. Keep in the same temperature until plants are large enough for the roots to fill the pots. Keep in a sheltered cold frame for the winter, and when frosts are forecast cover frame.

Pruning: Romneyas are borderline shrubs: in warm areas they will not be damaged by winter frosts, but in colder places the stems should be cut down in October. Plants caught by unexpected cold weather can be tidied up in late spring and left — new shoots will generally appear, though not necessarily near the parent plant.

Uses: As magnificent flowering plants, grow in a sunny, sheltered focal position. Flowers very short-lived in water, those of *R. trichocalyx* smell unpleasant.

Shrubs: Peter Chappell, Daisy Hill, Farall, Hilliers, Hopleys, Jackman, Knaphill, Marchant, Meare Close, Notcutts, Reuthe, Roger, Russell, Shepton, Sherrard, St. Bridget, Stonehouse, Toynbee, Treasure, Woodland, Wyevale.

Seeds: Chiltern.

ROSA — Rose *(Rosaceae).* To begin at the beginning, there are more legends and recorded history about roses than for any other flower in the world. Today's flowers are more beautiful than any other, but the first roses had to be practical plants, having evolved with sharp thorns to prevent, or at least deter, their consumption by those monster herbivores before man. This primitive rose had a sweet scent which attracted insects, thus ensuring pollination, and it had bright hips to entice the birds to eat and therefore spread its seed. Now it is loved and admired for its beauty alone, though, being a most practical gardener, I would like to add that a great deal of money has been made out of rose-breeding and all the various necessities essential to its well-being.

Before the history proper begins there were the myths — mostly Greek, as you would expect; these tell how the rose sprang immediately into being rather than by any evolutionary theory. Of course, the ancient gods had a hand in this, as they did in many other plant-beginnings. So, let us begin at the dawn of time.

Once upon this time the goddess Chloris was walking alone through the woods and meadows, admiring her work and making sure that everything was going along nicely. (Chloris was associated with spring flowers and with May-blossom in particular, and she is later identified with the Roman goddess Flora whose festival of flowers, the Floralia, was celebrated each year.) To her horror, Chloris tripped over the body of a dead nymph, whose beauty of form and feature were exceptional, even in those times of perfect loveliness. Abhorring waste, Chloris decided to change the life-less nymph into a flower, but as she could not envisage the shape or colour of this newest blossom, she called upon the other immortals for aid. From Aphrodite came even further beauty (though in flower-form, of course), from Dionysus, god of wine, came fragrant nectar; the Three Graces gave Charm, Joy and Brilliance; and Apollo, the Sun God, shone upon the new flower with warmth tempered by the gentle breezes of Zephyrus, the West Wind. With all these blessings it was no wonder that the newest flower was more beautiful than any other, so the gods crowned it as the Queen of Flowers and named it — the rose.

Another Greek beginning has it that once there was a mortal queen called Rhodanthe, who lived in Corinth (she was, of course, as beautiful as the day and was, in addition, very shy and modest). Being beautiful, unmarried and a queen, she was surrounded by suitors who plagued her with their attentions. Now Rhodanthe didn't care for this continual harassment because she found that she could not even leave her own home without being annoyed by her admirers. Rhodanthe venerated Artemis and had vowed to live a life of chastity out of respect and admiration for this goddess (she it was who had changed Actaeon into a stag, so that he might be torn to pieces by his own hounds because he had glimpsed her bathing). So Rhodanthe lived a rather shut-in sort of life until one fine day she felt she absolutely had to get out and take a walk in the fields and meadows. Wandering alone, peacefully gathering flowers and delighting in the sunlight and the scented breeze, she was able for a while to forget her persecuted existence; suddenly, she heard someone call her name — it was, of course, one of her suitors. Turning to run from him, she saw another barring her escape. The news of her emergence had spread and all the young men came running after her, wanting to speak with her, to touch her, to kiss her. They were promising eternal adoration and even greater ennoblement if she would only settle all this uncertainty by marrying one of them. Rhodanthe reacted to all this in terror and, casting aside her armful of flowers, she fled from her persecutors towards Artemis' temple in the distance. Being young and fleet, she outstripped the crowd of young men and ran through the temple gates, with just sufficient time to lock them after her. The suitors, now very annoyed by this behaviour, rushed up and flung themselves against the bolted gates, heaving

Above: Rhododendron ponticum and azaleas in a woodland setting
2. Below: Viburnum tomentosum 'Mariesii' (centre) makes a very handsome shrub when in full flower in late May

3. Above left: the lemon leaves of *Berberis thunbergii* 'Aurea' contrasting with the modern Dicentra 'Langtrees'

4. Above right: *Skimmia japonica* (male) against *Skimmia* x *Foremannii* (female): both are needed for fruits

5. Far left: *Corylopsis pauciflora* heralding spring

6. Left: The sunshine-yellow foliage of *Physocarpus opulifolius luteus* straying through *Phormium tenax*

7. Bottom left: *Sambucus racemosa* 'Plumosa Aurea' the yellow-leaved Elder against a dark wall

8. Bottom right: *Callistemon sieberi* flowering against dark foliage

9. *Above left:* Parthenocissus Henryana glowing against the shining dark leaves of the modern Hedera 'Green Ripple'

10. *Above middle:* The soft autumnal colouration of *Hydrangea* paniculata (centre) with *Cornus kousa* and Rh. 'Yakusimanum'

11. *Above right:* Erica arborea can give height

12. *Right:* Corylus avellana, the corkscrew hazel, at its best in late winter

13. *Below left:* An autumnal blaze of colour: *Pyracantha atlantioides* and *Parthenocissus quinquefolia*

14. *Below right:* Vitis coignetiae turning colour

15. Above left: *Clematis macropetala*

16. Above right: Camellia 'Donation'

17. Far left: *Cistus* x *pulvurulentus* and *Cistus* x *Skanbergii*

18. Left: *Deutzia scabra* 'plena'

19. Bottom left: Rose 'Dorothy Perkins' is set off well by the dark branches of a yew

20. Bottom right: *Lonicera periclymenum* and the modern rose 'Cupid' toning perfectly with their supporting wall

21. **Above left:** *Clematis Armandii* will grow vigorously in a sheltered position

22. **Above right:** *Cistus ladanifer* needs full sun

23. **Near right:** White Scotch Briars - *Rosa spinosissima* seen through a gate

24. **Far right:** The exuberant species rose 'Cerasocarpa' covering an old apple tree

25. **Below left:** *Olearia mucronatus*, the daisy-bush, is well-named

26. **Below right:** The hanging bells of *Pieris formosa* 'Forrestii'

27. Above left: *Philadelphus coronarius*, the Mock-orange, escaping over the garden wall

28. Above middle: Rich, raspberry-scented flowers of the old Bourbon rose 'Madame Isaac Pereire'

29. Above right: The huge, pale flowers of *Hydrangea arborescens*

30. Left: A summer entanglement - *Rosa Moyesii* and *Rosa Willmottiae*

31. Below left: Variegated ivies climb the porch pillars of the author's cottage

32. Below right: *Hibiscus rosa-sinensis* in a tropical garden

33. **Above left:** *Cytisus battandieri* has silver leaves and flowers that smell deliciously of fresh fruit salad

34. **Above middle:** *Hippophae rhamnoides* (centre) makes excellent hedging in coastal gardens

35. **Above right:** The silvery *Helichrysum splendidum* contrasting with *Allium moly* and golden marjoram

36. **Right:** *Berberis stenophylla* is always cheerful in early spring

37. **Below left:** *Rosa rubrifolia,* contrasting with the light green leaves of *Sorbaria aitchisoniae*

38. **Below right:** A mature *Ribes sanguineum* growing through the contrasting grey foliage of *Eucalyptus gunnii*

39. **Overleaf:** *Magnolia stellata* has pure white flowers in early spring

and pushing at them until they broke. In they poured, a frustrated throng in search of their quarry, overturning and breaking the furniture and sacred altars and generally behaving like vandals. Artemis was absolutely furious at this desecration and, to succour Rhodanthe, she turned her into a rose, which retained in its delicately flushed petals the blush of the harried maiden. To protect this loveliness, Artemis changed the suitors into thorns to guard this new flower for ever. Artemis obviously had what would later be called a Gilbertian sense of justice.

One more myth of many is again connected with Artemis. Another of the inexhaustible supply of beautiful maidens was called 'Roselia'. She was a priestess of one of Artemis' temples and as such her life was dedicated to the service of the goddess. But Roselia's beauty had been seen and she was desired by a rich young man, Cymedor, who persuaded Roselia's mother to take her away from the temple so that he could have her as his wife. Now, Artemis had to make a stand on this issue, was she not a goddess and total arbiter of the fates of all who served her? So she killed the innocent Roselia (instead of dropping a rock on her greedy mother) by stabbing her to the heart and leaving her to die. Cymedor found his dying love and clasped her to him (good theatre, this stuff), but instead of an expiring maiden he found that he was clasping a very thorny bush, whose flowers were of a new and exquisite perfection: this was the first rose. There are many such stories, usually involving the carryings-on of the old gods who really had too much time on their hands and nothing much (except the obvious diversions) to do.

Passing on to some of the stories associated with the red roses in particular, I will relate a few of the cleanest — those old gods really were a shocking lot. Aphrodite, the Goddess of Love, was herself in love with a handsome and beautiful mortal youth called Adonis (who, if one can trace a way through the behavioural tangle of cause and event, had been helped into the world by Aphrodite herself). He loved to hunt and spent all his time in the pleasures of the chase. Now Aphrodite had been quite happy with Ares, God of War, before she found Adonis. She had been wont to spend her life being beautiful for Ares alone (more or less) but now she followed the youth Adonis on the chase, through woods and thickets, up and down mountain-sides, crossing streams and rivers and getting more than dishevelled in her attempts to keep up with her apparently unheeding lover. Her clothes got torn, her lovely hair was tangled and full of knots and her face and arms were covered with scratches from the briars. The other gods laughed at all this, and waited to see the outcome — it relieved the tedium of their lives a little.

Now Ares was no fool and knew what was happening (how could he not, when Aphrodite was looking such a mess?). So he made his plans and waited until Aphrodite was away on a visit to one of her shrines. Adonis had gone out on one of his obsessional hunting trips, and Ares changed himself into a great wild boar. In this shape he lured Adonis' dogs away from their master, and then came circling back to where the young man was following the earlier trail made by Ares in the boar's shape. Luring Adonis on, far into the wilds of the forest, he turned and rushed at him, goring him fatally. As Adonis lay dying in a welter of gore, Aphrodite, sensing that something was very wrong, cancelled her engagement and turned her swan-chariot in the sky and flew back to where Adonis was lying. Leaping from her chariot, she ran to him, over the wild and white-flowered briars that grew all around. Her beautiful feet were torn by the thorns so that her blood stained the white blossoms, and that is how the first red roses came into being.

A Persian legend says that in the beginning all roses were white. A nightingale fell in love with a beautiful white rose and pressed its tiny breast against the cruel thorns until they pierced its heart. In dying, the nightingale's blood stained the white petals red.

But an early Christian story says that the first roses were all red. When Mary Magdalen wept at the death of Our Lord, her tears washed this colour all away. In the middle ages the Christians believed that the white rose signified purity and innocence, while the red rose represented evil.

As you may imagine, there are more myths than I have space for, and now it is time to pass on to the reality of rose history which is as tangled as the briars that surrounded Sleeping Beauty — a rose fairy-tale that everyone knows.

After the evolution of roses, things went unrecorded for a millenium or so by the very nature of things. The rose gradually became known to man and was used by him in art, religion, diet, medicine and in commerce: these uses developed at different times and in different civilisations, as I will tell you.

On the island of Crete, a fresco painting in a good state of preservation was found at Knossos by the archaeologist Sir Arthur Evans. The painting (which is dated at approximately 2000 B.C.) is very similar to the tomb-wreath rose, *R. sancta*, discovered in Egypt, of which more later. It appears that this painting is the oldest recognisable rose picture known.

One would have thought that the Egyptians, with their highly civilised life-style, might have been the first rose-growers, but this came much later on. Roses must have been grown since earliest times in the Middle East, though perhaps as just another scented flower, because what we like to think of as stylised representations of them start to appear in manuscripts, architectural decorations and on pottery and carpets. Many of these decorative 'roses' have 6 petals and may, of course, have had another or other flowers as their inspiration. The Bible is often quoted as an early reference, but the word 'rose' which appears in Isaiah, Ch. 35, v.1, could have been the translator's interpretation.

Whilst excavating the ruined city of Ur in Chaldea (Babylon) archaeologists discovered clay tablets dating back some 5000 years. These listed some of the campaign booty brought back to the city by Sargon, a Sumerian king of the period, on his return from battle. The list is translated as 'vines, figs and roses' but deeper delving elicits a plant description of 'sweet-scented flowers from which oil was extracted'. These were most probably roses because this method was known at that time, and the manufacture of the oil later became a considerable industry all round the eastern end of the Mediterranean.

The remains of a rose-garland or wreath was discovered by Sir Flinders Petrie in a tomb which dated from the time of Alexander the Great (356-323 B.C.). The flowers in the wreath have been identified as being composed of the rose that the Romans called *Rosa sancta*, which was always grown near temples, sacred buildings and, later, churches; this rose had pale pink petals and appears to be an early Gallica. It is assumed by Egyptologists that rose-growing was not practised at that time in Egypt because the cultural details of the lives of the Pharaohs are so well documented that, had there been large-scale rose-growing in some part of Egypt, pictures or tablets would have shown it. So, here we are during the time of the great Alexander — the extraction of rose-oil was well-known and therefore roses, and cultivated ones at that, must have existed. Staying in the same geographical area for the sake of convenience and clarity, you will remember that I began with some early Greek rose legends; it would appear that their actual use of the flowers was confined to religious and ceremonial ritual. They put rose-garlands on the graves of their dead and in certain parts of the world this custom is still practised, even though the Church later forbade it because of the rose's long association with the very improper carryings-on of the Romans (see later paragraphs on this).

The Greek philosopher Theophrastus (372-287 B.C.) was a keen observer of natural history. He wrote some very detailed descriptions — for those times — in his book *'Enquiry to Plants'* and his section on roses shows that he must have known them throughout their seasons. He says, 'Among roses there are many differences, in the number of petals, in roughness, in beauty of colour, and in sweetness of scent. Most have twelve petals, but some have twelve or twenty, and some a great many more of these; for there are some they say, which are even called 'hundred-petalled'. Many of such roses grow near Philippi, for the people of that place get them on Mount Pangaeus, where they are abundant, and plant them. However, the inner petals are very small (the way in which they are produced being such that some are outside, some inside). Some kinds are not fragrant nor of large size. Among those which have large flow-

ers those in which the part below the flower is rough are the more fragrant. In general, as has been said, good colour and scent depend on locality; for even bushes which are growing in the same soil show some variation in the presence or absence of a sweet scent. Sweetest-scented of all are the roses of Cyrene, wherefore the perfume made from them is the sweetest.'

Compared to the restrained use of roses by the Greeks, the Romans grew and used the flowers in excessive numbers. Their traders began bringing other species or varieties back with them from other countries and these, together with those already known to the Romans, were cultivated on a truly gigantic scale. Pliny the Elder wrote extensively on roses in 50 A.D. and it would seem that he knew of six or seven distinctly different types (though, as Theophrastus before him knew, and every serious rose-grower since would agree, the flowers can be made to seem different according to the way the plant is treated).

Roses were being use in medicine also and Pliny, who never stopped in his writings, fortunately for us, advocated different parts of the rose-bush used fresh or dry or in solution, for the following ailments: complaints of the uterus, for dysentery, for ear-ache, sores in the mouth and gums, for stomach-ache, for rectal problems, headache, insomnia, nausea, chafed thighs, fluxes of the eybrows(?), to check menstrual discharges, sore eyes, other complaints of the belly, hypochondria and, finally, to cure mange. He also recommended its use as an astringent, as a gargle and as an anti-perspirant. Roses were used by the ton. They were worked into garlands for the never-ending stream of returning warriors: the rank and file of the victorious soldiery would have marched through the streets through a rain of rose-petals, rather like a nice form of ticker-tape welcome. Great quantities of the petals were used at the games, for decoration and to carpet the floors at banquets, and more would descend in scented drifts from the ceiling at intervals during the feasting. (There is a tale, possibly apocryphal, that Nero smothered all his guests by this means at one particular function.) Since the cultivation of roses for this extravagant use had to be on a grand scale, rose-fields grew and grew in size. The Romans were very good gardeners in any case, and they even developed 'greenhouses' made of glass.

Glass had been invented or discovered in Egypt some time in the XVIIIth dynasty (though Pliny states that glass originated from Syria) and very beautiful artefacts were made which were better than much on sale today. However, sheet-glass was used in windows by the Romans and its presence must have been very much appreciated in the colder parts of their Empire, such as Britain. The glass for their greenhouses would not have been of the best quality, but, with their excellent hot-water systems, it would have sufficed to protect and bring on the roses and other plants so that they flowered much earlier. The Egyptians had at last caught up with all this, and had been growing roses for the 'winter trade' with the Romans for some time. The roses were exported (we do not know exactly how, but it would have taken many weeks by galley and sail) to Italy in order to keep up with the insatiable demand, and for a while the Egyptians had had a very nice market because their rose-season was two months earlier than that of the Romans. It is to be supposed that the large-scale construction and use of glassed-in buildings for the home-grown flowers (it must have looked rather like Guernsey from the air) would have made quite a difference to the economy in the Nile delta, where the Egyptian roses were grown.

Then came the decline and fall of the Roman Empire and the requirement for roses decreased almost to nothing. The rose, because of its association with past orgies and extravagance, became an impious flower for centuries, even after the Dark Ages.

The roses that the Romans grew with such skill would probably have flowered once only in their season, and it was in China that the new species were eventually discovered which flowered twice or even continuously. The Chinese had also been growing roses, even before Confucius (551-478 B.C.) wrote that in the library of the Emperor there existed many books on rose-growing. What a precious record these would have been to later rosarians. The Chinese used their scented roses to make a precious Attar of Roses, as did the Persians (the word comes from the Persian 'Atir') and later the Bulgarians, who called it 'Otto'.

During the Dark Ages, when, in any case, there are such large gaps in historical documentation, roses went into something of a decline. People still continued to put them on the graves of their loved ones, in preference to other flowers, in spite of edicts from the Catholic Church which plainly said 'Thou Shalt Not'. But in this, their last time of giving, the people often ignored the Church and therefore a gradual change in ecclesiastical thinking came about: the red rose (though there were no real red roses then) symbol-ised the blood of Christ and the white flowers stood for absolute purity, soon becoming one of the emblems of the Virgin Mary. Rosaries as an aide-memoire for the recitation of prayers came into being much later on, some time in the 15th century, though it is probable that some form of bead-string for the purpose existed before this. Buddhists and Mohammedans use a similar device. The rose became respectable at last, and wonderful 'rose-windows' were designed for the cathedrals and churches of Europe. The known roses were grown in monastery gardens for altar decorations on feast days, and for garlands, and for medicine. Nothing changes.

The Crusaders went off to their wars (a 13th century equivalent of national service, I suppose) but after the killing and the carnage they gathered many strange plants and brought them home in their baggage trains. The original Damask rose came to England from Damascus in this way and its date of introduction is given as 1270.

Most of the roses were grown for medicinal purposes and for the new French perfume industry, which was centred around the town of Provins, near Paris. Acres of roses, called 'The Provins Rose' were grown there. This was a Gallica and not to be confused with the blousy, many-petalled beauty from Provence, later called the Centifolia. The various preparations made from these Gallica roses were rose oil, rose-water, rose honey, rose vinegar, rose con-serve and rose-sugar (this last was very expensive in those days, even on its own, let alone when admixed with dried, pounded rose-petals, plus a manufacturing charge and maybe a middle-man as well to be paid). Here was another rose industry starting up, this time in northern Europe.

The rose in a stylised form became an important heral-dic device with many noble families in Europe incorpor-ating it (in various forms and colours) into their armorial bearings. The English Wars of the Roses were more or less settled, at long last, by the marriage of Henry Tudor (Henry VII) to Elizabeth of York (Edward IVth's daughter), and the white rose and the red symbolically became one under the description of the 'Tudor Rose' which has remained in its simplistic form to this day.

It is time to leave the myths, legends and the fascinating history of the rose in order to discuss the older roses in more detail. They are generally once-flowering, in a glorious burst at midsummer (with some exceptions, which are men-tioned). This to some people is their only drawback, but what gardener expects his Camellias, his Rhododendrons (or his daffodils, for that matter) to keep right on flowering. Almost all the old roses are very vigorous, usually much more so than the modern ones, with sturdy stems, interest-ing foliage and almost disease-free growth. Many have very beautiful and abundant hips. The shrubs themselves last in the garden far longer than the more modern kinds, whose life is generally only about 15 to 20 years or so, by which time an old rose will be getting into its stride, though it may have taken a few years to get going. Lastly (again, with a few exceptions) they need little pruning, except to give them a good tidy-out every four or five years. If you actually like pruning, and many gardeners do, then prune: you will get fewer but larger flowers. Many (but not all) old roses flower on the previous season's wood, which is one reason for having a light touch with the secateurs. Visit one of the historic rose-gardens in June and you will, I am sure, come away and want to re-plan at least part of your garden so as to make room for a few of these wonderful garden plants.

Species roses are what might be called 'wild' roses — that is, they have not changed or been changed by the hybridists since being discovered. Examples of these are the wild roses of the British Isles — *R. canina*, the Dog Rose, *R.*

arvensis, the Field Rose, *R. pimpinellifolia* syn. *R. spinosissima,* The Burnet or Scotch Rose, and the delicious *R. rubiginosa,* the Sweet Briar. All these may still be bought and are lovely in the wild garden, and all have been much used by rose-growers as parents for modern varieties. Other countries have their wild roses and we cherish these for their individuality as well as their strength and long-lasting vitality. A huge-growing rose is *R. brunonii,* the Himalayan Musk Rose, which will grow to a height of 40ft (12m) in ideal, warm conditions in Cornwall, the Scilly Islands or the south of France. From the sublimity of this giant among plants (though there are several others like it whose dates of introduction are too late for inclusion in this book) I would like to go to the other extreme in height. *R. spinosissima* is a very low-growing rose — I have seen it in roadside dust at a height of 9" (23cm) — which increases by means of thickets of suckering, thorny growths. This means that it is immensely useful to prevent soil erosion, which, further translated into mundane terms, means that it will stop the earth sliding down that bank of yours on to the drive and, because of the prickles, next-door's dog will go somewhere else for its natural functions. It is a sweetly scented little rose, with single, cream-yellow flowers and fat black hips. There are many roses of average height and average vigour (this means they will not take over more than twice their allocation of your precious garden space) and a brief list is given here.

Some species roses

R. Hugonis — Father Hugo's Rose (1899) has small single pale yellow, cup-shaped flowers and delicate ferny leaves. 7 x 6ft (2 x 1.8m) mid-May. Good as internal hedging, and loves a warm wall. Not really fussy as to soil, either.

R. primula — The Incence Rose (1910) Primrose-like yellow flowers paling with age in mid-May and scented young foliage. 6 x 8ft (1.8 x 2.4m).

R. ecae (1880). Named after Mrs E.C. Aitchison. Has flat, bright yellow flowers in late May, all over the brown branches. 5 x 4ft (1.5 x 1.2m) needs a warm or, even better, a hot place and good drainage.

R. rubrifolia (before 1830) has small clusters of charming, pointed-petalled bright pink flowers, but it is grown for its lovely blue-grey foliage which has a plum-coloured sheen. Pleasing brown hips. 6 x 5ft (1.8 x 1.5m) June.

R. rubiginosa — Eglantine has bright pink single flowers in June and red urn-shaped hips later. Delicious apple-scented foliage. 6 x 6ft (1.8 x 1.8m); good as internal garden hedging.

R. Moyesii (1894) has uniquely coloured single crimson flowers with golden stamens in June and July followed by scarlet flagon-shaped hips. A stiffly erect rose 9 x 8ft (2.7 x 2.5m) that associates beautifully with *R. Willmottiae* or *R. rubrifolia.*

The Gallica roses flower once, in the middle of the summer. They have bristle-bush stems and a great many suckers. A good example of how they grow is *R. officinalis,* the Apothecary's rose which is the probable Red Rose of Lancaster. I earlier mentioned that there were no red roses in former times — this deep cerise-pink was as red a red as it was possible to get in the days of the Provins rose-fields. The leaves are dry-looking, rather deeply-veined and a bright, characteristic jade-green. Another example is its sport, the lovely 'Rosa Mundi' which has raspberry-ripple striped petals in pink and white, no two petals ever coming the same. The Gallicas do not mind ordinary unenriched garden soil and are unfussy just so long as they have sun. 'Rosa Mundi' grows strongly, and makes a very beautiful internal garden hedge.

Some Gallica roses

R. officinalis — The Apothecary's Rose thought to be the Red Rose of Lancaster. Deep cerise-pink semi-double flowers in midsummer with red hips later. 4 x 4ft+ (1.2 x 1.2m+) (usually even more) suckering freely; it makes a good garden hedge or screen.

'Rosa Mundi' syn. **R. gallica versicolor** (before the 16th century). Said to have been named after Fair Rosamonde, Henry II's mistress. Since Henry's dates are from 1154-1189 it is very unlikely that either he or his mistress knew this rose as we see it today, as it would be about 800 years old. It is the palest of pinks, striped, spotted and splashed with cerise, with odd cerise petals or whole pale pink ones and has bright golden stamens. June. 4 x 4ft (1.2 x 1.2m). Good in wet weather, a strong and easy rose and lovely as a hedge.

'Tuscany' (very old) has velvety crimson-purple semi-double flowers with golden stamens. Midsummer. 4 x 3ft (1.2m x 90cm).

'Tuscany Superb' (before 1848) is a larger bush with larger, more double flowers, therefore the golden stamens have less impact. 4 x 4ft (1.2 x 1.2m).

'Charles de Mills' (Age not known). A fine very double flat rose with richly-coloured crimson-to-purple flowers with maroon shading in midsummer. 5 x 4ft (1.5 x 1.2m).

The Damask roses came later, with two lines of descent. The summer-flowering group has a Gallica rose as one early parent and a climbing species rose called *R. phoenicea* for the other. These roses have no real distinguishing marks to set them apart, though a real rosarian would spot one (out of bloom) at the end of someone else's garden. On the whole, they have rather soft and downy, greyish leaves, quite thorny stems and rather weak flower-stalks, so that the blooms droop. 'Léda' is fairly typical and in a good summer is very floriferous, with a cluster of carmine-edged white flowers. 'Ispahan' has a wonderful fragrance and is used to make Attar of roses. It has very pink flowers, with the characteristic weak stem, but these are so very pink, there are so many of them and they have such a wonderful scent that one can forgive it anything. 'Ispahan' started life in my garden as a bush but decided to aspire to more, so now, to keep it tidy, it has a 6ft (1.8m) post and is taller than this, so one could truthfully call it a pillar rose here, which it normally is not. However, grown in this way the flowers dangle attractively, and come at the same time as a blue pool of *Geranium ibericum* exactly beneath them. I have not pruned it in recent years and it seems the better for this, and certainly has more flowers than ever.

For such an historic rose, 'York and Lancaster' is not as nice as it should be, but it may be that I observed it first in a bad year, growing in the wrong soil — it likes plush conditions. It is a pink and white, or pink, or blush pink flower, with random all pink petals if the others are not. To me it is a dithering sort of rose, and I cannot for the life of me see what the fuss is all about. It could not possibly be the same flower which was said to have started the Wars of the Roses; if you read the speech (Henry IV, part 1) it seems that there were several rose bushes of different colours in the Temple Garden. On the other hand, in Shakespeare's sonnet XCIX there is a description of a rose which much better fits 'York and Lancaster' — it reads as follows:

'... The Roses fearfully on thorns did stand,
One blushing shame, another white despair
A third, nor red nor white, had stolen of both...'

But grow it, and see for yourself.

The other kind of Damask roses are called 'Autumn Damasks' and are late-flowering. The main example of this is the 'Quatre Saisons' Rose or *R. damascena bifera* which is not always a good garden plant now; it may well have been grown at Pompeii and has, if so, somehow survived through the centuries in cultivation. It has been much used as a parent by rose breeders because of its useful repeat-flowering habit.

Some Damask roses

'Ispahan' (age unknown). Clusters of bright pink richly-scented flowers for six weeks in midsummer. Used to make Attar of roses. Can be trained as a pillar rose and it will flower low down. 5 x 4ft (1.5 x 1.2m) — sometimes more.

'Léda' — the **Painted Damask** (age unknown). Has double white flowers reflexing, with the petals touched with crimson lake at the edges. Nice dark leaves. 3 x 3ft (90 x 90cm).

'Mme Hardy' (1832). White flowers, flat and quartered with a green pointel or 'eye'. Needs watering in dry weather or flowers will be smaller. 6 x 5ft (1.8 x 1.5m).

'Celsiana' (before 1750). Named after its French breeder, Cels. Fragrant semi-double pink flowers with yellow stamens. Grey-green foliage. A very beautiful rose. 5 x 4ft (1.5 x 1.2m).

'York and Lancaster' or **R. damascena versicolor** (before 1551). Said to be the bush from which the two flowers were picked at the start of the Wars of the Roses. The

flowers should be half pink and half white, but seem to be either all pink, or a mixture of pink and white petals. Needs rich soil and regular feeding. 6 x 6ft (1.8 x 1.8m).

'Quatre Saisons' — the **Autumn Damask, R. damascena bifera.** (probably Roman). Has richly fragrant double pink flowers of an indeterminate shape and two flushes of bloom, unlike the other Damasks. Interesting historically and much used by rose breeders. 4 x 3ft (1.2m x 90cm).

The Albas, or 'The White Roses' — though they are not all white — have grey-green leaves and flower once, at midsummer. They are a small group with some famous names, such as *R. x alba maxima* which is the Jacobite Rose, emblem of Bonnie Prince Charlie in the Jacobite rebellion. 'Celeste' or 'Celestial' is quite lovely with soft, clear pink flowers and delicious, appropriately named scent. These are strong-growing plants for gardeners who don't want to spend too much time on their roses, and it is as well, like most of the old roses, that they do not seem to suffer from disease. A beautiful rose for naughty old gentlemen (and young ones too) is 'Cuisse de Nymphe' or, more generally, 'Maiden's Blush' and so she should, because the literal translation of this name is 'Nymph's Thigh'. It is that sort of delicate flesh tone, with flowers of the typical old-fashioned, muddly shape.

Some Alba roses

R. x alba 'Maxima' — The **Jacobite Rose** or **The Great Double White** (very old) with flat white double flowers in a great burst at midsummer on a vigorous dark-leaved shrub. This tends to leaf more at the ends of the branches and can, if wished, be pruned hard back immediately after flowering so as to make it more compact. It looks nice against good modern red brick. 6 x 5ft (1.8 x 1.5m).

'Celeste' or **'Celestial'** (late 18th century). Soft, semi-double pink flowers in mid-summer with grey-green leaves. Absolutely beautiful. If you have space for only a few roses, this should be one of them. 6 x 4ft (1.8 x 1.2m).

'Cuisse de Nymphe' or **'Maiden's Blush'** (before 15th century). scented pale blush-pink double flowers in midsummer. 5 x 4ft (1.5 x 1.2m). There is a 'Great Maiden's Blush' which is larger — 6 x 5ft (1.8 x 1.5m).

'Königen von Dänemark' (1826) with clusters of small, very pink blooms paling as they age. Midsummer. 5 x 4ft (1.5 x 1.2m).

The China roses can be described as light, airy and delicate in their habit of growth. They brought the red, coral, flame and yellow part of the rose-spectrum to Europe, though few of the original plants remain to us as they were. You will remember that the China roses have been in cultivation for a very long time, probably for over 1000 years before their first introduction to the west in the 1800s. One very 'different' rose belonging to this group, suitable for small gardens, patios, or even a balcony, where it can be grown in good rich soil in a big tub, is *R. mutabilis* (called 'Tipo Ideale' elsewhere in the world) which is several roses in one. It is a small and dainty dark-stemmed rose with bronze young leaves that set off the fascinating flowers which are single, opening from beautifully-shaped flame-coloured buds that unfold to disclose cream-buff flowers, changing quickly to yellow, then to pink and, finally, to deep pink and crimson. Though single, the flowers are of even more interest because the petals behave in an individual way so that no two flowers on the bush are the same shape. The leaves are elegant and shining, and this plant can be kept as a small shrub or allowed to lean against a warm wall to mingle with other not-too rumbustious climbers that will not take too much light and air from it. I have it as a group with *Jasminum x stephanense* and a very pink honeysuckle, *Lonicera belgica,* whose peach and crimson flower tones, followed by the fat fruit clusters, go well with all the stages of this interesting rose. The Jasmine is pleasant with them, but looks better further along the wall where it meets a Solanum with its purple potato-flowers. Again, if you have space for only a few roses, this should be one of them because each day the flowers are a different colour.

Another curious rose, definitely for the flower-arranger, is *R. viridiflora* sometimes rather unkindly called *R. monstrosa)* The Green Rose. This seldom seems to lose its leaves in my garden and there are always flowers on the bush, except during November, December, January, February and March. In April it forms its very pleasing rather blue-green buds (quite the nicest thing about it) and from then it keeps right on until late October. The buds open to green 'flowers' which soon become tinged with tones of bronze and brown. These last for an obligingly long time because they are not flowers at all, but a conglomerate of petal-like scales. The 'flowers' last for an equally long time in water and are best arranged with other foliage than their own, as they will then show up better.

Some China Roses

R. mutabilis — 'Tipo Ideale' (before 1896). A dainty and elegant single rose for connoisseurs, opening from flame-coloured buds to creamy-buff which changes to yellow, pink, deep pink and then crimson. As a bush 3 x 2ft (90 x 60cm) or to 8ft (2.4m) on a wall, and will climb higher. Needs sun and regular spraying against black spot and aphis.

'Viridiflora' or **R. viridiflora** syn. **R. chinensis viridiflora — The Green Rose** (1855, probably earlier) has blue-green buds, opening to rather formless though interesting, long-lasting green flowers that are tinged brown. Buds very pleasing and early, flowers still coming in October. Good for green arrangements.

'Hermosa', 'Old Blush', Parson's Pink China, Monthly Rose, Old Pink Monthly etc. (age unknown). Clusters of pink blooms, deepening as they age to crimson. 4 x 4ft (1.2 x 1.2m) or much more against a wall.

The Centifolias, or the Cabbage, Provence or Provincial Roses are the bosomy roses that figure so largely in our imaginations and our illustrations of times gone by. They are not really very old, certainly the first of them would not be older than the end of the 16th century. Most of them were the products of the Dutch rose-breeders and this is why they appear so often in those magnificent, eye-filling Dutch flower-paintings. These roses are generally large plants and have (generally) lax-growing branches of heavy, many-petalled flowers, such as the very typical *R. x centifolia* with its almost spherical richly scented pink flowers. 'Tour de Malakoff' is another which needs the right kind of year to be happy and give of its best — the round crimson buds unfold to unpack a vast number of petals which, in good seasons, continue to open into a fine large flower that changes colour throughout the first day, from a brilliant rose cerise through tones of magenta and crimson until the outer petals pale to a delicate, veined grey-mauve (all this in one day — *very* hard to keep up with when painting it). In bad seasons the buds expand to a spherical shape but thereafter they stay that way, never unfolding to the true and characteristic form of this fine rose. This can, of course, be very disappointing — another year will have to pass before the rose's season comes again. 'Tour de Malakoff' is not a rose for the rain, and the unopened wet paper-bags will eventually have to be cut off. But in a good summer the pendulous branches bend with the further weight of the large and very beautiful flowers, and it is all worth waiting for. This rose should be planted where its flowers can be looked up at, as most of them dangle. 'Fantin Latour' (named after the great French painter) is quite exquisite, with an abundance of scented, pale pink, button-eyed, quartered flowers. It is one of the loveliest of roses and has quite a long flowering season.

Some Centifolia roses

'Tour de Malakoff' (1856) has large quartered blooms opening cerise and magenta, shading through crimson to lavender, pink, lilac and grey. Wonderful in a good hot year, a wet-paper-bag-bush in a bad one. Needs space to flop into, or a bank or low wall to drip over. 6 x 5ft+ (1.8 x 1.5m+).

'Fantin Latour' (age unknown) named after the French painter. Clusters of sweetly scented delicate shell-pink flowers, opening flat. Quite beautiful. 6 x 5ft (1.8 x 1.5m).

R. x centifolia, R. provincialis — Provence Rose, Provincial Rose, 'The Old Cabbage Rose' with scented, pink, many-petalled globular flowers in midsummer. 5ft x 4ft (1.5 x 1.2m).

'De Meaux' (before 1800) with small pink pom-pom flowers. An open and rather lax shrub but the little flowers on their nodding stems are lovely for cutting. 4 x 3ft (1.2m x 90cm).

'Robert le Diable' (age unknown) has fascinating and

shapely flowers of violet, purple, cerise, scarlet and grey. Again, best in hot summers. (Late-flowering.) A low-leafing bush to put in front of taller, more naked stems. 4 x 3ft (1.2m x 90cm).

Moss roses seem to epitomise old fashioned flowers, though they are not much older than the first 'sport' which came from Europe in 1727. The combination of soft green 'moss' and clear pink or white, perfectly-formed buds is irresistible. There are varieties with bronze or brown moss, and other flower colours, such as the rich crimson-purple flowers of 'Capitaine John Ingram' with green moss, and 'William Lobb' which has magenta to crimson-purple petals with lilac reverses, also with green moss. These are very colourful indeed, but it is the paler shades that people think of when moss roses are being talked about. I have 'William Lobb' on my now overcrowded pergola, with 'Vielchenblau' next to it, whose dozens of small blooms echo all of William Lobb's colours. Intertwined with this is the modern clematis 'Hagley Hybrid' with its mauve-pink flowers which might have come from the edge of the same palette. Of course, 'William Lobb' flowers at and on the top of the pergola, and is best viewed, precariously, from my tallest steps, but I know that it's all a glorious tumble of colour up there and that all of them tone, and that is what matters. 'Capitaine John Ingram' reaches out to grab me as I hang out the washing and this reminds me, painfully, that this year I will be strong about the Akebia there, which is suffocating both the Capitaine and the more precious 'Gloire de Dijon' further along.

Some Moss roses

R. x centifolia muscosa — The Common Moss Rose (1727) and still the best and most beautiful, having fragrant fat pink buds, later opening to flat flowers with a button eye. Green moss. 4 x 4ft (1.2 x 1.2m).

R. x centifolia muscosa 'alba' — Shailer's White Moss (1788). This rose is very beautiful when in bud, with its long mossy green calyces. The flowers open to a flesh-pink which fades to pure white. 4 x 3ft (1.2m x 90cm).

'Capitaine John Ingram' (1856) has flat, very dark crimson flowers with lighter mottling on the petals and lighter reverses. Green moss. A later-flowering rose of rich colour and scent, good against a light-coloured wall. 5 x 4ft (1.5 x 1.2m) and more against a wall.

'William Lobb' — Old Velvet Moss, Duchesse d'Istrie (1855). Both the last two names are better for this lovely rose, with all due respect to the orchid collector after whom it was named. A great flowering of crimson-purple, mauve and lilac, all of which fades gracefully to lavender. It has green moss. It cannot be persuaded to flower lower down and needs something in front of its naked, thorny stems; very good in a terraced garden where it can be seen from above. A tall rose, usually more than its listed height of 6 x 6ft (1.8 x 1.8m).

The Bourbons were born on the island of Réunion (formerly Ile du Bourbon) in the Indian Ocean, round about 1819. They apparently had their beginnings in a mixed hedge of China roses and with the Autumn Damask, which I mentioned as having been the progenitor of many of the repeat-flowering roses. At about the same time another natural cross happened, this time in Italy, between the same vigorous (though not lovely) Autumn Damask and *R. gallica officinalis*. This strain became the Portland Rose, and was named after the Duchess of Portland, who was a keen gardener. One very beautiful Bourbon rose is 'Madame Isaac Pereire' which has truly enormous, scented cerise flowers in August and September, with a first and not-so-good flush of bloom earlier. This rose produces magnificent blooms when grown in good rich soil and, though it flowers several times in the season, the later blooms are the largest and best, and often the weather is more settled so they are not ruined by the rain. The more modern 'Zigeuner Knabe' (Gipsy Boy) grows to a great round thorny bush, with hundreds and hundreds of scented dark plum-crimson flowers all at once. These are excellent for making an impact when cut in quantity, and look well in brass or copper vases.

'Zéphirine Drouhin', the Thornless Rose, belongs here with its scented cerise-pink blooms. It is a vigorous rose, generally trained round a post or over an arch, though it can be kept pruned down to a (strong-growing) shrub.

Some Bourbon roses

'Madame Isaac Pereire')1880) has enormous flowers packed with perfume and petals in a clear cerise-pink. It has flowers that are best described as sumptuous. Two main flushes of bloom, with intermittent bloom afterwards. This is a rose that deserves one of the best garden positions; you will also need extra and larger vases for the flowers when it gets going. Crimson young foliage and a raspberry perfume. 7 x 5ft+ (2.1m x 1.5m+).

'Zéphirine Drouhin' — The Thornless Rose (1868) has semi-double fragrant cerise flowers and a tendency towards mildew — plant it on an arch and not against a wall, though it will grow to 15ft (4.5m) against one. It is an easy-going rose and will do well providing you can spray regularly.

'Madame Pierre Oger' (1878) has beautiful flowers of cream and soft pink, deeper at the edges of the petals and flushing to an overall pink in the sun. A bush in full flower with all the different tones is a lovely sight. 6 x 3ft (1.8m x 90cm).

'Boule de Niege' (1867). A most lovely rose, with red buds that open to ivory-white flowers of great beauty and sweetness. 5 x 4ft (1.5 x 1.2m).

'Zigeuner Knabe' — Gipsy Boy (1909) has clusters of many-petalled flat, very dark crimson flowers in June in a great burst. These do not last long in water, but on an established bush there are hundreds more. Very thorny. 5 x 7ft+

(1.5 x 2m +).

'La Reine Victoria' (1872) has rounded, cupped pink flowers that are sweet scented and very delicate. A vigorous rose, but needs discreet support. 6 x 3ft (1.8m x 90cm).

A Portland rose

I could make a list, but few are now obtainable. However, the Duchess herself still is:

'The Portland Rose' — **Duchess of Portland** (before 1809) has semi-double crimson flowers. The rose is strong-growing and suckers freely, and is spectacular when in full bloom. Needs dead-heading, petals do not fall in the British climate. 2 x 2ft (60 x 60cm).

The Hybrid Perpetuals — a perfectly descriptive tough off-putting name for a large group of lovely roses, many of which were raised originally in French nurseries near Auteuil. This was at a time when rose-breeders were crossing everything that they had with everything that everyone else had and in most cases accurate records were not kept. It is known that one of the French growers, Laffey, raised over 200,000 seedlings, but as no proper register exists there are many genetic mysteries in this group. Quite a number of the roses have survived, and can be bought today, but do not be disappointed when you find that they do not actually flower perpetually — most of them flower well only twice in a season. Their colours are the pinks and purples, lilacs, cerise, red and crimson and some beautiful whites. These flowers of yester-year do not look well in association with the brighter-than-bright tones of the modern roses, so the beds are best kept well separated. A very interesting, though not typical, Hybrid Perpetual is 'Roger Lambelin' which has scalloped crimson petals with a white edge. I always put this in the same vase as 'Léda' which is the other way about. 'Baron Girod de l'Ain' is almost the same as 'Roger Lambelin' only more vigorous. Because of their mixed ancestry, Hybrid Perpetuals do not resemble each other, apart from their soft colouration, their scent and their repeat-flowering. They mostly produce long canes, which can be pegged down if space permits: flowers will then be produced all along the length of the cane.

Some Hybrid Perpetuals

'General Jacqueminot', **'General Jack'**, **'Jack Rose'** has fragrant long-stemmed double scarlet flowers and is a pleasure to grow and to give. 4 x 3ft (1.2m x 90cm).

'Frau Karl Druschki' — **'Snow Queen'**, **'White American Beauty'** (1901) has large and lovely pure white blooms and absolutely no scent. 5 x 4ft (1.5 x 1.2m).

Baron Girod de l'Ain (or **Giraud de l'Ain**) (1897) scented double crimson flowers whose irregularly white-edged petals are reflexed. 5 x 4ft (1.5 x 1.2m). Stronger-growing than:

'Roger Lambelin' (1890) which has fragrant crimson-purple petals that are 'deckle-edged' with white. This and the 'Baron' do not look alike when side by side, but in a

small garden there is generally only room for one of two rather unusual and similar roses. 'Roger' needs more than its share of rose-food.

'Reine des Violettes' (1860) has the cup-shaped form of the true old rose, with its soft yet brilliant colouration. The quartered flowers are purple, mauve and violet, with a button eye and are at their best (in hot years) in August and September. 6 x 5ft (1.8 x 1.5m).

'Vick's Caprice' (1891) has large double cup-shaped scented flowers of lilac-pink that are striped with white and crimson. A very eye-catching rose, good with other purples. 3 x 2ft (90 x 60cm).

The Tea roses were so called because their scent was supposed to be like freshly packed tea. This, of course, really does smell of tea, unlike the packets that we buy which may have been stored for many months.

The first of these roses came from China in the middle of the 18th century, by way of the East India Company, and was called 'Hume's Blush Tea-scented China' (later abbreviated to the more convenient 'Hume's Blush').

Tea roses are not grown much in the open air in the British Isles because they need better summers than we generally have, though the white-flowered 'Sombreuil' is hardy and shares a post in my garden with that most beautiful of roses, 'Climbing Lady Hillingdon', whose colour is like an orange sorbet.

The very beautiful 'La France' with its soft pink flowers was the first hybrid Tea rose; these became a more practical new group combining the lovely colours, shapeliness, scent and free-flowering of the Teas with the vigour of the Hybrid Perpetual. But all things change, especially with roses, and the Hybrid Perpetuals began to be crossed with the new Pernet roses from the Pernet-Ducher nursery at Lyon in France. This nursery was better organised, and records were kept. For many years the owner, Joseph Pernet, worked at a breeding programme to produce a good yellow rose. He used the Austrian briar as one parent and crossed it with a Hybrid Perpetual of his own — 'Antoine Ducher'. After many years of work, in 1900 he produced an important new rose, the famous 'Soleil d'Or', which had orange petals with a striking yellow reverse. These and other similar roses were known as Pernetianas, though this term is no longer in use. Much important work continued, to improve the colours and constitutions of the new yellow roses, and this work continued up to and after 1914. Many of the modern roses with their bright yellow and flame colours have Pernet sap in their stems.

Some Tea Roses

'Lady Hillingdon' (1910) has soft orange flowers with the typical and delicious tea-scent. Beautiful buds and crimson-bronze new foliage. 4 x 2ft (1.2m x 60cm). The climbing sport came later on and is now more generally grown.

'Hume's Blush' (1809). Scented double flowers in blush-white. A rather delicate rose, needs the warmest position in the rose garden. 3 x 3ft (90 x 90cm).

'Sombreuil' (1850). A climbing rose, placed here for convenience. Creamy-white flat, double, quartered flowers, blush pink in the centre on opening. Delicious scent. Vigorous and hardy for a Tea — to 20ft (6m).

The Rugosas or the Japanese roses came originally from Japan and China. The species is a strong-growing and lusty rose with large, semi-double pink-to-purple flowers followed by round red hips like small tomatoes; branches and stems are covered with sharp thorns and prickles and the plant suckers freely. A Rugosa that is not immediately recognisable as such is the delicate-looking *R. Willmottiae,* named after the rose-loving Ellen Willmott. This has charming small, flat, lilac-pink flowers with cream stamens and very attractive small-leaved ferny-looking foliage. *R. Willmottiae* makes a spectacular display when grown with the brilliantly coloured *R. moyesii.* I have them together in my garden, which is far too small for these now well-established shrubs, but the month of sheer pleasure when both are in flower together is worth all the spatial problems.

The first Rugosas were brought to Europe in 1784, but were not 'different' enough to find much favour with gardeners at that time. The species Rugosa was used (and still is) as breeding stock because of its strong constitution, willingness to grow in dry, sandy soil, perfumed flowers, good hips, good foliage and autumnal leaf colouration. Many of these qualities have, by careful selection, been passed down to its progeny, and among these are the famous 'Blanc Double de Coubert' which has large, almost single white flowers, and the equally famous 'Frau Dagmar Hastrup' with pale pink single flowers, lovely buds, handsome hips and jolly autumn colours. I have seen all this at one time on a bush, but one cannot count on it every year.

Some Rugosa Roses

'Blanc Double de Coubert' (1892) has large semi-double creased-paper white flowers like poppies on a thorny bush. 6 x 5ft (1.8 x 1.5m).

'Roseraie de l'Hay' (1901) has a succession of sweet-scented wine-red to purple flowers in loose clusters. 6 x 5ft (1.8 x 1.5m).

'Frau Dagmar Hastrup' (also 'Hartopp', 'Hastrop' and 'Haastrup') (1914) has very beautifully-formed single pink fragrant flowers, with fine fat round hips later and good autumn colour. A rose for a small collection, because of its charm and versatility, but perhaps not for a small garden. 5 x 5ft (1.5 x 1.5m).

'Fimbriata' (1891) has scented pink flowers that look like carnations, because the petals have serrated edges. A good rose for flower-arrangers. If it cannot be obtained, the later 'Pink Grootendoorst' (1923) is very like, though with deeper coloured pink flowers. 5 x 4ft (1.5 x 1.2m).

'Schneezwerg' (Snow Dwarf) (1912) has continuous clusters of neat, semi-double white flowers with golden stamens. Red hips follow, sometimes at the same time as the last of the flowers. 6 x 5ft (1.8 x 1.5m).

Climbers and Ramblers. All the taller-growing roses have to be placed together, rather irrespective of their parentage, because of convenience to growers, buyers and in cataloguing. There are languid leaners, no more than 6 or 7ft (1.8 or 2m), which are just too tall to be called shrubs or bushes, especially as their flowers often come well above eye-level.

In this group are to be found the real tree-climbing giants of the genus (though, alas, some of the best were found or bred after the time-scale of this book). There are no real 'climbers' as such among the roses, nothing twines insidiously like Ipomoea or suffocatingly like Russian Vine, but the climbers have all got good prickles or thorns that lodge their stems rigidly against a strong support like a tree, and so the rose can haul itself up to the light. A word of warning. The giants from the Himalaya truly are giants and should not be planted unless you can give them unlimited travelling space — upwards and sideways. One laburnum and a flowering cherry just will not do — these big roses really need a full-grown oak as a climbing frame, and even then they will need a little 'management'. My garden is too shaded by its over-sized shrubs, such as the huge Philadelphus, the matching Weigela, assorted well-grown old apple trees and an internal 'hedge' of lilacs, Forsythia and Chaenomeles, so for the moment there is some growing-space, though the day of reckoning will inevitably come. Most of these roses send out annual shoots of from 10-20ft (3-6m) once they have become established. They can be plaited into boundary hedges and treated as living barbed wire on walls, but the space available for this ploy will soon be used up. They are much too vigorous for house-walls.

What is the difference between a climber and a rambler? That great and knowledgeable rosarian and plantsman, Graham Stuart Thomas has defined it as follows, and I will here quote him: '. . . among the taller roses the 'ramblers' are the wild species and closely allied garden forms — flowering once only in the summer, as is normal with most species — and the 'climbers' are the large-flowered, highly-bred mainly repeat-flowering varieties'. And, as Mr Thomas goes on to say, the two groups of roses are being brought nearer together by the hybridists who are attempting to breed a rose that combines the best of both groups.

Some climbers (of mixed ancestry)

R. banksiae lutea (of unknown age, cultivated for centuries in China and introduced to this country in 1824) has delicate, falling clusters of very double yellow flowers (always at the top of the plant, whether it be on roof or tree). A very famous old rose, only really hardy in warm counties, the Scillies and the South of France. Flowers come on previous season's wood. 25ft + (7.5m +).

'Cécile Brunner, Climbing' ('Bloomfield Abundance') (1894) is a strong-growing rose which has tiny little flowers of great perfection, shading from pink to peach. These are perfect for small arrangements. Keep dead-headed and well-fed. Sporadic and welcome flowers after main flush. 20ft (6m).

'Gloire de Dijon' (1853) has buff-yellow-cream very double scented flowers from June onwards. Somewhat delicate, needs a warm place and good soil and a good start. Buy from a reputable nursery. 15ft (4.5m).

Some Rambler roses

'Albéric Barbier' (1900) is a comfortable old rose, and one that I and many other gardeners grew up with. It has creamy-yellow buds (almost the best part of the rose) that open to scented creamy flowers that do not last, either on the bush or in a vase (like those of 'Albertine'). These keep on and on, so long as the plant is dead-headed every day. Dark, glossy foliage.

'American Pillar' (1902) has bright clusters of shocking-pink single flowers, with conspicuous white centres. A vigorous, cheerful rose that needs little attention. Must have sun. Good on a fence or in a small old, thin-branched apple tree.

'Dr. W. van Fleet' (1910) has clusters of cerise buds opening to palest pink flowers. Dark green foliage. Flowers come on previous year's wood, so care must be taken with the pruning.

'Dorothy Perkins' (1901) has scentless clusters of small multi-petalled bright pink flowers. Lovely when scrambling into yew or up a conifer. Is now enjoying new popularity in the form of standards and in the more elaborate weeping form of these. Can be counted on to get mildew.

'Vielchenblau' (1909) has clusters of blue-violet flowers with a white centre and white streaks. These fade, at different rates, to pleasing mixtures of mauve, lilac and magenta. A lovely rose.

Requirements: All roses need sun to give of their best. As to soil, many, such as the Rugosas and the species roses, do not actually need the best that you can give them, as some of the other rose-groups do. When planting a single rose it pays to remember the old saying 'A £2-plant should go into a £10 hole', though inflation has now spoiled the alliteration. Rose beds, borders and gardens need good preparation because, in theory, you will only do it the once. In late August or September there is no substitute for double digging the whole area, adding well-decayed manure and garden compost to the top spit as you go. Take out any evil weeds like ground-elder, couch or bindweed, whose aerial parts will still be visible as a guide to their extermination. When this has been done leave the bed or border until the roses arrive, which should be in November, but can be at any time until February because of weather problems at the nursery. Container-grown plants (never as good, because they will have had their roots coiled round and round like a

spring) can be planted at any time, of course. For re-planting an existing bed or border in an old garden, it is better to take a good look at the occupants. If they are of manageable size they can all be lifted out in November, the bed dug over, fresh soil added instead of the existing top spit (the old rose soil can be usefully used somewhere else in the garden) and the whole thing rearranged while waiting for the new plants. Where previous roses have died of old age this renewal of the soil should always be carried out, taking up a square yard (1 sq.m) by about 2ft (60cm) deep where the old rose was. New roses should *never* be planted where old ones have died — the soil is said to be 'rose-sick'.

All roses need well-drained soil to do well, sour and acid soil in neglected gardens is often inherited with the purchase of a different house. In which case, let a season go by while you plan the garden, so that you can do the preparation at the proper time without hurrying. The roses will soon catch up that missed summer, I promise you.

Planting When the day comes, have ready all the things that you will need: spade, fork, rake, some buckets of rainwater, a bamboo cane, stakes if necessary, labels, secateurs and a barrowful of planting mixture, which should consist of 2 man-handfuls or 3 lady-handfuls of bonemeal to each 2-gallon pail of damp peat. Add some Hoof-and-Horn while you are about it, you need never use it again. Unwrap the first roses to be planted and put them in the buckets and, as each is planted, so put another in the water. Trim off any bruised or broken roots or branches with the secateurs or a sharp knife. Look at the shape of the roots and dig a (larger) hole to fit. In windy gardens, align the greatest area of root-ends to the windiest point, and it would be best to stake all your new roses in this case for the first year. Scatter some of the planting mix into the hole and put the can across it to indicate ground level. Spread out the roots, if you can. If the shrub is large, give it a short stake, just for that first summer; put it in now, while you can still see where the roots are, and set it so that it is to windward of the shrub. If you have someone to help from now on the job will be done better, but if not, use three hands or the fork to hold the rose upright while you are carefully filling in the hole with the planting mixture. Make sure that the 'union' (where the graft is) is just below the level of the soil — this is what the cane is for, to help you to visualise. Do the filling in carefully, it is very important. Water a little as you go, and when the rose is planted tread it gently in, then add more soil and rake it tidy. When planting climbers or ramblers, spread them out and tie the stems to the wires or other supports that you will, I hope, have already prepared.

Propagation: Some species roses will come true from seed — a good example of this is *R. rubrifolia*. Plant ripe seeds extracted from the hips in October, and grow on in the usual way.

Cuttings are successful with the true species, old shrub roses and for once-flowering ramblers. Take 12″ (30cm) heel cuttings in August or September. Strip off axilliary buds and leaves except for a few at the tip of the cutting. Dig a V-shaped trench 8″ (20cm) deep in a sheltered part of the garden, with no drip from trees. Put 1″ (2cm) of grit into the trench, dip the bottom end of the cuttings in hormone rooting powder and put them into the trench, against one of the sloping sides. Put the soil back and sprinkle the leaves with water, do the sprinkling every day, and in very hot weather water the ground nearby as well.

Cuttings of other types of roses are not really strong-growing and are better not attempted.

Commercial growers propagate their roses by means of 'budding', which is a skilled art. It is not difficult, but is hardly worth learning in order to produce the one-offs for the average garden. If the rose that you want does not seem to exist in any of the catalogues, write to a reputable grower, or the Royal National Rose Society for advice, to ask whether what you want can be specially budded for you. This will take some time, from one to three years, and will cost much more than an existing plant, but if you have set your heart on something I know how you feel.

Pruning:

Species: Need little pruning, except for the removal of old dead wood and crossing stems. With the large-growing bushes try to keep the centre of the bush 'open' for the circulation of air. If you have good soil, your roses may well grow larger than the measurements given, and you should ask yourself if you have the space.

Gallicas: These are strong-growing roses and need very little attention. The tangle among the suckering growth may need a little thinning, some of the side-shoots may need a little shortening (do the latter immediately after flowering, and the former in February, depending on the winter weather).

Damasks and Albas should be pruned after flowering: take off about two-thirds of all side-shoots and shorten main stems by one third. Cut to an outward-facing bud always.

Bourbons: Treat as for Damasks and Albas, except for repeat- or twice-flowering varieties: prune these in spring.

Chinas: Prune these lightly in winter or early spring.

Centifolias and Moss Roses have a lax habit of growth and it will be found that the weight of the flowers causes the canes to sink, so that the tips of the branches are apt to lie on gravel, grass or paving. Therefore the main shoots should be shortened after flowering, by about a third unless there is ample room for growth, eg. if these roses are being grown on wires as rose-hedges. Rain-wet branches are even heavier.

Rugosas: Strong-growing roses these, needing only an occasional tidy-up and a thinning-out.

Climbers: Do not expect these to produce much growth or flower until the second year. Prune in winter by cutting lateral shoots back to about two buds. Prune small-flowered climbers after they have flowered — take the whole plant away from its ties and supports, cut out the flowered shoots and tie in any new canes that have grown up.

Ramblers: Cut away most of the flowered shoots, leaving the new growth on which next year's flowers will form.

Hybrid Perpetuals: These should be treated individually and not all in the same way. For strong-growing roses, prune in winter or early spring, and treat as for the Damasks and Albas.

It will not matter if you miss out a year's care of these roses — they will hardly notice it, whereas modern roses need almost constant attention. If hips are wanted to brighten the winter garden, then the pruning, if any, can be done in early spring, when they are frost-blackened and past their best.

Mulching is of immense benefit to roses if they are grown separately from other plants. It is much easier to spread a thick, even coverlet of your chosen material, which will look neat for months and will deter weeds from sprouting. In mixed borders, the roses can still be mulched, but be careful not to smother nearby herbaceous plants which will not take kindly to this treatment. Water well before applying the mulch, which can be of spent hops, straw, compost, old well-rotted leaf-mould, peat (expensive, but looks wonderful, though provides no nourishment), lawn-mowings (do not use weed-killers on the lawn in this case) and do not allow the mowings to touch the stems of the roses, as this mulch gets hot in the process of decomposition. Manure and mushroom compost are very good in spring, but are not necessary every year unless your soil is poor or very light. Mulching conserves moisture, improves the soil, because it eventually becomes plant food, and prevents weeds from getting a foothold. Apply leaf-mould and compost in the autumn. Wood-ash from garden bonfires is very good; collect it all up in a dry shed, sift it and scatter it on, or sieve it through as it comes and scatter it on the rose bed.

Uses: Almost more than for any other flower. Shrubs for mixed shrub and herbaceous borders, or for collections of roses grown in beds and borders on their own. As specimens on lawns (where they must not have grass over their roots). In containers and tubs (where they will need more feeding). Ramblers and climbers for walls, fences, trees, pergolas, trellis, pyramids, posts and chains. As ground cover. Flowers for cutting and for pot-pourri.

Shrubs: Anderson, Austin, Ballalheannagh, Beales, Busheyfields, Cants, Daisy Hill, Fryer's Roses, Le Grice, Harkness, Hilliers, Marchant, Mattock Notcutts, Roger, Russell, Scotts, Sherrard, Smith, Southcombe, St. Bridget, Stonehouse, Toynbee, Treasure, Warley, Wheatcroft, Woodland, W.W., Wyevale.

Seeds: Chiltern, Thompson and Morgan.

ROSMARINUS — Rosemary *(Labiatae).* There is an old belief that if rosemary is used to scent a house (either by burning the branches or by sprinkling or spraying the fragrance) all who live therein will be protected from harm.

Perhaps this is why rosemary bushes were seen so often beside cottage doors. Shakespeare's Ophelia says 'That's Rosemary, that's for remembrance', even though the Victorian Language of Flowers gave its meaning as 'Your presence revives me'. And I will quote further from Robert Tyas's delightful book 'The Sentiment of Flowers':

'...This shrub yields by distillation a light, pale essential oil of great fragrance, which is imparted to rectified spirit. It was formerly recommended for strengthening the nervous system, for the cure of headaches, etc., as well as to strengthen the memory.

Rosemary has also been made the emblem of fidelity and used accordingly to be worn at weddings, and, on the same principle, at funerals. It is the principal ingredient in Hungary water, and is drank as tea for headachs, and for nervous persons...'

Here is an old recipe for 'the Queen of Hungary's Water' for which I am indebted to Jean Palaiseul. I will quote this also in full, since it is wholly delightful.

'In the city of Buda, in the Kingdom of Hungary, was found the present recipe in the Hours of Her Most Serene Highness, Donna Izabella, Queen of Hungary.

"I, Donna Izabella, Queen of Hungary, aged seventy-two, infirm of limb and afflicted with gout, have for one whole year used the present Receipt, which was given me by a Hermit I had never seen before, and have not seen since, which had so great an effect upon me that I recovered my health and regained my strength, and on beholding my beauty, The King of Poland desired to marry me; which I refused for the love of our Lord Jesus Christ, believing that this Receipt had been given to me by an Angel: Take 30 onces of spirit of wine distilled four times, 20 onces of rosemary flowers, put all together in a tight-corked vessel for the space of 50 hours, then distil in a bain-marie. Take one dram in the morning once a week with some other liquer or drink, or else with meat, and wash the face with it every morning, and rub the infirm limbs with it."'

So there you are. Please let me know if it works.

It is now known that a rosemary-bush is absolutely full of medicinal virtues. I will list a few of them: rosemary assists in the healing of wounds, being antiseptic; it helps to ease the pain of rheumatism and neuralgia; it is good for influenza, coughs and colds; it helps calm nerves that are stressed; it is good for aenaemia, also for indigestion, cirrhosis, gall stones, obesity, palpitations, migraine and it is a diuretic.

Rosemary-bushes are a law unto themselves when it comes to flowering times — you may be fortunate enough to have a shrub that flowers regularly during the winter and I know of several that do this.

The shrubs are part of the aromatic 'maquis' of Mediterranean islands and grow particularly well in sea-coast gardens; indeed, their name of 'Ros-marinus' means 'dew of

the sea' from the Latin ros, dew, marinus, of the sea. Sea-winds rub the branches together, thus releasing the fragrance. A low hedge of rosemary would do well in such gardens where plants are (almost) safe from frost, though because of the constant force of the wind it may be found that a shrub which would grow to 6ft (1.8m) in an inland garden will become a prostrate 9" (23cm) rock-clinger in cliffside gardens. It should not be confused with R. lavendulaceus which is naturally prostrate and is not hardy. This comes from North Africa and Spain and has a hairy calyx which will necessitate using a magnifying glass. The true plant is uncommon in any case, those being offered for sale usually being R. officinalis prostratum.

The culinary rosemary has been grown in the British Isles for over five centuries and was probably introduced by the Romans.

R. officinalis grows to 7ft (2.1m) with an angular spread of 5ft (1.5m) according to how it is cared for — or not, as is often the case. Pale lilac-blue flowers (usually) from April to May or even to September, according to luck. An aromatic evergreen shrub from S. Europe and Asia Minor for a warm, sunny place in inland gardens. For collectors and herb gardeners there are rosemaries with pink, white, pale, clear and dark blue flowers, also with more erect habits or variegated leaves. All, even R. officinalis, should be regarded as being from slightly to definitely tender.

Requirements: An open free-draining soil. Sun and shelter are essential in inland gardens.

Propagation: Take short cuttings and insert them into the ground in a shady border under closed cloches, or put them in a rooting compost of peat and sand in a cold frame, depending on the number of plants needed. When well rooted transfer into pots of John Innes No.1 and protect in the frame or cold greenhouse for the first winter. Or sow ripe seeds in boxes in a sandy seed compost in spring. Green fingered gardeners can plant likely looking woody cuttings directly into a sheltered part of the border in March, or in September in south and west gardens.

Pruning: Trim away winter-damaged shoots. R. officinalis will get straggly in old age. It can either be kept tidy or left to grow eventually into an interestingly gnarled specimen. The tidy-minded gardener can shorten all the shoots by half in April, this will keep the bush neat but a season's flowers may be sacrificed.

Uses: Very many. As a medicinal and culinary plant. As hedging in mild or seaside areas. As a container-plant for patios and sunny balconies. An essential and expected shrub in any herb garden.

Shrubs: Ballalheannagh, Barcock, Bees, Bodnant, Brackenwood, Busheyfields, Caldwell, Peter Chappell, Daisy Hill, Fairley's, Margery Fish, Goatcher, Hilliers, Hopleys, Ingwersen, Jackman, Knaphill, Knoll Gardens, Lime Cross, Marchant, Meare Close, Notcutts, Oak Cottage, Old

Rectory, Ottery, Parkinsons, Rampart, Reuthe, Robinsons, Roger, Rosemoor, Scotts, Shepton, Sherrard, Smith, Southcombe, St. Bridget, Stoke Lacy, Stonehouse, Toynbee, Treseder, Warley, Weald, Woodland, Wyevale.

Seeds: Fothergill.

RUBUS *(Rosaceae)*. To most people 'Rubus' means 'Bramble', to be hauled out as soon as the distinctive leaves are recognised, and an innocent-looking bramble-baby can have a long, strong and tenacious root which invariably vanishes under the impossible stems of a lilac or any large perchable shrub for birds. There is one very handsome though huge-growing species, *R. ulmifolius* 'bellidiflorus', which may be regarded as a permanent source of living barbed wire for those gardeners who need to strengthen their boundaries (ornamentally) against intruders, whether on two legs or four. This far-reaching briar has inch-thick thorny stems which grow to 20ft (6m) and more (both ways) with a proliferation of typical rather unattractive leafy branches. However, in July and onwards it comes into its full glory, with masses of pink powder-puffs that make this a really spectacular plant. These are pretty for short-term arrangements but will begin to drop their petals after 24 hours, less in warm conditions. The dreadful, armed stems are excellent as a deterrent when trained along fence or wall or in a hedge, and the briar sends out a constant succession of shoots which will root at the tip to provide new plants. My briar has swooped up into the old apple tree, from which it sends forth a cascade of blooms in July and August. In addition, I am training the great arching branches along the wall so that there will be more flowers in later seasons. Being very double ('bellidiflorus' aptly describes them) there are never any fruits.

R. laciniatus is another spiteful rambler with very ornamental deeply-cut leaves. It would be worth growing for these alone, as they look delightful on a pale or white wall, or climbing a porch or pergola posts, but in May there are single pale flowers followed in due course by excellent blackberries. In mild winters it retains its leaves, at least it does in its sheltered corner in my garden. Its spines are vicious.

R. Cockburnianus is a very large briar for a winter-focal point. It is not a plant for tidy gardens, growing as it does to a big leggy shrub. Its interest for collectors of the unusual lies in its winter stems, which look as if newly whitewashed. These can be very striking, especially when grown near dark evergreens, but this plant does need the right place to look as handsome as it can and is best planted in a large group and in association with red and yellow barked Cornus, the rabbits' tails of *Salix Wehrhahnii* and with the corkscrew Hazel, *Corylus avellana* 'contorta'. This makes a fascinating group, needing appropriate green ground-cover to set off the subtle colourations, and this could be *R. tri-*

color or a Hedera. The whole area should be thickly planted with Narcissus of several colours, which will flower before any of the shrubs comes into leaf.

R. tricolor is a fascinating and little-known member of this family with much gentler manners. It is a low, creeping, spreading plant, shiningly evergreen, with attractive, burnished leaves and rather frightening stems which appear to be a mass of bristling red thorns but which in reality are just fuzzily soft. This Rubus travels busily and quickly, rooting as it goes, and makes excellent ground-cover in shady, difficult places. It is the most unfussy plant, thriving in dry corners under trees and equally dry places in full sun. I have seen it planted to mound up round an old tree-stump, whose removal would have caused too much upheaval even if it had been possible. The Rubus looked wonderful in the sun with its healthy, glossy leaves and red stems; the stump was in the middle of a gravel drive so the briar was something of a focal point and was quite worthy of its position. I would think that somebody must have gone round it fairly often to nip off some of its exuberance, but it was an elegant and inspired planting association.

The little-grown Japanese wineberry, *R. phoenicolasius*, is a handsome shrub for larger, wilder gardens. It has very attractive clusters of scarlet fruits with matching whiskery sepals; these, picked as they are on the branch, look most unusual in autumnal arrangements. The flowers, though small, are a very bright pink, and the stems are covered with bristly red hairs. It is an unusual shrub, liking damp gardens, and the fruit is delicious. I must warn you that the clumps grow larger and larger with the years, which is why it is not for small gardens.

R. Cockburnianus (1907) grows to 10ft (3m) and as much through, with pure white stems. Small purplish flowers in June followed by black fruit, which are a bonus, because it is for its startling stems that this plant is grown. A deciduous shrub from China for the larger garden.

R. laciniatus — Cut-leaved Briar grows to 8ft (2.4m) and as much sideways with white or pale pink flowers in June followed by fine black fruit. Very ornamental leaves. A spiny fruiting briar from China for fences, walls, posts and hedges in full sun.

R. phoenicolasius — Japanese Wineberry (1876) grows to 10ft (3m) and as much through, with small bright rose-pink flowers in June followed by most attractive and tasty scarlet fruits in August. A deciduous shrub from China and Japan with very hairy red stems.

R. tricolor (1908) grows only to 1ft (30cm) unless it is leaning against a support. White flowers in June (sometimes) followed by red fruits in July. An always good-looking trailing and spreading ground-cover plant with fuzzy scarlet stems for shady places, from China. Very vigorous.

R. ulmifolius not generally grown, but is the parent of *R. ulmifolius* 'bellidiflorus' which grows to 20ft + (6m +) with a spread of 30ft (9m). Very double pink pom-poms from July to August. A semi-evergreen briar (in sheltered places) for large or wild gardens. Very vigorous and thorny, excellent on boundaries.

Requirements: Briars grow in any free-draining garden soil in full sun. Fruiting kinds are better against warm walls.

Propagation: Take half-ripe cuttings in August and September of all except *R. ulmifolius* 'bellidiflorus' and insert in a rooting compost of peat and sand in a cold frame for the winter. When rooted they may be planted out in a nursery area in spring to grow on. Divide *R. phoenicolasius* in spring as needed, or take off a clump of its suckering growth. *R. tricolor* roots as it goes, so a pot of compost can be placed beneath runners for them to root into (peg down firmly). *R. laciniatus* grows quickly from seed. *R. ulmifolius* 'bellidiflorus' sends up arching wands of new growth, peg these down into a pot in August, or at any time they are needed. They will take about six months to root and can then be severed and grown on for a season.

Pruning: Be strong minded about *R. ulmifolius* with matching shears, one cannot pussy-foot about with this giant. Take off all the flowered shoots that you can reach and thin out the stems, though this need not be done every year. Cut out fruiting stems of *R. laciniatus* and tie in new canes. Cut out fruiting canes of *R. phoenicolasius*. Tidy up *R. tricolor* once a year or its attractiveness can be lost. Cut out dead stems of *R. Cockburnianus*.

Uses: This large genus is full of character, with interesting species and varieties and a collection can be made of them, but only in a large garden. The thorny ones are almost intruder-proof in hedges and on fences and walls. Flowers, fruit, foliage and stems make them interesting for decor.

Shrubs: Ballalheannagh, Bodnant, Brackenwood, Caldwell, Beth Chatto, Hilliers, Hopleys, Ingwersen, Jackman, Kaye, Marchant, Marten's Hall, Notcutts, Otter, Reuthe, Roger, Rosemoor, Shepton, Sherrard, Smith, Southcombe, St. Bridget, Toynbee, Treasure, Treseder, Woodland, W.W., Wyevale.

Seeds: Chiltern.

RUSCUS — Butcher's Broom *(Liliaceae)*. *R. aculeatus* is only a 'borderline shrub' and shouldn't be in this book by rights because it has no real woody stems. It is called 'Butcher's Broom' because being such a stiff scratchy plant it was said to have been bound into brushes and brooms with which to scrub butchers' chopping blocks and tables. Ruscus is exceedingly useful in a tree-shaded garden because it positively needs to grow under trees. It is an apparently leafy sub-shrub; the 'leaves' are interesting in that they are flattened cladodes or stems, with minute flowers appearing on the upper surface of the cladode. If male and female plants are set together there will be fine red berries on the females but it is not always easy to get such certified plants,

but keep asking and refuse the new hermaphrodite form which will doubtless be offered you. They are quite unfussy as to soil type and will grow on chalk, clay and acid loams. They have been rather spoiled for some of us by being seen for sale painted silver or gold, in gipsies' baskets. It is even possible to buy plastic Ruscus which is the ultimate awfulness.

R. aculeatus — Butcher's Broom, Knee-holly grows to 3ft (90cm) with minute greenish flowers in March and April, followed by red berries when both sexes of the plant are grown together. An 'evergreen' European sub-shrub for interest under trees, berries very conspicuous in ideal conditions.

Requirements: Any soil, sun, semi- or quite dense shade. Plants of both sexes.

Propagation: Lift established clumps in April and divide. Or sow seeds (not easy to buy) in September when ripe, in John Innes seed compost. Leave in a cold frame indefinitely, they will take from one to two years to germinate. If and when they do, transplant carefully into a nursery area and grow on until large enough to be planted out. Sow some of the seeds directly into the garden and mark the place, these may germinate more quickly.

Uses: As strangely interesting plants to grow in tree-shaded places. Berried plants rare, don't pick too many for arrangements.

Shrubs: Hilliers, Holden Clough, Ingwersen, Marchant, Meare Close, Notcutts, Roger, Russell, Scotts, Sherrard, Treseder, Wyevale.

SALIX — Willow, Pussy Willow *(Salicaceae)*. The genus is a large one, consisting of many trees, but there are a number of interesting shrubs of varying sizes to correspond with similar gardens. The word 'willow' makes most gardeners think 'Ah, damp soil — I haven't got damp soil', but most of the genus will do almost as well in ordinary earth which is just as well because over-exuberant growth, due to lush living, is usually unplanned and may be difficult to cope with. Some of the really dwarf kinds are delightful plants for open areas near paving — their stems and small leaves associate well with rocks in summer, and in winter a mature shrub reveals its interesting form. *S. lanata*, the Woolly Willow, is a cosy shrub in spring and summer, producing typical 'pussies' in late spring which are closely followed by the emergent silvery, felted foliage; the golden catkins surrounded by the woolly leaves are most attractive in the sun. Another dwarf shrub, slow growing (for a willow) is *S. x boydii* which has a rigidity very reminiscent of bonsai. It is gratifyingly small — 3ft (90cm) — and stays that way, with rounded, crinkled, silvery leaves. These get greener as the season advances, but are always interesting. It is a very focal shrub (or dwarf tree) and should be planted in association with delicate bulbocodiums, cyclamen and plants that have a restrained elegance, rather than the wild, rushing growth of annuals or the huge herbaceous plants which may be sensibly slow to emerge in spring but which put on an astonishing amount of growth later in the season. For interesting ground cover in a damp rockery the tiny *S. herbacea* is appealing, it grows only to 4″ (10cm) and has stemmy subterranean shoots with leaves on the end as well as catkins in spring. Another dwarf type, also very suitable to rock gardens, is *S. retusa* which has creeping branches that root as they go. It is seldom more than a few inches (cm) high, and presents its 'pussies' in neat rosettes of leaves in early summer.

S. gracistyla is a very attractive not-too-large shrub which has long, brushy 'pussies' which are red and grey when they open, later turning to yellow. The leaves are silvered with down to begin with, later becoming green. There are so many types that, as with many other shrubs, it is a good idea to visit an established arboretum, such as Hilliers at Winchester, during the early part of the year. Willows are wonderful for wet gardens, and it is possible to establish the rare and curious saprophyte, *Lathraea clandestina* on their roots which takes several years to achieve and is a cultural triumph when successful.

S. x boydii (1901) grows to an erect 3ft (90cm) or less, with a similar spread. Small catkins in April. A small deciduous shrub with very attractive silvery, crinkled leaves for the rock garden or a focal position near water or stone-work.

S. gracistyla (1895) grows to 10ft (3m) with colourful red and grey 'pussies' in spring. A deciduous shrub from Korea and Japan for the spring garden.

S. herbacea — Dwarf Willow grows only to 4″ (10cm) with catkins in April. A deciduous creeping shrub of the northern hemisphere for damp rockeries and similar gardens.

S. lanata — Woolly Willow, grows to 3ft (90cm) with golden 'pussies' in May and silver-furred young foliage at the same time. A deciduous shrub of N. Europe and N. Asia for a focal position in the spring garden.

S. retusa (1763) grows only a few inches (cm) tall with erect 'pussies' coming with the leaves in May and June. A useful and attractive prostrate spreading shrub for the rockery or at the edge of a path.

Requirements: It must be said that most willows prefer damp soil, but this is not necessary except with specific types which will languish without it. Regular watering will suffice with the others, especially in unexpectedly long dry periods when other garden work demands your attention. At these times go round and water *all* the climbers on any walls or buildings as well as any willows that you may have. All shrubby willows prefer sunny situations. Any good garden soil.

Propagation: Take woody cuttings appropriate in length to the species and insert in a rooting compost of peat and sand in October. Keep in a cold frame for the winter and transfer to

individual pots of John Innes No.1 in spring and grow on, or if appropriate plant out in a nursery area.

Pruning: None generally needed except to take off dead branches in spring.

Uses: As interesting shrubs for focal places, backgrounds, rockeries and as ground cover. As bee plants in spring. Branches of 'pussies' for arrangements.

Shrubs: Ballalheannagh, Barcock, Bodnant, Brackenwood, Bressingham, Broadwell, Caldwell, Peter Chappell, Beth Chatto, Dobbies, Goscote, Highfield, Hilliers, Holden Clough, Ingwersen, Jackman, Knaphill, Marten's Hall, Notcutts, Otter, Robinsons, Roger, Russell, Scotts, Shepton, Sherrard, Smith, St. Bridget, Stonehouse, Toynbee Treasure, W.W., Wyevale.

SALVIA — Sage *(Labiatae)*. The common sage — so much a part of Sunday dinners — is a pretty powerful herb. Too much of it in the stuffing and the bird is ruined because a small amount only is needed. A jar of dried sage leaves would last for ever (and often does, alas) if one used it at the normal rate. But to give of its best, sage should be this year's dried leaves, so throw the ten-year old contents of that jar of yours out on to the roses and go and call on a friend with a herb-garden. There are several different kinds and colours of shrubby sage and all of them can be used in the pot. *S. officinalis* is the one that ends up in all those jars and packets, but it is a most attractive plant when in flower and does well in a hot dry place, and it positively loves drought years. *S.o* 'aurea' has yellow leaves and looks most attractive when set next to *S.o.* 'purpurea', which has dark plummy leaves, or *S.o.* 'tricolor' which has delightful leaves (too nice to eat) in purple, green and white or red, grey-green and white. *S.o.* 'icterina' is an unusual variety having gold and green leaves, and a mature plant is a handsome thing in a sunny corner. I have heard it called 'The Lizard Sage', which is a very good name for it because the markings resemble a lizard's colouration. Sages vary in hardiness, 'tricolor' being the most tender and apt to give up in a bad winter. If you have room for one only, grow *S.o.* 'purpurea' or 'icterina', the latter being a trifle more hardy.

There are some nice old rhymes about sage. One is:

'He that would live for aye

Must eat Sage in May.'

Sage was an important herb in ancient times, believed to confer longevity even if only growing in the garden, and where sage flourishes then the woman of the house rules.

Another belief in earlier times was that as the owner's business prospered, or the reverse, so would the sage wax or wither. In England, as in France, the plant was supposed to assuage grief and it was formerly planted on graves in country churchyards.

The French had a verse about the virtues of sage and, when translated, it said:

'Sage helps the nerves and by its powerful might
Palsy is cured and fever put to flight.'

In addition, the herb was supposed to be very effective against the bitings of serpents, though I am not sure whether you wore it as an amulet or ate it as a preventative: either way, it wouldn't be wasted because Gerard said:

'Sage is singularly good for the head and brain, it quickeneth the senses and memory, strengtheneth the sinews, restoreth health to those that have palsy, (there, I said it wouldn't be wasted) and taketh away shakey trembling of the members.'

Medicinally the plant has been in use since ancient times as a remedy for dyspepsia and sore throats; sage tea was used in the West Indies to calm fevers and the Chinese were said to prefer this above their own tea. It was formerly used in homeopathic medicine in cases of typhoid fever, biliousness, measles, quinsy (an old name for tonsillitis) headache and pains in the joints. Real sage was once used in tooth powders, and externally a strong infusion was used to darken hair; hot poultices of the leaves were very effective to ease pain. It is no wonder that in the Middle Ages (when Latin was the common language) there was a saying 'Cur monatur homo cui Salvia crescit in horto?' (Why should a man die whilst sage grows in his garden?).

S. officinalis (1597) grows to 2ft (60cm) with blue-purple flowers in June and July. A short-lived aromatic evergreen shrubby herb from southern Europe for a sunny sheltered bed in the garden.

Requirements: Any ordinary free-draining garden soil and a place in the sun.

Propagation: Take short heel-cuttings in August or September and insert into a rooting compost of peat and sand. Put pots in a cold frame until rooted, then transfer into individual pots of John Innes No.1. Protect in frame for first winter. In the following spring, once growth starts, pinch out tips to encourage bushiness.

Pruning: Nip off winter-damaged branches and replace plants that get old and lax.

Uses: Culinary and medicinal, as ornamental foliage plants and as pot-plants for balconies or window boxes (not indoors).

Shrubs: Brackenwood, Bressingham, Daisy Hill, Margery Fish, Hilliers, Hopleys, Jackman, Kaye, Knoll Gardens, Marten's Hall, Meare Close, Notcutts, Oak Cottage, Old Rectory, Parkinsons, Robinsons Russell, Scotts, Shepton, Sherrard, Southcombe, Stoke Lacy, Stonehouse, Treasure, Treseder, Warley, Weald, Wyevale.

Seeds: Suttons.

SAMBUCUS — Elder, Golden Elder (*Caprifoliaceae*). Much history and many legends surround the elder and as I have written of this in other books I do not wish to repeat myself. However, because I love to see the great flat plates of creamy flowers in midsummer (which can be eaten in fritters and sorbets) and wonder why the pendant sprays of black, black fruits are so seldom picked for good wine and good health, I cannot resist this opportunity to tell you just one or two superstitions and some of the wilder remedies, in the hope that you will spare the old elder at the bottom of the garden, which is a tree, of course, and not a shrub; but blood is thicker than water, or sap in this case, and the Scots' rhyme says:

'Bour-tree, bour-tree, crookit rung,
Never straight, and never strong
Never bush and never tree,
Since Our Lord was nailed t'ye.'

There is a belief that Our Lord was crucified on a cross made of elder-wood and ever since the elder has been neither bush nor tree, and has been feared for centuries for its other associations; this is certainly a case of 'give a dog a bad name'.

There is an old 17th century recipe for a most useful substance to be used as an anodyne, or pain killer. The recipe does not say whether this substance is for drinking or for application, and I will leave you to decide. Here it is:

'Of quick (live) snails, newly taken out of their shelly cottages; of Elderberries dried in the oven, and pulverized; and of common salt, of each as much as you will; put it in the straining bagg, called Hippocrates sleeve, making one row upon another, so oft as you please; so that the first be of the snails, the next of salt, and the last of the berries; continuing so till the bagg be full; hang it up in a Cellar, and gather diligently the glutinous liquor that distils out of it little by little.'

Because each elder, whether bush or tree, is supposed to shelter its own spirit (good or bad according to the luck of the draw), one is supposed to ask permission when fruit, flowers, bark or leaves are to be gathered. You should say: 'Elder, Elder, may I pluck thy branches?' and if all is quiet this means assent, and you should spit three times, after which you can fill your basket.

I feel that the elder has long been neglected and it is time that the pendulum of fashion swung back in its favour. It is, forgetting all the superstitions, a very useful tree indeed and will grow absolutely anywhere, including gale-torn cliffside gardens where it will survive to become a useful (and lovely) wind-break — for which seaside gardeners would gladly wave a magic wand (elder-wood, of course). I do not say that it will be a large tree, because in these conditions, it cannot grow as symmetrical as one of the same age in a peaceful Dorset dale, but it will have tremendous character and, in time, lichen will form on the gnarled, fissured trunk and the twisted branches. The leaves often colour well in autumn when the plant grows on chalk.

There are some very ornamental forms of Sambucus, particularly the green-leaved *S. racemosa* which has delicate saw-edged foliage with pointed cones of cream flowers, followed by red fruits instead of black. *S. racemosa* 'plumosa aurea' is exquisite, having finely-cut golden-yellow leaves in early summer. There are two choices of position — shade will keep the colour lighter longer, but in a sunny place it will glow as if touched by Midas himself. I know of a large one that is planted in a sunny place, where it stays yellow throughout the summer, getting a little bleached as the months go by but contrasting always against the darker green of the forest trees behind it. It is at least 15ft (4.5m) (I think more) high which always makes me smile when I read the descriptions on the plant label in the garden centres: most of them say 'grows to 6ft (1.8m)' because the mention of actual height would terrify people too much. I installed mine (from the same garden centre) which was a beautiful baby of some 3ft (90cm) two years ago; it is now a bigger baby 7ft (2.1m) tall. I must add that, as usual, it has had a disturbed life because I tried it in the shade for a season, where it looked quite lovely in front of the new brick wall with blue Rue at its feet, but this position was too shaded and the wonderful yellow tones turned very quickly to a pleasant light green which was certainly not what I wanted. So in due course, and at the proper time, it was moved and it now conceals the fearsome armed stems of the *Rubus ulmifolius* 'bellidiflorus' which are in no way attractive. Here the Sambucus has much more sun and it stays nicely yellow commensurately longer. It is planted in a neutral free-draining soil.

S. racemosa — Red-Berried Elder, Mountain Elder (since the 16th century) grows to 10ft (3m) with cream panicles of flowers in April, which should be followed by scarlet berries. (This shrub does not fruit reliably in England, though it does so in Scotland and near Paris.) *S.r.* 'plumosa aurea' (1895) has panicles of toning creamy flowers with spectacular cut-leaved yellow foliage, especially beautiful in spring and early summer. There are several very garden-worthy varieties of *S. nigra*, notably:

S.n. aurea — Golden Elder (1883) with yellow foliage (not like *S.r.* 'plumosa aurea').

S.n. var. 'laciniata' with linear, pointed lobes.

S.n. 'marginata' syn. **'albovariegata'** with white-bordered leaves.

S.n. 'Aureomarinata' with yellow-edged leaves.

S. racemosa is a deciduous shrub of the northern hemisphere for the larger garden.

S.r. 'plumosa aurea' is a deciduous shrub for a focal position.

Requirements: Any good garden soil and a sunny position.

Propagation: Take half-ripe cuttings with a heel in July and August and insert them in a rooting compost in the proportions of one of peat to two of sand. Put into a cold frame and leave there for the winter. Plant out in a nursery area in spring. Transplant to final positions in late autumn or in February. The leaf-buds of *S.r.* 'plumosa aurea' are formed almost as soon as the leaves fall and may be damaged by frost.

Uses: *S.r.* 'plumosa aurea' as a focal garden shrub.

Shrubs: Bees, Brackenwood, Bressingham, Caldwell, Peter Chappell, Daisy Hill, Dobbies, Fairley's, Margery Fish, Goatcher, Goscote, Great Dixter, Hilliers, Hopleys, Jackman, Kaye, Knaphill, Lime Cross, Marchant, Marten's Hall, Meare Close, Notcutts, Otter, Reuthe, Roger, Rosemoor, Russell, Shepton, Sherrard, Smith, Toynbee, Treasure, Woodland, Wyevale.

Seeds: Chiltern.

SANTOLINA — Cotton Lavender (and, wrongly, **French Lavender**) *(Compositae)*. Santolina is still in use, after many centuries, as low hedging in herb-gardens or wherever such formality is appropriate. It is a pleasing silver grey throughout the year, though much whiter in hot weather and when grown in sandy soil. The yellow button-like flowers are very attractive when the plant is grown as an individual, but are quickly sheared off by the aesthete herb-gardener who wants no distractions (though there may well be a clump of Santolina busily flowering away somewhere else so that the 'collection' is totally representative of the herbs in all their stages). It is not really a medicinal plant, though it certainly smells like one. Its most useful function in former days was as a vermifuge and it was used as a stimulant. Dried, it was and is a good plant to put with woollen goods to keep away moths, but there are stronger, nicer-smelling plants for this. In former times, when people lived closer to the land they had much more to do with animals, and it would seem that they were often bitten. Certainly, the old herbals tell us that many plants were used to heal the 'bitings of venomous beasts' and Santolina was one such. It is an essential plant for the 'white' garden.

S. Chamaecyparissus — Cotton Lavender (1596) grows to 2½ft (76cm) with yellow button-like flowers in July and August. An 'evergrey' from southern Europe, with stiff pinnatisect leaves and white stems. Young leaves and winter appearance green. *S.C.* 'nana' is the dwarf form, nice in rockeries and as contrast among alpines.

Requirements: Full sun, sandy, very free-draining soil.

Propagation: Take short half-ripe cuttings of lateral shoots from July to September and insert in a rooting compost of peat and sand. Put into a cold frame. In spring transfer rooted cuttings into pots of John Innes No.1 and plunge in a nursery area. Potted plants can be set out in final positions at any time.

After flowering: Cut off flowering stems.

Pruning: Clip hedges to shape as needed. Old plants get lax with open centres, especially if snow has lain on them in winter. In April cut them hard back and they will (usually) respond with new basal growth. Discard large untidy plants.

Uses: As low hedges for parterres, herb and rose-gardens. Foliage and flowers for arrangements; aromatic leaves as moth repellant; as foliage contrast shrubs.

Shrubs: Ballalheannagh, Bodnant, Brackenwood, Bressingham, Broadwell, Busheyfields, Caldwell, Beth Chatto, Cunnington, Daisy Hill, Dobbies, Fairley's, Margery Fish, Goatcher, Highfield, Hilliers, Hopleys, Jackman, Kershaw, Knaphill, Knoll Gardens, Marchant, Marten's Hall, Meare Close, Notcutts, Otter, Reuthe, Roger, Russell, Scotts, Sherrard, Smith, Stonehouse, Toynbee, Treasure, Treseder, Warley, Weald, Woodland, Wyevale.

Seeds: Chiltern, Thompson and Morgan.

SARCOCOCCA — Christmas Box, Sweet Box *(Buxaceae)*.

Sarcococcas are neat-leaved evergreen shrubs that thrive in shady places. This in itself is gratifying, but in addition they have tiny fragrant cream 'flowers' in winter. It is a good idea to try to place all the winter-blooming plants in the same area, rather than spotting them about: the sight of Hellebores, Viburnums, Daphne, Hamamelis, Chimonanthus, Jasminum, Vinca, Bergenia and the first bulbs — Narcissus, Crocus, Leucojum and Galanthus — all together and (on kind days) scenting the air around makes spring come to your garden sooner; once these flowers are out there are others coming along behind, with ruffles of green foliage or the fat, promising spears of the new season thrusting up through the ground. Each day there will be some new buds that were not there previously, or two or three unfolding leaves. So, start your garden's spring early by designating a suitable area, and move the plants and shrubs to this in their dormant period. It is quite a lot of work and may take two seasons to achieve in a small and overcrowded garden, but it is so worth while. Being a practical gardener I face with fortitude the knowledge that sometimes the winter and early spring weather will freeze the flowers, frost the foliage, and blast the bulbs, but the good years are worth it.

To return to the Sarcococcas. They are what I term polite plants, thriving in quite dense shade, always glossily green, with their small and so-welcome flowers that begin to open from December onwards.

Most of them are low and can therefore be used to fill up the middle part of a shady area which they will furnish admirably, and the pointed leaf-shape is good in winter with larger plants, such as Aucuba, the always invaluable Bergenia, the delicate Epimediums and the pleasing forms of Tolmiea, Tellima and Cyclamen. Most years the previous season's berries remain on the branches throughout the winter, along with the forming flower buds. The 'flowers' have no petals and are not conspicuous — their charm lies in their mid-winter scent. Its consonantal name comes from *sarkos*, fleshy, and *kokkes*, a berry.

S. Hookeriana (1908) grows to 6ft (1.8m) with small scented white flowers from September to November. An evergreen shrub from China for the shady garden.

S. humilis (1907) grows to 2ft (60cm) with scented pink and white flowers from January to March. A dwarf evergreen from China with a dense suckering habit. Black berries in winter. For shady places. (Sometimes sold or grown as *S. confusa.*)

S. ruscifolia (1901) grows to 3ft (90cm) with scented white flowers from December to March followed by crimson berries. A neat, glossy-leaved evergreen from China for shaded gardens.

Requirements: Sarcococcas are unfussy about soil and general conditions, usually giving more than they get. They need a shaded position, free-draining soil and appreciate a mulch of leaf-mould in spring. Water in dry seasons. They will do well on chalk.

Propagation: The genus is rather like Butcher's Broom (Ruscus) and increases by means of suckering growths which may be divided off in spring. Or take half-ripe cuttings in July and insert in a rooting compost of peat and sand and place in a cold frame. When well rooted transfer into individual pots of John Innes No.1 and grow on. Sow seeds in spring in individual pots of seed compost and place in a cold frame.

Uses: Excellent as healthy greenery under trees; flowering branches for scent indoors in winter.

Shrubs: Ballalheannagh, Barcock, Bodnant, Bressingham, Caldwell, Chappell, Goatcher, Goscote, Hilliers, Ingwersen, Jackman, Knaphill, Knoll Gardens, Marchant, Marten's Hall, Notcutts, Otter, Reuthe, Rosemoor, Russell, Scotts, Shepton, Sherrard, St. Bridget, Stonehouse, Toynbee, Treasure, Woodland, W.W., Wyevale.

SAROTHAMNUS — Broom, Common Broom, Scots Broom *(Leguminosae)*.

This is the yellow-flowered broom of myth, legend and usefulness, whose branches were formerly made into besoms and brooms. A hillside in full flower is a wonderful sight and is quite a noisy place to be on a hot day, with all the ripened pods exploding sharply to fling the shot-like seeds in all directions. The wild native broom grows quickly and easily from seed and this is the best way to propagate it rather than to move a young shrub and watch it die by inches.

All kinds of fairy folk live in broom bushes, with powers to give useful advice and help to any who ask — if they ask properly. Sometimes the answers might not be to the taste of the supplicant — there is a nice little story about a good-wife of the 13th century who asks of the fairy in the broom bush:

> 'Tell me, being in the broom
> Teach me what to do
> That my husband
> Love me true...'

To which the being tartly replies:

> 'When your tongue is still
> You'll have your will.'

Nothing at all has changed in seven centuries — what a

comfort.

Broom was much used medicinally in former times, and still is in homeopathy today.

S. scoparius syn. **Cytisus scoparius** grows to 8ft + (2.4m +) with a spread of about 6ft (1.8m) and bright yellow pea-flowers in May and June. A European wild shrub for sunny gardens. Does well on acid soil. *S. scoparius* var. 'Albus' (before 1830) has white flowers and *S.c.* 'Andreanus' (1884) has crimson-brown yellow flowers.

Requirements: Full sun, any well-drained poor to average soil but best in acid, sandy conditions. Rich soil does not suit it.

Propagation: Broom bushes are short-lived as a rule and die by degrees, untidily. So, after about twelve years of pleasure from whatever broom (or Cytisus) you have, take some of its seeds (if it is a species) and sow them in a sandy seed compost in April. Put the pots in a cold frame and when large enough transfer into 4" (10cm) pots of John Innes No.1 and keep in the frame for a month until they are large enough to be plunged out of doors in a nursery area. Or take heel cuttings in August or September and put into a rooting compost of peat and sand. When well rooted, pot on carefully in John Innes No.1 and grow on. Plant out in autumn.

Pruning: If necessary prune after flowering, cut away previous summer's growth only. When whole sections of the shrub turn brown it must be discarded, there is no cure for anno domini.

Uses: Beautiful in the mass on a bank. Flowering branches for cutting. In homeopathic medicine and therefore has a place in the herb garden. Ultimately for besoms.

Shrubs: Goatchers, Hilliers, Notcutts, Russell, Scotts, Sherrards, St. Bridget, The Weald, Wyevale.

SENECIO *(Compositae).* This large genus seems to need as much unravelling (at least, in some of its more popular species) as kitten-tangled knitting wool, as readers of my previous book, on old-fashioned flowers*, will notice. The shrubby Senecios confuse nurserymen, growers and garden-centre staff alike, not to mention the most important person of all — you, the gardener. Let us try to sort it out. *S. Greyii* is what most people think they are familiar with — a handsome evergreen with yellow daisy-flowers and silver white stems and undersides to the leaves, which make it a smart looking shrub when properly cared for. But, and here we go, the shrub that they are given is usually *S. laxifolius* or, in some cases, a hybrid of *S. Greyii* and *S. compactus*. The true species of *S. Greyii* is a taller, wider less hardy shrub with certain distinct foliage differences. Where a certified specimen does exist it is a very fine and floriferous shrub. What is called *S. laxifolius* may well be the plant that you are offered; this does not (generally) grow to more than 4ft (1.2m) high, and when well grown it should have 8" (20.5cm) long panicles of yellow daisy-like flowers. It does

well in seaside gardens, where it is taken for granted along with Griselinea, Hydrangea, Potentilla and Olearia. It is not hardy in the midland counties and, as the true plant is seldom seen in the British Isles, what you may actually get under either name is one of the hardier *S.* 'Dunedin Hybrids' which, according to W.J. Bean 'cover all cultivated senecios which derive apparently from hybridisation between *S. compactus*, *S. Greyii* and *S. laxifolius*, including backcrosses'. He goes on to say 'From typical *S. laxifolius*, the hybrids may be distinguished by their relatively broader, more rounded leaves; from typical *S. Greyii*, by the leaves at the first forks of the inflorescence having a narrowed stalk-like, not a sessile expanded base and from *S. compactus*, by their larger leaves, laxer habit and the absence of a conspicuous white margin to the upper surface of the leaves'. The earliest known specimens date from 1910-1913 and originated from the Dunedin Botanic Garden, New Zealand, hence their name. So there you are, they are as bad as Asters when it comes to moral standards. I find all this most interesting but do not really mind what plant I get just so long as it is not too floppy in its habits, has leathery dark green leaves edged with white which are also white beneath, white stems and sprays of yellow daisies in midsummer. It would seem that in this case particularly it is best to go to a reliable grower who has propagated the plants himself, and he can then discuss their pedigrees with you.

S. compactus grows to 2ft (60cm) high and spreads to 4ft + (1.2m +) with bright yellow flowers in July and August. A tender evergreen from New Zealand with white-felted undersides to its leaves, for a hot sunny corner in southern gardens and by the sea. Not hardy near and north of London.

S. Greyii syn. **S. Greyi** — true species grows to 8ft (2.4m) in the wild (less in gardens) with a similar spread. Yellow flowers in June and July and again later. A tender evergreen shrub from New Zealand with white shoots, stems, undersides and margins of pointed leaves.

S. laxifolius grows to 4ft (1.2m) with a similar spread and yellow flowers with red-brown centres in June and July. Larger leaves and a laxer growth habit. An evergreen shrub from New Zealand, species slightly hardier than the others.

Requirements: Full sun and ordinary free-draining soil. Good in seaside gardens, where they are used for loose hedging or as ground cover. Senecios do not mind wind.

Propagation: Take half-ripe cuttings of unflowered lateral shoots in August and insert in a rooting compost of peat and sand. Place in a cold frame and in the following spring transfer to individual pots of John Innes No.1 and plunge in a nursery area.

Pruning: Cut back straggling branches in April. For coastal hedging the flowered stems should be cut back as far as a good leaf.

After flowering: Cut off flowered stems.

Note: *Lys de Bray's Manual of Old Fashioned Flowers, published by Oxford Illustrated Press Ltd., 1984

Uses: As excellent long-lasting foliage in arrangements, particularly good forms with white-margined leaves. Flower sprays for cutting in season. As a contrast shrub in the garden, especially against carefully chosen backgrounds. As loose 'hedging' in coastal areas and for cliffside gardens.

Shrubs: Ballalheannagh, Barcock, Bees, Bodnant, Brackenwood, Bressingham, Busheyfields, Caldwell, Peter Chappell, Beth Chatto, Daisy Hill, Dobbies, Fairley's, Farall, Margery Fish, Goatcher, Great Dixter, Highfield, Hilliers, Holden Clough, Hopleys, Jackman, Kayes, Kershaw, Knaphill, Lime Cross, Marchant, Meare Close, Notcutts, Otter, Ramparts, Reuthe, Roger, Rosemoor, Russell, Scotts, Shepton, Sherrard, Smith, St. Bridget, Stonehouse, Toynbee, Treasure, Treseder, Warley, Woodland, W.W.

SKIMMIA *(Rutaceae).* These are solid, comfortable looking bushes which seem never to be out of bloom or berry. There is no airy delicacy about a Skimmia, it has the comforting solidity of a tea-cosy in the bare winter garden, though in bad winters the leathery evergreen leaves may be damaged by frost. Skimmias are sociable shrubs, and for the berries it is essential to have at least one male to a harem of five female plants. Male flowers are usually sweeter-smelling than the female and sometimes these last are not at all nice to be near. If there is only space in your garden for one bush then it will have to be *S. Reevesiana,* which is the bi-sexual form. If you should find that you have more space than you thought you had, plant two hermaphrodite forms together for better berries on both. Skimmias have long-lasting compact panicles of flowers, male plants having more of these than the females. The solid-looking clusters of berries turn colour from green to red at the same time as the conspicuous buds are forming. This genus occasionally produces hermaphroditic flowers in some years on a female plant, though afterwards it will revert to its proper station in life. With the most popular species it is best to buy certified male and female plants and to hand-pollinate these yourself if the bees do not seem to be doing this job for you. The female plants (which I hope you will keep labelled as such until their appearance is familiar) have flowers which can be differentiated from the male flowers by the prominent ovary and stigma (take a magnifying glass and compare male and female just as you did in school biology lessons), and then take a soft paintbrush (I would use a sable hair No.4, because I have them to hand, but don't buy one especially: improvise, borrow or steal, it's cheaper). On a good sunny day, when the dew has dried, test with cotton wool to see if the pollen is loose enough on the male flowers; if it is, then rub the brush gently over the male flowers to collect the pollen and transfer this to the female flowers. The job will take some time if you are not to miss out any of the ladies, and you might have to ration out the male pollen rather carefully, but a little goes a long way. The bees will generally assist you, and the resulting crop of berries will be worth it. I do this with the flowering *Prunus cerasifera* 'Pissardii', which is too tall now to attend to properly; this means that I have to tie my brush to a cane and dab about in the blossom, precise 'painting' being difficult when perched on a step ladder. I do it because the flowers come so early (before the bees really get out and about), and I like the delicious little round red plums that this ornamental tree produces with such assistance. Also, I like the plums to be where I can get at them, not 15ft (4.5m) up.

The naming of the Skimmias as they were discovered became very confused because male and female forms were found separately and introduced at different times. The first to be found was *S. japonica,* which was seen by Engelbert Kaempfer in 1712. It was the male form, grown by the Japanese for its sweet scent. They called it *'Mijama Skimmi'* or *'Sikimi'* which means 'harmful plant' in Japanese. The seeds within the fruits have an occasional tendency to sprout whilst still on the plant. Altogether this is a queer genus and well worth cultivating for its odd habits, its scent (except for the smelly females), the wonderful long-lasting berries and the well-upholstered appearance of the bushes in general — added to which there is their willingness to be beautiful in semi-shade if necessary.

Carl Peter Thunberg (1775-1828) was a Swedish physician and botanist employed by the Dutch East India Company. Whilst working with them, he was able to purchase maps of the area which had hitherto been prohibited to earlier Europeans. He was even allowed to buy seeds and also plants from Japanese nurseries, which he cared for on the artificial island of Deshima; this had been created by the Japanese for the European traders who were not allowed to enter Japanese ports at that time. Thunberg was thus able to send home, via the Dutch ships, live plants in pots, some of which survived the long sea voyage across the Indian Ocean, round the Cape of Good Hope, and so to Europe. He was so assiduous in his search for new plants to record that he even examined the hay (that was provided daily for the livestock kept on Deshima) to find new species of Japanese flora. A thorough man, and a keen observer of everything around him, his comments are as valid today as they must have been in long-ago Japan. He approved of the well-made and maintained Japanese road system, and of their 'most excellent rule, that travellers should always keep on the left-hand side of the way'. He was of the opinion that the accident toll in the Europe of his time was occasioned by being 'rode and driven over by the giddy sons of riot and dissipation'. This was written almost exactly 200 years ago and with all our sophisticated modern thinking and equipment we are even better at killing proportionately more travellers.

In 1784 Thunberg wrote *Flora Japonica* but this, though more comprehensive, did not have the same impact as Kaempfer's earlier *'Amoenitates Exoticae'* written in 1712, of which only one of the five sections was devoted to plants. However, in this section is to be found the first description of the skimmias, and some of the main species are listed here with male or female named clones.

S. japonica (1838) grows to 5ft (1.5m) and more wide, with fragrant white flowers in April and May followed (on the female plants) by clusters of round red berries. A rounded, evergreen shrub with aromatic leaves from Japan for a fairly sheltered area in the garden in sun or semi-shade, on chalk or acid soils, good in sea coast gardens and tolerant of urban pollution. Female clone is 'Foremanii', syns. 'Fisheri', 'Veitchii'. Male clones are 'Fragrans' and 'Fragrantissima' which are sweet-scented; 'Rubella' has red-toned buds and white flowers in March and April.

S. Reevesiana (1849) grows to 2ft (60cm) high, more in width with white (hermaphroditic) flowers in May, followed by clusters of red fruits that are still on the shrub in spring when the new flower panicles are forming. An evergreen shrub from China with (sometimes) pale edged leaves. For any good garden position except on chalk.

Requirements: Good, free-draining garden soil, very good in acid or peaty conditions. Will flower and fruit in semi-shade so long as there is not too much competition from tree roots. Hand pollination sometimes necessary. Protection afforded by other shrubs from chilling winds or frost.

Propagation: Take unflowered lateral heel cuttings in July or August and insert in a sandy rooting compost in a cold frame. When well rooted, by the following spring, they can be potted up individually to grow on for a couple of seasons. Mark each cutting according to its sex. Or sow seeds as soon as ripe (in autumn) in pots of seed compost in a cold frame. When large enough they can be pricked out into boxes or individual pots. Transfer to a nursery area to grow on for two years before planting in final positions. Sex of the plants will not be known until the group begins to flower.

Uses: As neat, dome-shaped evergreen shrubs for winter berries and good foliage. Berried branches for winter decor.

Shrubs: Ballalheannagh, Barcock, Bodnant, Brackenwood, Bressingham, Busheyfields, Caldwell, Peter Chappell, Daisy Hill, Dobbies, Margery Fish, Goatcher, Goscote, Great Dixter, Highfield, Hilliers, Jackman, Kaye, Knaphill, Knoll Gardens, Lime Cross, Marchant, Meare Close, Notcutts, Otter, Reuthe, Roger, Russell, Scotts, Shepton, Sherrard, Smith, St. Bridget, Toynbee, Treasure, Treseder, Warley, Woodland, Wye.

Seeds: Chiltern, Thompson and Morgan.

SOLANUM — Potato Vine, Chilean Potato-tree *(Solanaceae)*. *S. crispum* is a semi-hardy scrambler which has loose clusters of violet flowers with golden-yellow 'beaks' in the centre of each. It looks particularly pleasing when seen dangling out of another tree whose flowers are either over or have been chosen to complement the Solanum. In west-country areas it grows and flowers prolifically, covering itself with its striking flowers during the whole summer, and it can climb to 30ft (9m) if it has a mind to and if the conditions are right. There is a beautiful white-flowered variety and the two together make a very lovely picture. In warm counties where a climber is not wanted it can be treated as a shrub by pruning it as such in spring, and though it will still cover itself with flowers it will have lost the grace and character that it has as a climber. It will not survive really bad winters when planted to face east and it needs shelter and protection as a matter of course. I know of a fine plant that is many years old, which climbs up into a hawthorn sending its vine-like shoots to the top of the tree from which it cascades floriferously for the whole of the summer. Its roots and part of the twining stems are protected by a 3ft (90cm) wall, and even though it looks to the east its rootstock is well protected. My plant died in the dreadful winter and spring of '84-'85 and, because it twined toningly with Rosa 'mutabilis', a summer jasmine, and the mossed mauve-pink blooms of the centifolia rose 'William Lobb', I have planted another in its place; but every time the frost glitters on the grass I shiver for the solanum and I shall move it in the spring — if it survives.

S. jasminoides is a strong-growing climber with prehensile petioles like those of Clematis. With these it hauls itself up trellis or wires and produces large clusters of white or pale blue flowers with yellow centres. It is even more tender than *S. crispum* but, once established, it will spring up again from the ground after a hard winter even if the upper parts have been badly damaged.

S. crispum — Potato Vine (1824) grows to 20ft+) (6m+) with trailing clusters of blue-purple flowers with bright yellow anthers from June to September. A rather tender semi-evergreen twiner from Chile for walls, pergolas and scrambling up and through climbing roses and small trees. If space can be found in a cold greenhouse (or, better still, a slightly warm conservatory) the plant will luxuriate (maybe too much so in a small place). Good in chalk areas.

S. jasminoides — Jasmine Nightshade, Potato Vine (1838) grows to 15ft+ (4.5m+) with slightly scented pale bluish-white flowers and golden anthers from July to October. A semi-tender fast-growing evergreen from Brazil for a warm south-facing wall. Climbs trellis quickly by means of petioles. White flowered var. is *S.j.* 'Album' with yellow anthers.

Requirements: Any soil and full sun. Both plants and their varieties need careful siting, a warm south-facing wall is best or a sheltered tree to grow up into. *S. jasminoides* is more tender and may well be cut to the ground in hard winters. Protect *S. crispum* in winter. Both may be grown as greenhouse climbers.

Propagation: Take short cuttings of lateral shoots in August or

September; insert in a rooting compost of peat and sand in a propagator set at 13-16°C (55-61°F). When well rooted transplant into individual pots of John Innes No.2 and keep in a frost free greenhouse for the first winter. Plant out in May. If grown as greenhouse plants they will need trellis or wires to grow up.

Pruning: Fortunate gardeners in south western counties can prune *S. crispum* back in spring by cutting the previous year's growth back to 6" (15cm). *S. jasminoides* will need thinning and tidying in April. Less lucky gardeners can uncover *S. crispum* and nip off the frost damage, while *S. jasminoides* will need thinning after mild winters and prayerful patience after bad ones to see if the new growths will come up from the ground.

Uses: As beautiful 'twiners' on their own or to grow in association with other plants. Flower trusses lovely in arrangements.

Note: Berries are poisonous.

Shrubs: Ballalheannagh, Brackenwood, Busheyfields, Goscote, Great Dixter, Hilliers, Knaphill, Knoll Gardens, Marchant, Meare Close, Notcutts, Otter, Reads, Russell, Scotts, Shepton, Sherrard, St. Bridget, Stonehouse, Toynbee, Treseder, W.W., Wyevale.

Seeds: Chiltern.

SOPHORA — Kowhai, New Zealand Laburnum *(Leguminosae).* Members of this beautiful genus are seldom seen outside botanic gardens, though better-known but far more tender plants are carefully protected through our winters. If Sophoras had no flowers at all they would still be beautiful, especially the small-leaved kinds, but the dangling branchloads of blossom, followed by the rather exotic-looking pods are a true bonus. *S. tetraptera microphylla,* the Kowhai or New Zealand Laburnum, is properly classed as a tree *or* large shrub and so can appear in this book. It seldom achieves more than 15ft (4.5m), and that rather slowly, and is a very beautiful plant with its zig-zag branches bordered on each side by a flat, even row of minute and perfect leaves, tiny enough to please a fairy. These leaflets are described as numbering 7 or 9 on young plants (which is what I have in a pot at this time) but on adult specimens they can number 80 or more. The young plant has a characteristic juvenile phase where it grows into a tangled, wiry bush with interlacing branches.

S. tetraptera microphylla syn. **S. tetraptera — Kowhai** (1774) grows to 10ft+ (3m+) with a spread of 7ft (2.1m). Clusters of pendant yellow flowers in April and May followed by 8" (20.5cm) beaded pods. A tender deciduous shrub from New Zealand for a warm wall in a warm garden in south-west England. Exquisite foliage.

Requirements: Any good well-drained garden soil, a sheltered south-facing wall and some trellis or wires.

Propagation: Sow seeds in seed compost in March in greenhouse. When big enough to handle, prick out into individual pots of John Innes No.1. When larger they can be planted out in a sheltered sunny corner to grow on for a year or two before planting in final positions.

Uses: As delicate and different warm wall or greenhouse shrubs. Beautiful ferny foliage for arrangements.

Shrubs: Bodnant, Brackenwood, Great Dixter, Hilliers, Hopleys, Knaphill, Knoll Gardens, Marchant, Marten's Hall, Sherrard, St. Bridget.

Seeds: Chiltern, Thompson and Morgan.

SPARTIUM — Spanish Broom *(Leguminosae).* This is a tall-growing shrub to grow for its rush-like green stems which are clothed with yellow broom-blooms from June until September. It is a lonely plant in the taxonomic order of things — the botanists found that it had structural differences from the closely allied Genista and Cytisus genera and therefore it was given a genus all to itself, where it reigns alone. It is a sculptural plant when not in flower (even more so when it is) with erect, apparently leafless stems. It needs careful placing so as to make the most of both its shapes — the one, glorious with yellow blossoms for quite a while, and then for the rest of the year a tall leggy shrub that looks like the Strewwelpeter of the border. It likes hot, dry banks and needs to be planted either where one cannot see its legs or with something round and plump like a Cistus, Potentilla or Hypericum in front of it. Spartium is a helpful plant both to itself and to the bees; when they press on the sensitive upper edge of the keel the stamens spring out, flinging a little cloud of ripe pollen into the air which then lands on the insect. Doorstep delivery in reverse, so to speak.

The plant has had a long and useful history. The ancient Greeks made marine cordage from the plant when they discovered it in Spain in 238 B.C. And, being Greeks, they already had a word for it — Spartum — which they had previously given to ropes made from rushes. Hemp and flaxen ropes had been made for centuries before that, but it was found that the new plant was admirably suited for nautical use.

In dry and barren parts of Europe, Spartium was still being grown right up to the end of the 19th century. It was made into thread and cloth in areas too infertile to grow flax or hemp.

S. junceum — Spanish Broom (1548) grows to 10ft (3m) with apparently leafless stems that burst into a fountain of yellow flowers from June to September. A tall, sculptural and interesting shrub from the Mediterranean region for hot, dry banks and poor soil. Good in coastal gardens.

Requirements: Sun and average well-drained soil. Young plants can be killed by frost in exposed positions in inland gardens.

Propagation: Sow seeds (soak these for 24 hours in tepid water) in a sandy seed compost. Transfer into individual pots of John Innes No.1 when large enough, then pot on until ready for planting in final positions. Do not set out in a nursery bed, it is after all a broom and all brooms hate root disturbance.

Pruning: None needed, it destroys the very individual character of this shrub. I have read that it can be clipped over in early spring (March) before new growth starts. Whilst this does not harm the shrub, there is little purpose in such interference. Spartium is a gaunt, green-stemmed leafless shrub and this is its character for three-quarters of the year — leave it so.

Uses: As a very sculptural garden shrub that can be planted to fountain with sun-yellow flowers from behind a sombre conifer. Cut branches for arrangements.

Shrubs: Ballalheannagh, Barcock, Bees, Bodnant, Brackenwood, Busheyfields, Daisy Hill, Farall, Goatcher, Goscote, Great Dixter, Highfield, Hilliers, Jackman, Kaye, Knaphill, Knoll Gardens, Lime Cross, Marchant, Meare Close, Notcutts, Otter, Reuthe, Roger, Russell, Scotts, Shepton, Sherrard, Smith, St. Bridget, Toynbee, Treasure, Warley, Woodland, Wyevale.

Seeds: Chiltern, Thompson and Morgan.

SPIRAEA — Garland Flower (*Rosaceae*). The taller spiraeas are most useful at the back of the border, where their many sprays, corymbs or panicles of tiny flowers make a good contrast to the strong shapes of the summer flowers. But, as with all gardening statements, there are exceptions in the genus, both in height and flowering time, and all are useful, lovely and usually of very easy temperament.

Taking some of the earliest-to-bloom species first — those that flower on bare branches are delicate and cheering in the spring garden because they come with many of the Narcissus. *S. Thunbergii* is often seen from a distance as a froth of tiny, insubstantial white flowers on a graceful, wiry bush, invisible against a background of other leafless shrubs. This spiraea is one of the first to flower and its prettiness is the more appreciated, especially if it is near early pink Prunus with some scillas, puschkinias and *Anemone blanda.*

Later to flower is the old fashioned 'Bridal Wreath' or 'Foam of May', *S. x arguta,* which was a chance seedling raised around 1884. I will digress here to say that spiraeas and asters are as bad as each other and it is a marvel that we still have the proper species plants, but no surprise that there are so many modern hybrids. The genus Spiraea formerly included many more species such as the herbaceous Aruncus and the familiar meadowsweet, now Filipendula. Shrubs now deleted from the genus are Holodiscus, Leutkea, Petrophytum and Sorbaria, which are among those not included in this book for reasons of space. To return to 'Bridal Wreath' it is an appropriately named plant with arching masses of white flowers in late April and May. These, when examined, turn out to have the typical separate, mounded cluster-shape of so many of the genus, though

from a distance they appear to be a single cascade. They form on the upper part of the slender branches and look exactly like a bride's sheaf or shower. The most familiar variety 'Anthony Waterer' belongs to the species *S. x Bumalda,* though the botanists cannot agree on this point and the purists among them say that *S. Bumalda* itself is a synonym of *S. japonica.* As Shakespeare said 'What's in a name?' and this sort of thing can get wearisome. However, to come back to 'Anthony Waterer', this is the variety we all know and grow because it can be utterly relied on to produce its profusion of rose-coloured flowers each summer. The foliage is a soft unremarkable green, broken here and there on the shrub by irregularly occurring sprays of pink, cream or yellow leaves. These are a genetic heritage from its parent, *S. x* 'Bumalda', which had variegated or yellow shoots. *S. x Bumalda's* other parent is not known, *S. japonica* being the legitimate part of the family tree (or bush, in this case).

S. japonica's progeny mostly have pink, rose or carmine flowers and are very beautiful, especially the small-growing variety *S. x bullata* which is seldom more than 15" (38cm) and is therefore a nice plant for rockeries, rock banks or as part of the herbaceous border, particularly as it is in its glory in July when parts of the border seem to revert to tonal green.

The early flowering spiraeas have white flowers and the later ones are in shades of pink or crimson, which is useful to remember when planning a shrub or combined border. Some types such as *S. x arguta, S. x Bumalda, S. japonica* and its many progeny, *S. Menziesii,* and *S. Thunbergii* make excellent flowering hedges and as many are composed of a mass suckering growths then no gaps will appear at the bottom.

Spiraeas have been grown in this country for centuries, the earliest being the willow-leaved *S. salicifolia* with its spikes of tiny pale flowers (in the species). This one took to our soil and settled itself in, becoming naturalised in separate parts of the British Isles, and its incidence seems to be increasing. It is found from Eastern Europe and Asia to Japan, and it was noticed and commented on by one early writer who said somewhat poetically that it 'springs in the deserts to cheer the banished Muscovites, whom the tyranny of despotic rulers sends to waste their bloom of manhood in the dreary regions of Siberia'. (From this it would seem that it might not be safe to let it loose in the smaller garden.)

Spiraeas need to be carefully pruned according to the species to which they belong, because some flower on the present season's growth and some on that of the previous year. If they are not cared for they will get thin and 'unprosperous' with smaller and less flower clusters. Many shrubs need no pruning at all and are better left to grow into their characteristic shapes, but spiraeas are a genus that does need such annual attention. They can be treated in two ways to keep the shrubs at their best. The first group flowers on shoots grown in the previous season, it includes *S. arguta*, *S. Thunbergii*, *S. x Vanhouttei* and *S. Veitchii* and these need to have older stems and weak growth removed after flowering. The second group flowers later in the year on the same season's shoots and includes *S. japonica*, *S. Douglasii*, *S. salicifolia*, etc., which need to be cut hard back in late winter or early spring, removing all worn-out branches at ground-level. The thicket-forming groups get very crowded in time and in the tidier parts of the garden they might need to be dug up in their entirety and thinned out, with the outside portions replanted into improved soil, much as one does with some herbaceous plants. This is for gardeners with strong backs — the rest of us can plant this type of spiraea in sunny parts of the garden that are more remote from the manicured portions; such species or varieties make excellent screens, though you can be sure that ground elder will get among the stems in the end.

S. x arguta — Bridal Wreath, Foam of May (before 1884) grows to 8ft (2.4m) with a similar spread and tiny pure white flowers on bare branches in April and May. A deciduous shrub for masses of spring flowers.

S. betulifolia (1812) grows to a rounded 2ft (60cm) or a little more with a similar spread and corymbs of white flowers in June. A deciduous shrub from N.E. Asia and Japan for the rock garden or border.

S. x Bumalda grows to 4ft (1.2m) with a similar spread and corymbs of crimson flowers in July and August. 'Anthony Waterer' has similar flowers and variegated shoots. Both flower on current season's growth.

S. chamaedryfolia (1789) grows to 6ft (1.8m) and as much through, with white flowers in May. A deciduous suckering shrub flowering on previous season's shoots; cut out old growths to leave room for new ones.

S. Douglasii (1827) grows to 6ft (1.8m) and as much or more through in a dense thicket; deep rose-purple flowers in panicles in June and July. A deciduous, strong-growing shrub for large gardens or as a summer-flowering screen. Previous year's flowering shoots should be cut out in February or March. Likes natural pond or stream-side situations. Needs splitting up every few years; improve or replace soil at this time.

S. japonica (1870) grows to 5ft (1.5m) and as much through, with wide corymbs of rose-pink flowers in July and August. A deciduous shrub from Japan. Prune in spring by cutting out some of the old wood which crowds the new growths; shorten all to within 6″ (15cm) of the ground. (Some sources of reference and nurserymen list the cv. 'Anthony Waterer' here, also *S. x Bumalda*.)

S. Menziesii (1838) grows to 5ft (1.5m) and as much or more through, with large pyramid-shaped panicles of rose-purple flowers in July and August. A deciduous shrub from W.

North America for the larger garden.

S. salicifolia — Bridewort, grows to 6ft (1.8m) and spreads widely in suckering clumps. Pale pink or white panicles of flowers in June. A deciduous shrub of S.E. Europe, Asia and Japan. Needs sorting out by lifting and splitting every few years. Improve soil at this time.

S. Thunbergii grows to 6ft (2.4cm) with a spread of 8ft. White flowers on bare ranches in March and April. A (usually) deciduous shrub from China and Japan. Needs a hot summer to ripen the wood for good flowers in the following year.

S. Vanhouttei (1862) grows to 6ft (1.8m) with clusters of white flowers in June. A deciduous shrub with a graceful habit. Cut out older wood after flowering to make room for young growth.

Requirements: Spiraeas are amongst the easiest of all flowering shrubs to grow, needing only full sun and average free-draining garden soil. Early flowering species and varieties may get nipped by frost, so plant these in sheltered places.

Propagation: The species that have suckering growth are easily split up in March, or before growth starts. Take good rooted portions. Or take half-ripened lateral cuttings in July or August and place in a sandy rooting compost in a cold frame. Plant out in a nursery area the following spring and grow on for several seasons.

Pruning: As previously described.

Uses: As very easy, reliable and beautiful flowering shrubs and for internal garden hedges. Dwarf species and varieties for rockeries and herbaceous borders. Flowers for arrangements.

Shrubs: Ballalheannagh, Barcock, Bees, Bodnant, Brackenwood, Busheyfields, Caldwell, Daisy Hill, Dobbies, Fairley's, Goatcher, Goscote, Highfield, Hilliers, Hopleys, Ingwersen, Jackman, Kaye, Kershaw, Knaphill, Knoll Gardens, Lime Cross, Marchant, Meare Close, Notcutts, Otter, Reuthe, Roger, Russell, Scotts, Shepton, Sherrard, Smith, Southcombe, St. Bridget, Stonehouse, Toynbee, Treasure, Warley, Woodland, Wyevale.

STACHYURUS (*Stachyuraceae*). Stachyurus is hardy and there seems to be no real reason why it is not seen as often as it deserves to be. It has delightful 4″ (10cm) long flower tassels like short strings of beads which swing from the leafless branches. The shrub is so pretty then that when it flowers it deserves to be seen in isolation. In later months the leaves are not unattractive, so if it forms part of a summer border these will still be of interest, unlike those of the hazel tribe — *Corylus avellana* and *Hamamelis mollis* which, alas, are just plain dull in summer.

S. praecox (1864) grows, usually, to 5ft (1.5m) in the British Isles, more in its native country. Pendant racemes of yellow flowers in February and March. A deciduous shrub from Japan for a winter focal position in the garden.

Requirements: Best in acid conditions with plenty of humus but will grow in neutral soil. Add plenty of peat and leaf-mould to heavy soils when planting, and mulch annually with leaf-mould. Stachyurus prefers full sun or partial shade from sheltering trees or other larger shrubs. The flower buds form in autumn and are seldom damaged by normal winter conditions, though too-early warmth followed by a further wintry spell will take toll, as it does with other brave early-flowering shrubs.

Propagation: Take half-ripe cuttings with a heel in July and insert in a rooting compost of peat and sand. Place in a propagator set at 13-16°C (55-61°F) and when rooted transfer into individual pots of John Innes No.1. Keep in a cold frame for the winter and plant out in a nursery area to grow on for a couple of seasons before planting in final positions.

Uses: As a winter-flowering shrub; branches (when there are sufficient to spare) for arrangements.

Shrubs: Bodnant, Hilliers, Hopleys, Marchant, Notcutts, Otter, Reuthe, Russell, Sherrard, St. Bridget, Treasure, Treseder, W.W.

STAPHYLEA — Bladder-Nut, European Bladder-Nut, St. Anthony's Nut *(Staphyleaceae)*.

Not to be confused with Stapelia, the Carrion flower, which is fascinating to some and odious to others. Staphyleas are largish shrubs, occasionally small trees. They are grown mainly for their interesting fruits or nuts, though the drooping clusters of flowers are attractive in early summer, some kinds being more eye-catching than others. For example, the wild *S. pinnata* has an extra long flower-stalk which makes the dangling inflated fruits look very decorative. This species has naturalised itself in rather localised places in the British Isles. They are good shrubs for the larger, wilder garden because they are undemanding and grow quickly. When medicine operated on a rather hit-or-miss basis in earlier times, the Doctrine of Signatures was used as some kind of a guide, with like plants being used in an attempt to cure diseases or ailments that resembled them. 'Bladder-Nuts' then called *Nux Vesicaria,* were administered for bladder problems, but it would seem that even then there was a doubt as to their efficacy and Parkinson says 'Some Quack-salvers have used these nuts as a medicine of rare value for the stone, but what good they have done, I never yet could learne'.

S. colchica (1850) grows to 10ft (3m) with erect panicles of white flowers in May followed by the characteristic 'bladders'. A deciduous shrub with handsome foliage from the Caucasus for the larger garden. 'Coulombieri' is larger, very floriferous with bigger leaves but smaller bladders.

S. pinnata — Bladder-Nut (1596) grows to 15ft (4.5m) with dangling white flowers in May followed by the decorative fruits and autumnal colour. A deciduous European shrub

for the gardener who likes something 'different' that is easy to grow and not fussy about its situation.

Requirements: Ordinary free-draining garden soil and sun or semi-shade.

Propagation: Take heel cuttings in July and August and insert in a rooting compost of peat and sand. Place in a cold frame until well rooted and then transfer into individual pots. Protect for first winter. Or sow seeds.

Pruning: None needed except to remove winter-damaged branches.

Uses: Decorative in flower and fruit for arrangements.

Shrubs: Hilliers, Marchant, Notcutts, Sherrard, St. Bridget.

Seeds: Chiltern.

STAUNTONIA *(Lardizabalaceae).*

Stauntonia was named after the Irishman Sir George C. Staunton (1737-1801), who travelled with Lord Macartney on his embassy to China in 1792.

This is a strong-growing evergreen climber which, when established in a sheltered garden, will give great pleasure. It has scented white flowers flushed with violet, though these do not appear until the plant is sure of itself and its surroundings. It is not hardy except in the gardens of the south-west though, owing to prayer and protection, my infant plant survived the cruelties of the '84, '85, '86 winters which was a true test of endurance when other quite mature shrubs and climbers succumbed. It was an expensive time for gardeners and growers alike. Stauntonias and Holboellias are difficult to tell apart except to a botanist with a magnifying glass: leaves and flowers are similar to the naked eye, as is their habit of growth and cultural requirements. They are both unusual climbers and if it were possible to see them growing side by side, or in the same garden, then one could make a choice; but, as this is an unlikely event, just take the first healthiest plant that you can get, give it what it needs and forget about the other species. Both are of vigorous growth when established and the evergreen, leathery leaves are very handsome. You may, of course, be given one plant wrongly named for the other and, until it flowers, you will not be able to tell the difference. In the Stauntonia genus the stamens are united, whereas in Holboellia they are free. Since it may be some time before my plant flowers I, too, do not know the difference at the time of writing this.

The flowers are unisexual and are produced together in an attractive raceme (as in Akebia, to which these plants are related). In good, hot years there may be edible 2″ (5cm) round to oval fruits.

S. hexaphylla (1874) grows to 30ft (9m) with scented white and purple flowers in April. An evergreen twiner from Korea and Japan for a warm south or south-west wall. Not hardy except in the south-west.

Requirements: A sheltered and warm south or south-west wall.

Ordinary free-draining garden soil. Strong trellis to tie to. Protection of the lower parts of the climber with bracken and/or hessian in winter.

Propagation: Take short half-ripe cuttings in July or August and insert in a rooting compost of peat and sand. When rooted transfer into individual pots of John Innes No.1, each with a cane. Plunge in summer but protect for first winter in a frost-free greenhouse or frame. Or layers may be pegged down in April and May; these can be severed a year (sometimes less) later.

Pruning: In borderline gardens where frost damage happens, cut back some of the luxuriant growth in autumn or early winter. It need not be wasted, and will be long-lasting and beautiful in a vase indoors.

Uses: As a handsome and unusual climber. Foliage and (eventually) flowering sprays for arrangements. Excellent in an unheated conservatory, where it may become too exuberant.

Shrubs: Hilliers, Marchant, Sherrard, St. Bridget.

STEPHANANDRA (*Rosacea*). Stephanandras are graceful shrubs that are easy to grow. They need little attention once planted, and the species *S. Tanakae* has such brilliant orange foliage in autumn that it should be placed where its days of glory can best be appreciated. The flowers are pleasing though not exciting, and it is really for the fine autumnal colouration that these shrubs should be sited in the garden. They look best when planted against dark conifers or any evergreen, and if one of the autumnally scarlet Berberis tribe is nearby it will be a very warming spectacle in October.

S. incisa syn. **S. flexuosa** (1872) grows to 7ft (2.1m) with a spread of 5ft (1.5m) and panicles of greenish-white flowers in June. Elegant foliage, turning yellow in autumn. A deciduous shrub from Korea and Japan for autumn colour.

S. Tanakae (1893) grows to 7ft (2.1m) with a spread of 6ft (1.8m). Panicles of dull white flowers in June and July. A deciduous shrub with good orange autumn colour.

Requirements: Any good garden soil and sun or partial shade.

Propagation: Is by the removal of the suckers as in Spiraea. Or take woody cuttings in October and set in a prepared bed. Inspect in spring and grow on for a season or so until needed.

Uses: Plant for autumn colouration in the garden or for elegant cutting foliage. Flowers, though unexciting compared to those of Spiraea, can be used in green-toned arrangements. Bare stems in winter are rich brown.

Shrubs: Bodnant, Caldwell, Dobbies, Goatcher, Hilliers, Hopleys, Kaye, Knaphill, Knoll Gardens, Marchant, Meare Close, Notcutts, Otter, Roger, Scotts, Shepton, Sherrard, Smith, Toynbee, Treasure.

STEPHANOTIS — **Madagascar Jasmine, Madagascar Chaplet Flower, Clustered Wax Flower** (*Asclepiada-*

ceae). The Stephanotis seen in florists' shops will have been grown under perfect conditions to produce the dark leathery leaves and the waxy white flowers with the wonderful scent. This is what sells the plant, though without the perfume it would still be a lovely thing. So there you are with your beautifully wrapped Stephanotis which, without proper care, will quite quickly deteriorate. Stephanotis are demanding plants so, unless you have a heated greenhouse, these plants are not for you and they are certainly no good as house plants except for special-occasion appearances when they are at their best. Much better to grow on a plant in the greenhouse and pick the flowers, then you will have (almost) the best of both worlds. The scent is heavy and sweet, as befits its tropical origins, and the Victorians loved it as they loved all heavily perfumed flowers, such as the Gardenias, jasmines and tuberoses that they grew so well in their great warm stove-houses. In the Language of Flowers, Stephanotis means 'will you accompany me to the East?'. Florists use the blossoms to add scent to wedding bouquets and I sometimes wonder if the bride knows what her flowers (carefully chosen for sentiment and to match The Dress) actually mean. Most of us love yellow roses, for example, as being less trite than a dozen unidentifiable red ones: but the Language of Flowers says that yellow roses mean 'decrease of love' or 'jealousy'. (I'm sure you'll wish I hadn't told you that.)

S. floribunda — **Madagascar Jasmine** (1839) grows to 10ft (3m) with clusters of pure white perfumed flowers from May to October. An evergreen twiner from Madagascar for the heated greenhouse or conservatory.

Requirements: Stephanotis are just-so plants and their care has to match or leaves will fall off and buds will not form. Repot the purchased plant into a slightly larger pot of John Innes No.2 — about 5-6" (12.5-15cm) — or in a prepared part of the greenhouse border which has had its soil taken out and replaced with John Innes No.2. If the plant is in a florist's pot it will be tied to an ornamental cane shape such as a figure-of-eight, which will admirably show off blooms and foliage without damage to either, or taking up too much space. This arrangement is fine for a few months, though it does look as if it has 'just come from the shop' and therefore may be irritating after a while. If the plant has come from a nursery it will be wound round canes, and the ties can be undone and the canes removed to reveal that it is probably 6ft (1.8m) tall already. Arrange appropriate trellis or wires (which can be extended later) in the greenhouse and tie the plant to these, all without damaging the wonderful wax-like flowers which look artificial enough to repose under a glass cover. The temperature of the greenhouse should not be lower than 10°C (50°F) but this is mere survival, it would be happier at 13°C (55°F). During the so-called summer of these islands, the external day and night temperature should be watched, and that of the greenhouse should never drop below 18°C (64°F) which is asking a lot. 'Bud-drop' can happen if there is too great a difference between day and night temperature. In summer, Stephanotis need plenty of water and humidity (they do well as paying guests in orchid houses, of course), and they need light shading of the roof glass during the brightest months, though they should have as much light as is available at other times of the year. If they are being grown in pots they should be fed fortnightly from May to September. After this cease feeding (though not abruptly) and water less often, keeping the soil moist but not wet. They should be potted on one size each year in April until they are into 9" (23cm) pots, then at two or three year intervals (put a date label in the pot or on the plant, time flies in a greenhouse). Keep roots of plants in shade.

Propagation: Take cuttings of lateral non-flowered shoots from April until June and insert into a rooting compost of peat and sand. Place these in a propagator set at 18-21°C (64-70°F). When rooted transfer into individual pots of John Innes No.2.

Pruning: In February cut out weak growth. If plants have flourished they may well be getting too large, which is a credit to you but hard on the other plants in your greenhouse. Cut back alternate lateral growths to 6" (15cm) and shorten leading shoots by a third, or more if space is limited.

Pests: As with many greenhouse dwellers, Stephanotis suffers from the infestation of scale insects and mealy bugs. Wiping, spraying and fumigation will solve these difficulties for a while.

Uses: As sweetly perfumed cut flowers, potted plants in flower indoors for short periods, though they will not care for the dryness of our human habitations.

Seeds: Butcher, Chiltern.

STEWARTIA (see Stuartia)

STRANVAESIA *(Rosaceae)*. The Stranvaesia was named after an aristocratic botanist, William Thomas Horner Fox Strangways, Earl of Ilchester (1795-1865). This is a small genus of evergreen shrubs and trees with shiny leaves, flat corymbs of white flowers and bunches of scarlet berries in autumn, which for some reason the birds do not see. *S. Davidiana* (after Père David) was discovered in 1869, though not introduced to this country until 1917. It is the species which is most often grown, being of a vigorous disposition and amiable temperament. In autumn some of its dark green leaves turn red, not many and not in groups, just isolated ones here and there on the shrub, toning nicely with the berries. The young shrubs send up rather angular shoots which can be shortened for symmetry if liked. It is a quietly good-looking shrub for gardeners who have not the energy to be out attending to everything all the time. I find that well-scrubbed gardens are admirable and often enviable

for their neatness and good order, but they are not allowed to have surprises.

S. Davidiana (1917) grows to 18ft+ (5.5m+) with a spread of 12ft+ (3.7m+) (can grow to 30ft (9m) in ideal conditions). White flowers in June followed by clusters of dangling red berries along the branches. A large and handsome evergreen shrub from China for a focal position in sun or semi-shade.

Requirements: They grow best in full sun in an acid soil but will be reasonably content in neutral conditions and semi-shade, but may not flower and fruit as well.

Propagation: Take half-ripe heel cuttings in July and insert them in a rooting compost of peat and sand. Place in a propagator set at 16-18°C (61-64°F) until rooted. Transfer into individual pots of John Innes No.1 and keep in a cold frame for the winter. In spring they may be planted out in a nursery area to grow on for two years (or potted on into larger pots). Lift in late October or November in mild weather and plant in permanent positions.

Pruning: None needed.

Uses: As very ornamental foliage and berry shrubs; berried branches for arrangements.

Shrubs: Ballalheannagh, Bodnant, Brackenwood, Bressingham, Busheyfields, Caldwell, Dobbies, Goatcher, Goscote, Highfield, Hilliers, Hopleys, Jackman, Knaphill, Knoll Gardens, Marchant, Notcutts, Otter, Reuthe, Roger, Russell, Scotts, Shepton, Sherrard, St. Bridget, Stonehouse, Toynbee, Treasure, Treseder, Woodland, W.W., Wyevale.

Seeds: Chiltern.

STREPTOSOLEN — Orange Browallia *(Solanaceae)*. This is a colourful greenhouse leaning shrub, not quite a climber, not a twiner and not really able to stand on its own stems. It has bright orange flowers that are rather like those of Lantana and in tropical countries it flowers without stopping the whole year round. For those who like strong colour contrasts it looks electric with Ipomoeas climbing through it. Keep it away from the pure blue of Plumbago, but try it with red-flowered Abutilons, white Cobaea, or the yellow annual Black-eyed Susan (Thunbergia). Toning apricot or cream Begonias in baskets would look just right hanging nearby. It is not a very particular plant and will respond (with flowers) to a little kindness from a greenhouse gardener who is willing to keep frost at bay (this is encouraging to the greenhouse gardener whose Stephanotis buds have just dropped off). Streptosolen flowers are luminously bright, so do not grow it if you don't care for orange.

S. Jamesonii — Orange Browallia (1847) grows to 6ft (1.8m) with a similar spread. Cascades of bright orange flowers from May to July in these latitudes. A floppy evergreen shrub from Colombia for a cool greenhouse or conservatory with a minimum temperature of 7°C (45°F).

Requirements: Streptosolens are greedy plants and, to produce all the flowers of which they are capable, they need to be planted in John Innes No.3. They can be grown in large pots (which can come out for part of the summer when the nights are warm) or in the greenhouse border. They need plenty of ventilation during the summer and light shading from above (this is where *Jasminum polyanthemum* comes in useful, also Cobaea again).

Water well in growing and flowering season, decrease watering in September and keep fairly dry in winter. Feed fortnightly from April to September. They will need potting on into a larger size in March.

Propagation: Take short cuttings of non-flowering shoots in March or April, insert into a rooting compost of peat and sand and put into a propagator set at 16-18°C (61-64°F). When well rooted transfer into pots of John Innes No.1 and pot on as necessary, working up to John Innes No.3. When the cuttings are beginning to grow pinch out tips to encourage bushy growth. Give potted plants a cane to grow to at first, a 'wigwam' of three will be necessary later to support the weight. Arrange wires or trellis on greenhouse walls for plants in the border.

Pruning: After flowering cut back all growth by a third.

Uses: As patio tub-plants (only in settled warm summers), as colourful greenhouse shrubs and as exotic-coloured flowers for arrangements. Plant pots of red and orange dwarf nasturtiums to flower near patio plants, or use climbing varieties of nasturtium nearby.

Shrubs: Bodnant.

STUARTIA, STEWARTIA *(Theaceae)*.

I find myself saying again that 'this genus' — Stuartias or Stewartias — should be planted more often. They are easy shrubs, even small trees in maturity, with very lovely white and gold flowers in July and August, which is the doldrums time in the garden. Many people spend more time and effort on roses (which, of course, are very demanding prima donnas) than they do on the rest of the garden put together, though I except the vegetable growers from this statement. It is so nice to visit another garden and see a totally different plant or shrub in full flower and to have no idea of its name or country of origin. One walks past roses most of the time without comment or enquiry simply because one can recognise them, whereas many easy enough shrubs that could be grown are not. There is more credit to a gardener who tries something new each year, providing it suits his soil, than to those folk who constantly plant the safe and the familiar.

Stuartias are named after John Stuart, Earl of Bute (1713-1792). He was a keen botanist and assisted Augusta, Princess Dowager of Wales, when she extended Kew in 1759-60. The mis-spelling of the attribution must have annoyed the Scots family greatly — all Scots are most particular about spelling. The error came about because the botanical artist Ehret painted *S. Malacodendron* from a specimen growing in the London residence of the Earls of Bute, then Caenwood House (now Kenwood House). The painting was sent to Linnaeus by Isaac Lawson who misspelled the Stuart name in his dedication, and ever since there has been confusion in the catalogues.

S. Malacodendron is very beautiful when in flower, with blossoms as much as 3½" (9cm) across, but this species is best grown only in the warmer south-western counties. The flowers are large (up to 4" (10cm) wide according to the species), white or creamy-white, with prominent golden stamens. Individual flowers do not last long but there is a constant succession of them during the flowering period. The seed heads are unusual and attractive, as is the winterbare bark of *S. pseudocamellia* and *S. sinensis* (these are trees, so not for this book).

S. Malacodendron (1742) grows to 15ft (4.5m) with a spread of 10ft (3m). Large — 3½" (9cm) wide — wide white flowers with purple stamens in June and July. An unusual and beautiful deciduous shrub or small tree from S.E. United States for a sheltered situation in acid soil shaded at midday. Good in warm years and best in S.W. counties.

S. ovata syn. **S. pentagyna** (1785) grows to 15ft (4.5m) with a spread of 10ft (3m). Large white single flowers 4" (10cm) across in July and August. A large deciduous shrub (or small tree in nature) from the E. United States, with yellow autumnal colour.

Requirements: Stuartias need warm conditions, so are best not attempted in the colder northern or east-coast counties. They require a sheltered sunny situation though with their roots shaded at mid-day with, for example, Ericas or dwarf Azaleas. They need plenty of water during hot or drought years, so a moist, acid soil is best or, failing this naturally, a moist neutral soil with plenty of peat and leaf-mould incorporated. They will not thrive in alkaline conditions. Once planted, they should never be moved.

Propagation: Is best from ripe seeds sown in autumn in a lime-free seed compost. Prick off seedlings into pots of John Innes No.1 (without lime) and grow on in a cold frame. Since this genus dislikes moving house at any time, it is best to pot on young plants until they are big enough to be set out in their final positions.

Cuttings are difficult to strike but may be attempted by taking short, unflowered lateral wood heel-cuttings in July or August. These should be inserted in a very sandy rooting compost of two parts of sand to one of peat, try some in pure sand. Put a seed-box cover over them and place in a shaded cold frame. Protect rooted cuttings for first winter in the frame.

Uses: As very beautiful late summer flowering shrubs. Flowering and fruiting branches for arrangements and autumn colour.

Shrubs: Caldwell, Peter Chappell, Dobbies, Hilliers, Marchant, Otter.

SYMPHORICARPOS — Snowberry, Indian Currant,

St. Peter's Wort *(Caprifoliaceae).* This is a plant from the New World which has taken so happily to our soil that it is now found growing in all sorts of wild places throughout the British Isles. *S. rivularis* is the commonest species, which has the familiar and appropriately named 'Snowberries' that form in white clusters in autumn and last on the bare branches throughout the winter. They look most attractive when arranged with the black berries of privet and ivy, some crimson ones (no shortage of this colour), the turquoise-blue ones from *Viburnum Davidii,* or Dianella, some yellow or golden-toned ones from Pyracantha and some of the jolly Pernettya marbles. I am not suggesting the whole lot all together in one vessel, it is merely that the milky whiteness of Symphoricarpos goes so well with all of these and many more. If Snowberries are seen alone against a dark background they look very beautiful — the stems vanish and the waxy berries look unreal.

Some Symphoricarpos have pink, coral or purplish fruit and, if space permits, a group with different berries is interesting and cheering during the early winter months because the birds do not take them. Symphoricarpos is vigorous in growth, spreading by means of suckers which will need firm control. The leafy tangle at the bottom of a Snowberry hedge is a whole conservation area for hedgehogs, mice, voles and shrews, not to mention a frog or two in summer when they abandon their pools. This is another shrub whose (small) nectar-rich flowers are beloved by bees; Symphoricarpos goes on blooming until September, so it can be used as part of mixed hedging or planting near beehives. The plants make interesting hedges and can be relied on to grow and fruit well in shade, despite drip from overhead foliage and competition from the roots of nearby trees or other shrubs.

S. albus syn. **S. racemosus** (and sometimes confused with or sold as **S. rivularis**) (1879) grows to 2½ft (76cm) and spreads to 8ft (2.4m) with inconspicuous urn-shaped pink flowers from July to September followed by abundant clusters of round white berries lasting through the winter. A deciduous thicket-forming shrub from E. North America for the shrub border, hedging and shady situations.

S. orbiculatus — Coral-berry, Indian Currant (1730) grows from 2-6ft (60cm-1.8m) with a spread of 10ft (3m). Clusters of pink flowers from July to September followed by oval coral, red or rose-purple berries along the stems. A shrub from the United States for similar situations. Berries well after hot summers, otherwise it can be disappointing.

S. rivularis — Snowberry (1817) grows from 3-10ft (90cm-3m) high with a similar (usually greater) spread. Inconspicuous pinkish-white flowers from July to September followed by clusters of white berries. A deciduous shrub from N. America for almost any soil and any garden situation in sun or shade.

Requirements: Because Symphoricarpos will oblige by growing and fruiting in almost any garden situation, it is sometimes scorned and often abused. But give it better, slightly moist soil and a pleasant airy situation that is not closed in and it will respond with even more abundant clusters of berries that will weigh the branches down most gracefully. The shrub will grow in any garden soil and sun, semi-shade, or the shade beneath deciduous trees, and is most useful for filling difficult corners. Restrict its living quarters in good soil or it will spread invasively. This is best done by setting sheets of corrugated iron on edge in the ground, or by planting the shrub or shrubs at the edge of a path or against a wall. Symphoricarpos ignores fences, the other side of these will probably have better berry-bearing plants.

Propagation: Divide suckering growth in winter or remove selected portions. When a quantity of plants is wanted for hedging, take 12″ (30cm) woody cuttings from October onwards and plant (right end up) in a prepared trench. Examine in spring, dispose of corpses and grow remainder on for a season or until needed. Or sow seeds as soon as ripe in boxes of seed compost. Leave in a cold frame for the winter, then treat as usual.

Pruning: This usually consists of removing large quantities of the extra suckering stems with which this shrub surrounds itself. Thin out crowded growth in early spring. For hedging, pinch out growing tips of small plants to encourage early bushiness. If there is a large number of plants to pinch, use shears instead. Hedges will need clipping twice a year, though this may mean sacrificing berries. Plant the related *Lonicera periclymenum* among the hedging plants for its sweet scented flowers and subsequent scarlet berries among the white. Make sure the Lonicera is watered well in dry years, it is a 'woodland' plant.

Uses: Multitudinous. As hedging, screening, as specimen shrubs, for winter interest, as shady-place plants and for arrangements.

Shrubs: Ballalheannagh, Bees, Brackenwood, Caldwell, Beth Chatto, Daisy Hill, Dobbies, Margery Fish, Goatcher, Highfield, Hilliers, Hopleys, Jackman, Kaye, Kershaw, Knaphill, Knoll Gardens, Lime Cross, Marchant, Marten's Hall, Meare Close, Notcutts, Otter, Reuthe, Roger, Russell, Scotts, Sherrard, Smith, St. Bridget, Stonehouse, Toynbee, Treasure, Woodland, W.W., Wyevale.

Seeds: Chiltern.

SYRINGA — Lilac *(Oleaceae).* Lilac in the rain evokes an instant picture of an English cottage garden (in often typical English weather), but like so many of our pictorial images these flowering shrubs are an importation from other lands. The colour range is beautiful — violet, purple, wine-red, crimson, rose-mauve, lavender, 'lilac', blue-grey, pink, cream and white, with either single or double flowers. The lilac, or Syringa, that has this sumptuous colour range is *S. vulgaris,* which came originally from eastern Europe in the

16th century, though at that time the flowers would have been the 'lilac' colour from which the descriptive adjective is taken. (So many of our flower-colours have to be described by those of other flowers: 'rose', 'pink', 'lavender' blue, 'primrose' yellow, 'violet', 'geranium' red — the list is a longer one, and there are no substitutes.)

Lilacs are divided into two groups — *Ligustrina* or tree-lilacs, which resemble privets, and the true lilacs which are sub-divided into two sections, *villosae* and the *vulgares*: the flowers of the *villosae* section are borne on the current year's shoots in June, and those of the *vulgares* on the previous season's growths, on bare branches in May. The first lilac (the common one) was brought back to Vienna in 1562 by Ogier Ghiselin de Busbecq (along with the Philadelphus), when he returned from Constantinople; Gerard had them in his garden 'in very great plentie' by the time he made his famous and important list in 1597. The 'Persian Lilac', *S. persica*, was in cultivation long before this in the gardens of Persia and India, possibly since before 800 A.D. It did not reach Europe until about 1614 (again through the enthusiasm of an ambassador, this time a Venetian one) and, for a while, it was called a 'Persian Jasmyn' possibly because of its sweet scent which was one of the methods by which the early botanists attempted to classify the new plant discoveries. These were the only two lilac species (with a hybrid and a few varieties) to be found in English gardens until well into the 19th century. White lilac was known, though mostly by repute, and the double white was first catalogued in 1823. The hybrid between *S. vulgaris* and *S. persica* was raised in the Botanic Garden at Rouen round about 1777 and it was named, logically, the Rouen Lilac; it can still be bought today, though it is now called *S. x chinensis*. *S. emodi* had been found in the Himalaya in 1848 and in 1885 *S. villosa* was discovered in China. In Hungary, round about 1830, a botanically-minded baroness, Rosalie von Josika, noticed that there was a distinctly different form of lilac growing wild in her locality (in addition to the already-known *S. vulgaris*). This plant was afterwards named *S. Josikaea* in her honour and it was later used as an important part of a lilac-breeding programme in Ottawa in the 1920s.

In the early part of this century new species of lilacs were discovered by the plant-hunters in China; some are very fragrant, others not so, and one or two are dwarf types (for lilacs) that are very suitable for the smaller garden *(S. microphylla, S. julianae* and the later *S. Mayeri* of 1920).

Lilacs can withstand winter cold well, they develop thicker trunks for insulation, and for this reason they are very popular in Canada. They are resistant to urban pollution and are therefore good in town gardens.

French people have always loved the scent of lilac and forcing the shrubs for out-of-season blossom began as early as 1774. The plants are coerced into bloom in heat and darkness, and coloured varieties come out a better white

than pale kinds, though if required the colour can be 'restored' by admitting light. Such skill was acquired in this unnatural but very remunerative form of horticulture that, by the 1880s, lilac blossom could be had in every month of the year except for the holiday months of July and August, when the French leave Paris in a lemming-like rush for the sea and *'fermeture annuelle'* obtains.

Lilacs are easily and quickly grown and are excellent for large, new or empty gardens. They need a sunny situation and do well on chalk. Because many of the early lilac colours were mauve-toned (though not all — there was a very rare red variety in 1659) and therefore the colour of half-mourning, there are sad superstitions attached to the flowers in some countries where it is associated with death, bereavement or partings. Walt Whitman wrote:

'Here, coffin that slowly passes
I give you my spray of Lilac
O death I cover you with roses and lilies
But mostly and now the lilac, that blooms
                                    the first...'

In Persia it meant 'the forsaken' and was said to be given by lovers to their mistresses on the termination of the liaison. This, to me, seems the height of Victorian silliness because in Moslem countries there were no such civilised arrangements — men had wives, as many of these chattels as they could afford, and those that did not had boys or prostitutes according to their tastes, affluence or lack of it. In England and America nobody ever wore lilac because it was unlucky; for a girl to wear it meant that she would never wear a wedding ring. A trace of the Persian meaning existed here — a spray of lilac sent to a fiancé/fiancée meant that he or she wished to break off the engagement. But the English Language of Flowers gives the meaning of mauve lilac as 'the first emotion of love', because of the abundance of blossom on the bare branches (conveniently forgetting that most lilacs come into leaf at the same time as they come into flower) and white lilac meant, simply, 'Youth'.

S. x chinensis — Rouen Lilac grows to 10ft (3m) and as much wide with fragrant 'lilac' coloured flowers in May. Varieties have single or double flowers of rosy-mauve, purple, purplish-red and white. A deciduous shrub for any sunny garden position.

S. emodi — Himalayan Lilac (1840) grows to 15ft (4.5m) with purple tinged white flowers on current year's shoots in June. A deciduous shrub from the Himalaya. Scent not an asset of this plant.

S. x hyacinthiflora and its varieties are early-flowering, sometimes by the end of April, and may therefore be frost-damaged. Many colours: the earlier ones were 'Descartes', mauve; 'Lamartine', mauve-pink; 'Mirabeau', mauve (very early); 'Necker', rose-pink; and 'Vauban', double mauve-pink. A deciduous hybrid shrub.

S. Josikaea — Hungarian Lilac (1830) grows to 12ft (3.7m) with a spread of about 9ft (2.7m) and deep violet-mauve flowers in June. A deciduous shrub from Central and East Europe.

S. microphylla (1910) grows to 5ft (1.5m) with a similar spread. Fragrant 'lilac' flowers in June and again in autumn. A deciduous small shrub from China with rounded leaves, for a focal position in a rockery, small garden or patio. The Chinese called it 'Four Seasons Lilac' because with them it flowers more often.

S. persica — Persian Lilac (1640) grows to 7ft (2.1m) with a similar spread. Sweet-scented 'lilac' flowers in May. A deciduous shrub from W. Asia to China.

S. Sweginzowii (1914) grows to 12ft (3.7m) and as much through with large very fragrant panicles of rosy 'lilac' and white flowers in June. A deciduous shrub from China.

S. villosa (1885) grows to a bushy 10ft (3m) and as much through with large panicles of fragrant 'lilac'-pink flowers in May and June. A deciduous shrub from N. China.

S. vulgaris — Common Lilac (16th century) grows to 20ft (6m) with typical double panicles of fragrant flowers in many colours in May.

Note: The charming 'Canadians', with their very distinctive flowers (raised by Isabella Preston of Ottawa) were born too late for inclusion in this book.

Requirements: Lilacs are not fussy plants but they must have a sunny situation for good flowers. Chalk-to-neutral soils suit them well; acid conditions do not generally. Established hedges will need watering in drought years and all kinds will say thank you to feeding, every other year, with a barrow load of well-rotted manure or compost, with bone-meal dug in in alternate years. One is inclined to forget about lilacs, they are so undemanding. Though they will grow in almost anything, rich, moisture-retentive soil will ensure bigger and better flower-panicles. After moving a lilac (other than container-grown plants) it is best to remove most of the flower buds for the first two years to help them to establish themselves more quickly. It will be some years, in any case, before the flower trusses achieve their full size.

Propagation: Is not easy except under mist. Layers will root and can be detached after two years. Or heel cuttings may be taken in July or August and placed in a rooting compost of peat and sand in a propagator set at 16°C (61°F). When well rooted transfer into individual pots of John Innes No.2 and grow on in a cold frame. Plant out in a nursery area in spring and leave for two or three years before transplanting to flowering positions; they will grow very slowly.

Seed will grow well when sown in the normal way but is unlikely to come true, and as it will be some time before the plants flower it is a long time to wait for a possible disappointment.

Purchased plants of *S. vulgaris* vars. are sometimes grafted on to privet stock, for two reasons: lilac is slow growing and privet is not, so stocks for sale can be more quickly built up in this way; *S. vulgaris* suckers at its base (and often far beyond) whereas privet does not. But this is not a good practice because the scion will not last as long in the garden as it would if it were on its own roots. It all depends on how deep the union is below soil level — the scion is supposed to form its own roots in time, but does not always do so effectively.

Pruning: With *S. vulgaris* all suckers should be cut away when seen, it may well be that a better variety has been grafted on to pale mauve stock, which will in time overwhelm the scion. Take away weak or old branches in winter (mark them before leaf-fall, it is easy to amputate the wrong limb). Cut off the dead flower trusses as soon as these are over, in any case they turn brown and are sometimes unsightly and can be an unwelcome reminder of autumn in mid-summer. As the shrubs get taller consider investing in a pair of long-handled shears with which you can sort out just about everything in the garden without any further risk from falling off the steps. Shorten the branches of *S. x hyacinthiflora* by about a third after flowering.

Uses: As specimen shrubs whether of a single colour or as a planned group. As hedging or screening (not for close-clipping, of course). Flowers for arrangements.

Shrubs: Ballalheannagh, Barcock, Bodnant, Brackenwood, Caldwell, Daisy Hill, Dobbies, Fairley's, Goatcher, Goscote, Great Dixter, Hilliers, Jackman, Kaye, Knaphill, Knoll Gardens, Lime Cross, Marchant, Notcutts, Otter, Reuthe, Roger, Russell, Scotts, Shepton, Sherrard, Smith, Southcombe, Stonehouse, Toynbee, Treasure, Warley, Woodland, Wycvale.

Seeds: Chiltern.

TAMARIX — Tamarisk *(Tamaricaceae)*. Tamarisk bushes, pink-plumed and wind-blown, are an essential part of seaside scenery. These graceful shrubs seem to thrive in a salt-laden environment and have adapted to it through the millenia. Though they appear quite happy growing in beach sand or where they are diurnally drenched with salt-laden spray, they do not actually need these conditions to do well inland. They have adapted to salinity, which adaptation prevents too much transpiration, therefore in other situations they need (unexpectedly) good deep soil.

Tamarisk was once thought to be something of a cure-all for ailments ranging from serious bladder infections to chilblains, and the ancient Greeks believed that drinking from a cup made from the wood of tamarisk would be sufficient '. . . as though the drincke which was given them out of such cups should doe them good'.

In earlier centuries the cure was often more of a killer, it seems, than the disease; for afflictions of the spleen, the apothecaries of the times used poisonous 'bowes of ughe' (yew) until they learned of a type of tamarisk with which they treated their patients.

Pliny called tamarisk 'the unluckie tree' because it set no fruit; it was used, mockingly, to garland criminals and in the Language of Flowers it represents 'crime'. More recently the Cornish fishermen have used its supple branches to make lobster-pots, probably now a lost art since the invention of plastic.

T. anglia — English Tamarisk grows to 10ft (3m) except in very windy areas when it will be shorter. Racemes of pinkish-white flowers from July to September or later. A scaly-leaved shrub for a sunny situation, as seaside screens or hedges, or in inland gardens.

T. gallica — French Tamarisk grows to 12ft (3.7m) (sometimes more) with racemes of pink flowers in June and August. A large-growing shrub from the coastal regions of France and Portugal for similar situations where extra height is needed.

T. pentandra (1880) grows to 15ft (4.5m) with a similar spread. Crowded racemes of tiny pink flowers from August to September. A scaly-leaved shrub from S.E. Europe with a pale green appearance for coastal gardens, hedges and as a graceful specimen plant.

Requirements: Full sun in all situations, any soil in coastal areas, better in inland gardens.

Propagation: Is as easy as with willows. Take some cuttings about ⅜" (1cm) thick and about 8" (20.5cm) long and plant them to two-thirds of their depth in a prepared bed in early winter.

Pruning: None is needed if the graceful, sweeping branches of tamarisk are admired. Take out any winter-killed shoots. Hedges may be cut back in late winter if they have become too tall.

Uses: As contrast plants in an inland garden, as sea-coast hedging or screening and for arrangements.

Shrubs: Barcock, Bodnant, Brackenwood, Busheyfields, Caldwell, Dobbies, Goatcher, Highfield, Hilliers, Jackman, Knaphill, Lime Cross, Marchant, Meare Close, Notcutts, Otter, Reuthe, Roger, Russell, Scotts, Shepton, Sherrard, St. Bridget, Stonehouse, Toynbee, Treasure, Warley, Woodland, Wyevale.

Seeds: Chiltern, Thompson and Morgan.

TEUCRIUM — Germander *(Labiatae)*. The Teucriums are probably named after Teucer, the Trojan king who is believed to have been the first to use the genus medicinally. The shrubs are not spectacular in any way but are, nevertheless, very useful as contrast, rockery or edging plants. *T. Chamaedrys* is a small, stolid upright little plant with shining evergreen leaves (very similar to those of *Dryas octopetala)* that are grey beneath. It has rather quiet pink labiate flowers in summer and I find it most attractive as a contrast and background shrublet which spreads sideways so as to fetch up against my rockwork where it looks pleasingly natural. Not all plants can have the flamboyance of poppies or dahlias, alas, nor the grandeur of an ancient Wisteria in full bloom.

T. Chamaedrys or Germander was used to alleviate gout in former times; it was the essential ingredient in a preparation called Portland Powder with which an 18th century Duke of Portland was reputedly cured of his sufferings. Difficult to believe, when one thinks of the cellarage in those great houses. However, it had also been part of a (vinous) decoction administered to the Emperor Charles V which, with some other herbs, was taken for sixty successive days. The 'vinous' part of the decoction might have made it just about potable but perhaps would have had a somewhat negative effect on the cure. I find that herbalists once used the plant, when gathered and dried in the right conditions, as a stimulant, a tonic and a diuretic; Culpeper lists a number of ailments that the Teucrium reputedly cured, and finishes with 'it is also good against diseases of the brain, as continual headache, falling sickness (epilepsy), melancholy, drowsiness and dulness of spirits, convulsions and palsies'. So this unassuming little shrub has more to it than one would think, and would have had a place in a medieval herb garden. It was used, like so many other plants, to heal 'the biting of all serpents' and I now feel well protected from these as I weed that part of the rockery where the Teucrium lives. *T. fruticans* has most attractive and very distinctive orchid-like flowers but it is too tender to grow well in the British Isles, unless it is tucked into a warm-walled corner.

T. Chamaedrys — Wall Germander grows 9" + (23cm+) and spreads to 15" (38cm) with small pink flowers from July to September. A small European evergreen sub-shrub for sunny banks, walls, rock-pockets, edges and in the herb garden.

T. fruticans — Shrubby or **Tree Germander** (1869) grows to 5ft (1.5m) and spreads to 4ft (1.2m) with unusual lavender-blue orchid-like flowers from June to September. Silvery stems and undersides to leaves. A tender shrub from S. Europe for a warm-wall corner in south-western counties.

Requirements: Ordinary to poor garden soil and full sun for *T. Chamaedrys* and a very sheltered sunny corner for *T. fruticans,* or a cold greenhouse.

Propagation: Take half-ripened cuttings of lateral shoots of *T. Chamaedrys* in May and insert in a rooting compost of peat and sand. Keep in a cold frame until rooted, then grow on in separate pots of John Innes No.1. Plunge for the summer and winter and plant into final positions in the following spring. For *T. fruticans* take half-ripened heel-cuttings of lateral shoots in July and August. Insert into a rooting compost of peat and sand and put into a propagator set at 15°C (59°F). When well rooted transfer into pots of John Innes No.1 and keep in a frost-free place for the winter. Plant out in summer or grow on as a cold greenhouse shrub. Tie shoots to wires in either case.

Pruning: Tidy up *T. fruticans* in spring and shorten new growth by half after flowering.

Uses: *T. Chamaedrys* as a quiet evergreen background shrub. *T. fruticans* as a delicate wall shrub with branches for arrangements.

Shrubs: Ballalheannagh, Broadwell, Daisy Hill, Margery Fish, Goatcher, Hilliers, Hopleys, Ingwersen, Kaye, Knoll Gardens, Marchant, Notcutts, Old Rectory, Otter, Potterton and Martin, Ramparts, Reads, Robinsons, Rosemoor, Scotts, Shepton, Sherrard, Smith, St. Bridget, Stonehouse, Toynbee, Treasure, Treseder, Weald.

Seeds: Chiltern, Thompson and Morgan.

THYMUS — Thyme *(Labiatae)*. Difficult to think of the tiny thymes as 'shrubs', but shrubs they are, especially when you fall over a wiry-stemmed hummock in the paving on a dark, wet night. The hummock is quite able to take care of itself and, having tripped you up, it will be quite unscathed. There are a great many species of this genus (the botanists do not actually agree on this, or on an estimate of their number), but only a few of several hundred are grown to make those nice aromatic hummocks in the paving that trip you so effectively on dark, wet nights. Most of these are varieties of the species *T. Serpyllum,* of which *T. Drucei* is the common wild thyme that Shakespeare knew so well. I will say here that the botanists and taxonomists did not distinguish *T. Drucei* as a separate species until 1924, but I cannot pretend (though I would like to) that I did not know this. As Shakespeare said… and it is wearisome to need to be so precise.

To return to the chalk downlands where the rabbity turf is studded with little jewel-like flowers — Centaury, Ladies' slipper, Autumn Felwort, Eyebright and tiny Veronicas and, of course, thyme. Thyme grows here in perfumed cushions on old molehills and disused ants' nests, though look carefully before you sit, those little yellow ants have a disproportionately large amount of venom. The thyme recently formed part of the unique life cycle of the now-thought-to-be-extinct Large Blue butterfly, *Maculinea arion.* This butterfly's habitat was grassy downland slopes with short turf and low scrub and such areas are, alas, becoming rarer. The butterfly laid its eggs on the wild thyme, *T. Drucei.* The eggs hatched and the caterpillars or larvae fed on the thyme-flowers, though these larvae were a bloodthirsty, cannibalistic lot and would eat each other for preference. (This first stage is called an instar.) After the first instar the surviving larva or larvae moult (because their skins do not stretch) and sensibly turn pink to match the thyme-flowers, to avoid being eaten by larger predators. This is the second instar. Then the larva (now no longer so cannibalistic) moults again and drops to the ground where it is found by a special type of ant, usually *Myrmica sabuleti* which 'milks' the larva's honey-gland. The larva does not mind this and, after a while, the ant picks up the larva and carries it off into its nest where it feeds on ant-larva until it is half-grown, when it hibernates for the winter inside the nest. In spring it starts to feed again; the whole larval stage lasts for ten months. Then it pupates and the metamorphosis takes about three weeks; the butterfly hatches inside the ants' nest and crawls to the open air before its wings expand. This astonishing life-cycle involves this kind of butterfly only, the wild thyme and the Myrmica ants.

The culinary thyme is *T. vulgaris* which is large — to 15″ (38cm) high — and wiry and not very lovely except in miniscule quantities in the pot. It was formerly grown as a medicinal plant and is always seen in herb gardens, simply because it always grew there in former times, though it is not much used today.

Herb-garden catalogues list quite a number of species and varieties which make lovely, scented paving plants most of which are flat enough not to trip one up, though they are strong enough to withstand the tread of untrained garden visitors. In fact, thymes are almost wasted when treated only as rock garden plants, they look best when grown on a large paved area, where their flowers and different foliage types will combine to make the most delightful aromatic carpet which will best release its fragrance when stepped on. I am not suggesting that this planting scheme be carried out where there is busy traffic, or on a patio or terrace where the legs of garden furniture are constantly scraping to and fro, or where children play; it all depends on your priorities which have a habit of changing as the years go by. Thymes love and need the sun, and grow very well in pre-arranged gaps left when paving is laid. A thyme lawn as such is not usually successful — the thymes grow at different heights and weeds will get in among them, necessitating a constant effort which is tiresome. Thymes in paving are better because the surface is pleasant and dry to walk on throughout the year and there is little space for weeds to get established. Also, the various foliage colours of the thymes show up much better against brick, stone paving or even concrete than they do against earth.

T. x citriodorus — Lemon-scented Thyme grows to 12″ (30cm) high with a similar spread, and (usually) pale lilac flowers from July to August. An evergreen sub-shrub with several varieties such as 'aureus' with golden leaves and 'Silver Queen' with variegated foliage, both of which may revert to green. An aromatic herb plant for sunny places.

T. Drucei syn. **T. Serpyllum — Wild Thyme, Mother of Thyme** grows to 3″ (7.5cm) with a spread of 24″ (60cm). Flowers in domed clusters of lilac-pink in the true wild species and pink, crimson, mauve and white in the varieties, from June to August. A slow, mat-forming evergreen herb with wiry stems to grow as a paving plant, as edging, on banks, in rock and herb gardens, and in pots and troughs on patios and balconies. It must always have full sun.

T. Herba-barona (1908) grows to 5″ (12.5cm) with a spread of 15″ (38cm) with elongated pale lilac flower-clusters in June.

A caraway-scented mat-forming dark green herb from Corsica for all similar situations.

T. pulegioides grows to 12″ (30cm) and spreads to 24″ (60cm) with many varieties which have been given separate and sometimes conflicting names, eg. the red-flowered form, *T. pulegioides* var. *Chamaedrys* f. *kermesinus,* is usually grown and sold as *T. Serpyllum* var. 'Coccineus'.

T. vulgaris — Garden Thyme, Culinary Thyme grows to a springy, bushy 15″ (38cm) with a spread of 12″ (30cm) and lilac flowers in June. A variety with coloured leaves is *T.v.* 'Aureus' with yellow leaves. An aromatic evergreen sub-shrub for herb-gardens, culinary and medicinal use.

Requirements: Thymes are more tender than is realised and a cold wet winter may kill them. Plant in sheltered, sunny places. Thymes do well on chalk soils and dislike being moved in maturity, so plan your thyme pavement on paper first. They love the reflected warmth from paving.

Propagation: Large clumps can be divided in spring, but it is better and safer to take cuttings of *T. vulgaris* in May or June. Take lateral unflowered cuttings with a heel and insert in a rooting compost of peat and sand in a cold frame. When well rooted transfer into John Innes No.1 and grow on. Or sow seeds of *T. vulgaris* in spring in the usual way.

Pruning: Thymes are not really 'pruned' though their wiry stems are too strong to pick. Tidy away dead winter-killed shoots in spring. Old plants get bare and leafless in the centre and should be discarded.

Uses: Many. As very ornamental flowering plants for paved areas, edges, rockeries, banks, walls, troughs and sinks (colours should be planned on paper before planting when large areas are involved). As traditional herb-garden plants, for homeopathic medicine and in the preparation of beauty products. In the wild garden it is a good bee and butterfly plant.

Shrubs: Broadwell, Beth Chatto, Cunnington, Margery Fish, Glenview, Great Dixter, Hopleys, Ingwersen, Marten's Hall, Old Rectory, Parkinsons, Potterton and Martin, Robinsons, Scotts, Stonehouse, Weald.

Seeds: Chiltern, Fothergill, Suttons, Thompson and Morgan.

TRACHELOSPERMUM (*Apocynaceae*). This is a rather rare climbing shrub which has scented flowers that look like pale periwinkles. Trachelospermum has all the assets except true hardiness, but what can we expect in these latitudes when a plant comes originally from the Far East. The shrub is ever-green and has pale-coloured perfumed flowers and it is a very different climber to grow for gardeners in the southern counties of the British Isles. It is happier (and perhaps safer) in a large frost-free conservatory where it will clothe a wall with its glossy leaves spangled with sprays of white or pale yellow fragrant flowers. There is a very large-growing and vigorous species, *T. majus,* which lives up to its name; this will grow like ivy and will cover a whole house wall but

only, alas, in the South of France.

T. jasminoides syn. **Rhyncospermum jasminoides** (1844) grows to 12ft (3.7m) with a similar spread. Sprays of fragrant white flowers in July and August. A rather tender evergreen twining climber from China for a warm south or west-facing wall.

Requirements: A south or west-facing wall and acid soil; or space in a large cold greenhouse in southern counties, or a heated one in northern areas.

Propagation: Take short nodal cuttings from lateral shoots in July or August and insert in a rooting compost of peat and sand. Place in a propagator with gentle heat. When well rooted transfer into individual pots of John Innes No.1. Protect in a frost-free greenhouse for the winter. Plant out in late spring. Give young plants twiggy sticks for early support, these will soon be hidden.

Pruning: Thin out shoots in March or April. Dead-head faded blooms after flowering.

Uses: As an unusual and exotic evergreen wall-climber in sheltered gardens and large conservatories. Scented flower sprays for arrangements.

Shrubs: Ballalheannagh, Bodnant, Brackenwood, Busheyfields, Farall, Hilliers, Knoll Gardens, Marchant, Notcutts, Otter, Rosemoor, Sherrard, St. Bridget, Stonehouse, Wyevale.

TRICUSPIDARIA (see **CRINODENDRON**).

ULEX — Gorse, Furze, Whin (*Leguminosae*). Gorse is one of the loveliest of shrubs, which may seem an odd statement to make considering its prickly nature. But this is forgettable when you see a hillside all a-golden with flowers in spring, and during our odd-climate mild winters it blooms almost as exuberantly, presumably thinking (along with the birds who sing in the middle of the night in such unseasonable weather) that spring is here. Judging by the considerable amount of blossom seen in December recently, I wonder what the shrub does when the days lengthen and spring really arrives? Unlike many plants less capable of survival, I would think that the gorse will flower again; and as 'kissing's out of season when the gorse is out of bloom' it should be a good year for young — and not-so-young — love.

The scent of gorse in bloom on a hot hillside is glorious — it is a mixture of almond and orange with a trace of coconut. To lie on the grass in such a place, with the scent heavy all around and with the song of an invisible lark above in a cloudless blue sky, is my idea of perfect bliss.

The wild gorse seeds itself about with cracking abandon, as broom does and, if you sit on the same hillside on a hot summer's day a few months later, the ripe pods will be exploding all about you in an irregular cannonade. The seedlings come up without spines and are not immediately recognisable as those of gorse. The double-flowered garden variety smells the same but, of course, has no progeny which, though I love gorse dearly, can be too much of a problem in a small garden. Whether wild or 'cultivated', gorse makes an excellent hedge, screen and windbreak, though it will become barish and brownish at the base in old age. It can be planted as part of a hedge in a wild garden to keep out cows and sheep.

Though wild gorse is apparently so common, it is not always hardy and can be killed in bad winters. It is not a plant for constant low temperatures and does not do well in the colder parts of Europe. Linnaeus admired it greatly, so much so that he tried to keep a plant going in a greenhouse. When he visited England in 1736 he saw great sheets of golden gorse in bloom and is said to have fallen to his knees in an ecstasy of pleasure (the same reaction is told of other visiting botanists such as Dillenius in 1721 and Kalm in 1748, though the latter is said to have expressed his admiration in a more restrained fashion).

The Victorians liked the story of Linaeus' reaction to our gorse and a poetess called Emily Carrington wrote these lines for 'Aunt Judy's Magazine' entitled:

Linnaeus and the Gorse

'Over the heath the golden gorse is glowing,
and making glad the breeze;
And lo, a traveller by the wayside going
Falls low upon his knees,
And thanks God for such a glorious vision,
and such a rich perfume,
As met him in what seemed a dream Elysian,
far from his northern home.

So felt the great Linnaeus when before him
the yellow gorse spread out . . . '

The double flowered kind is more compact for gardens and even more floriferous in season, if this is possible.

U. europaeus — Gorse, Furze, Whin grows to 8ft (2.4m) with a similar spread. Golden yellow flowers in spring but intermittently and unseasonably throughout the year. A spiny native shrub for the wild garden or hedging. *U.e.* 'plenus' is smaller and more compact, with rich golden flowers like scrambled duck eggs.

Requirements: Full sun, poor to average soil. Not really suitable for cold inland areas.

Propagation: Sow seeds of the wild *U. europaeus* in pots of seed compost in spring. Put into a cold frame until seedlings are well up. Thin out and grow on, transfer into larger pots and plunge for the summer. Ulex does not like root disturbance, so keep plants in pots until needed. For *U.e.* 'plenus' take short cuttings of current season's shoots in August or September and insert in pots of a rooting compost of peat and sand in a cold frame. Keep in frame for winter and pot on in spring into John Innes No.1. Plunge for the summer and plant out in autumn.

Pruning: Is done with difficulty. (Do not allow shrubs to become tall, leggy and bare at the bottom.) Cut back every March to encourage new basal growth.

Uses: *U.e.* 'plenus' among the spring flowering shrubs and as impenetrable garden hedging. Wild gorse as a wild garden shrub or on dry sunny banks where it provides good cover for birds. Flowers for pot-pourri.

Shrubs: Ballalheannagh, Busheyfields, Caldwell, Goatcher, Hilliers, Jackman, Kershaw, Knaphill, Notcutts, Otter, Roger, Scotts, Shepton, Sherrard, Smith, Southcombe, St. Bridget, Stonehouse, Toynbee, Warley, Woodland, W.W., Wyevale.

Seeds: Chiltern, Thompson and Morgan.

VIBURNUM *(Caprifoliaceae).* This is a large genus of flowering shrubs for widely diverse garden positions. There are useful and handsome-leaved evergreen varieties, beautiful spring flowering kinds, bright-fruited types for autumn interest and some that have sweet-scented winter flowers on bare branches. No garden should be without at least one viburnum — they are all so different and most of them are beautiful. It is difficult to know where to start, but January seems as good a month as any with which to begin. The very hardy *V. fragrans* will have been in bloom for months on the bare branches, and in mild spells scented eddies will surround the shrub and its clusters of pink-tinged white flowers that keep on forming until March when the leaves come. This viburnum is so hardy that it was formerly grown by Chinese who lived at such a high altitude that corn could not be relied upon to ripen. The plant was found and described by several plant-hunters in turn, first by William Purdom in 1909 and again by Reginald Farrar in 1914. Farrar was about to send home more seed of this shrub (it seldom ripens its seeds in the British Isles) and had made an arrangement with His Highness Yang Tusa, Prince of Jo-ni, who was to let him have the kernels when his viburnum fruits were harvested. But the voluble Farrar had a disagreement with His Highness, who took umbrage and 'set to, and sedulously ate up all the viburnum fruits in his palace garden, and threw away the seed'. One wonders what the quantity involved was, and what effect this fit of pique had upon the Royal digestion. In shaded corners, the old fashioned 'Laurustinus' or *V. Tinus* will also be in flower, with its prim, neat corymbs of pink-budded white flowers that are so useful in winter arrangements. This shrub is an evergreen and its character always reminds me of a Victorian governess, because it is long-suffering, enduring, and can be put almost anywhere in the garden where it will cheer up draughty, shaded corners. It withstands haphazard clipping, too, which it is subjected to because it grows unexpectedly well even when disadvantaged. I am attempting to redress the balance a little and have planted a new small shrub where I can appreciate it, directly opposite my studio door, and I am hoping that my warm and appreciative thoughts as I go to and fro will compensate for the lack of sunlight because it is in a semi-shaded place.

V. Davidii is a fine evergreen shrub with deeply-veined shining dark green leaves. These alone are sufficient to earn it good garden space, but it has neat flowers in winter similar to those of *V. Tinus* and 'when two or more are gathered together' then (providing the gender selection is right) brilliant sapphire-blue berries will form and colour in late autumn to last through the winter. When I began to plant up this garden I forgot to collect the 'other half' of this pair, so have had to content myself with admiring other people's berries. But last November I moved my lonely chap to a bigger space and have chosen a plump little wife for him.

V. Opulus is the wild species, with hydrangea-like flat corymbs of fertile flowers surrounded by large sterile bracts. This is the Guelder-Rose of summer hedges, where its occasional flower heads look beautiful among honeysuckle and the late blooms of *Rosa arvensis*. If planted as a group in an open situation they can look magnificent in autumn, with red and yellow foliage and brilliant scarlet berries that the birds do not eat. They need to be planted close together to be sure of a good crop of fruits. I saw such a group of shrubs about five years ago, and I can remember that golden October day and the brilliant fire-coloured shrubs with their red and yellow leaves; when the wind blew it was as if small flames were flickering among the branches.

V. Opulus 'sterile' is the 'Snowball bush', easy to grow, tremendously effective in the garden and more so in a vase. *V. tomentosum mariesii* is one of the handsomest of the reliable flowering shrubs. I could say that it is one of the handsomest of all, but then I would tangle with Camellia, rose and Rhododendron lovers. But for those whose soil is not right for such definitely calcifuge plants then *V. tomentosum mariesii* is excellent. It has tiers of branches from which stand up double rows of flower buds. The stems extend and the buds unfold until each branch is surmounted by flat, Hydrangea-like creamy flowers clustered like a snowfall all along the top of each branch. The effect is stunning on all those who have never seen a good specimen in full blast in May. My own plant came as a legacy from the garden of a dear friend who died and who is still sorely missed by colleagues and companions. She played in a symphony orchestra and was brave, cheerful and uncomplaining right up to the end; what better memorial could anyone have than this lovely shrub.

V. Carlesii (1902) grows to 8ft (2.4m) and as much through, with very fragrant convex heads of white flowers which form in autumn and remain all winter to open in April and May. This deciduous shrub is now superseded by its more modern hybrids.

V. Davidii (1904) grows to 4ft (1.2m) with a spread of 5ft (1.5m).

Pink-budded white flowers in June (continuing into late autumn with me) followed by brilliant sapphire-blue berries that last through the winter. An evergreen shrub from China with very handsome, shining deeply veined leaves; needs another plant of a different sex in order to berry well. Hand pollinate as a belt-and-braces measure. Single plants very good-looking, though no berries will be borne. Plant in a sunny, fairly sheltered situation, bad frosts can damage the large leaves.

V. fragrans (1909) grows to 15ft (4.5m) and as much through, with white, tinged pink, or all pink clusters of very fragrant flowers from November through the winter to March. A deciduous shrub from N. China for the winter flower garden; frost damages the flowers but others will come to replace them. Several modern varieties exist, the best is *V. x bodnantense* 'Dawn' (1935).

V. lantana — Wayfaring tree grows to 15ft (4.5m) in a hedge, with white flowers in May and June, followed by clusters of berries which are red and black in the same cyme. A native deciduous plant for informal hedging or as a specimen shrub. Excellent on chalk.

V. Opulus — Guelder-Rose grows to 15ft (4.5m) and as much through, with flat hydrangea-like heads of white flowers in May and June. A deciduous native shrub with excellent autumn colour and dangling clusters of scarlet berries that remain on the shrub all winter. Var. 'sterile' is the Snowball Tree or Bush, with spherical clusters of white flowers in June. A focal shrub for its flowers.

V. Tinus 'Laurustinus' (1560) grows to a rounded 15ft (4.5m) and as much through, with neat posies of pink-budded white flowers from December to April, sometimes followed by blue berries. A handsome, glossy-leaved evergreen for the winter flower garden and for hedging in milder counties. Will tolerate some shade but flowers better in sun. Any soil.

V. tomentosum f. **plicatum** grows to 10ft (3m) and spreads to 15ft (4.5m) according to type. The wild form has horizontal branches in layers with closely set double rows or lace-cap, hydrangea-like white flowers in May and June. The var. 'Mariesii' is the best form. A deciduous shrub from China for a focal sunny place in the garden. Good as a single specimen plant on a lawn.

Requirements: Good garden soil and full sun. *V. lantana* is best on chalk. Set early-flowering species and varieties where their flowers will not be damaged by cutting winds or early sun on frosted buds and shoots.

Propagation: Take lateral heel cuttings in June or July and insert in a rooting compost of peat and sand. Or take softwood cuttings at the same time and root in a propagator set at 16°C (61°F). When cuttings are rooted transfer to individual pots of John Innes No.1 and keep in a cold frame for the winter. In the spring, plant cuttings in a nursery area and grow on for two or three seasons. Or layer appropriate branches or long shoots in September and sever a year later.

Pruning: Thin out old, damaged or overcrowded·branches of evergreen species and varieties in spring. Deciduous kinds can be tidied up in the same way after flowering. Move evergreen species from November onwards in suitable weather, or in early spring. Move deciduous species when dormant.

Uses: As specimen shrubs, and for the shrub border; *V. Tinus* for informal hedging. Flowers, foliage and berries for arrangements.

Shrubs: Ballalheannagh, Barcock, Bees, Brackenwood, Bressingham, Busheyfields, Caldwell, Peter Chappell, Daisy Hill, Dobbies, Fairley's, Goatcher, Goscote, Great Dixter, Highfield, Hilliers, Holden Clough, Hopleys, Jackman, Kaye, Kershaw, Knaphill, Knoll Gardens, Lime Cross, Marchant, Meare Close, Notcutts, Otter, Reuthe, Roger, Rosemoor, Russell, Scotts, Shepton, Sherrard, Smith, Southcombe, St. Bridget, Stonehouse, Toynbee, Treasure, Warley, Woodland, W.W., Wyevale.

Seeds: Chiltern, Thompson and Morgan.

VINCA — Periwinkle, Band-plant *(Apocynaceae)*.

The trailing stems and leathery leaves of Vinca (or periwinkle) are evergreen and enduring, and I suppose that this is one reason why it has been planted so much in poor places in deep shade, where it does not have the chance to show what it can really do, though because it roots as it goes a good patch of it is useful for anchoring soil on sloping banks.

The early gardeners thought it was a kind of Clematis, and Turner said '. . . it hath prety blew floures . . . and the herbe crepeth upon the grounde very thicke, one braunche woven about an other'. Several other colours were being grown by the beginning of the 18th century, including a rather exciting one which is described by Tournefort as follows: '. . . Or, to the Delight of the Eye, the violet Flower is striped with a milky Line from the Extremity of each Segment to the Bottom, which is likewise found in the double or multiplied Flower'.

Vinca, or Periwinkle, Pervenche, Pervinca and such similar and recognisable permutations on the spelling, was a very magic herb — the French called it 'Violette des Sorciers'. It had strong powers in matters amatory. It was always used in herbal medicine, Turner advising: 'perwincle chewed stauncheth the tuth ache', while Bacon said that stems of periwinkle tied round the calf of the leg were thought to ease the pain of cramp (hence 'band-plant'). One of its cousins, the pink-flowered Madagascar Periwinkle, *Catharanthus roseus*, has now been found to have considerable use in modern medicine, with a potential value in the treatment of cancer.

There are quite a number of Vincas of different colours, with or without variegated foliage. Some are old varieties, rediscovered early this century, whilst others are of more recent origin. A long bank of Vincas of different kinds is a pleasant sight, particularly as all are evergreen, though of varying degrees of hardiness. The most vigorous of them is, of course, *V. major*, which will suffocate the lot in a season if not watched, but this can be planted where its bounding vitality can be utilised, such as to lean its way up through deciduous shrubs at the top of the bank, and in very mild winters there will be flowers throughout the coldest months.

V. major — Periwinkle, Band-plant grows to 12" (30cm) though stems will climb to 3 or 4ft (90cm-1.2m) against or up through shrubs. Blue-mauve flowers in spring until June, and from November onwards in mild winters or counties. A very vigorous trailing evergreen perennial, useful (though generally mis-used) for clothing difficult places and corners, where it will not flower as well. It likes sun as much as any other plant. Does well in ordinary to poor soil. Var. 'Elegantissima' has cream and green leaves, with paler flowers and is less vigorous.

V. minor grows to 4" (10cm) with a spread of 3-4ft (90cm-1.2m). It has darker green leaves and purple, mauve, blue, wine or white flowers from March to July, and intermittently throughout the year. A European perennial for better soil and situation than *V. major*.

Requirements: More flowers are always produced in sunny situations, though *V. major* will grow green almost anywhere. Variegated kinds are always best in sunny positions.

Propagation: *V. major* roots at the tips and nodes of the trailing stems. Allow these to root and settle, then sever the umbilical stem and transfer the new plant. Peg down varieties of *V. minor* over pots of seed compost, into which it will root.

Pruning: Shear over *V. major* and thin out some of the twining stems when necessary.

Uses: As good evergreen ground cover for walls, banks, hedge bottoms, woodland areas, rockeries (the choicer kinds only) and edges of borders in light shade or full sun.

Plants or 'shrubs': Peter Chappell, Beth Chatto, Highfield, Hillier, Holden Clough, Ingwersen, Kelways, Robinsons, Scotts, Southcombe, St. Bridget.

VITIS — Glory Vine, Grape Vine *(Vitaceae)*.

Vines of all kinds are beautiful, because of their handsome leaves which overlap each other like tiles on a roof. Being a practical gardener, I would grow a grape vine primarily for its leaves and would consider that ripe fruit was a bonus. In drought years, of course, you can look smug as you distribute those perfect bunches of grapes, but drought years are well spaced out between the wet ones, so I would learn to love the leaves. Grape vines will in time grow quite enormous, much bigger than people realise. Therefore, please do not plant one unless you can give it all of a two-storey house wall (south or south-west facing) to itself. It will, in time, have a huge root and it will always be hungry and thirsty. But if you are prepared to devote quite a lot of time to the care of your grape vine it will repay you most handsomely. When I was a child of twelve, I was admiring a fine vine in a greenhouse, festooned with dark bunches of ripe grapes. I was told that to make sure the vine got off to a good start in life, a body of some kind, such as a dog, a pig or a sheep 'or something larger' had to be buried under the planting hole to feed the vine's roots. Being a curious child I asked what this old gardener had buried for the vine to feed on, and he wouldn't tell me. The mystery has remained with me ever since and perhaps, one day, I'll go back to see what the skeleton is, or was, under the vine. He also said that it was best for vines to be planted outside the greenhouse, through a hole in the brickwork, and I have noticed that many old vines are grown like this. If beautiful leaves are required to set off the wine-dark fruits, then grow the crimson-leaved varieties such as *V. vinifera* 'Brandt', or *V.v.* 'Purpurea' (Teinturier grape) which has been grown in Britain for centuries. Small-growing vines, complete with fruit, are very beautiful on pergolas or archways. Such a one is *V.v.* 'Apiifolia' syn. *V.v.* 'Laciniosa', the Cut-leaved or Parsley vine, which has delicately cut leaves and small fruits.

A full size grape vine wants to grow to 50 or 60ft (15-18m), so do think about the space available first. Grapes have been grown in our so-called unsuitable climate since the Romans brought them, as is testified by all the historic reference, and though the summers were hotter in past centuries there is no reason why you cannot grow grapes for the table or to turn into your own vintage. Since there will generally be space for one plant only, consider whether you want to eat the fruit or drink them, or whether you want autumnal coloured leaves, or just a large and lovely plant. That being decided, the rest is easy. There are one or two other 'grape vines' that are grown for their ornamental leaves and fruit, such as the Fox Grape, *V. Labrusca*, which is a very vigorous climber with dark leaves that are downy beneath and blackish-purple musk-flavoured fruit. *V. riparia* syn. *V. vulpina* is the American 'Riverside' or 'River-bank Grape', which is a vigorous plant with large leaves, sweet-scented flowers and bloomy, black-purple fruits. There are many other ornamental grape vines which are grown for beauty rather than utility; for true viticulture, a work devoted entirely to the subject is best consulted.

V. Coignetiae is a fine and beautiful climber, with large, matt, deeply veined, heart-shaped leaves in summer. But come the early autumn, these leaves begin to stand out from all the other foliage, turning first to an apricot-rose and then to brilliant tones of red and crimson. This climber looks well on a pergola but even better with a background of conifers or dark yews, or it may be planted to climb them, but see note on ultimate size first.

V. Coignetiae — Glory Vine (1875) grows to 80 or 90ft (24 or 27m), with large — up to 8 or 12″ (20.5-30cm) — ribbed, lobed leaves which change to brilliant scarlet autumn shades. A vigorous deciduous climber for a large support, such as a big pergola or a full sized evergreen tree.

V. Labrusca — Fox Grape (1656) grows vigorously with tendrilled shoots and dark leaves that are downy beneath. Black-purple grapes, musk flavoured. A hardy American species much used as a parent.

V. riparia syn. **V. vulpina — Riverbank** or **Riverside Grape** (1656), grows high — to 30ft (9m) — or scrambles very vigorously with sweetly scented flower racemes in summer. Glossy, green leaves and bloomy black-purple fruits. Var. 'Brandt' (1886) has bronze-red autumn foliage, with veins remaining green or yellow. Dark black-purple grapes, good for fresh juice.

V. vinifera — Grape Vine (about 60 centuries old). Many species grown according to soil type, climate, aspect etc. Some old varieties are var. 'Apiifolia', the Parsley or Cut-leaved Vine, with deeply cut leaves sometimes with the divisions stalked; var. 'Purpurea' sometimes sold as and confused with the ancient Teinturier grape. The leaves are a plummy purple during the summer, darkening to rich purple in autumn, with darker purple (very sour) grapes.

Requirements: Grape vines can be grown for ornamental purposes in ordinary good garden soil, though lime at a recommended rate should be added to acid soil. Dig over the soil deeply before planting and add well-rotted manure or compost at this time. Prepare strong wires with vine-eyes for house walls. Pergolas are excellent for vines because they are easier to get at for general maintenance. If grown into trees this ceases to be possible. A high warm south or south-west wall for fruit to ripen if this is of importance. Water well in hot weather and feed each year with well-decayed manure.

Propagation: *V. Coignetiae* has to be layered in September or October: choose one-year-old shoots for this. Sever a year later. For true vines, take half-ripe heel cuttings in July or August and insert them singly in pots of sandy compost. Place in a propagator set at 13-16°C (55-61°F). When rooted, pot into John Innes No.1 and grow on in a cold frame, potting on into larger pots as necessary and supporting each with a cane.

Pruning: None needed for *V. Coignetiae*. For the true vines, the young shoots are shortened back once or twice during the summer. In December or January, cut shoots back to one or two buds. This pruning is for the ornamental vines. For the production of fruit, allow three or four stems or 'rods' to develop for the first season. In September cut away two-thirds of the main stems and continue in this way until the vines fill the available space. Do not let the vines fruit until they are three years old, after that, each lateral shoot should have one bunch only. Pinch out tips of lateral shoots on first-year plants at 24″ (60cm). In later years and on mature plants, stop the lateral growth at two leaves after the flower stems, on sub-laterals at one leaf.

Uses: As very ornamental climbers for foliage and fruit, on and up large pergolas, fences, walls and trees. Fruit for juice, wine and for the table.

Shrubs: Barcock, Bodnant, Brackenwood, Bressingham, Busheyfields, Daisy Hill, Dobbies, Goatcher, Highfield, Hilliers, Jackman, Kaye, Kershaw, Knoll Gardens, Lime Cross, Marchant, Meare Close, Notcutts, Otter, Reuthe, Roger, Russell, Shepton, Sherrard, Smith, St. Bridget, Stonehouse, Toynbee, Warley, Woodland, Wyevale.

WEIGELA — (wrongly, **Weigelia**) *(Caprifoliaceae)*. The genus Weigela was named after the German botanist Christian Ehrenfried Weigel (1748-1831), professor at Greifswald in northern Germany and author of *Flora Pomerano-Rugica* in 1769. Weigela was at one time included in the genus Diervilla, and may be found under this name in some nursery catalogues or at garden centres.

The most popular and easy-growing member of this now smaller genus of hardy shrubs is *W. florida* in all its colours and forms, many of which, alas, are too recent for inclusion in this book. The species plant is being superseded by these, though large and established specimens are to be seen in old gardens. When I say large, I do mean this — my own inherited shrub is over 12ft (3.7m) high and over 16ft (4.8m) wide; it is a fountain of pink blossom in May, with intermittent flower-sprays throughout the summer until the frosts. I know that this is not characteristic, but much that grows in my garden is not. I must admit to a certain pride in the size and beauty of this ancient specimen, but just because of this I feel that it must surely soon begin to deteriorate; I have not heard that Weigelas are noted for longevity. The species was first seen by Robert Fortune in a Mandarin's garden on the island of Chusan, and he was able to buy a similar plant from a nursery in Shanghai, which he sent to the Horticultural Society in 1844. When he returned to the same nursery the proprietor asked him how the Weigela and other plants bought at the same time were doing. Fortune replied 'I told them that most of the plants had arrived safely in England, that they had been greatly admired, and that the beautiful Weigela had even attracted the notice of her Majesty the Queen. All these statements, more particularly the last, seemed to give them great pleasure; and they doubtless fancied the Weigela of more value ever afterwards.' (Fortune, Gard. Chron., 1850, p.757).

The buds of Weigelas are formed in autumn and are carried through the winter and prolonged late frosts will spoil the blossom, though this does not often happen. There is a small and gentle yellow-flowered species called *W. Middendorffiana,* which needs partial shade and a very sheltered place for its earlier flowers to bloom in safety. This is much less of a giant than *W. florida* and is a real acquisition for a semi-shaded corner, where its sulphur-coloured flowers stand a better chance of achieving undamaged maturity in the dangerous late-frost times of April and May. The interesting hybrid *W.* 'Looymansii Aurea' has really yellow leaves, finely edged with red, and pink flowers. This is not a vigorous shrub and is best in partial or dappled shade where it will be a patch of sunlight in itself. I do not like the pink flowers with the yellow leaves; as an artist I find that they have almost the same colour-value and therefore they cancel each other out, but the beauty of the foliage, together with the brightness and impact of the shrub in a shaded place (of which I have too many) makes me take to it in spite of my comment. The variegated leaved Weigelas are the most beautiful shrubs, almost ethereal in their prettiness, with green and white or pale green and cream leaves and paler pink flowers. This is a colour harmony of real delicacy and perfection that does not jar on the sensibilities in any way.

The Chinese gardeners esteemed their Weigelas and named them severally as 'Silk Ribbon Flowers', 'Embroidered Belt Flowers' and 'Hair on the Delicate Side-Temples'.

W. florida syns. **W. rosea, Diervilla florida** (1845) grows to 9ft (2.7m), with a similar spread. Groups of rose-pink funnel-shaped flowers along the branches in May and June. Other (later) varieties have variegated, purple or golden leaves, with pink, cream, white or crimson flowers. A hardy deciduous shrub from China for a good position in sun.

W. Middendorffiana syn. **D. Middendorffiana** (1850) grows to 4ft (1.2m) with a similar spread. Sulphur-yellow flowers, tinged orange in April and May. A tender deciduous shrub from China, Manchuria and Japan for a position in partial shade and sheltered from frosts.

W. x 'Looymansii Aurea' (1873) is an interesting and rather special hybrid having golden leaves edged with red, and pink flowers. A deciduous shrub for a sheltered position in dappled or semi-shade.

Requirements: Any good, well-drained garden soil and full sun. Partial shade for golden-leaved varieties.

Propagation: Take half-ripe lateral non-flowered heel cuttings in June or July: insert in a rooting compost of peat and sand and place in a propagator set at 16°C (61°F). When well rooted transfer into individual pots of John Innes No.1 and grow on. Keep in a cold frame for winter, plant out in a nursery area for a season before transferring to flowering positions.

Pruning: Take out one or two whole stems to ground level from mature plants after flowering.

Uses: Foliage of gold, purple and variegated leaves for arrangements (flowering branches do not last long).

Shrubs: Ballalheannagh, Barcock, Bees, Bodnant, Brackenwood, Bressingham, Busheyfields, Caldwell, Peter Chappell, Beth Chatto, Daisy Hill, Dobbies, Fairley's, Margery Fish, Goatcher, Goscote, Great Dixter, Highfield, Hilliers, Holden Clough, Hopleys, Jackman, Kershaw, Knaphill, Knoll

Gardens, Lime Cross, Marchant, Marten's Hall, Meare Close, Notcutts, Otter, Reuthe, Roger, Rosemoor, Russell, Scotts, Shepton, Sherrard, Smith, Southcombe, St. Bridget, Stonehouse, Toynbee, Treasure, Treseder, Warley, Woodland, W.W., Wyevale.

Seeds: Chiltern.

WISTERIA, WISTARIA (*Leguminosae*). Fools and first time gardeners have better luck with growing things than those with more experience. I have seen things planted upside down or in uncongenial aspects and they grew as if they had been set in the ground by the loving hand of a master. For example — with Wisterias you never know whether, or if, they will ever flower; a decade more or less means nothing to them. I planted one against a wall, all unknowing, and within two years it was flowering well and I wasn't even surprised. This was many years ago, when I made my first garden (to do it I had to burn down three garages and break up the concrete floors with a pick-axe, which I did, single-handedly — but that is another story). Since then I have seen many such youthful plants, and some that are not so young, growing with grace and exuberance but with never a flower. Their owners, or rather the gardeners who planted them, stand cursing and threatening in some cases, or just resignedly sad in others. There is no telling what the Wisteria thinks: it will flower when it is ready and not before, and it will not be hurried — you should remember that these plants will undoubtedly outlive you, since there is a specimen in Japan that is said to have been planted over 1000 years ago. Its trunk is 32ft (17.6m) in diameter, it covers an area of about 400 square yards (33.5 sq.m) and it will have over 80,000 flower racemes in a season. *Festina lente* with a Wisteria, it makes haste slowly. A Wisteria should not be planted unless it can have a house-front, a whole long pergola or a sturdy structure of some kind all to itself, because as well as being long-lived the Wisteria is very vigorous indeed.

The first plant was described by a French Jesuit missionary who wrote about it in 1723; this was *W. sinensis*, the Chinese Wisteria, which was seen growing in the garden of a Cantonese merchant about a century later. He had been given it by his nephew who had brought the plant from a more northerly province, then called Fukien. The merchant was persuaded to propagate it by John Reeves, chief tea-inspector for the East India Company for over twenty years. At that time, 'foreign' traders and officials of all kinds were not permitted to live in Canton except when the merchant fleet was in port; during the rest of the year they lived at Macao, where there were fewer restrictions and sufficient space to have gardens. Reeves made the most of this facility because he had been asked by Sir Joseph Banks at Kew to collect plants for the Horticultural Society, and the plants that he acquired were kept in pots in his garden on Macao

until they could be sent home on a merchant vessel. This was a further gamble, because few sea-captains had the skill to keep the plants in good condition during the six-month's voyage, which included two Equator-crossings and rounding the Cape of Good Hope; the climatic fluctuations on these voyages are difficult to comprehend today. The plants spent the voyage in 'plant cabins' on the poop-deck (to be out of the way of the salt spray) and when the weather was bad, as it so often was, these rather heavy cabins were blamed by the captains for the effect they had on the trim of the vessel and, in times of danger, the cabins (like small greenhouses) were hurled overboard, together with their precious contents.

The first Wisteria plants propagated from that of the Cantonese merchant (whose name was rendered as 'Consequa') arrived in England in 1816, first on the vessel 'Cuffnels' and within a month the 'Warren Hastings' had made port with another plant collection aboard. These plant collections had been commissioned by those patrons of gardening Charles Hampden Turner of Surrey and Thomas Carey Palmer of Kent. Turner's ship, the 'Cuffnels', came in first and therefore he received the credit for the introduction, together with a medal from the Horticultural Society, though the early care of this first plant was almost enough to kill it, as it was planted in a heated peach-house to begin with and then moved into a pot in a cold greenhouse where it and the pot were frozen through three times during the first winter. It says much for the plant's iron constitution that it survived to flower in the following spring, later to be illustrated in the *Botanical Magazine* in 1819.

Reeves sent another plant to the Horticultural Society in 1818 which had a better time of it; by 1838 it had grown to 11ft (3.4m) high with side-branches of 90ft (27.5m) one side and 70ft (21.3m) on the other. Robert Fortune found the white-flowered Wisteria, which he discovered on the island of Chusan on his expedition of 1843-46. These Chinese Wisterias can be trained as standard 'trees' which display their beautiful flowers admirably. The Japanese species is *W. floribunda* 'multijuga' with very long flower racemes — sometimes as much as 5ft (1.5m). This needs to be trained as a standard, or on overhead trellis, in order to show off these amazing blooms.

The ageing 'trunks' of venerable specimens of Wisteria sometimes become hollow and decayed, but this does not seem to affect their vitality in any way. The stems of *W. floribunda*, the 'Japanese Wisteria', twine in a clockwise direction, while those of *W. sinensis* twine in an anti-clockwise way.

Thomas Nuttal named the genus after Caspar Wistar (1761-1818), Professor of Anatomy at the University of Pennsylvania, 'a philanthropist of simple manners and modest pretentions'. We do not know whether it was his error or that of the printer to spell the generic name 'Wisteria', or whether he was imitating the way in which the professor pronounced his name.

W. floribunda — Japanese Wisteria (1830) grows to 30ft+ (9m+) with fragrant violet or purple-blue 10″ (25.5cm) racemes of flowers in May and June. Var. 'Alba' is white with 2ft (60cm) racemes. *W.f.* 'Multijuga' syn. *W.f. macrobotrys* has racemes 3ft (90cm) long in the British Isles. A wonderful twining deciduous climber from Japan for a sunny wall, large pergola, bridge, trellis or tree. Flowers open from the base downwards; the leaves having between 11 and 19 leaflets.

W. sinensis — Chinese Wisteria (1816) grows to 100ft (30m) with fragrant deep lilac racemes of flowers 12″ (20cm) long opening simultaneously and before the leaves, which usually have 11 leaflets. An even lovelier (and larger) twining deciduous climber from China for a sheltered sunny wall, large pergola, or any large and permanent structure such as a bridge or iron cage.

Requirements: A good garden loam and sun on their roots. Space in which to grow (both below and above the ground) and the provision of strong, long-lasting supports (ordinary wooden trellis will not do). When Wisterias are planted to grow into trees, choose a south-west aspect.

Propagation: Is by layering, which should be done in May. Though seeds can sometimes be obtained, these do not produce reliably good plants.

Pruning: Should be done in February; cut back all growth to about two or three buds of the start of the previous year's growth. If you inherit a large specimen, which can get impossibly tangled very quickly once neglected, cut this season's new growth back to within five or six buds of its base during July or August. Train and tie in shoots to cover framework, trellis or wires as appropriate. To grow standards in the open, stake the young plants firmly to start with and spur back each year as described.

Uses: As the finest climber possible on a house front, providing you have time to wait for it. Or on walls, arches, bridges, and into large trees (very beautiful into full grown dead ones, but these may one day need to be removed). The lilac-blue flowers and pale bronze-green new season's foliage are beautiful in arrangements, though of short duration.

Shrubs: Barcock, Brackenwood, Bressingham, Busheyfields, Daisy Hill, Fairley's, Goatcher, Goscote, Highfield, Hilliers, Jackman, Kaye, Kershaw, Knaphill, Lime Cross, Marchant, Meare Close, Notcutts, Otter, Reuthe, Roger, Russell, Shepton, Sherrard, Smith, Southcombe, St. Bridget, Stonehouse, Toynbee, Treseder, Wyevale.

Seeds: Chiltern.

YUCCA — Adam's Needle, Spanish Bayonet, Spanish Dagger *(Agavaceae)*. These are very sculptural plants, even if they never flower for you. Some species, such as *Y. glori-*

osa, get their timing wrong and produce magnificent flowering stems in November which in colder counties may fail to open or, sadly, are ruined by winter weather. I had a very fine clump of these which someone planted in exactly the right place to receive the full weight of the snow which falls on (and slides off) our thatched roof. Most years there is no problem, but in very bad winters when the ground freezes to a depth of several inches, the yucca-stems freeze as well, and then the whole plant snaps off like a cabbage. This can be heartbreaking, until I did an inquest when clearing away the corpse — the disaster had happened many times before, as could be seen by the remains of old, old stems. When a Yucca has been in one place for over fifty years, as this one had, it never really gives up and spiky young plants have been coming up from the subterranean roots ever since. I shall soon have to re-plant that part of the garden to make room for the new generation. And when *they* have reached maturity and begin to flower, which will not be for about five years at least, then there will come another roof slide and history will repeat itself. Yuccas harbour snails all the year round and more especially in winter, so put on your spectacles or some sunglasses (to protect your eyes from the devilish spines) and have a clear-out every so often among the dry debris beneath their armoured canopy.

These are wonderfully sculptural plants that look their best against a formal background of stonework or brick. They start off as neat rosettes of strap-shaped or spiny leaves but they soon produce offsets which can spoil their previously perfect symmetry. If this matters to you, grow box or yew which can be controlled, Yuccas cannot, and in old age they sometimes fall over sideways in a rather haphazard way, though they still keep on growing, and flowering.

In the wild (the south, west and eastern parts of the United States) future generations of most Yuccas depend on the Pronuba or Yucca moth, *Tegeticula yuccasella*. The female moth has evolved specialised mouth-parts with which she gathers pollen from the night-opening flowers of the Yuccas. She collects sufficient pollen to form a pollen ball from the flowers on one plant and then flies to another flower on a different plant. There she deposits her eggs in the ovary with her ovipositor. Having done this she forces the collected pollen ball into the stigmatic chamber of the ovary thus ensuring cross-pollination. The eggs hatch into larvae that begin to feed on the ovules or swelling seeds, which develop in sufficient numbers both to feed the larvae and leave the plant with some viable seed. In this remarkable way the continuation of both plant and insect is ensured for the next and succeeding generations.

Y. filamentosa is a sculptural but more docile plant than the dangerously rigid and steel-spined *Y. gloriosa*. It is smaller, has softer leaves fringed with filaments (hence its name), does not grow so large, and sensibly flowers in

August. *Y. recurvifolia* is a graceful plant for all such similar positions, having graceful, drooping leaves (still armed at the end of each) and tall spikes of earlier flowers. It withstands the British winter climate well, enduring the succession of wet/cold/freeze/snow and thaw that is so familiar and so cruel to the gardener's soul as he watches his treasures succumb one by one. This Yucca in particular endures urban pollution well, and can be used for gardens whose owners are often away. It, like all the Yuccas, simply loves a drought year and will flower accordingly. Its stem or trunk is much longer than other Yuccas thus allowing the reflexed leaves to fall in a graceful curve without lying on the ground; this should be remembered when choosing the species to plant. If space permits an informal grouping of several species is very interesting, but for truly formal and exactly regular design one type should be chosen. *Y. flaccida* is a smaller, less rigid species, suitable for matching gardens and as a patio plant, where its long down-curving leaves are handsome at all times of the year.

Y. filamentosa — Adam's Needle (1675) grows to 3ft (90cm) with creamy spires of flowers in July and August, often on young plants (in suitable soil and position). An evergreen shrub from the S.E. United States for a warm position in full sun.

Y. flaccida (1816) grows to 3ft (90cm) and as much wide with creamy-white spires of flowers in July and August. A low evergreen shrub from the S.E. United States with down-curving softer sword-leaves for a hot, sheltered position in full sun. Plant out of the wind, which can damage the leaves.

Y. gloriosa — Adam's Needle, Spanish Dagger, Spanish Bayonet (1550) grows to 5ft (1.5m) (foliage) with tall — to 6ft (1.8m) — panicles of creamy, pink-tinged bell-shaped flowers from July to November. An evergreen shrub from the S.E. United States with straight fiercely spine-tipped sword-leaves. A handsome and architectural plant, best not planted near paths. Does not flower every year and is subject to frost damage.

Y. recurvifolia (1794) grows up to 6ft (1.8m), with thick stems, like elephants' legs, and a mop of down-curving sword-leaves each from 2-3ft (60-90cm) long. Cream spires of bell-shaped flowers from August to October. The hardiest species.

Requirements: All Yuccas thrive best in hot, even arid situations in a sandy, free-draining loam. They are desert dwellers in nature and are good in low-maintenance gardens (this terms is synonymous with neglect).

Propagation: Most Yuccas can be easily propagated from pieces of rhizomatous underground stem, which generally send up new plants around the old parent (when this is in a border). These can be potted up into 6" (15cm) pots of ordinary garden soil to grow on until large enough for planting out. Protect such small plants in winter in a cold frame and reduce watering to a minimum. Hand-pollination can be attempted, this was done most successfully by J.B. Deleuil of Marseilles in 1874, and later by Carl Sprenger in Naples. Small Yuccas can be cut off and set in pots of sandy soil, when they will form roots (the lower leaves should be trimmed off when this is done), but this method is rather an extreme measure. The decapitated trunk (often under the skirts of a mature plant) may grow new leaves, but small shoots are more likely to appear from the base. Dead leaves should be removed as they will form a safe winter residence for hibernating gastropods.

Pruning: None required. The stems of some old plants lengthen, as in *Y. gloriosa*, and are then more fragile in bad winters, or the whole plant may lean, or be forced sideways by the rigid leaves of the central rosette. One cannot train a Yucca, so grow some young plants as replacements if this very natural occurrence disturbs your eye.

Uses: As very exotic and almost always hardy architectural plants for patios, terraces, paved areas and (small ones) in containers. Flower and seed magnificent in arrangements.

Shrubs: Ballalheannagh, Barcock, Bees, Brackenwood, Busheyfields, Caldwell, Peter Chappell, Beth Chatto, Daisy Hill, Dobbies, Goatcher, Goscote, Great Dixter, Highfield, Hilliers, Hopleys, Jackman, Kelways, Knaphill, Knoll Gardens, Lime Cross, Marchant, Meare Close, Notcutts, Otter, Roger, Russell, Scotts, Shepton, Sherrard, Smith, Southcombe, St. Bridget, Toynbee, Treasure, Treseder, Woodland, Wyevale.

Seeds: Butcher, Chiltern.

BIOGRAPHICAL NOTES

CLUSIUS — Jules Charles de L'Ecluse (1526-1609) — born in what was Flanders, at Arras. A botanist who spoke eight languages. Met Sir Francis Drake and through him obtained some of the first American plants. One of the founders of the bulb-growing industry in the Netherlands.

NICHOLAS CULPEPER (1616-54) — an apothecary and a Puritan who fought in the Civil War, where he was severely wounded. In spite of his faith he believed in the powers of astrology, linked to plants that were governed by the planets. He wrote *The English Physician Enlarged* (published in 1653) which was very popular.

DIOSCORIDES — Pedanios Dioskurides — (*circa* AD 40 to *circa* AD 90). His most important work was *De Materia Medica* which was about the identification and use of medicinal plants. This was still in use over 1000 years later. A manuscript copy (dated AD 512) is in Vienna.

REGINALD FARRER (1880-1920) — was a great gardener, traveller and plant collector, visiting Japan, the Himalayas and Burma. His most famous book is *The English Rock-Garden* though this is, of course, outside the time scale of this book. His name is commemorated in all the plant varieties named 'Farreri'.

ROBERT FORTUNE (1812-80) — became a 'botanical collector' to the Royal Horticultural Society in 1842. He went to China in 1843 where he discovered many plants and flowers that bear his name (Fortunei). He returned to a post as curator to the Chelsea Physic Garden and began writing his books, but returned to China as an employee of the East India Company and found many more plant species.

JOHN GERARD (1545-1612) — born in Cheshire, England. Became a Barber-Surgeon in 1569 and was a garden-planner. His book, the *Herball or Historie of Plantes* (1597) was 'borrowed' from Dodoens. Important because of the list of his own garden plants that he made in 1596 and 1599.

WILLIAM HANBURY (1725-78) — became rector of Church Langton in Leicestershire in 1753. Was famous for his extensive tree plantations, his garden and his writings on gardening. He wrote *The Complete Body of Planting and Gardening* a fortnightly publication that sold at 6d. a copy. This ran from 1769-73.

GERTRUDE JEKYLL (1843-1932) — 'Artist-Gardener-Craftswoman' — these words on her memorial stone sum up her abilities. She wrote many books about plants and gardening and is famous for her herbaceous borders and beautiful planting schemes.

LINNAEUS — Carl von Linné (1707-78) — the Swedish botanist who is famous for the plant classification system and the binomial method of nomenclature that is still in use today. Though most of his work was with plants he also classified insects, birds and animals.

JOHN CLAUDIUS LOUDON (1783-1842), **JANE LOUDON** (1803-58) — John Loudon was a landscape gardener who wrote many gardening books, in spite of the fact that he had the partial use of his left arm only — his right had been amputated in 1825. Jane Loudon knew nothing of gardening when she met her husband but studied so that she might understand his work and help him as much as possible. She wrote several books for learner-gardeners. They lived in Bayswater Terrace in London, and had only a moderate-sized garden.

HENRY LYTE (1529-1607) — born in Somerset, England. He wrote *A Nievve Herball* in 1578 which was a translation from Clusius. He was married three times and had a large family of 13.

PHILIP MILLER (1692-1771) — had a small nursery-garden in London. Was the protégé of Sir Hans Sloane who later made him the first curator of the Chelsea Physic Garden. He wrote several books, the most important being *The Gardener's Dictionary* (published 1731). He employed only Scottish gardeners.

JOHN PARKINSON (1567-1650 — an apothecary, becoming the Warden of the Society of Apothecaries in 1617. His famous garden was in Long Acre. Wrote *Paradisi in Sole, Paradisus Terrestris*, an illustrated book on plants whose title was a pun on his name — 'Park in Sun'. Became Botanist to King Charles I.

PLINY the Elder — Gaius Plinius Secundus — born in AD 23 at Como, died in AD 79. His death was attributed to the sulphurous atmosphere during a great eruption of Vesuvius. He held many public offices and was a most industrious man, spending each day in writing and learning throughout his life.

WILLIAM ROBINSON (1838-1935) — a rather violent Irishman who left his first employer under dubious circumstances. His second job was in London, where he was put in charge of a collection of English wild flowers. These so influenced him that he pioneered the 'Wild Garden' or more natural form of gardening. He was a contemporary and friend of Gertrude Jekyll. His name is commemorated in the many plants named after his Gravetye Manor. He designed and promoted rock gardens that looked like natural rock-strata. He detested the formal Victorian form of gardening and in particular he hated 'carpet-bedding'.

THEOPHRASTUS (Greek) — born at Lesbos in about 370 B.C. Said to have lived to the age of 107. A friend of Alexander the Great. Wrote several books including the earliest still-surviving botanical work *Enquiry into Plants*.

J. PITTON DE TOURNEFORT (1656-1708) — his father wished him to enter the Church but he became Professor of Botany at the Jardin du Roi. Louis XIV sent him on an expedition to discover new plants in 1700, and he visited Crete, many of the Greek Islands, the Black Sea coast, Tiflis, Erzerum and Smyrna. He was a great botanist of his day.

JOHN TRADESCANT (the Elder) (d. 1638) — began a 'career' as a gardener, first to the Earl of Salisbury, then to Lord Wotton, the Duke of Buckingham and finally to King Charles I. He went with Sir Dudley Digges to Russia in 1618, and afterwards travelled to Algeria to fight the Corsairs. He began an extensive collection of natural curiosities which was the foundation collection of the Ashmolean Museum.

WILLIAM TURNER (c. 1508-68) — a student at Cambridge where he began to classify British flora, the nomenclature of which was in a state of confusion. Exiled (twice) voluntarily because of his religious beliefs, he utilised the time abroad to take his degree in Medicine at Bologna. Published first part of *A New Herbal* in 1551 and the second part in 1562. Finally became Dean of Wells.

NURSERIES, SEEDSMEN AND BULB MERCHANTS

The species and varieties described in the book are all obtainable from the nurseries, bulb merchants and seedsmen listed here. But it should be remembered that nurseries are not garden centres — they actually grow what they sell and may not be geared for visitors. Some of them are mail-order only, whereas others sell plants in containers to visitors on certain days (usually at weekends). Some sell only to visitors and do no mail orders at all. So it is as well to write (enclosing an S.A.E.) or telephone first to find out how they do things. All of them produce catalogues, which can cost from 30p to about £1.50p, plus postage. If seeking particular plants, it is essential to peruse the catalogues before ordering or visiting as not all the nurseries have all the plants.

The smaller nurseries (often with the most interesting plants) operate with minimum staff, so do not be surprised if the telephone bell goes unanswered at first. Just keep on trying, and choose a different time of day to make your next call. Nurseries are run by fascinating individuals who are in themselves collectors' items. If you are genuinely interested in their plants they will be most helpful. Many British nurseries are licensed to export their plants or bulbs, but as each country of destination has different agricultural import rules, it is as well to check. Many nurseries, bulb-merchants and seedsmen exhibit at the Royal Horticultural Society shows, where you can see the standard of their plants. Go early — they always run out of catalogues.

NURSERY AND SEEDSMEN DIRECTORY

Anderson's of Aberdeen — Anderson's Rose Nurseries, Cults, Aberdeen, Scotland. Tel: Aberdeen (0224) 868881.

David Austin Roses — Bowling Green Lane, Albrighton, Wolverhampton WV7 3HB. Tel: Albrighton (090 722) 2142.

B & H M Baker — Bourne Brooke Nurseries, Greenstead Green, Halstead, Essex CO9 1RJ. Tel: Halstead (0787) 472900.

Ballalheannagh Gardens — Glen Roy, Lonan, Isle of Man, British Isles. Tel: Laxey (0624) 781875.

F G Barcock & Co — Garden House Farm, Drinkstone, Bury St Edmunds, Suffolk IP30 9TN. Tel: Rattlesden (044 93) 249.

Peter Beales Roses — London Road, Attleborough, Norfolk NR17 1AY. Tel: Attleborough (0953) 454707.

Bees (Sealand Nurseries Ltd) — Sealand, Chester CH1 6BA. Tel: Sanghall (024 458) 501.

Bodnant Garden Nursery — Tal-Y-Cafn, Colwyn Bay, Clwyd LL28 5RE. Tel: Ty'n-y-Groes (049 267) 460.

Brackenwood Nurseries — 131 Nore Road, Portishead, Avon. Tel: (0272) 843484.

Bressingham Gardens — Diss, Norfolk IP22 2AB. Tel: Bressingham (037 988) 464.

Busheyfields Nursery – Herne, Herne Bay, Kent CT6 7LJ. Tel: Herne Bay (022 73) 5415.

Thomas Butcher Ltd — 60 Wickham Road, Shirley, Croydon, Surrey CR9 8AG. Tel: (01 654) 3720.

Caldwell & Sons Ltd — The Nurseries, Knutsford, Cheshire WA16 8LX. Tel: Knutsford (0565) 4281.

Cants of Colchester Ltd — Agriculture House, 305 Mile End Road, Colchester, Essex CO4 5EB. Tel: Colchester (0206) 844008.

Peter Chappell — Spinners, Boldre, Lymington, Hants. Tel: Lymington (0590) 73347.

Beth Chatto — White Barn Housse, Elmstead Market, Colchester, Essex. Tel: Wivenhoe (020 622) 2007.

Chiltern Seeds — Bortree Stile, Ulverston, Cumbria LA12 7PB. Tel: Ulverston (0229) 56946.

Church Nurseries — Church Street, Woodhurst, Huntington, Cambs. Tel: Ramsey (0487) 823333.

Crarae Woodland Garden — Cumlodden Estate Office, Crarae, Inveraray, Argyll PA32 8YA. Tel: Minard (0546) 86633.

J Cunnington — Engelberg Nursery, Bulls Lane, Brookmans Park, Hatfield, Herts AL9 7AZ. Tel: Potters Bar (0707) 58161.

Daisy Hill Nurseries Ltd — Newry, Northern Ireland. Tel: Newry (0693) 2474.

Dobbies — Melville Nurseries & Garden Centre, Lasswade, Nr Dalkeith, Midlothian, Scotland. Tel: (031663) 1941.

Jack Drake — Inshriach Alpine Plant Nursery, Aviemore, Inverness-shire. Tel: Kincraig (054 04) 287.

D and M Everett — Greenacres Nursery, Bringsty, Worcester WR6 5TA. Tel: Bromyard (0885) 82206.

Exbury Gardens Ltd — Exbury, Nr Southampton SO4 1AZ. Tel: Fawley (0703) 891203.

Fairley's Garden Centre — Cairneyhill, Fife, Scotland. Tel: (0383) 880223.

Farall Nurseries — Roundhurst, Nr Haslemere, Surrey. Tel: Haslemere (0428) 53024.

The Margery Fish Nursery — East Lambrook Manor, East Lambrook, South Petherton, Somerset. Tel: South Petherton (0460) 40328.

Fisk's Clematis Nursery — Westleton, Nr Saxmundham, Suffolk IP17 3AJ. Tel: Westleton (072 873) 263.

Mr Fothergill's Seeds Ltd — Gazeley Road, Kentford, Newmarket, Suffolk CB8 7QB. Tel: Newmarket (0638) 751161.

M G Frye — The Willows, Poors Lane North, Daws Heath, Thundersley, Essex SS7 2XF. Tel: Southend (0702) 558467.

Fryers Roses — Fryers Nurseries Ltd, Knutsford, Cheshire. Tel: Knutsford (0565) 2642.

Glendoick Gardens Ltd — Perth, Scotland PH2 7NS. Tel: Glencarse (073 886) 205.

Glenview Alpine Nursery — Quarryhill, By Forfar, Angus, Scotland DD8 3TQ. Tel: Foreside (030 786) 205.

A Goatcher and Son — The Nurseries, Washington, Sussex. Tel: Ashington (0903) 892626.

Goscote Nurseries — Syston Road, Cossington, Leics. Tel: Sileby (050 981) 2121.

Great Dixter Nurseries — Northiam, Sussex. Tel: Northiam (079 74) 3107.

Le Grice Roses — Norwich Road, North Walsham, Norfolk NR28 0DR. Tel: North Walsham (0692) 402591.

R Harkness & Co Ltd — The Rose Gardens, Hitchin, Herts SG4 0JT. Tel: Hitchin (0462) 34027.

Highfield Nurseries — Whitminster, Gloucester GL2 7PL. Tel: Gloucester (0452) 740266.

Hillier Nurseries (Winchester) Ltd — Ampfield House, Ampfield, Romsey, Hants SO5 9PA. Tel: Braishfield (0794) 68733.

Holden Clough Nurseries — Bolton-by-Bowland, Nr Clitheroe, Lancs BB7 4PF. Tel: Bolton-by-Bowland (020 07) 615.

Hopleys Plants Ltd — High Street, Much Hadham, Herts SG10 6BU. Tel: Much Hadham (027 984) 2509.

Hortico — Spalding, Lincs PE12 6EB. Tel: Spalding (0775) 5936.

Hydon Nurseries Ltd — Hydon Heath, Godalming, Surrey. Tel: Hascombe (048 632) 252.

W E Th. Ingwersen Ltd — Birch Farm Nursery, Gravetye, East Grinstead, West Sussex RH19 4LE. Tel: East Grinstead (0342) 810236.

Reginald Kaye Ltd — Waithman Nurseries, Silverdale, Carnforth, Lancs LA5 0TY. Tel: Carnforth (0524) 701252.

Kelways Nurseries — Langport, Somerset TA10 9SL. Tel: Langport (0458) 250521.

Kent Country Nurseries Limited — Challock, Nr Ashford, Kent TN25 4DG. Tel: Challock (023 374) 256.

Charles Kershaw — The Nurseries and Garden Centre, Halifax Road, Brighouse, W.Yorks. Tel: Brighouse (0484) 713435.

Knap Hill Nursery Ltd — Barrs Lane, Knaphill, Woking, Surrey GU21 2JW. Tel: Brookwood (048 67) 81212.

The Knoll Gardens — Stapehill Road, Stapehill, Wimborne, Dorset BH21 7ND. Tel: Ferndown (0202) 873931.

Lea Rhododendron Gardens — Matlock, Derbyshire. Tel: Dethick (062 984) 380.

Lime Cross Nursery — Herstmonceux, Hailsham, East Sussex BN27 4RS. Tel: Herstmonceux (0323) 833229.

C J Marchant — Keeper's Hill Nursery, Nr Stapehill, Wimborne, Dorset BH21 7NE. Tel: Ferndown (0202) 873140.

Marten's Hall Farm — Longworth, Abingdon, Oxon OX13 5EP. Tel: Longworth (0865) 820376.

John Mattock Ltd — The Rose Nurseries, Nuneham Courtenay, Oxford OX9 9PY. Tel: Nuneham Courtenay (086 738) 265.

Meare Close Nurseries Ltd — Tadworth Street, Tadworth, Surrey KT20 5RG. Tel: Tadworth (073 781) 2449.

Notcutts Nurseries Ltd — Woodbridge, Suffolk IP12 4AF. Tel: Woodbridge (039 43) 3344.

Oak Cottage Herb Farm — Nesscliffe, Nr Shrewsbury, Shropshire SY4 1DB. Tel: Nesscliffe (074 381) 262.

The Old Rectory Herb Garden — Ightham, Kent TN15 9AL. Tel: Borough Green (0732) 882608.

The Orchard Nurseries — Stone Street, Nr Petham, Canterbury, Kent. Tel: Petham (022 770) 375.

Otter Nurseries Ltd — Gosford Road, Ottery St Mary, Devon EX11 1LZ. Tel: Ottery St Mary (040 481) 3341.

Parkinson Herbs — Barras Moor Farm, Perran-ar-Worthal, Truro, Cornwall. Tel: Truro (0872) 864380.

Potterton and Martin — The Cottage Nursery, Moortown Road, Nettleton, Caistor, Lincs LN7 6HX. Tel: Caistor (0472) 851792.

Ramparts Nursery — Bakers Lane, Colchester, Essex CO4 5BB. Tel: Colchester (0206) 572050.

Read's Nursery — Hales Hall, Loddon, Norfolk. Tel: Loddon (0508) 46395.

G Reuthe Ltd — Foxhill Nursery, Jackass Lane, Keston, Nr Bromley, Kent. Tel: Farnborough (0689) 52249.

Robinsons Hardy Plants — Greencourt Nurseries, Crockenhill, Swanley, Kent. Tel: Swanley (0322) 63819.

R V Roger Ltd — The Nurseries, Pickering, N.Yorks YO18 7HG. Tel: Pickering (0751) 72226.

Rosemoor — Torrington, Devon EX38 7EG. Tel: Torrington (080 52) 2256.

L R Russell Ltd — Richmond Nurseries, Windlesham, Surrey GU20 6LL. Tel: Ascot (0990) 21411.

Scotts Nurseries (Merriott) Ltd — Merriott, Somerset. Tel: Crewkerne (0460) 72306.

Shepton Nursery Garden — Old Wells Road, Shepton Mallet, Somerset. Tel: Shepton Mallet (0749) 3630.

Sherrards — The Garden Centre, Wantage Road, Donnington, Newbury, Berks RG16 9BE. Tel: Newbury (0635) 47845.

James Smith (Scotland Nurseries) Ltd — Tansley, Matlock, Derbyshire DE4 5GF. Tel: Matlock (0629) 3036.

Southcombe Gardens Plant Nursery — Widecombe-in-the-Moor, Newton Abbot, Devon TQ13 7TU. Tel: Widecombe (036 42) 214.

Speyside Heather Garden Centre — Skye of Curr, Dulnain Bridge, Inverness-shire, Scotland PH26 3PA. Tel:Dulnain Bridge (047 985) 359.

St Bridget Nurseries — Old Rydon Lane, Exeter, Devon EX2 7JY. Tel: Topsham (039 287) 3672.

Stoke Lacy Herb Garden — Bromyard, Herefordshire. Tel: Burley Gate (043 278) 232.

Stonehouse Cottage Nurseries (Arbuthnotts) — Nr Kidderminster, Worcestershire. Tel: Kidderminster (0562) 69902.

Suttons Seeds Limited — Hele Road, Torquay, Devon TQ2 7QJ. Tel: Torquay (0803) 62011.

Thompson and Morgan Limited — London Road, Ipswich IP2 0BA. Tel: Ipswich (0473) 218821.

F Toynbee Ltd — Barnham, Bognor Regis, West Sussex PO22 0BH. Tel: Yapton (0243) 552121.

Treasures of Tenbury Ltd — Burford House Gardens, Tenbury Wells, Hereford & Worcester. Tel: Tenbury Wells (0584) 810777.

Tregrehan Camellia Nurseries — Par, Cornwall.

James Trehane & Sons Ltd — Camellia Nursery, Stapehill Road, Hampreston, Wimborne, Dorset BH21 7NE. Tel: Ferndown (0202) 873490.

Treseders' Nurseries (Truro) Ltd — Resugga Farm Nursery, St Erme, Truro. Tel: Mitchell (087 251) 567.

Unwins Seeds Limited — Histon, Cambridgeshire CB4 4LE. Tel: Histon (022 023) 2270.

Ward's Nurseries — Eckington Road, Coal Aston, Sheffield S18 6BA. Tel: Dronfield (0246) 412622.

Warley Rose Gardens — Warley Street, Great Warley, Brentwood, Essex CM13 3JH. Tel: Brentwood (0277) 221966.

The Weald Herbary — Park Cottage, Frittenden, Cranbrook, Kent TN17 2AU. Tel: Frittenden (058 080) 226.

Wheatcroft Roses Ltd — Landmere Lane, Edwalton, Nottingham NG12 4DE. Tel: Nottingham (0602) 216061.

Whitehouse Ivies — Hylands Farm, Rectory Road, Tolleshunt Knights, Maldon, Essex CM9 8EZ. Tel: Maldon (0621) 815782.

Woodland Services & Supplies Ltd — Brooklands, Mardy, Abergavenny, Gwent NP7 6NU. Tel: Abergavenny (0873) 5431.

W W Nurseries — Westend House, Wickwar, Wotton-under-Edge, Gloucestershire GL12 8LB. Tel: Wickwar (045 424) 208.

Wyevale Garden Centre — Kings Acre, Hereford. Tel: Hereford (0432) 265474.

HORTICULTURAL SOCIETIES DIRECTORY

Details of the activities of these Societies may be obtained from the Secretaries; the names and addresses are correct at the time of going to press.

American Societies

American Camellia Society: P.O.Box 1217, Fort Valley, GA 31030, (912) 967-2358, (Milton H. Brown, Ex.Sec.)

The American Ivy Society: c/o Cox Arboretum, 6733 Springboro Pike, Dayton, OH 45449, (513) 434-9005, (Sabrina Mueller Sulgrove, Pres.)

American Magnolia Society: P.O.Box 129, Nanbet, NY 10954, (914) 354-3981, (Richard B.Figlar, Sec.)

American Poinsettia Society: P.O.Box 706, Mission, TX 78572, (512) 585-1256, (Mrs T.L.Tuncan)

The American Rhododendron Society: 14635 S.W. Bull Mountain Road, Tigard, OR 97223, (503) 639-5922, (Fran Egan, Ex.Sec.)

American Rose Society: P.O.Box 30,000, Shreveport, LA 71130, (318) 938-5402, (Harold S. Goldstein, Ex. Dir.)

Azalea Society of America, Inc: P.O.Box 6244, Silver Spring, MD 20906, (301) 946-5526, (Alice Holland, Sec.)

Gardenia Society of America: P.O.Box 879, Atwater, CA 95301, (209) 358-4251, (Lyman Duncan)

British Societies

Alpine Garden Society, E.M.Upward, Lye End Link, St. John's, Woking, Surrey GU21 1SW.

Heather Society, K.H. Farran, 7 Rossley Close, Highcliffe, Christchurch BH23 4RR.

Herb Society, The Executive Secretary, 34 Boscobel Place, London SW1.

International Camellia Society, (UK rep.), H.J.Toobey, Acorns, Chapel Lane, Bransford, Worcester WR6 5JB.

International Dendrology Society, Mrs Eustace, Whistley Green Farmhouse, Hurst, Reading, Berkshire RG10 0DU.

National Association of Flower Arrangement Societies of Great Britain, 21a Denbigh Street, London SW1V 2HF.

Northern Horticultural Society, Brian Booth, Harlow Car Gardens, Harrogate HG3 1QB.

Royal Horticultural Society of Ireland, Thomas Prior House, Merrion Road, Ballsbridge, Dublin 4.

Royal National Rose Society, The, L.G. Turner, Chiswell Green Lane, St Albans, Herts AL2 3NR.

Scottish National Sweet Pea, Rose and Carnation Society, Ken Wayt, Rosebank, 7 Brown Street, Motherwell ML1 1LJ.

Scottish Rock Garden Club, Mrs I. Simpson, 2 Dalrymple Crescent, Edinburgh EH9 2NU.

BIBLIOGRAPHY

Art of Botanical Illustration, The — Wilfred Blunt, Collins, 1971.

Atlas of the British Flora — Ed. by F.H.Perring and S.M.Walters, Thomas Nelson, 1962.

Book of the Rose, The — Michael Gibson, Macdonald General Books, 1980.

Botanic Garden, The — B.Maund F.L.S., Simpkin and Marshall, 1825-6.

Climbing Roses Old and New (revised edition) — Graham Stuart Thomas, V.M.H., J.M.Dent and Sons Ltd, 1978.

Colour Schemes for the Flower Garden — Gertrude Jekyll, Antique Collectors' Club, 1983.

Complete Guide to British Butterflies, A — Margaret Brooks and Charles Knight, Jonathan Cape, 1982.

Complete Herbal — Nicholas Culpeper M.D., Thomas Kelly, 1828.

Concise British Flora in colour, The — W.Keble Martin, George Rainbird, 1969.

Concise Flowers of Europe, The — Oleg Polunin, Oxford University Press, 1974.

Dictionary of Garden Plants, The — Roy Hay and Patrick M.Synge, Ebury Press and Michael Joseph in collaboration with the Royal Horticultural Society, 1969.

Dictionary of Shrubs in colour, The — S.Millar Gault, Peerage Books in collaboration with the Royal Horticultural Society, 1984.

Early Gardening Catalogues — John Harvey, Phillimore, 1972.

Early Nurserymen — John Harvey, Phillimore, 1974.

Encyclopaedia Britannica, Eleventh Edition — Cambridge University Press, 1911.

Englishman's Flora, The — Geoffrey Grigson, Paladin, 1975.

Essential Earthman, The — Henry Mitchell, Farrar, Straus & Giroux, 1983.

Fantastic Garlands: An Anthology of Flowers and Plants from Shakespeare — Lys de Bray, Blandford Press, 1982.

Field Guide to Australian Wildflowers, A — Margaret Hodgson and Roland Pain, Rigby Limited, 1973.

Field Guide to Rocky Mountain Wildflowers, A — John J.Craighead, Frank C.Craighead, Jr., Ray J.Davis, Houghton Mifflin Co., Boston, 1963.

Field Guide to Trees and Shrubs, A — George A.Petrides, Houghton Mifflin Co., Boston, 1972.

Flora of the British Isles — A.R.Clapham, T.G.Tutin & E.F.Warburg, Cambridge University Press, 1962.

Flowering World of 'Chinese' Wilson, The — Daniel J.Foley, Macmillan, 1969.

Flowers of the World — Frances Perry, illustrated by Leslie Greenwood, Hamlyn in collaboration with the Royal Horticultural Society, 1972 .

Gardening in the Shade — Margery Fish, Faber and Faber, 1983.

Garden Shrubs and their Histories — Alice M.Coates, Vista Books, 1963.

Gardens for Small Country Houses — Gertrude Jekyll and Lawrence Weaver, Papermac, 1983.

Georgian Gardens — David C.Stuart, Robert Hale, 1979.

Gerard's Herball — The Essence thereof distilled by Marcus Woodward from the edition of T.H.Johnson 1636, Gerald Howe, 1927.

Grandmother's Secrets: Her Green Guide to Health from Plants — Jean Palaiseul, Barrie and Jenkins, 1973.

The Greek Myths: 1 — Robert Graves, Penguin Books, 1962.

The Greek Myths: 2 — Robert Graves, Penguin Books, 1962.

Hillier's Manual of Trees and Shrubs (5th edition) — David and Charles and Van Nostrand Reinhold Co. Inc., 1981.

History of England — G.M.Trevelyan, Longman, 1981.

Holy Bible, The — Collins, 1954.

Illustrated Herbal Handbook, The — Juliette de Baîracli Levy, Faber and Faber, 1974.

International Book of Wood, The — Mitchell Beazley, 1979.

Ivies — Peter Q.Rose, Blandford Press, 1980.

Language and Sentiment of Flowers — Compiled and edited by L.V., Frederick Warne, 1866.

Life of Linnaeus, A — Wilfred Blunt, Collins, 1971.

Modern Herbal, A — Mrs M.Grieve, F.R.H.S., Jonathan Cape, 1974.

My Garden in Autumn and Winter — E.A.Bowles, M.A., David and Charles, 1972.

My Garden in Summer — E.A.Bowles, M.A., David and Charles 1972.

New Illustrated Gardening Encyclopaedia, The — Edited by Richard Sudell, F.I.L.A., A.R.H.S., Odhams Press,

Old Shrub Rose, The — Graham Stuart Thomas, V.M.H., J.M.Dent & Sons Ltd., in association with the Royal Horticultural Society, 1979.

Perennial Garden Plants, or the Modern Florilegium — Graham Stuart Thomas, V.M.H., J.M.Dent & Sons Ltd., 1982.

Plants of Colonial Williamsburg — Joan Parry Dutton, The Colonial Williamsburg Foundation, 1979.

Quest for Plants : A History of the Horticultural Explorers — Alice M.Coates, Studio Vista, 1969.

Reader's Digest Encyclopaedia of Garden Plants and Flowers — Reader's Digest Association, 1975.

Reader's Encyclopaedia — William Rose Benet, A.C.Black, 1972.

Royal Horticultural Society's Dictionary of Gardening — Edited by Fred. J.Chittenden, O.B.E., F.L.S., V.M.H., and Patrick M.Synge, M.A., F.L.S., Oxford University Press, 1977.

Sentiment of Flowers, The — Robert Tyas, F.R.B.S., Houlston and Stoneman, 1844.

Simon and Schuster's Complete Guide to Plants & Flowers — Edited by Frances Perry, Simon and Schuster, Simon and Schuster,

Southern Garden, A — Elizabeth Lawrence, Chapel Hill, 1984.
Trees and Shrubs hardy in the British Isles (eighth edition) — W.J.Bean, C.V.O., I.S.O., V.M.H., John Murray, 1980.
Trees and Bushes of Europe — Oleg Polunin and Barbara Everard, Oxford University Press, 1976.
Victorian Flower Garden, The — Geoffrey Taylor, Skeffington, 1952.
What Flower is that? — Stirling Macoboy, Omega Books Limited, 1984.
Whitakers Almanack (114th edition) — London, 1982.
Wild Flowers of Australia — Thistle Y.Harris, B.Sc., Angus and Robertson Limited, 1952.
Wild Flowers of the World — Barbara Everard and Brian D.Morley, Octopus Books, 1975.
Wild Garden, The — William Robinson, Century Publishing, 1983.
Wild and Old Garden Roses — Gordon Edwards, David and Charles, 1975.
Wood and Garden — Gertrude Jekyll, Antique Collectors' Club, 1981.

INDEX